'These are the facts and notes taken by a soldier on campaign, written daily, sometimes in a tent, sometimes in a canoe, today in the presence of the enemy, tomorrow in conference with a tribe of savages.' This succinct description is taken from the original French edition of the journal of Comte Maurès de Malartic. It offers a fascinating glimpse into the daily life of a French soldier. Malartic, *aide-major* of the Régiment de Béarn, sailed to the North American colony of New France in 1755 as France responded to British forces sent out to Virginia in the same year. As war escalated, he remained in the colony for the next six years and was present at all the major engagements in what came to be known as the French and Indian War, or Seven Years War. Until now many historians have relied on the English translations of Bougainville for an account of the French in North America. Bougainville was another French officer who later found fame as an explorer of the Pacific Ocean. Although written in a much plainer style than Bougainville, Malartic's writings provide clarity, balance and contrast to this tumultuous time. Unlike his contemporary, Malartic's journals continue right through the war and conclude with his transportation back to France as a prisoner in a British vessel. Although serving as one of General Montcalm's aides, Malartic was not part of his clique and presents us with a more independent minded view of events and the man, than the impressionable Bougainville.

Available now for the first time in English, Malartic's recollections illuminate the reader to the great pains and efforts undertaken by the French army in America to preserve New France under immense pressure. Energy-sapping journeys and logistical efforts are recorded as Malartic kept his journal almost every day during the campaign season. Not only does he describe his military duties but continues his observations into the cold winters spent in Montreal and Quebec, organising lodgings for his regiment and watching the helpless population become reduced to starvation while the elite gambled away huge fortunes. His recollections record many other aspects of daily life, of a more mundane nature and of the sort so often omitted by other memorialists, that will prove invaluable to the student of the 18th Century, New France and the Seven Years War.

William Raffle lives and works in Derbyshire and has been studying colonial North America for many years. He is currently part-way through an MA in Early Modern History at the University of Sheffield with a focus on the Seven Years War and its transformative power on the nations and cultures who experienced it. This current project evolved as a spare-time project in between his career as a music teacher and is part of the resurgence of interest of the history of New France in the English-speaking world.

Glories to Useless Heroism

The Seven Years War in North America from the French Journals of Comte Maurès de Malartic, 1755-1760

Translated and Annotated by William Raffle

Helion & Company

Helion & Company Limited
26 Willow Road
Solihull
West Midlands
B91 1UE
England
Tel. 0121 705 3393
Fax 0121 711 4075
Email: info@helion.co.uk
Website: www.helion.co.uk
Twitter: @helionbooks
Visit our blog at http://blog.helion.co.uk/

Published by Helion & Company 2017
Designed and typeset by Mach 3 Solutions Ltd (www.mach3solutions.co.uk)
Cover designed by Paul Hewitt, Battlefield Design (www.battlefield-design.co.uk)
Printed by Lightning Source Ltd, Milton Keynes, Buckinghamshire

Cover: Malartic in later life, in the uniform of a general officer (Painting after Jean Tanisch circa 1800-1825, reproduced with the permission of the Musée Leon Dierx, Ile de La Réunion).

ISBN 978-1-911512-19-6

British Library Cataloguing-in-Publication Data.
A catalogue record for this book is available from the British Library.

For details of other military history titles published by Helion & Company Limited, contact the above address, or visit our website: http://www.helion.co.uk

We always welcome receiving book proposals from prospective authors.

Dedicated to Jo. Thank you for putting up with me.

ANNE JOSEPH HIPPOLYTE
Cte DE MAURES DE MALARTIC
Lieutenant Général des Armées du Roi
Commandeur de St. Louis _ Gouvr. de l'Ile de France
1730 - 1800

Contents

Translator's Preface

The Seven Years War in North America has received a good deal of attention in recent years. It has been recognised as a root to some of the causes of friction during the American Revolution and a time of great change for the continent. Despite the interest, sources from the French side of the conflict frequently remain underutilised by Anglophone historians. The most-used accounts translated into English are the memoir by Captain Pouchot and the vivid journal of Bougainville.

This new translation of Malartic is unique in its depth of everyday detail. Unlike Pouchot and Bougainville, Malartic recorded events day by day without introducing opinion or judgement to the events he witnessed. He also maintained the journal throughout the entire war, right up until disembarking at La Rochelle in the November of 1760. Military life is at the forefront. Malartic puts across the difficulties of travel and supply in New France, the harsh winters and quarrels within the army. He kept his journal daily during the campaigning season and it is fairly detailed during the winter months too, showing glimpses of civilian life and the logistical problems of lodging hundreds of men in small habitations.

This translation is based on the printed edition of 1890 which was a transcription of the original manuscripts, which were still held by the Malartic family. This edition contains many footnotes made by Paul Gaffarel, the original editor, which contextualise and sometimes quote heavily from other French sources. These are often highly biased and full of conjecture, however I have retained those which contain contemporary quotes from participants or other points of interest rather than simply opinion. Each footnote of the original is marked 'Note by Gaffarel -' to differentiate from my own. Gaffarel's citations are often vague but details of most of his printed sources can be found in the Bibliography. Malartic added his own occasional footnotes which are preserved, mostly to explain the definition of words which may have been unfamiliar to a metropolitan reader. Despite Gaffarel's partisan nature, his poetic language did supply me with the title for this volume. In his call for a greater recognition for this period of history in France, he hoped that this journal would provide 'glories to the useless heroism and fruitless dedication of their ancestors.'

I have tried to keep sentence structure fairly true to the original. This can often lead to long passages separated by commas and semicolons in place of full-stops. This was common at the time and I felt should be preserved where possible. I have tried to keep word order similar to the French unless the result becomes too difficult to comprehend. French names for English places are retained although English alternatives are noted in their first instance. I have tried to include every place mentioned on the accompanying maps, scale allowing. If I have been unable to locate them then a note has been made of a possible location. Malartic's spelling of the names of people and places varied greatly. In cases of near similarity, they have been standardised; if substantially different, the original is given with correct spelling in square brackets. I have used square brackets for my own comments in the text and Gaffarel's footnotes. To better understand Malartic's references to the military organisation in New France, the account has been prefaced with a short summary of the different troops that served in North America and their organisation. An appendix of French/English Indian tribal names are given, as is a list of French weights and measures used in the text.

Whenever possible, biographical notes have been provided for individuals mentioned by Malartic in the text. Unless otherwise cited, this information has been sourced from the *Dictionary of Canadian Biography* and from Marcel Fournier (ed.), *Combattre pour la France en Amérique: Les Soldats de la Guerre de Sept Ans en Nouvelle-France* (Montreal: Société Généalogique Canadienne-Française, 2009). The biographical note on Malartic which follows this introduction is a truncated version of Gaffarel's with some extra detail from the *Dictionary of Canadian Biography.*

William Raffle
February 2017

Explanatory Note – The French Military in Canada

The French Army

The forces sent to Canada during the Seven Years War from the regular army were referred to as the *troupes de terre*. What many Anglophone historians forget or do not realise is that the colony of Canada came under the jurisdiction of the Ministry of the Marine, therefore supreme military command was given to the Governor General of New France, the Marquis de Vaudreuil. As such, strategic decisions were made by Vaudreuil with the army generals (Dieskau, Montcalm and then Lévis) being subordinates until late in the war. After passing review on arrival in Canada, Captain Pierre Pouchot described the regular soldiers were 'saddened' at now being under the authority of the Ministry of Marine and 'looked upon the event as worse than passing under an absolute foreign prince.'[1]

During this time, regiments of the French army had differing numbers of battalions ranging from one to four, but most had two. The battalions sent to North America were as follows:

New France:

The 2nd Battalions of Béarn (667), Guyenne (672), Languedoc (553) and La Reine (558) were sent to New France in 1755.

The 2nd Battalions of La Sarre (613) and Royal-Roussillon (631) were sent to New France in 1756.

The 2nd and 3rd Battalions of Berry (Total 1,169) were sent to New France in 1757.

Small complements of officers and men of the Royal-Artillerie and the Corps de Génie (52) were sent to New France in 1755, 1757 and 1759.

Louisbourg:

The 2nd Battalions of Artois (634) and Bourgogne (573) were sent to Louisbourg in 1755.

2nd Battalion of Cambis (599) was sent to Louisbourg in1758.

2nd Battalion of the Volontaires Étrangers (708) was sent to Louisbourg in 1758. A force of 150 of the volunteers also went to New France in 1757.[2]

1 Pierre Pouchot, *Memoir upon the late war in North America,* trans. Franklin Benjamin Hough, (Roxbury, Massachusetts: W. Elliot Woodward, 1866), vol. 1, pp. 31-2.

2 The number in brackets is the total number of officers and men of each battalion on arrival

Battalions in the French army were formed in various ways. Regiments such as Guards or foreign raised regiments often held onto archaic organisations and the 1750s was a time when new regulations were ordered throughout the army in an attempt at standardisation. According to the most recent army regulation of May 1754 before the troops departure for New France, each battalion should be formed of 16 companies of *fusiliers* or *soldats* (soldiers) and one company of grenadiers.[3] The grenadiers were the best men picked from the rest of the regiment and, as can be seen throughout Malartic's journal, they were often selected for important combat roles. When the battalion was formed in line they were placed on the right flank of the battalion; the place of honour and seniority. The other sixteen companies would be formed up in pairs to make *pelotons* or platoons.[4] Malartic describes a total of sixteen companies of the Béarn Regiment disembarking along with their grenadiers in June 1755 so it seems that these 1754 regulations were adhered to.

Battalions also had another temporary form of company called a *piquet*. It was formed up when the battalion assembled and 3 fusiliers from each company were designated to it, theoretically for their marksmanship and nimbleness.[5] It formed the left flank of the battalion when in order of battle and is the precursor to the later light or *voltigeur* companies found in the French army. As can be seen from Malartic's journal, sometimes more than one *picquet* was formed and detached for garrison and other duties. Regiments were instructed that if their grenadiers were absent that they should form two *piquets*.[6] As well as these forty-eight men, the piquet included a captain, lieutenant, two sergeants and a drummer, making it a slightly larger unit than the other companies with a total of fifty-two men. The other companies were formed thus;

Rank and Category	Disposition	No.
Fusilier Compagnie		
Capitaine	Compagnie Commander	1
Lieutenant	Second in Command	1
Sergent	Sergeant-Major	1
Sergent	Quartermaster	1
Caporal	Escouade (Squad) Leaders	3
Anspessade[1]	Escouade Leaders	3
Fusilier	Battalion Gun[2]	1
Fusilier	On detachment to *Picquet*	3
Fusilier	Company Escouades	27
Tambour (Drummer)		1
Total		42

in America. All data from Marcel Fournier (ed.), *Combattre pour la France en Amérique: Les soldats de la guerre de Sept Ans en Nouvelle-France*, (Société généalogique canadienne-française: Montréal, 2009), pp. 59-77.

3 *Instruction sur l'exercice de l'Infanterie*, (Paris: L'Imprimerie Royale, 1754), pp. 17-8.

4 Ibid., pp. 17-8.

5 Pengel, R.D., and G.R. Hurt, *French Infantry Regiments 1740-1762* (Doncaster: Imperial Press, 1982), Part 3, pp. 19-20.

6 *Instruction sur l'exercice de l'Infanterie* (Paris 1754) p. 22.

Rank and Category	Disposition	No.
Grenadier Compagnie		
Capitaine	Compagnie Commander	1
Lieutenant	Second-in-Command	1
Sous-lieutenant	Third-in-Command	1
Sergent	Sergeant-Major	1
Sergent	Quartermaster	1
Caporal	Escouade leaders	3
Anspessade	Escouade leaders	3
Grenadier	Company Escouades	36
Tambour		1
Total		47

Both tables taken from Pengel and Hurt, *French Infantry Regiments 1740-1762*, Part 3 pp. 19-20.

Notes

1 *Anspessade* translates literally as 'lance' in old French and is a rank senior to a fusilier but lower than caporal. In the 1762 this rank was replaced with one named appointé. Charles-Pierre-Victor Pajol, *Les Guerres sous Louis XV* (Firmon-Didot: Paris, 1881), vol. 7, pp. 442-3.

2 At various times in the 18th century, each battalion was supplied with a small cannon for support, however in New France there were no guns attached to the infantry in this way.

The *escouade* or squad was a small group of five or six soldiers, led by a *caporal* or *anspessade*. Soldiers were put into squads once they had achieved a standard of basic training and had been considered good enough to pass into the first class which brought with it the privileges of being required to do less drill.[7] Despite these regulation figures the number of men varied from one battalion to another and they were rarely at full complement.[8] The regulation strength of a battalion was around 720, including staff officers. Even on arrival in Canada most battalions were more than 100 men below this total. By the time of the Battle of the Plains of Abraham in 1759, the average strength of the regular battalions was around 450 men.[9]

Malartic's rank was of *aide-major*, this was equivalent to a captain although the role was different to that of a company commander, being focussed on the administration and logistics of the battalion. The most senior administrator of a regiment was the major, however for the battalions of New France, their majors remained in France and so it fell to those officers like Malartic to look after their battalion's food, clothing, pay and lodgings. The prefix '*aide-*' to rank signifies that it is a lower designation of the rank that follows. Thus Malartic was an 'under-major' and Bougainville was an *aide-maréchal des logis général de l'armée*. (The post of *maréchal des logis général* was roughly the equivalent to major general or chief of staff. In 1760 this

7 *Instruction sur l'exercice de l'Infanterie*, (Paris: L'Imprimerie Royale, 1754), pp. 9-10.

8 Lee Kennett, *The French Armies in the Seven Years War* (Durham: Duke University Press, 1967), pp. 29-30.

9 C.P. Stacey, *Quebec 1759: The Siege and the Battle*, (Montreal: Robin Brass Studios Inc., 2002), Appendix H: Order of Battle and Strength, French Land and Naval Forces at Quebec, 1759, p. 251.

rank was renamed *chef d'état-major général de l'armée.*)[10] Malartic would have regularly had to deal with was the *commissaire de guerre*, who was in charge of all the logistics of New France, roughly equivalent to quarter-master general. This office was first held by André Doreil and then Benoît-François Bernier.

The Marine

When Malartic refers to marines or colony troops he is referring to the *Compagnies Franches de la Marine.* This establishment of colonial troops, distinct from marines serving aboard ships, was created in the seventeenth century to provide a permanent armed force for New France. *Compagnies Franches* translates literally as 'free companies'. As such they were independent units with no battalion structure, each one commanded by a captain and under direct control of the Governor General. From 1750 to 1757 there were 30 companies of marines in New France, each composed of 43 *soldats,* 1 *cadet-soldat* (a young gentleman in training to be an officer), 2 *sergents,* 3 *caporals,* 1 *cadet à l'aiguillete* (a more senior cadet) and 1 *tambour.* The cadets were young gentlemen, usually adolescent, who were introduced to military service in the ranks to train with the other soldiers and learn how to become an officer for their future career. This practice seems to have been unique to Canadian troops of the Marine and was started in the 1680s. Companies were commanded by a *capitaine,* a *lieutenant* and a *sous-lieutenant.* From 1757 ten more companies were raised with the complement of men being raised to 65. 1757 also saw the first instance of Marine companies being formed together. In the campaign against Fort William Henry, Montcalm put his available companies together to form a battalion of 525 men. This practice continued up to the Battle of Sainte-Foy when two battalions of Marines were formed, one under chevalier de la Corne and the other under de Vassan.[11]

Artillery and Engineers

The overall commander of artillery in New France was Captain François-Marc-Antoine Le Mercier who had at his disposal a company of gunners, called the *Canonniers-Bombardiers.* Under Mercier it was commanded by a *lieutenant,* and was composed of an *enseigne,* two *sergents,* three *caporals,* two *tambours* and twenty-two *canonniers.* A second company was added in 1757.[12] The men were drawn from the soldiers of the Marines: sailors of the ship the *Léopard* and also soldiers from the army during 1756. In 1757, gunners and officers from the *Corps Royal de l'Artillerie et du Génie* were incorporated (20 *canonniers* and 6 officers) and in May 1759 another twenty-five *canonniers* and two *sergents* arrived. It seems the officers of this unit

10 Charles-Pierre-Victor Pajol, *Les Guerres sous Louis XV,* (Paris: Firmon-Didot, 1881), vol. 7, pp. 537-8.

11 Fournier, *Combattre,* pp. 106-9. This source also mentions *Enseignes* and *Enseignes-en-second* (ensigns and second-ensigns) in the Marines although this rank is not listed in the company establishments. It was possibly introduced as a response to the lack of opportunity for the sons of the Canadian military nobility.

12 René Chartrand, *The French Soldier in Colonial America,* (Ontario: Museum Restoration Service, 1984), p. 27.

held commissions with the *Corps royal de l'Artillerie et du Génie,* the artillery regiment of the French regular army, although the *Canonniers-Bombardiers* were a part of the *Compagnies Franches de la Marine.* According to one historian, this mixture of army and marine soldiers posed 'problems'.[13]

Militia and the Administration of New France

There were three administrative centres, or *gouvernements,* in New France: Quebec, Montreal and Trois Rivières. Each had their own Governor (Quebec's also being the Governor General, Vaudreuil). The militia [*Milice*] included all men from 16-60 capable of bearing arms and was called upon in times of war and for security.[14] Under the town governors were the king's lieutenants who acted as lieutenant-governors. These individuals were primarily concerned with military administration and acted as governor when that official was absent. The position of king's lieutenant was established in Québec City in 1692, Montréal in 1697, and Trois-Rivières in 1715.[15] Below the king's lieutenant was the rank of town major. The position of town major of Montréal was the oldest in New France, the first dating from 1648. The rank brought the responsibility of the town's military administration and particularly the lodging of troops.[16]

13 Fournier, *Combattre,* p. 107.
14 René Chartrand, *Canadian Military Heritage,* (Montreal: Art Global, 1996), vol. 1, pp. 107-8.
15 Ibid., p. 108.
16 Ibid., p. 108.

Biographical Note

Anne-Joseph-Hippolyte de Maurès, comte de Malartic, was a descendant of an ancient family from Armagnac. It can be traced back to Odon de Malartic, a squire living in 1209 and father of Arnaud de Malartic, a crusader who was present at Joppa in 1252. Arnaud had a brilliant military career and an equally important role in the judiciary.

Anne de Malartic was born in Montauban on 3 July 1730 and was the second son of Pierre-Hippolyte-Joseph de Maurès de Malartic, comte de Montricoux,[1] and Antoinette-Charlotte de Savignac de Sainte-Urcisse. They had ten children during their marriage, four daughters and six sons, three of whom became generals.[2] Anne's father, Pierre, was an officer in the Gardes Française. He left his parents while still young, and was sent with two of his brothers to Nanterre College, near Paris, where he was raised. He left at age fifteen to join the La Sarre Regiment as a *sous-lieutenant*. A little later, he obtained a newly raised company in the Béarn Regiment, in which he, as captain, took part in the campaigns in Flanders, Italy and Provence. He fought at the Battle of Plaisance and was promoted to *aide-major* in October 1749.

In 1755 we find him with the force sent to New France in response to the British expedition under General Braddock. The troops were placed under the orders of the governor, Vaudreuil, and commanded in the field by Baron Dieskau. While Dieskau took the offensive south from Montréal, down Lake Champlain towards Albany. Malartic's regiment was placed on the defensive to the west at Fort Frontenac on Lake Ontario, where he got his first impressions of this new country and its people. After his capture at the Battle of Lake George, Dieskau was replaced by General Montcalm. Malartic accompanied this general in all his actions in the coming years: Oswego in 1756 where he acted as an aide-de-camp to Montcalm; Fort William Henry in 1757; Carillon in 1758 (where he was wounded and received the cross of

1 His father, Jean de Malartic had been authorised by patent letters from King Louis XIV, in February 1690, to receive the name and arms of the house of Maurès, registered with the Parliament of Bordeaux on the following 21st April. The name came from Anne de Maurès, comtesse de Montricoux, his maternal aunt.

2 Amable, named comte de Montricoux, first president of the Sovereign Council of Roussillon; – Anne, named comte de Malartic, governor of ile de France; – Charles, a priest, doctor of the Sorbonne, Provost Marshall of Montauban cathedral, Vicar General of Perpignan, Commended Abbot of the Royal Garde-de-Dieu Abbey; – François, named as marquis de Malartic, lieutenant-colonel of the Vermandois Regiment; – Joseph, *aide-major* to the Bourbonnais Regiment; – Ambroise-Eulalie, named vicomte de Malartic, *maréchal-de-camp* and mayor of La Rochelle, deputy in the States General in 1780; Jean-Vincent, *maréchal-de-camp*, entered into holy orders after the death of his wife, became honorary canon of Nancy and the director of the seminary at that town.

Saint-Louis for his conduct), and he was present at the Battles of Montmorency and the Plains of Abraham in 1759. General Montcalm met his end at this fateful battle but Malartic fought on with the army. He was wounded once more at the final battle at Sainte-Foy in 1760, spending the next few months in charge of the wounded French in the hospital and spending some time in Québec negotiating with the British commander, James Murray, and awaiting the inevitable approach of three British armies which would force the capitulation of New France. After the final surrender, Malartic returned to France with the rest of the army.

In the family papers, a letter was found by Gaffarel, written on 22 August 1761 by the marquis de Monteynard, who was charged with inspecting the battalions returned from Canada.[3] It speaks very highly of Malartic and his conduct;

> I received the memorandum of M. de Malartic which you recommended by Madame d'Alzan. I have seen few officers of M. de Malartic's age who have shown the talents that he has: he was known and praised by all the troops who returned from Canada, the seven American battalions speak unanimously to his advantage; he was in charge of their interests in Canada, he was commissioned to the Court where he has made a trip since they returned to France. I will be very anxious to perform the services which depend on me to render him the just reward he is due, and outline to the minister that which I have seen of him and that the battalions with which he has served has said.

In April 1763, Malartic was named Major of the Royal-Comtois Regiment. But Choiseul, the Minister of War, did not believe this to be sufficient reward for his loyal service and proposed his promotion to the King who named him Colonel of the Vermandois Regiment in June 1763. Four years later, newly embarked with his new regiment, he was ordered to go to the Antilles where he was named commander in chief and governor of Guadeloupe, with the rank of *brigadier*, on 3 January 1770. On his passage there he stopped at Martinique and Saint-Domingue to aid the Prince of Rohan in quelling uprisings on those islands.

Returning to France, his regiment was detached at Corsica. When he was recalled he was promoted again to *maréchal de camp* on 3 March 1780 which kept him in constant service up until 1792. It was during this period that Malartic compiled his memoirs, as detailed in his introduction. On 27 January 1792, Louis XVI named him *lieutenant-general* and Governor of the French Establishments in the East of the Cape of Good Hope, with the Ile de France [Mauritius] for residence and capital of his government. The revolution was far away from the Indian Ocean and conflicting news filtered through. The comte de Machamara, commanding the French fleet in the Indian Ocean, was a staunch loyalist and tried to instigate a counter-revolution in 1790. This failed and he was brought before the National Assembly and was hacked to death while trying to escape. By the time Malartic reached the island it

3 Louis-François, marquis de Monteynard, was a *lieutenant-general* and veteran of the Battle of Minden. He was born in 1713 and began his military career as a lieutenant in the Royal des Vaisseaux Regiment in 1728. He was later made governor of Corsica in 1772. M. Lainé, *Généalogie de la maison de Monteynard* (Paris: Moquet, 1840), pp. 91-7.

had suffered from an outbreak of smallpox and the mood was calmer. His policy was to act as Chairman of the Colonial Assembly and to reject any decrees which were judged not to be appropriate to the government of the islands. As such no revolutionary decrees were enacted.

With a modern eye on Gaffarel's biography, one can appreciate his obfuscation of some aspects of Malartic's life. Ile de France and Isle de Bourbon [renamed Réunion in the revolution] were both plantation economies. The revolution declared an end to slavery which Malartic refused to endorse, as Gaffarel recorded:

> In July 1796 two commissioners, Baco and Baruel, were sent to Ile de France to enact the laws whose execution had been suspended and announce the dismissal of the Governor. All the members of the Assembly and its worthy chief protested their attachment and respect for France, but they firmly declared that neither the Colony nor its Governor would submit to the will of the French government, not in order to disobey them, but only because the consequences of what they required would be fatal to the interests of the colonies as to the Motherland.
>
> The object of the claims and demands of the two Directory envoys, having reached the public, stirred up fury and to remove them from their wrath they were hastened to embark on board a corvette destined for Europe. The crowds burst into joy having regained their leader, carrying him in triumph to his palace on the shoulders of a thronging crowd hailing him as a father, by whose wisdom had maintained peace and happiness. After this event, despite complaints, claims and reports by agents sent by the transient powers which succeeded each other in the Metropolis, the tranquillity of the island was not troubled further.[4]

Mauritius was besieged by the British fleet during the Revolutionary and Napoleonic Wars and Malartic, despite wishing to return to France was never granted that request. He died on the island on 28 July 1800 at the age of seventy. On his death, the British squadron which blockaded Port-Louis, ceased fire and, proposing a suspension of hostilities, bowed their yard-arms, giving military honours to the colony in memory of its governor, and firing a shot every half an hour. His body was interred in a mausoleum on the Champ de Mars back in France on the first anniversary of his death. His portrait, used for the cover of this book, hung on the wall of Réunion's only church throughout the nineteenth century with the inscription, 'We give this to the dedication of the saviour of the two colonies'.

Malartic was obviously a great pragmatist, avoiding persecution in the revolution as an aristocratic army officer and holding fast to his objectives and duty at whatever the cost.

4 From Gaffarel's original *Notice Biographique*, pp. xv-xvi.

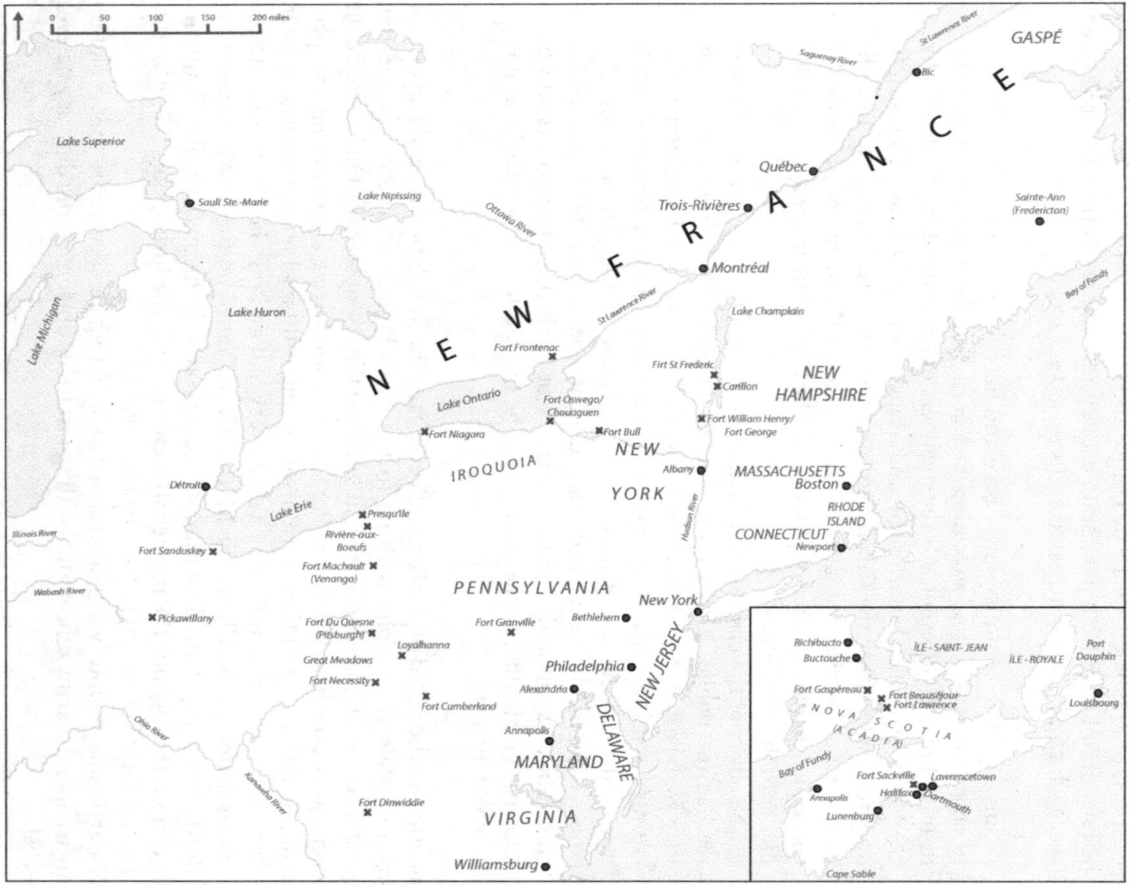

Map 1. The Seven Years War in North America.

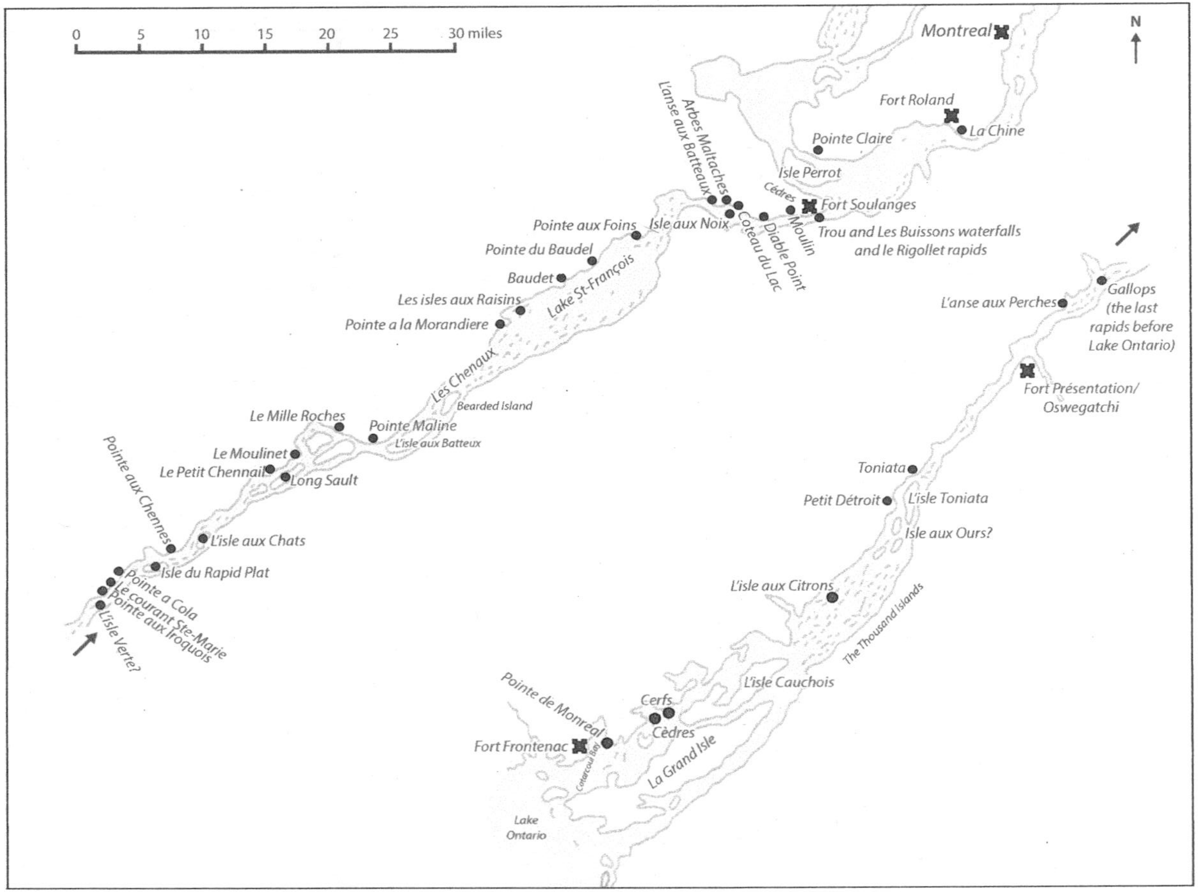

Map 2. Montréal to Frontenac.

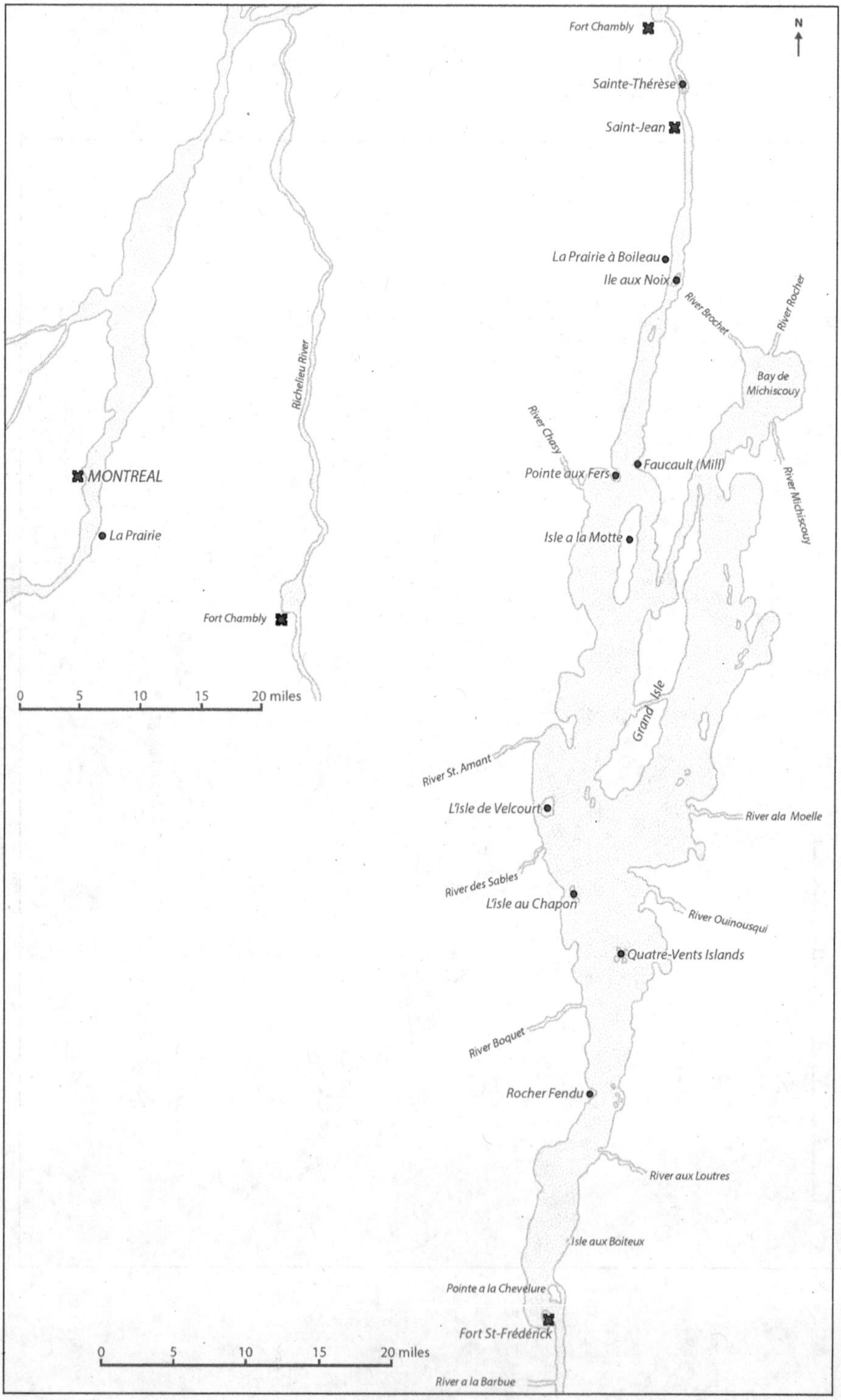

Map 3. Montréal to Carillon.

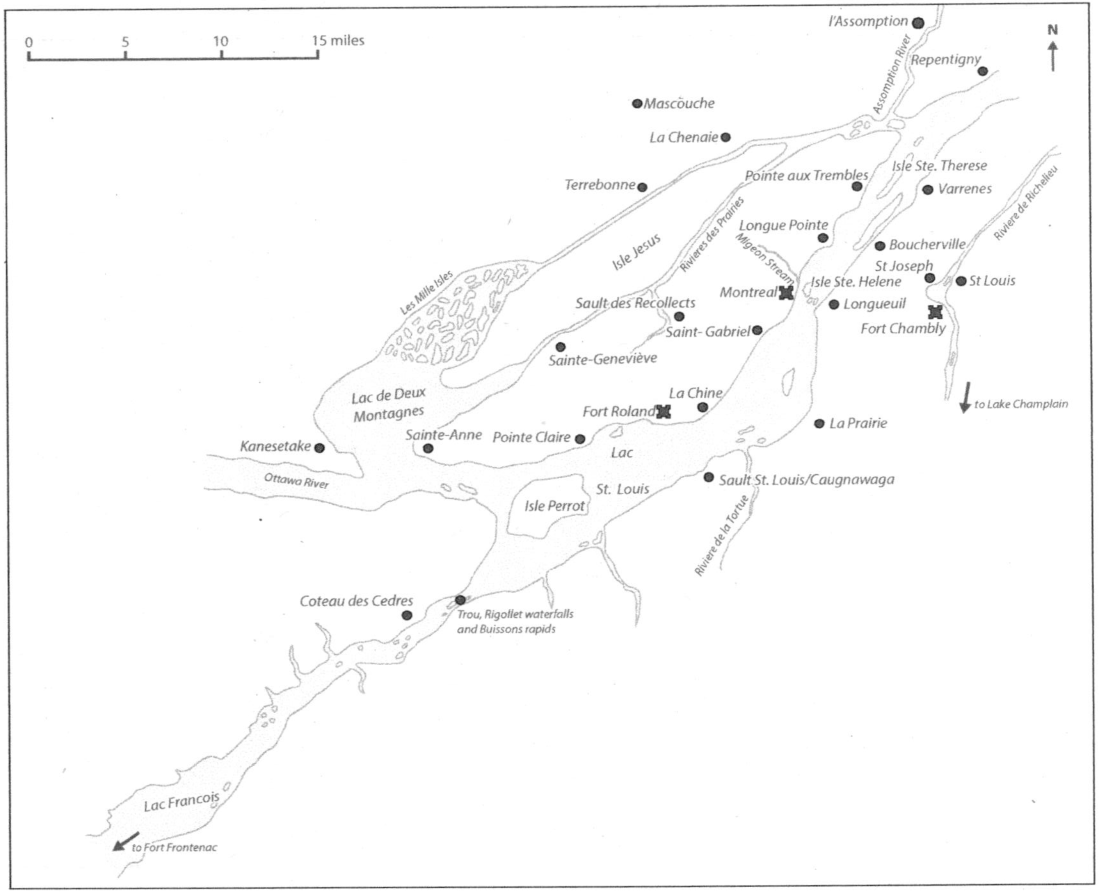

Map 4. Montréal and Surrounding Parishes.

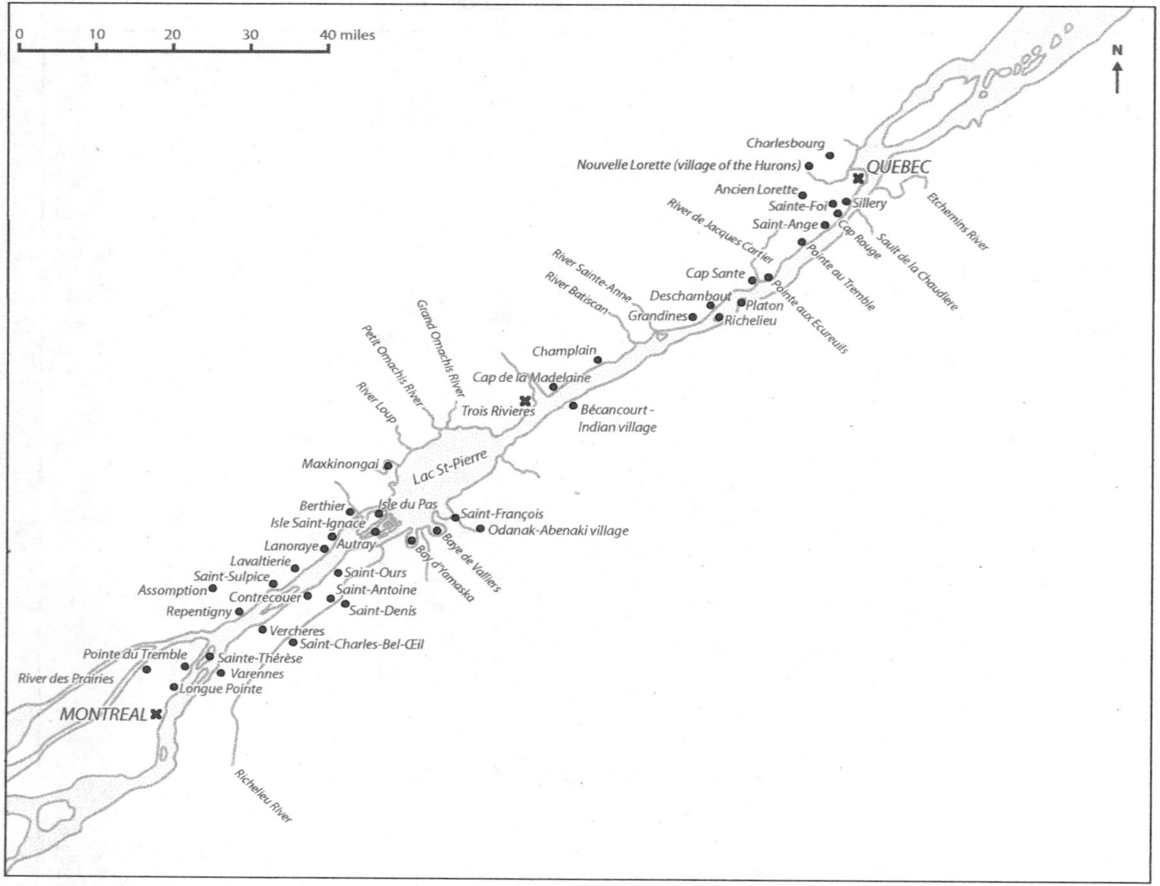

Map 5. Montréal to Québec.

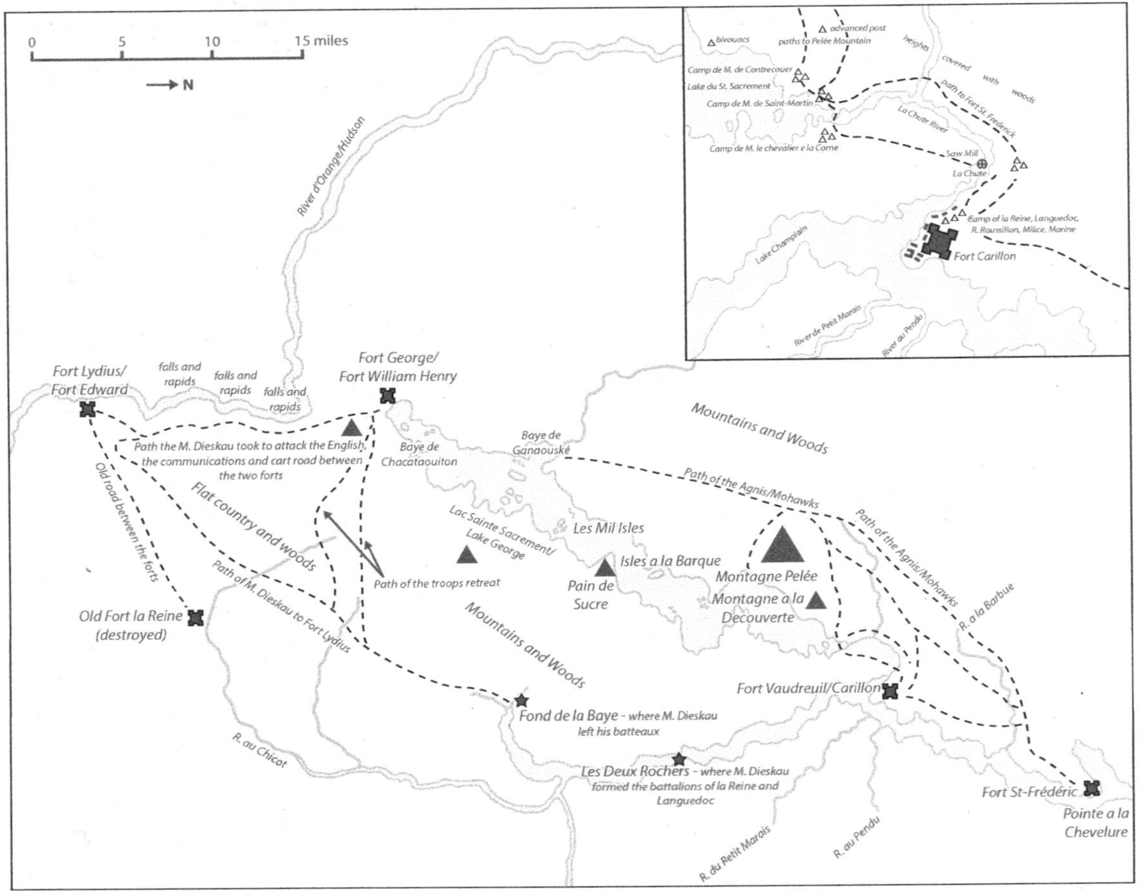

Map 6. Fort Carillon to Fort William Henry.

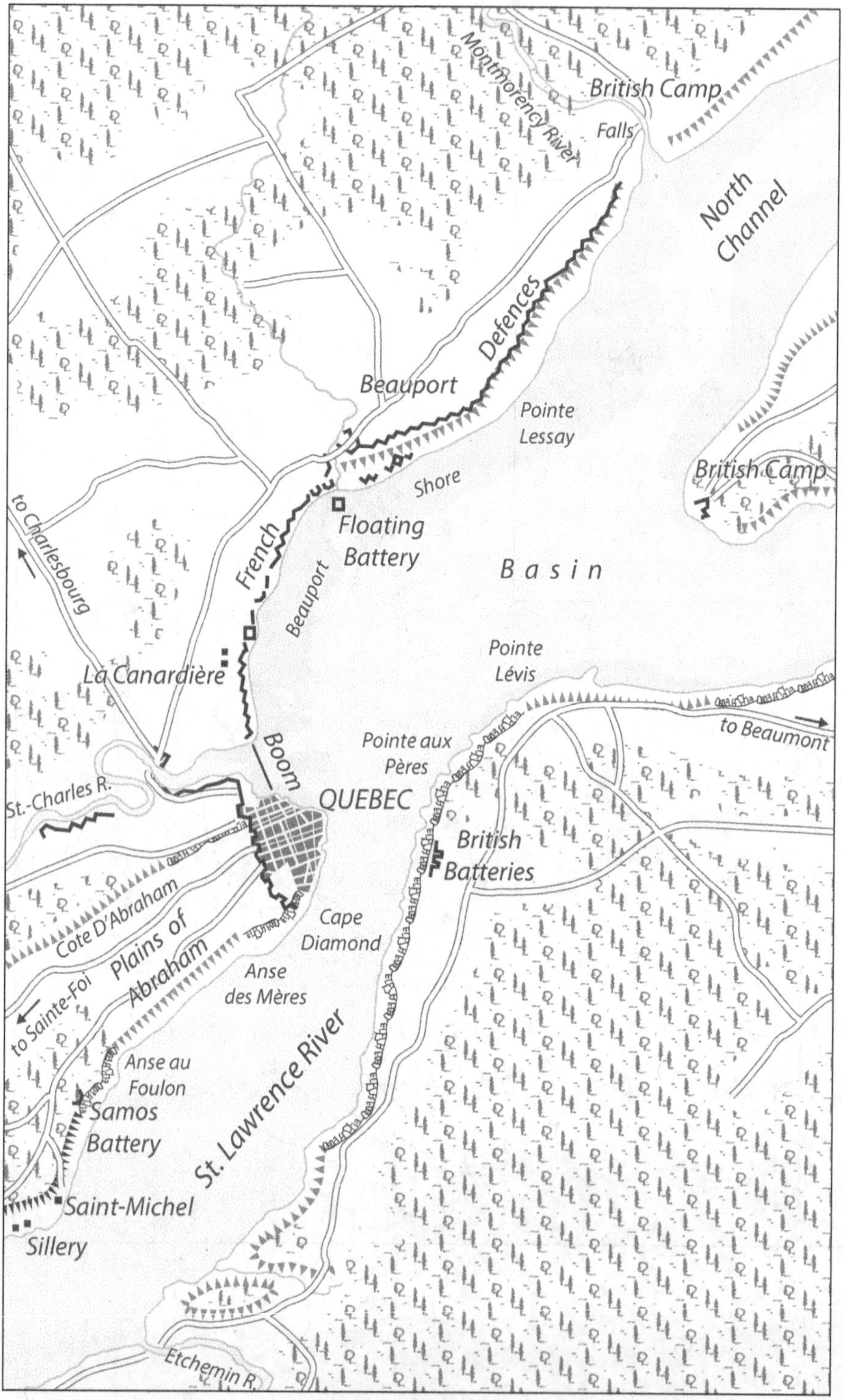

Map 7. City of Québec.

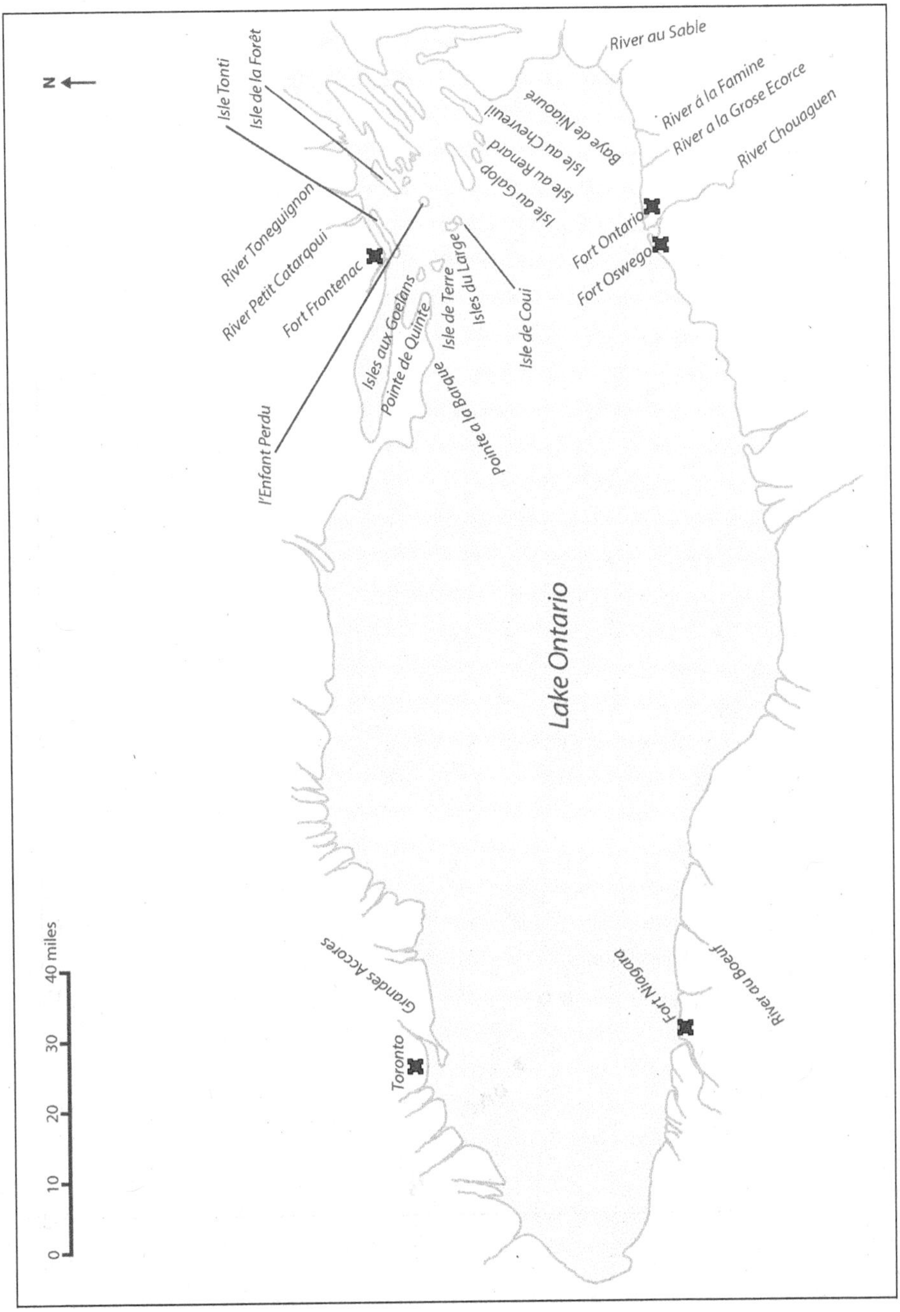

Map 8. Lake Ontario.

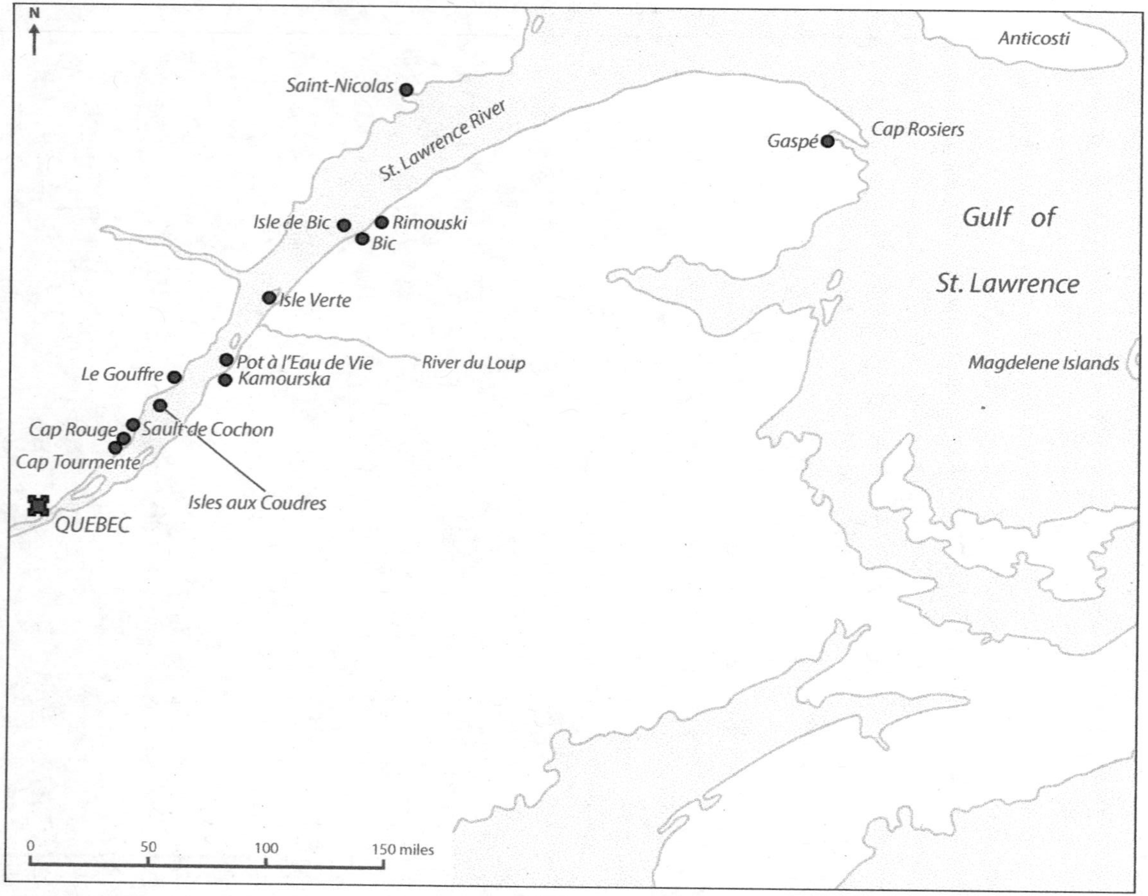

Map 9. North of Québec.

Introduction

Here follows Malartic's original introduction to his memoirs.

When I wrote this journal, I did not intend for it to be read; it was simply for me to remember what had happened in Canada. In 1780 an old comrade of mine of the reformed Béarn Regiment informed me that he was compiling a history of the regiment, and asked if he could use my memoirs to show what happened to the second battalion, from the 8th of April 1755 when it embarked for Canada, until the 25th of November 1760 when it left. I said I would be happy to furnish him with the details and set about reducing an extract to one hundred pages. M. le chevalier de Pontgibault, *aide-de-camp* to M. le marquis de Lafayette, knew that I had served in Canada, and spoke to me sometimes about what had happened during the last war and how he agreed with the insurgents and was astonished that no one had written about this war, as it would prove interesting and instructive. Busy with my extract and remembering conversations with M. de Pontgibault, I decided to pass my journal amongst my friends as I wrote each scene. I should perhaps have deleted small facts, but when one goes to war a thousand miles away, everything is of interest. I could have ignored the personal details, but shouldn't you know of all the details and work of the *aide-major*? I can assure you that they are multiple and often the whole day was not sufficient to accomplish them. I do not intend to aggrandise myself, I have never had any other motivation than to serve the state with vivacity. I hope that the general and senior officers I have served under have approved of me and that I did them justice. The military advancement I have made proves to my young comrades that if you love your job and do your best you will arrive there yourself eventually. More than once I experienced the inconvenience of having my cadets advance before me, while I was hurt I kept quiet. Although I felt strongly I did not murmur, and my time arrived. I must say to those of you who fear to travel the sea as I do, that I embarked on it twice, and was twice offered the chance to remain in France. When the second battalion of Béarn left for Canada, M. le chevalier de Valence, colonel of the regiment, said it would be easy for me to be kept back in France; I prayed that he let me follow the battalion to which I was attached. When the Vermandois Regiment, which I had the advantage of commanding for seventeen years, was ordered to embark for Guadeloupe, M. le duc de Choiseul said that although sending all of the regiment to the islands was advantageous he hinted that it would be easy to just send one battalion. I had the honour to respond to him that I would go to any destination whether convenient or troublesome to me, that my life was at the service and order of the king and ready to leave to whichever country his Majesty would send me to, that I would like best to have the whole regiment in the islands rather than half, as long separations are not good for the corps. I have been well rewarded for my service, by the graces and honour of the king.

Author's Note: I have put some expressions of the Indians and Canadians into the text which seemed appropriate.

1

The Year 1755

The year 1755 saw the escalation of the North American War between Britain and France. After an engagement in the Ohio valley between a force of Virginia Provincial soldiers, led by a young George Washington, and a French-Canadian force, the leader of the latter, Ensign Jumonville, was killed. This caused a diplomatic incident between the two countries as France declared Jumonville had been assassinated. No official hostilities were declared but French intelligence had heard of the embarkation of an expedition of British regular soldiers under the command of General Braddock. In response France dispatched five of their own regular battalions. Braddock led an ill-fated campaign inland through Virginia against Fort Duquesne in the Ohio Valley, but the French regular troops, slowed by the late thawing of the St. Lawrence, would not be able to reach that deep into New France. Instead they were divided to protect the two main approaches to the St. Lawrence valley settlements, guarding Lake Champlain at the newly constructed Fort Carillon and the mouth of Lake Ontario at Fort Frontenac.

The first nine companies of the second battalion of the Béarn Regiment embarked on the 8th of April 1755 on the 64 gun vessel, *l'Opiniatre*, armed *en flûte*, and sailed on the 3rd of May from the harbour of Brest.[1] They arrived before the city of Québec on the 19th of June and disembarked on the 20th, they were lodged with the towns-folk as the barracks had recently burnt down; in the city they found the *etat-major ordinaire* and the Intendant.[2] The Governor General was at Montréal and the Bishop

1 The *Opiniatre* was a 64-gun ship of the line, launched in 1750 at Brest. It was wrecked in January 1758. Details of this and other warships mentioned in the text are from "Three Decks – Warships in the Age of Sail", at http://threedecks.org/index.php. *En flûte* is literally 'as a flute' indicating that the guns have been removed so the vessel could be used as a transport ship. The empty gun ports evidently were reminiscent of the holes of a flute. The Béarn Regiment was, until 1759, the 71st most senior regiment of the French army. They wore the French army uniform of a white coat with red cuffs and yellow metal buttons, a red waistcoat and white breeches. They had a gold laced black tricorn and wore black gaiters. R.D. Pengel *French Infantry Regiments 1740-1762* (Doncaster: Imperial Press, 1982) pp. 3-4 & René Chartrand *Louis XV's Army (2): French Infantry* (Oxford: Osprey 1996) p. 21. They arrived to New France with 38 officers and 629 men. Marcel Fournier, ed., *Combattre pour la France en Amérique: Les Soldats de la Guerre de Sept Ans en Nouvelle-France* (Montreal: Société Généalogique Canadienne-Française, 2009), p. 59.

2 The *etat-major* was the body of French military staff-officers. The Intendant of Canada was the famous Bigot, a controversial figure. In the role of Intendant, he was responsible for finance in the colony and undoubtedly abused his position to become a profiteer. Traditionally he has

at Trois-Rivières.[3] Having established their lodgings, these companies were issued food for four days, which was a ration of a *livre* and half of bread, a *quarteron* of salt pork or a half-*livre* of fresh meat for each man per day. the Intendant gave a dinner for the ships officers, those of the regiment and a party of colony officers.

The city of Québec is divided into the upper and lower parts, the lower bordering the river is inhabited by the merchants of this country and those of France who they call foreigners. They come to spend eight to ten years here to manage the affairs of their company. The upper part is on a cliff, the bottom forms the right bank of the Saint-Charles River. The principal buildings are the government, called the chateau, in the highest part of the town, the Intendant's palace at the foot of the cliff and the Bishop's palace situated midway between the lower town and the chateau. In the main, the houses are built of wood, which is the cause of frequent fires. The Jesuits have a fine house in the cathedral square.[4] The Recollets have a convent near the chateau, the Hospitaliers were in the same neighbourhood which was very nice, but was burnt in the fire along with the barracks. The nuns of St. Benedict have a very nice hospital, called the General Hospital, outside the city, near the suburb of Monréal.[5]

21st June

The officers of the colony gave a very grand dinner to the officers of the marine and Béarn. We made pleasant visits and were received by many ladies who were beautiful, spirited and kind.

22nd June

The Béarn Regiment supplied a guard of 50 men to the ship *Algonkin*, which brought the first nine companies of the second battalion of La Reine, which anchored at 4 in the afternoon at the harbour.[6]

---

been seen as someone whose corruption was so great that New France's eventual fall was a direct result of his actions.

3 Founded in 1634, Trois-Rivières was on the left bank of the Saint Lawrence River, between Québec and Montréal, and was the third biggest settlement in New France. There were rich iron deposits nearby and in 1733 the only ironworks in the colony was established. René Chartrand, *French Fortresses in North America 1535-1763* (Oxford: Osprey 2005), pp. 30-1. The Governor General was the marquis Duquesne. He was in the process of being replaced by the marquis de Vaudreuil de Cavagnac, who would arrive on 23 June 1755. The Bishop of Québec was Henri-Marie Dubreil de Pontbriand, in office since 1741.

4 The Jesuits arrived in Canada in 1622.

5 The Recollects were established in New France in 1615. The Hospitaliers described were Augustine nuns who had founded a hospital in 1639, called the Hôtel-Dieu. It was destroyed by fire in the 7th of June 1755 and the sick relocated into the monastery. The General Hospital or the Hôpital-Genéral de Québec, was founded in 1692 by the Bishop of Québec. He requested that the Augustines run it and four canonesses formed it as an independent monastery in 1701. Despite Malartic's observations there do not appear to have been any Benedictines in Canada at this time. Greg J. Humbert, *A Compendium of the Catholic Health Association of Canada* (Ottawa: CHAC, 2004), Appendix 3, pp. 2-3.

6 The *Algonkin* was a 72 gun ship of the line, built and launched at Québec in 1753. By 1758 it was reclassified as a hulk.

23rd June

The ship *Illustre*, which carried the first nine companies of the second battalion of Guyenne; the *Léopard*, which brought the last four companies of the Béarn battalion; the *Apollon*, which served as hospital, and the frigates the *Siréne* and the *Fidéle*, anchored at the harbour in the morning.[7] M. le Marquis de Vaudreuil, who came to replace M. le Marquis Duquesne as the Governor General, disembarked with them. M. le Baron Dieskau, *maréchal de camp* commander of the army, disembarked at two o'clock with his staff.[8] The companies of La Reine and the battalion of Guyenne entered the town at three o'clock.[9]

24th June

The company of grenadiers and the last three companies of Béarn disembarked.

25th June

All the troops presented their arms for the reception of M. le Marquis de Vaudreuil, and gave him the same honours as a Marshal of France. The Béarn Regiment passed by in review.

---

7 The *Illustre* was another 64 gun ship of the line, commissioned in 1750 and condemned in 1761 after being present at the Battle of Pondicherry in 1759. The *Léopard* was a 62 gun ship, launched in 1727. It was burnt after an epidemic on board at Québec in 1756, which 'carried off the captain, first lieutenant, an ensign, the chief surgeon, the chaplain and about sixty men, both soldiers and sailors, of this ship, three officers and about thirty regular soldiers who were on board, a sickness coming, they say, from the antiquity of the ship and the captain's lack of maintenance and provision for ventilation'. Louis Antoine de Bougainville, *Adventure in the Wilderness,* (Norman: University of Oklahoma Press, 1964), p. 8. The *Apollon* was a 56 gun ship, launched in 1740. It remained as a transport and was at the later siege of Louisbourg where it was sunk as a blockship on the 17 June 1758. The *Siréne* was a 30-gun frigate. Launched at Brest in 1744 it was later captured in an action off Cuba in 1760. The *Fidéle* was another frigate of 24 guns. It was acquired by the Navy in 1748 and later, in company with the *Aquilon* (50), involved in an action fought on 17 May 1756 near Rochefort with the British warships *Colchester* (50), and *Lyme* (28). The *Fidéle* ended up at the siege of Louisbourg and like the *Apollon* was sunk as a blockship.

8 Dieskau was a protégé of Marshal de Saxe and held the rank the equivalent to that of major general. Born in Saxony in 1701 he had a long career in the military. Judged harshly by his contemporaries for his defeat at Lake George, historians have re-evaluated his performance in North America more sympathetically: see Ian Castle, *Fort William Henry 1755-57* (Oxford: Osprey 2013) p. 10. Governor General Vaudreuil was the first of his rank to have been born in the colony. His father had been Governor General in the early 1700s. Vaudreuil had previously been Governor of Louisiana. His role was the highest in the colony and he was responsible for all the military decisions and diplomatic relations of New France. There was great tension between the officers of the regular army and the colonial troops which extended to the top. Vaudreuil and, after the brief command of Dieskau, Montcalm grew to despise each other. Historians have been polarised in their views on this relationship.

9 The Béarn battalion had also arrived with those of Guyenne, Bourgogne, Languedoc and La Reine, all of which were the second battalions of their respective regiments and formed of nine companies each.

27th June

The ship *l'Actif*, which carried the first nine companies of the second battalion of Languedoc, for whom we had become concerned, moored beside the others. These companies disembarked the same day.[10]

29th June

All the troops presented their arms for the arrival of M. Duquesne, who returned from Montréal. The Béarn Regiment were warned to be ready to leave for Montréal.

30th June

The first seven companies embarked in 28 bateaux, each carrying 11 or 12 soldiers, and 3 Canadians to guide them.[11]

1st July

The company of grenadiers and the last five companies embarked in 24 bateaux which were propelled with oars when there was enough water, and with poles where it was shallow. They are steered with oars. They made two or three halts per day to let the rowing soldiers rest and the Canadians smoke. Two hours before nightfall, they dragged the bateaux on to the land to make a wind break. The soldiers stayed in houses or camped under the sails and tarpaulins of the bateaux, which are two halves of canvas, five or six *aulnes* long, used to protect the baggage from rain.

I left the same day by land to go to work on the establishment of housing at Montréal. I crossed the rivers of Cap Rouge, Jacques Cartier and Sainte-Anne, and stayed at a house on the left bank of the River Batiscan.

2nd July

I crossed the rivers of Batiscan, Champlain, and the channels of Trois-Rivières, dining at the house of the Bishop. I enquired if the four days food I had ordered given to the regiment at their passing, could be expedited. This town is jolly and agreeably sited. I left at 2 o'clock, filled with courtesies from M. de Pontbriand, the Bishop, and crossed the River Massis, and at the end of this embarked on the Loup, where I crossed the north channel, to sleep in a poor habitation.

---

10 *L'Actif* was a 64 gun ship of the line, launched at Brest in 1752. It was present with the *Illustre* at the Battle of Pondicherry, fighting against Admiral Pocock's Royal Navy Squadron. It was broken up in 1767.

11 In this context, a bateau (pl. bateaux) refers to a shallow draught small boat, constructed from planks. They were used by most Europeans on North American rivers. They were stronger than native canoes and took less expertise to construct. However, they were much heavier and required greater manpower to portage around rapids and falls.

3rd July

I set off at 3 o'clock and arrived at Chicot. I passed the Assomption river and arrived at 3 o'clock at Montréal, without being tired by the swift voyage made by *calèche* and bateau. The *calèche* is what we would call in France an open cabriolet. The horses were changed every two leagues. One pays 20 francs per league per person or 40 francs for two. One does not find an inn or village, but the road is dotted with homes that are almost all habitable, where one is welcomed and can find food and drink. I alighted at the house of the King's Lieutenant, M. de Cantagnac, an old Languedocian, and M. de Noyen, major, a friendly and intelligent man who offered me his services.[12] I left to go and see the lieutenant-general of police to ask for lodgings.

Montréal is a city which has been well sited on the left bank of the river, divided into upper and lower parts and is surrounded by a stone wall forming five very thin bastions, with seven gates and many loopholes; nearby to the chateau or Hôtel de Vaudreuil, where the Governor General lives, a *cavalier* which is better than all of the *faubourgs* of Québec.[13] The Jesuits have a house where two or three of them stay to correspond with their missions. M. de Saint-Sulpice, *seigneur* of all the island of Montréal, owns all the priest houses in the city, and has a very large house in town; their church is beautiful as the parish. The Recollects have a convent; the Sisters of the Congregation, a house for raising young girls. There are two hospitals, one in the city for the military, run by the sisters of the order of St-Benedict, and one outside, for the poor, run by the Grey Nuns.[14] There are three suburbs, that of Québec, St-Laurent and La Chine.[15]

12 Pierre-Jacques Payen de Noyan was an old soldier, born in 1695 who had been in the colonial regular troops almost all of his life. He had been appointed major of Montréal in 1749 and would see a brief period of active service again before his retirement in 1759.

13 A cavalier is a fortification built within a larger fortification which is higher than the rest of the work. A faubourg is approximate to the meaning of suburb, quite often an agglomeration built up outwards from the city gate.

14 Again this reference to the Benedictines is confusing. There was only one recorded Hospital in Montréal at this time, run by the Nuns Hospitallers of Saint-Joseph and called the Hôtel-Dieu de Saint Joseph. Jeanne Mance, a spirited individual, instigated the hospital at the height of the Iroquois Wars in 1642. Mance appealed to the Hospitallers to come over from France and officially took on the running of the hospital in 1659. Humbert. *Catholic Health Association of Canada*, Appendix 3, pp. 2-3. The Hospital outside the city walls was the Hôpital Genéral and was an institution for the care of the elderly and destitute rather than a medical facility like the Hôtel-Dieu. It was taken on by a congregation of nuns who had received their Royal sanction in 1753 who took on the rights and privileges of the previous order of Brother Hospitallers who had gone bankrupt. *Les grises* or grey nuns got their name from their habits but also the unfortunate reputation of the husband of their founder, Marie-Marguerite d'Youville, who was a renowned bootlegger – *'gris'* is vernacular for drunk. See http://www.greynun.org/who-we-are/our-colorful-name/.

15 Note by Gaffarel – La Chine, today called Lachine, is on the island of Montréal, 13 km Southwest of Montréal, on the left bank of the St. Lawrence, opposite the village of Caughnawaga, Iroquois Falls or St. Louis. This singular name comes from what the first explorers of Canada firmly believed, that the St. Lawrence communicated off to the west with the South China Sea. La Chine was once the port of departure and arrival of travellers from the upper country or hunting in the northwest.

I can appreciate the difficulties of establishing lodgings, the people try to avoid housing officers and soldiers who they dread without knowing why: after I had made arrangements the best I could, I paid polite visits, where I was welcomed and took lunch and supper in several houses.

6th July

The Lieutenant of the King asked me to attend a council to be held with the savages.[16] I called at his house at two o'clock, where I was met by thirty savages; they were told I was the officer they were waiting for; they seemed pleased to see me. They sat on benches and each had a *calumet*, which we know as a pipe, in their mouths. The speaker, who always talks on behalf of the nation, was often applauded by his brothers. When he said something they found to their liking, they rose, and presented a string of wampum to wipe away tears, cover over the death of warriors of two nations or open the throat and unclog the ears. They spoke that their young men had been at council at Orange;[17] that the English had shown them all the preparations they are making against the French, and that it would take little to ensure that they would be masters of Canada. The Lieutenant of the King presented them with three strings of wampum and answered that the great Ononthio, their name for the King of France their father, has sent troops for their defence, and in a few days there will be as many soldiers as there are leaves on the trees, which is an expression that they use for a number they cannot count to. The savages showed their great joy to know that their father had not abandoned them, and that they would be loyal; they reckoned that for giving their help they would like a little milk from the left breast, as that is the one they like the best as it is closest to the heart, by which they mean *eau-de-vie*,[18] and to be given bread and meat. They then took their leave, after having extended their hand, to each of the officers present.

All councils begin with the presentation of strings of wampum which are pieces of shell made into beads and put together in Virginia, and which the savages make much of; these are also made into collars which are given and received at the councils, when they make a promise or promise something; it is this that they call being bound by the collar.

These savages are tall, well made and robust, they have the same skin as us, but theirs is burnt by the strength of the sun and which they spoil with the different colours they use to stain themselves. When they come to council or leave for war, they pluck their beards. In the summer they wear a shirt and breech cloth, which is a piece of cloth which goes around the hips. In winter, they wear a capot, like a

16 The word 'savage' carries a great deal of negative connotation today. The eighteenth century definition should be considered when reading the text as it is not totally interchangeable with that of today. The French contemporary meaning of the word '*sauvage*' is closer to 'wild' and was associated with thoughts of forest spirits comparable to the English ideas of the 'Green Man'. It implies a lack of laws and civilisation rather than simply cruelty. See Peter N. Moogk, *La Nouvelle France: The Making of French Canada – A Cultural History* (Lansing: Michigan State University Press, 2000), pp. 17-20.

17 The name the French gave to Albany, New York after its original Dutch appellation, Fort Orange.

18 Literally 'water of life'. A clear colourless brandy derived from various fruits.

redingote,[19] and *mitasses*, which are two pieces of cloth, one wrapped round each leg. They like blankets which they wrap around them when travelling and to sleep in. The women are dressed in much the same with a piece of cloth around them larger than the breech cloth, called *maxtikote*. The men wear their hair very short, and intertwine it with pieces of bone or ivory, they split the ears, and put in small plates of silver and pieces of binding wire. The women wear their hair long and behind them and cover it in sleeves made of leather and decorated with silver. Men go to war and hunting. Women follow them to carry their things, take care of the cabins, which are a type of tent made with tree bark, and to the *chaudière*,[20] which means getting the dinner, otherwise they remain in the villages to cut the Indian corn that they love and watch over the wellbeing of the family.

7th July

The first division of the Béarn Regiment arrived today and the second on the 9th. The habitants came in crowds to see them go and seemed astonished at their marching and quality.

11th July

The regiment provided the guard of 30 men.

12th July

M. le baron de Dieskau arrived, warning us to prepare ourselves to take the field, and we learned the acts of hostility the English have made in taking Fort Beauséjour, in Acadia.[21]

13th, 14th and 15th July

The officers and soldiers were distributed with the equipment for the campaign.[22]

---

19 From the English, riding coat.

20 Archaic French for cauldron or kettle.

21 Acadia, now Nova Scotia and New Brunswick, had been settled by the French over the seventeenth century. It was sparsely populated compared to the Saint Lawrence valley settlements; however, by virtue of the Treaty of Utrecht signed in 1713, the British maintained it was their territory. A British expedition was launched under Monckton in 1755. After some brief fighting, Fort Beauséjour, the key strategic point controlling the isthmus of Chignecto, surrendered on 16 June. Guerrilla fighting continued with raiding by allied Micmac Indians, despite in the infamous deportation of over 10,000 Acadians. Chris M. Hand, *The Siege of Fort Beauséjour 1755* (New Brunswick: Goose Lane Editions, 2004).

22 Note by Note by Gaffarel – The arms distributed to the soldiers at their departure from France were defective. In a letter from Dieskau to comte d'Argenson, minister of war (29 April 1755): 'The guns which I had the honour to receive some time ago are becoming worse… This disadvantage is most embarrassing, and to remedy this then we must be sent more next fall, and if it is possible, that they be new guns and ramrods, as those that we received break like glass'.

For each man there was a *Capot de Cadix*,[23] a wool blanket, two cotton shirts, a breech cloth, *mitasses*, needles and thread, a pair of tanned shoes, a *livre* of tobacco; a *marmite* for each officer, a tent for four, two per battalion for the servants, and four tents and a *marmite* for each company.[24]

16th July

M. le marquis de Vaudreuil arrived at 10 at night.

17th July

The troops presented their arms for the reception of M de Vaudreuil. M de l'Hôpital received the order to send the battalion in three divisions to camp at Fort Frontenac.[25]

18th July

The first division left by land to go to La Chine three leagues away. They arrived there at 9 o'clock and embarked at noon in twenty four bateaux which carried six soldiers and four Canadians each, food for fifteen days, a ration of two *livres* of bread and one and a half of biscuit, a half *livre* of salt pork and four *onces* of peas for each man per day, and two jars of wine for the journey in addition to munitions of all kind to deliver to Fort Frontenac. After an hour they went to camp at the top of La Chine, a league and a half away.

19th July

They decamped at 5 o'clock, leaving from point Claire lés le Perron,[26] with Fort Roland to the north, unloading the bateaux to go up the Trou, le Rigolet and les Buissons.[27] We were obliged to get in the water and push. I saw that the soldiers were reluctant, so I took my shoes off and began to push the first bateau. I ordered the sergeants to do the same, which restored and maintained order. The division that took the effects disembarked at the bay and re-embarked at les Buissons where we camped at 6 o'clock.

---

23 *Cadix* is a type of woollen cloth. A *Capot* was the hooded, blanket-like coat, synonymous with Canadian troops of the time.

24 A *marmite* is a metal cooking or stock pot.

25 Laurent-Charles Hurault de l'Hôpital was Lieutenant-Colonel of the Béarn Regiment. He was born in 1693 and died in 1757 at Fort Carillon after becoming ill.

26 It seems there could be a transcription error here. Point Claire is next to Isle Perrot, just off Montréal Island.

27 These are the first three waterfalls from Montréal up to Lake Ontario. See Map 2 for the route of the following journey.

20th July

We embarked at 7 o'clock, leaving Fort Soulanges to the north, unloading the bateaux at Moulin, going up the flats [rapids] of Cèdres and dragging the bateaux, we camped at midday on the Soulanges heights where we reloaded the bateaux.

21st July

We set out at six o'clock, went past two points, where it was necessary to haul with ropes, the current being very rapid, passed Diable Point, unloaded the bateaux at the side of the lake, made the portage with the baggage, dragged the bateaux, reloaded them, launched the bateaux, traversing from north to south and south to north until we reached camp at l'Anse aux Bateaux in a clearing in the woods, at the mouth of the lake at 5 o'clock.

22nd July

We embarked at 5 o'clock, traversing l'Anse aux Bateaux, entering onto Lake St-François,[28] but were greatly hampered by the wind from the south west, it being so strong we had to shelter in a cove of Pointe du Baudel. We camped in a pretty meadow at 4 o'clock.

23rd July

We traversed the lake and camped in thick woods at 4 o'clock.

24th July

We set off at 5 o'clock, leaving some beautiful islands and that of la Savatte to the south, going up five rapids where the bateaux had to be pulled and camped at the foot of Long Sault, in a clearing, at 5 o'clock.

25th July

We set of at 5 o'clock, going up Long Sault, which is very long and whose current is very fast. It took 30 men to pull each bateau. We camped at the head of the Sault in a meadow after half a league.

26th July

We embarked at four o'clock, leaving l'Isle aux Chats and some other nice islands to the south, going up many rapids and camping on Pointe aux Chennes, in a pretty wood, at 6 o'clock.

---

28 The name used where the St. Lawrence widens upriver from Montréal.

27th July

We set off at six o'clock, went up several rapids, le Plat, where the current is dangerous, whereon my bateau drifted, and camped at Pointe aux Iroquois, at 6 o'clock.

28th July

We left at 5 o'clock, went up the two rapids of the two Gallops,[29] passed Pointe a l'Ivrogne, and travelled from north to south to get to camp at Fort Présentation, which saluted us with three volleys from five muskets, a habit observed in the colony to impress the savages. This fort is a square flanked by four bastion shaped buildings joined by a curtain wall made of upright stakes. There is a garrison of 30 men. The four buildings are occupied firstly by the commandant, the second by the garrison, the third by the missionary and is a chapel and the fourth is the guard magazine. In all the forts there is a magazine paid for by the King stocked with the necessary effects to give to the savages as presents.[30]

29th July

We embarked at 7 o'clock, passed two points, where we were hampered by the contrary wind, and camped on the Pointe aux Barils in a nice wood, at 3 o'clock.

30th July

We embarked at 4 o'clock, passing islands and the River Toniata, the wind was adverse. We camped on an island facing the Petit Détroit.

31st July

We left at 4 o'clock, made two traverses, and met two canoes laden with furs. From the pilots of these canoes we learned of the defeat of the English on the Ohio River.[31] We passed several islands to the south, landing on l'Isle aux Citrons. Seven Nipissingués joined us to discuss the defeat of the English. M. de l'Hôpital gave them wine and thanked them. We re-embarked to camp in a meadow of l'Isle Cauchois, at 7 o'clock.

29 The Gallops, or Isle au Galop, were a group of islands in the river. See Map 2.

30 Note by Gaffarel – The village of Présentation was founded in 1749 by a Sulpician, Father Piquet. This priest was here during all events of the campaign. He returned to France after the conquest, and died on 14 July, 1781. Fort La Présentation is now an archaeological site at Lighthouse Point, Ogdensburg, New York, at the mouth of the Oswegatchie River. This post was also called La Galette by both the French and English.

31 This was Braddock's defeat at what became known as the Battle of the Monongahela, 9 July 1755.

1st August

We left at 5 o'clock, passing Pointe du Petit Rocher, passing the islands of Cerfs and Cèdres to the south, passing the Pointe de Monréal, to go into Cataracoui Bay, where [Fort] Frontenac saluted us with three volleys of five muskets, we all got out to camp with our right to the river and the left to the fort. The bateaux which had carried us departed in the evening to return to Montréal.

2nd August

The second division arrived at 7 in the evening; a cadet detached from the commander on the Ohio River to carry news of the victory over the English to the Governor General arrived, reporting that the English under General Braddock had been marching to attack at the same hour as M. de Contrecoeur, commander of the Belle Rivière frontier,[32] was holding a council of war with his officers as to the best way to defend the frontier. MM. Beaujeu and Dumas, both Captains, proposed to go and stop the English, scout and lay an ambush; this was unanimously approved; M. Beaujeu, who had come to reinforce M. de Contrecoeur, who could not abandon the fort, would take command. He left with MM. Dumas, Lignery, both captains, many lieutenants and ensigns, and a large party of soldiers, Canadians and savages, who had arrived with him, to take a passage which would be favourable to their plan.[33] He met the English vanguard three leagues from the fort and attacked them with vigour, and was received in the same way, and was killed after the third shot. The English cannon unnerved the Canadians and savages a little. M. Dumas, taking command, perceived this and cried: *Vive le Roi,* rallied the Canadians and the wild savages who were beginning to waver, by proving to them that the cannons were more noise than evil and that by shooting at their gunners the pieces would soon be silenced. They followed this advice with much skill and success. The commander, having regained the men's courage, made a charge which broke the English. Then the savages fell upon them from both sides, the *casse-tete* [hatchet] in hand; at this moment, there was a full scale rout, in which everyone who resisted was massacred: General Braddock did what he could to avoid this, but was forced to retire injured with those who had been able to escape the carnage, he went to die at Fort Necessity, with the regret of ignorance, he said, of those who had beaten him. Colonel Dunbar, commanding the rear guard who did not reach the action, did not try to start a second. It is estimated that the English have lost at least 1,200 men. They abandoned their artillery, their standards and equipment, which enriched the Canadians and Indians. We had only 200 soldiers, many Canadians and 600 Indians. M. de Beaujeu, two other officers, 40 soldiers and Canadians were killed and 100 wounded.

32 The Ohio region was called Belle Rivière by the French.

33 There were 108 officers, cadets and men of the Marine, 146 Canadian militiamen, and 6-700 Indians of various nations. David Preston, *Braddock's Defeat: The Battle of Monongahela and the Road to Revolution*, (Oxford: Oxford University Press, 2015), p. 222.

3rd August

The cadet from the Ohio left at 7 o'clock. The third division arrived at 11 o'clock. Provisions were given to the regiment, the rations were the same size as on the journey.

4th August

The regiment finished establishing the camp. They did not seem tired after the painful voyage and very different from when the troops are in France. The soldiers still carried the oars and poles. They are needed to get into the water to unload the bateaux, drag and reload them while in the rapids. Here is a description of the voyage from Montréal to Fort Frontenac, a distance of 70 leagues. The country is populated up to the Cèdres, a remote parish 15 leagues from Montréal. At Frontenac you can see nothing but water and the forest, nice and flat in certain parts, others treacherous and steep; from Présentation up to the Cascades, the river is very fast flowing without being deep, which is the most difficult part of the journey; from Présentation to Frontenac the water is tranquil and is possible to sail or row with oars as the river has little power.

Eight grenadiers were sent today and yesterday a league ahead along the wooded river bank up to the mouth of Lake Ontario but had no news to report.

7th August

I began to exercise the regiment. The savages brought us venison.

8th August

Some other savages traded some venison for bread, powder and lead. We found this very favourable.

9th August

The savages brought us four deer. The regiment was exercised to my satisfaction. The first division of the Guyenne Regiment entered into the bay at 2 o'clock, disembarked and camped to the right of the regiment.

10th August

At 10 o'clock in the evening the guards fired on some canoes that came from the straight whose guides did not respond.

11th August

Canoes arrived here from Montréal this evening. The last division of Guyenne arrived at 11 o'clock. Three canoes arrived from the straight, which sold some bear skins. Canoe is the name used for the small boats of the savages made from tree bark. They are a lot lighter than wooden bateaux and serve to carry them about all of the *pays d'en haut*.[34] They seat three, five and eight. At their largest they can carry up to twelve men. They are set in motion with oars or poles and unloaded at rapids. Two men remain in to go up them using poles, or they carry them on their shoulders to the top of the rapids. Overnight they take them out of the water to protect them from the wind and waves.

12th August

The Guyenne Regiment provided the guard and Béarn was exercised.

14th August

M. de l'Hôpital, commandant of the camp, learned, at 2 o'clock in the morning from a courier from M. Dieskau, that he would not be joining the troops on this front. The general ordered him to entrench the camp, and not to fear the enemy, but impressed on him that he believed they had more troops than us.

15th August

The new camp was marked out, the right flank to the fort, the left to the river, the forest ahead and the bay to the rear.

16th August

The battalions occupied the new camp and worked all day at establishing it and communications.

17th August

The powder was carried ahead to the centre. The front and wings of the camp were cleared of stones.

18th August

The guard posts were changed. The guard captain would look out on a point on the river bank, where he could see the river mouth, the guard lieutenant in a cove where he could see the captain, and the sergeant at the large cove, all three in front of the

34 'The "*pays d'en haut*" or Upper Country: under the French Regime, this name described the basin of the Great Lakes, upriver from the St. Lawrence, where fur traders, missionaries, and military men ventured beginning in the early seventeenth century. Beyond the 1660s, their visits became more regular. Outposts multiplied, in several cases giving birth to flourishing settlements. That of Detroit, between Lakes Erie and Huron, became something of a capital for the region.' Canadian Museum of History – *The Virtual Museum of New France* http://www.historymuseum.ca/virtual-museum-of-new-france/population/pays-den-haut-and-louisiana/

woods, so they could take cover in them to retreat. At noon a courier arrived from Détroit, leaving an hour later for Montréal.[35] An officer of Béarn, a ship builder and some soldiers arrived in the evening from Montréal, in four bateaux loaded with munitions for the fort.

19th August

The ship builder was charged with building a barque loaded with 12 guns.[36] He sent out a bateau to Montréal to seek out tools and instruments. We began to mark out entrenchments. The savages brought us fish.

20th August

Two bateaux were sent to go to Montréal to bring provisions that are lacking in camp. It was ordered that each company make thirty *saucissons*.[37]

21st August

A larger number of *saucissons* were ordered to be made. The construction workers went to fell trees on the Isle au Cochon, dragging the largest pieces behind their bateaux.

22nd August

The regiments began work on the entrenchments, Guyenne on the right and Béarn on the left.

23th August

A canoe and a bateau arrived from the Ohio.

35 Detroit (literally, the straight) was established between Lake Huron and Erie in 1701 by Antoine de la Mothe Cadillac. It was an important trade site between the French and Natives.

36 A Barque, 'a settee or three-masted vessel with lateen sails.' From the section on French terminology in William Falconer, *An Universal Dictionary of the Marine* (London: T. Cadell, 1769) p. 370. Fort Frontenac was also the French naval base on Lake Ontario. The French already had two transport ships on Lake Ontario, The *Victor* and the *Louise*. This new barque was to be armed and named the *Hurault* and carried eight 6lb and four 4lb cannon. French ships maintained superiority in the early war over the rival British base at Oswego whose ships were not well built or supplied. D. Peter. MacLeod, 'The French Siege of Oswego in 1756: Inland Naval Warfare in North America'. *The American Neptune* 49 (1989): 264–7.

37 A *Saucisson* (literally, sausage) is a double length fascine, around 18-21 feet and 10-12 inches in diameter. A Fascine is a tight bundle of sticks used to build up or reinforce earth walls. Brian Leigh Dunnigan, *Siege 1759: The Campaign Against Niagara* (Niagara Falls: Old Fort Niagara Association, 1996), p. 139.

24th August

Very stormy and heavy rain.

25th August

Much work achieved. A canoe came from Montréal, which carried three men and two women, alighting at the camp.

27th August

Heavy rain. Ten savages, coming from Niagara in a big canoe, disembarked behind camp with two sick who had been covered in the canoe. After carrying them to land, they spread out all their wares brought back from the Belle Riviére.

28th August

Steady work. At four in the morning, three canoes loaded with furs arrived at the fort and left after two hours for Montréal. These canoes belong to the merchants who pay the Governor General 500 *livres* for a license, which grants permission to send canoes loaded with merchandise to trade with the savages of the *pays d'en haut*. The Governor General uses the profits of these licenses to reward families who receive little help from the nobility.

30th August

Four bateaux loaded with furs from Détroit, landed at eleven at the fort and left at two for Montréal. After this arrived twelve canoes of savages loaded with game and fish, which was sold cheaply. There was deer, sturgeon, several good white fish, teal and plovers.

31st August

A drunken savage hit a sentinel, who wisely defended himself without beating him and waited until the corporal arrived to relieve the nuisance. Many canoes and cattle which arrived here departed this morning. Left behind are eight drunken savages who play the devil.

1st September

The savages, regaining their reason, departed. Then more arrived, bringing game and ducks.

3rd September

The builder put up the keel of the corvette.[38] Very bad weather.

4th September

The bad weather continues. The patrols were augmented and slept under bivouacs of four grenadiers, to go and reconnoitre two bateaux which were passing between the islands.

6th and 7th September

Bad weather. The savages brought game and duck.

9th September

Bad weather. At 11 o'clock, five Algonkins arrived, very alarmed at having lost two comrades and a woman who they had left guarding their canoes, near to Chouaguen;[39] their panic did not last long: some hours later they arrived in a small bateau stolen from the English.

11th September

The two regiments performed firing exercises.

12th September

The Abbé Piquet, superior of the mission at Présentation arrived with forty savages.[40]

38 This corvette was to be named the *Marquise de Vaudreuil.* It was not launched until 1756 but would be larger than the *Hurault* carrying eight 8lb and eight 6lb cannon. D. Peter. MacLeod, 'The French Siege of Oswego in 1756: Inland Naval Warfare in North America'. *The American Neptune* 49 (1989): 264–7.

39 Chouaguen, on the southern shore of Lake Ontario, was in Iroquois territory, and had been established as a trading post called Oswego by the British in 1727. Its intention was to lure in Indians from the west away from French traders. The governors of Canada repeatedly protested this incursion. It became fortified over the years and provided a natural harbour to establish a ship yard in an attempt to rival Fort Frontenac.

40 Abbé François Picquet was a Jesuit priest who had been in New France since the 1730's. He founded la Présentation in 1749 with 25 Frenchmen and 4 Indians. By Autumn there were more than 300 Indians there. Picquet saw himself as a holy warrior and when war was declared he was everywhere with 'his' Indians, bringing the fight to the enemy. He quietly slipped out of Montréal before its surrender in 1760, travelling south to New Orleans and then to France.

13th September

The savages sang the war song, forming a circle. Each sings the song in turn, recounting his exploits.

14th September

After a report of the savages, who assured that a flag had been seen on the Grande Isle yesterday, the commandant sent seven of them with as many grenadiers, to go and make a patrol. They returned four hours later, without discovering anything. At four o'clock, the savages believed they saw an English *barque*, but it was our own that the strong wind had pushed wide. A clerk of the marine arrived from Niagara in a small canoe with two Outaouas and took the office of commissary.

18th September

An Iroquois, suspected of being strongly attached to the English, left at 10 o'clock in his canoe. At noon twenty men embarked in two bateaux. They caught up with him at the l'Isle au Cochon, where they brought him back.

19th September

Twelve bateaux arrived from Niagara loaded with furs and other items. They carried some sick.

20th September

The bateaux left. The Béarn Regiment exercised.

21st September

The two regiments were exercised in firing.

22nd September

Very bad weather. The savages got drunk and became devilish. The commander was almost beaten by one to whom he had refused drink.

23rd September

The regiments fired by palisades.[41]

41 A drill to efficiently present a continuous fire from a firing step at a fort.

24th September

The Béarn Regiment began a supporting wall to enclose the left of their camp.

25th September

At 2 in the morning, two couriers arrived despatched from Montréal. The first carried orders for the Guyenne Regiment to leave to go and reinforce the army of M. Dieskau, which had retired to Fort St-Frédéric,[42] the second carried contrary orders in which we learned that M. Dieskau, had taken forward a corps of 1,500 men composed of troops from the army, the colony, the Canadians and savages, and encountered a detachment of one thousand English. He forced them back to their entrenchments with considerable loss, he wished to storm their defences, was repulsed, dangerously wounded and taken prisoner by thirty men. We lost three officers, forty soldiers or Canadians, and had two hundred wounded: we do not know the English losses. They are believed to be considerable, as the corps which pushed them back to their defences punished them severely.[43] M. de Vaudreuil has decided not to withdraw troops from the Frontenac frontier, fearing that the English may move into these parts or on Niagara, which is a poor fort at the entry to Lake Ontario, and is the mouth to the upper country. M. de Villiers, captain of the colony, currently with five hundred men, left at daybreak, after being given orders from a cadet in a bark canoe.

The savages arrived at two in the afternoon with two prisoners they had taken from Chouaguen. They say they killed three men. The prisoners reported that General Shirley is at Chouaguen with 2,000 men; that they have constructed four corvettes or boats, two with twelve cannon and the others with eight, and are deciding whether to attack Frontenac or Niagara. At nine in the evening, the sergeant of grenadiers, who commands the bivouac, gave a report that he had seen four full sailed canoes coming, which tacked and changed course, after they shouted 'who goes there?'. At eleven o'clock, twelve grenadiers and also some Canadians went to reconnoitre and search the reeds of the bay of the Petit Cataracoui. Here they found four canoes of Mississaguès women, who they said were very afraid.

26th September

The detachment that left last night returned, followed by the four canoes. Abbé Piquet left with the savages and prisoners.

---

42 Construction of this fort was begun in 1731 in response to intelligence that the English were planning on taking the land on Lake Champlain which they called Crown Point. Initially only a wooden stockade, it was rebuilt in stone by 1737. Like most forts of this period it was built to withstand an assault, not a siege and by the 1750s and the prospect of heavy artillery being used in the American interior, it was judged to be in a poor site, overlooked by surrounding heights. René Chartrand, *The Forts of New France in Northeast America* (Oxford: Osprey 2008), pp. 31-2.

43 Dieskau was defeated at the Battle of Lake George on 8 September, was wounded and taken prisoner to New York.

27th September

The cadet who left for Niagara has returned giving his report that he travelled to the l'Isle Tonti, he surveyed the land and returned without being discovered, seeing some fires surrounded by the English. M. de l'Hôpital sent M.M. Wolff and Carpentier, partisan officers, into the field, supported with twenty soldiers taken from the French regiments, sixty seven Canadians and fourteen savages in six bateaux, their orders were to disembark with great care and to remove the enemy from the island.[44]

28th September

A violent wind from the south forced the fourteen recently departed savages to rest up at the Petit Cataracoui.

29th September

M.M. Wolff and Carpentier have returned with their detachments, reporting that they discovered, on the 28th in the morning, at the Isle de Coui, twelve bateaux and their pilots who assured them that it was they who had camped on l'Isle Tonti the day the cadet had left. The officers of the bateau party said they had not encountered any enemy on the lake.

30th September

The bateaux, after having been refitted, left for Montréal.

1st October

The Béarn Regiment was exercised, then at 6 in the evening Guyenne received an order by courier who had left Montréal on the 27th, to leave immediately for Niagara, to work on the fortifications of the post and to make barracks to house four hundred men. M. de l'Hôpital also received orders from the same courier to send M. de Pouchot, captain of the Béarn Regiment and a good engineer, to Niagara, to direct the fortifications there, and to reduce as much as possible the extent of Fort Frontenac's entrenchments and build barracks to lodge 300 men.

44 Both Wolff and Carpentier had travelled with the regular troops. Both were *lieutenants réformés*, essentially officers attached to the army without a company, but both with the specific role of partisan officers, hence the job they were given. It is interesting to note that both men had risen from the ranks as sergeants. Wolff had come from the Bentheim Regiment and was German in the service of France, while Carpentier was from the Piedmont Regiment. They served readily in various sized groups, often in command of militia groups or raiding parties and were praised by General Lévis at the end of the war. See Bob Bearor, *Leading by Example* (Bowie: Heritage Books, 2007), Vol. 3, pp. 119-132.

2nd October

We began preparing the bateaux necessary to carry the Guyenne Regiment and their munitions, and armed and loaded the two *goelettes* in the bay which have not yet been used this year.[45]

3rd October

A courier from Détroit told us that there is nothing new in those parts. We sent a courier to Niagara. A lieutenant of artillery, commanding a convoy of six bateaux loaded with guns, came to present M. de l'Hôpital with packets of letters from M. de Vaudreuil, and then returned to his convoy which had arrived during the night.

4th October

The Guyenne Regiment have taken supplies for 15 days. The bateaux not entirely equipped will leave tomorrow. The lieutenant of artillery moved the artillery of the fort, which he found to be in a poor state.

5th October

Guyenne embarked at 10 o'clock, in forty-five bateaux and have left 60 men to guard the two *goelettes*.

7th October

The *goelettes* sailed at 11 o'clock, saluting the fort which returned the gesture, and moved out into the bay with a good north wind, after an hour the wind abated and they were obliged to anchor at the Pétit Cataracoui.

9th October

M. de l'Hôpital has drawn up plans for twelve large rooms, which can hold around twenty-five to thirty men each. I loaded up two bateaux.

10th October

I took orders from the commandant and have embarked with a sergeant, twelve soldiers and eight Canadians, to go to Montréal to make representations to M. de Vaudreuil, to provide equipment and the needs of the detachment. We stopped

45 *Goelette* is French for Schooner, defined as 'a small vessel with two masts, whose main-sail and fore-sail are suspended from gaffs reaching from the mast towards the stern, and stretched out below by booms, whose foremast ends are hooked to an iron, which clasps the mast so as to turn therein as upon an axis, when after ends are swung from one side of the vessel to the other.' Falconer, *Universal Dictionary*, pp. 277-8. These are presumably the *Louise* and *Victor*, the transports mentioned above, that made runs between Frontenac and Niagara.

overlooking the Isle Cauchois, above Isle aux Citrons, to let the soldiers and Canadians eat and smoke. We found some Mississaugués who gave us deer in return for bread and we encamped in a small cove overlooking the strait, at eleven o'clock.

11th October

We embarked at six o'clock, descended onto the Isle aux Ours, at the Toniata Islands we met bateaux going to Frontenac, stopped at the outpost of these islands to make a fire, and we went to sleep in Fort Présentation; I found the commandant at table with eight savages of the Five Nations who carry wampum collars for M. de Vaudreuil.[46] The eight did not have the men to lead our bateaux down the rapids so I went around them. At eight o'clock, I spotted to the north, some bateaux passing through the rushes, I made my own bateau cross to meet them. I asked the pilots to guide the front and rear of my bateau, they gave me two who were very good taking us through the rapids to the south of the island. We disembarked at l'Isle Verte to make a fire, we crossed to the north to speak to the Iroquois who were in cabins, they gave us deer for our bread; we went over the Plat Rapids, we were assailed by thick snow and a contrary strong north-east wind. We descended on a small island to let the weather clear with a long bank ahead of us, which we crossed slowly two hours later, and encamped on an island below Pointe Maline, after fifteen miles.

13th October

We embarked at seven o'clock; at the entrance to the channels we met a *bateau du cent*, from whom I took two sacks of biscuit for fear of going hungry because, as usual, we had not been given enough supplies for four days. The northeast wind was very blustery and at ten o'clock we were forced to land on the Isle aux Noix; the soldiers picked many nuts which were as good as those in France but very difficult to crack. *Bateaux du cent* are those which carry provisions or ammunition, carrying a weight of seven thousand *livres* and are piloted by four or five Canadians.

14th October

Very bad weather. At midday the wind dropped, the guides hoped it would change, we embarked an hour later and crossed Saint-François Lake without rest, fearing we

46 Five Nations was another name given to the Iroquois confederacy who were made up of the Mohawk, Oneida, Onondaga, Cayuga and Seneca tribes. By this time, though, there were six nations as the Tuscaroras had been brought into the league in 1722. The Iroquois confederacy was a powerful union whose territory spread from the Mohawk River in the east to Niagara in the west. Traditional enemies of the French, they were more disposed to France during the Seven Years War than previously as their treatment from Britain had worsened. Scholars now refer to them with their own name, the Haudenosaunee rather than Iroquois which is derived from the name the French gave to them. See Daniel K. Richter, *Ordeal of the Longhouse: The Peoples of the Iroquois League in the Era of European Colonization* (Chapel Hill: University of North Carolina Press, 1992).

would be forced onto another island and die of hunger. We landed at Côteau du Lac, my bateau grounded on a rock which flipped it over, we had trouble getting out, and righted it by pulling the top of the crossbeam. We arrived very wet at the first houses of Cèdres at ten o'clock.

15th October

We embarked at seven o'clock, crossing the Cèdres flats, while the bateaux were brought over I went to see the officers of the Guyenne Regiment who were going to Niagara, who gave me many letters. As soon as I knew the bateaux were at the bottom of the falls, I ran to get on board to profit from the good wind blowing from the south west and within three hours we passed La Chine. At the King's magazine I returned the register of the bateaux and tents which would be necessary for our return journey, and I walked on foot to Montréal where I arrived at five o'clock.

18th October

My soldiers who I had allowed to rest a La Chine, arrived at eight o'clock. I stayed five days at Montréal to distribute that which I had been asked by the officers and soldiers who would spend the winter at Frontenac, and to make provisions that I thought necessary for these comrades who would have to spend eight months in a deprived country, and to take these from the commissary of marine who was not lacking in these indispensable things.

21st October

I took orders from M. le Marquis de Vaudreuil, who overwhelmed me with pleasantries and marks of friendship; I had sent my soldiers to La Chine yesterday and I went to join them on the 22nd at eight in the morning. We embarked at 9 o'clock, and stopped at midday at Pointe Claire to warm ourselves. A very contrary wind forced us to stay there.

23rd October

The wind permitted us to leave at 2 in the afternoon. We made our way to the Isle Perrau [Perrot] where we slept; I lodged with the *seigneur* who had a very nice commodious house.

24th October

We left at eight o'clock. We traversed the falls, unloading the bateaux at the base of the falls. I sent for carts to carry their cargo to the top of the Cèdres, so that our bateaux could return that evening and make the journey in one day which would normally take two. The carts arrived at six o'clock. I went to the last houses to prepare food and drink for the soldiers and Canadians who were very tired.

25th October

It was snowing heavily at daybreak so that we could not leave until nine o'clock. We went past two bad points and then past Pointe Diable, unloaded the bateaux at Cote du Lac, went up le Rigolet, made the portage, stopped for half an hour to warm ourselves and let the men dry who were soaked with water, rounded Pointe du Côteau and camped there in a pretty wood; there we met the guides of the *bateaux du cent* who were awaiting men to replace some of theirs that had contracted small-pox and been dismissed.

26th October

We left at seven o'clock, going up the Côteau rapids, travelling from north to south and from south to north to get up to the Arbres Maltaches. Arriving at the cove, where we discovered a fire and supped with the soldiers who were travelling by land; we entered the St-François Lake, rounded the Pointe aux Foins, and disembarked on that of Baudet. Here one of my guides fell ill. I found he had the symptoms of small-pox, so I covered him well and placed him comfortably in a bateau to wait for a favourable time to send him back. We went to camp on Pointe a la Morandiere, where my bateau was punctured, which filled it with much water.

27th October

We perceived a bateau going down river; we signalled him with a flag to come to us but he pretended not to understand and went wide. I took fifteen men and embarked in my second bateau where I ordered them to fire on the fugitive, but not to injure, just to scare him. They executed the commands skilfully; having fired two shots, a ball pierced the sail and another hit an oar; the master of the bateau came up and tacked to join us. He gave me many excuses, that he had attempted to comply but had become stuck on a tree so he could not obey our signal; fearing he may take vengeance on my sick man, I apologised, and asked him for a man to replace my sick one. We separated at 8 o'clock and went past the Pointe aux Joncs, les Isles aux Raisins, entered into les Chenaux, where we discovered two bateaux which we pulled up to approach; they had the wind behind them though and continued on their route, we saw a third bateau at the edge of an island which we perceived to be changing its course. I made my bateau set course to cut it off. We continued to chase, and approached close enough to fire two musket shots. One ball hit the arm of the sail which brought them out, they came to us and we followed them. I proposed to the pilots that they take my bateau as it took on too much water to finish the journey and they give me theirs. We loaded the baggage from one into the other and separated happily. We went to camp on the Isle a la Traverse. The soldiers had killed some partridges and these small birds were very good. The partridge resembles a grouse and is very tasty. Six Iroquois of Présentation who were returning from carrying wampum of the Five Nations to the general, camped with us.[47] I gave them some bacon and a little *eau-de-vie*.

47 Malartic is referring to Governor Vaudreuil as the general, who was commander-in-chief, above Dieskau and later Montcalm, a point often missed by Anglophone historians.

28th October

We embarked at seven o'clock, passing three points which had a violent current, passed by the Tiensagué River, le Mille Roches, le Moulinet, la Grande-Batture, le Petit Chenail, we went up Long Sault, one bateau after another, and we camped on its plains.

29th October

We decamped at 8 o'clock, rounding two points which had a strong current, we stopped and made a large camp to wait for the soldiers who came by land, leaving the Isle aux Chats to the south, the peninsula, went past its point and rapids, and encamped a league from la Grosse Roche.

30th October

We left at 7 o'clock, passing three points, going up the Plat Rapids, the Pointe a Cola, passed the Rideau River, la Pointe and le Courant Ste-Marie and camped 2 hours later.

31st October

We departed at 7 o'clock, and passed three difficult points, we went up the two Gallops, disembarked into l'Anse aux Perches, made the traverse from north to south to arrive at Présentation, where we arrived at 2 o'clock. I was very astonished to find the two officers of the Guyenne Regiment that I had seen at Buissons, and I had much amusement that I had caught up with them before they had reached Frontenac. M. Duplessis, who was commander of Niagara, arrived at 10 in the evening.[48]

1st November

I embarked at 8 o'clock. I gave passage to the two officers of Guyenne and M. Duplessis who followed us. We stopped at the Pointe au Baril, we entered into the Toniata Islands and went to camp at the Toniata River in ugly terrain.

2nd November

We embarked at 7 o'clock, meeting up with bateaux from Frontenac which were making a sortie of the islands, we disembarked on the Isle aux Ours where we took a large quantity of bustards and ducks, stopping at a small straight to find a tolerable camp; we could not find anywhere so we went to establish one on the Isle aux Citrons, where M. Duplessis did not arrive.

48 François Lefebvre Duplessis Faber was a career officer of the colonial troops. He had served in Louisiana in his youth and commanded various posts, receiving the Cross of St. Louis.

3rd November

We embarked at seven o'clock, stopping at the Isle Cauchois. A contrary wind from the south west impeded our travel, we were forced to rest up at Petit Rocher until 3 o'clock. We passed the Couiard Bay, where M. Duplessis caught up with us and we arrived at camp at 4 o'clock. I was received with open arms by my comrades who gave me no time to disembark but carried me away to learn the news and what had become of our detached officers; after having given M. de l'Hôpital his packets and given him an account of my voyage, I told him that M. de Vaudreuil had decided we should leave Frontenac which would be left manned by three piquets commanded by the three junior captains. He seemed happy to hear this and I was to be ready to return in thirteen days if we had good weather.

4th November

I examined the corvette which had been launched during my absence; this was loaded with provisions as well as the two *goelettes*, for Niagara. The ship builder received the order to build another stronger one during the winter.

5th November

I distributed to the officers and soldiers the effects I had brought. I oversaw works on the barracks.

6th November

I made a tour of the retrenchments which had been perfected during my absence. They were composed of a grand redoubt at the head of Guyenne's camp joining to the fort with a great branch of palisades, all sharpened, then two smaller palisades at the front of the Béarn camp, like those of Guyenne, linked with a curtain wall to the fort, and a supporting wall which extends to the bank of the river, all sharpened.[49]

7th November

Three bateaux were equipped to go to Présentation carrying boards used for covering the barracks; five *bateaux du cent* arrived.

9th November

I equipped a bateau in which I was to leave in the following day with a man from each company, to establish lodgings for the regiment over winter. I gave money on account to the officers and soldiers who were to remain at Frontenac over winter. We were obliged to unload the corvette as it had become grounded due to it being

49 Sharpened refers to the ends of the logs which made up the wall, giving a spiked appearance.

loaded too close to shore; we were supplied with a guard of thirty men commanded by a lieutenant.

10th November

I embarked at 8 o'clock. I will not repeat the details of the journey having done so above. I arrived at Montréal in the evening of the 13th. The *commissaire de guerre* told me the regiment was to occupy the parishes of Longueuil, Prairie and Boucherville.[50]

I rested on the 14th, 15th and 16th. It is much quicker to travel from Frontenac than it is to return. It is a voyage of three or four days barring any mishaps by sail or rowing. At the falls and rapids, the guides at the prow and stern of the bateaux steer with their oars, so as to follow the path of the water, the current being so fast that it is not possible to count the trees along the river banks. It is said that the bark canoes descend in the same manner but they can be fully loaded.

17th November

I travelled on the river to visit the parishes we had been assigned. I landed at Boucherville, going to sleep at Longueuil which is two hours away. On the 18th I went along to la Prairie which is three hours from Longueuil; these three parishes are on the right bank of the river and are very nice. I returned to sleep at Montréal.

19th November

M. de Vaudreuil invited me to l'Isle Sainte-Hélène to dine with the Agent General of the Compagnie des Indies.

20th November

I sent two soldiers to La Chine, one of them returned to tell me that a bateau of the regiment had arrived.

21st November

At 6 in the evening, a soldier came to tell me that the regiment's lieutenant of grenadiers had returned to La Chine and would be followed presently by the rest of the regiment. I went to inform the general and ask his permission that the regiment

50 The *commissaire de guerre* [commissary of war] was independent from other military leaders, empowered by the King and reported to the Minister of War. They were present at councils of war to advise the leaders, were responsible for provision for the troops, barracks, guards and other military buildings, excluding fortifications. Pajol, *Guerres*, vol. 7, p. 473. The *commissaire de guerre* was André Doreil, who had come out with the French army in this year. Doreil was promoted to *commissaire ordonnateur des guerres* in 1756 which meant he was authorised to make financial decisions. He appears to have taken a genuine interest in the troops' welfare and to have taken his role seriously. He was ambitious and capable, and was granted recall to France in 1758.

could come and stay at Montréal. He agreed and I left at 10 o'clock to take the order to M. de l'Hôpital. Along the way I commandeered four soldiers, carriages, horses and carts for the next day to carry the officers and their equipment.

23rd November

There was a great snow fall. Half of the horses and carts ordered did not arrive. I deposited all the effects and campaign utensils we had brought back in the Royal Magazine. The regiment marched at 8 o'clock and arrived in town at 11 o'clock very wet. Myself and many of my comrades made the journey on foot.

The regiment stayed the 24th and 25th. Here the clothing which should have been received before our departure from Québec was received. The soldiers, being deprived of wine for so long, were expected to be drunk, but were mainly sober.

26th November

I went early to see if all the bateaux necessary for the transport of the regiment had arrived. I found several lacking and so sent two sergeants with their soldiers out onto the water to look for them. I gave supplies for eight days to those companies designated to stay at Boucherville, where there are no purveyors. The regiment assembled at 10 o'clock at the magazine to embark. The companies of the *etat-major* left together for Longueuil, followed by five for Boucherville; the five designated for la Prairie could not leave because the bateaux were without guides and loaded too heavily to go up the rapids so they returned to town. I left at midday and arrived at Longueuil at 1 o'clock. We were barely able to leave, the *bordages* being solid (the name *bordages* is given to the banks of the river that have been frozen). I stayed until the 27th to see that the three companies were established.

28th November

I went to Boucherville and on the 29th to la Prairie, to see that the officers and men had found good lodgings. These three parishes are good and rich. Many houses border the river, the others are at the entrance of the woods, two leagues from the river, these occupy nine leagues of the country.

30th November

I went to Montréal to catch those returning and present to the *commissaire de guerre* an order to receive the money owed to the regiment. I stayed here on the 1st and 2nd of December.

3rd December

The Marquis de Vaudreuil, worried about the return of the Guyenne Regiment due to the ice which would make for a dangerous journey, learnt that they had arrived at La Chine at midday. The La Reine Regiment, destined to be garrisoned in Montréal, disembarked two hours later having had a difficult crossing of the river. A bateau which came from the Montréal prairie carrying twenty-two men of Québec hit a rock at the Normand Falls which split it in two and sunk. 11 men were drowned.

4th December

The Guyenne Regiment were to be billeted in the parishes of Longue Pointe, Pointe au Tremble and Pointe des Prairies, all three of them islands. They arrived at Montréal where they stayed. M. le General informed us that the Languedoc Regiment would stay in the parishes of the Rive de Chambly, where they would spend the winter.[51] After having received these general orders, I left in a carriage for Québec to make the accounts of the regiment. At Pointe au Tremble I was obliged to change my carriage as the snow prevented the wheels from turning. I took with me a grenadier to act as escort in a *cariolle* or sled. We dragged this to the end of the island, where we embarked in a small wooden canoe to traverse the Assomption River; we disembarked at the banks of Repantinie. I took a *cariolle* which carried us to the first houses of Saint-Sulpice, we passed Lavalliere and arrived at 9 o'clock in Berthier having travelled 15 leagues. When I left from Montréal I was sure this would only take until six. At Saint-Sulpice I had met Monsieur Pean, *aide-major* of Québec, who carried letters to M. le General from two *goelettes* sent from Louisbourg.[52] They were carrying the cargo of the *Montrosier* as that ship did not want to enter the river in late autumn. The two *goelettes* had become trapped in the ice at Kamouraska and ordered to wait until it had melted.[53] I lodged with the captain of the parish. In all parishes there are one or two companies of militia, made up of all those able to carry arms, from 16 to 60. They are commanded by the most intelligent or notable of the inhabitants, who are then nominated by the Governor General as Captains. They march with the men of their company when they receive orders to be sent to war or some fatigue duty. They then receive the same equipment as the soldiers and are fed at the expense of the King; all the duties of carting and others are paid for.

5th December

I took advantage of a *cariolle* from Maxkinongai, in which we departed at 5 o'clock. We traversed the ice over the Rivers of Chicot and Maxkinongai without having to leave our transport, we travelled on foot over that of the Loup, taking a *cariolle* from the first house, changing at Massis [Omachis] and arriving at Trois-Rivières at midday; after giving the King's Lieutenant a packet of letters, I re-embarked at 1

51 Malartic is referring to the Richelieu River which joins the Saint-Lawrence at Sorel. Travelling upstream leads to the parishes and Fort Chambly.

52 Michel-Jean-Hugues Péan was born in 1723 and had risen swiftly through the ranks of the colony troops. He used his position as *aide-major* of Québec to enrich himself. He worked with Intendant Bigot in using government funds and contracts in procurement to make his fortune. Once the scandal came out after the fall of New France he was banished for nine years for his part in the affair.

53 Kamouraska is just south of Riviere-du-Loup on the south bank of the Saint Lawrence. See Map 1.

o'clock in a small canoe to traverse the three channels. We were badly hampered by the wind; we had barely made the base of the Cape [Cap de la Madelaine], which we ascended with much difficulty up a steep and slippery slope to the first house. We could not find a sledge and so were obliged to wait for the captain who procured one for us which arrived at four o'clock which we took to Champlain. There I took two *cariolles* which left us on the right bank of the river as they dared not cross so we went on foot probing the ice, and slept at the house on the left bank.

6th December

We left at 6 o'clock with a *cariolle* of the captain that we replaced at a habitant's on the right bank of the Batiscan. We waited for daylight to cross on foot; at 7 o'clock we took a *cariolle* from the left bank then we crossed the Sainte-Anne and went up to Grandines, we made Cape Sante on the right bank of Jacques Cartier. The inhabitants did much praying before setting out to cross the river; I decided then that I would pay them well. We descended a bad coast tied to their canoe, we had much difficulty pushing through the water and we could not have held on without a strong rope which I had brought. We set off to traverse the river which we found had become very dangerous due to the ice that had formed; we landed on the other bank using our hatchets to anchor us to the ice. Our two guides did not want to come up the bank and left us there with our equipment without asking for payment. I found myself in difficulty as we had to ascend a slippery bank with no one to help pull us up. I tried to gain ground and climb a less steep part but slid back each time I tried. I told the grenadier to climb the bank and go and look for help. I tried again to climb the bank and was successful. The grenadier returned and said that the first house was uninhabited. I told the grenadier to guard the equipment and I would go up the coast and procure a vehicle. I discovered nothing at the first house. Likewise the second but I saw a sled coming out of the woods led by a child, who I asked to go and seek out the grenadier. He set off immediately while I sought out a house where I could get warm and eat as I was starving and thirsty. The grenadier joined me at three o'clock. We left when he had warmed up and reached the Pointe au Tremble at night fall. We took two *cariolles* which led us up the Saint-Ange coast, and arrived in Québec at 10 o'clock at night, covered in snow.[54]

7th December

I gave the Bishop, the Lieutenant of the King and the Intendant the packets I had brought for them.

8th December

I worked with the Intendant who gave me everything I asked for the regiment.

54 Saint-Ange is probably Saint-Augustin. See Map 5.

9th December

I completed the accounts with the treasurer. I asked the Intendant to give me some strong boxes that I could transport the money I would be taking.

10th December

I sent the boxes to be filled by the treasurer with the grenadier in a *cariolle.* I told him to wait for me at the first river as it would be difficult to cross. I went to finish my work with the Intendant, enchanted at the ease with which he works. There was terrible weather all day.

11th December

I could not leave until 9 o'clock. I took pouches loaded with letters. If I had set off an hour later I would have had enough to fill a trunk, there being no courier between Québec and Montréal. I changed horses at Sainte-Foi and at Pointe au Tremble, which I left at 2 o'clock. Along the path I received a letter from the grenadier which said he had stopped by Jacques Cartier River, which he could not cross on the ice or by bateau. I joined him at 4 o'clock in the last houses of Ecureuils. I slept there in the expectance that the frost would strengthen the ice overnight.

12th December

At 7 o'clock I put the boxes of money into a *cariolle*, and I went with the grenadier in the other equipped with rope; we were followed by three Canadians, who would attempt to cross over on foot where men had walked the previous day. We unloaded the *cariolles* and I attached the boxes to small sleds at both ends so that if the ice was weak it could be pulled from either side. I passed one after another until they had all crossed successfully. When I saw that all the money was out of danger I took the path to Cap Santé to send for vehicles to carry us. I found one half way. The driver assured me he could carry the whole load. I went to wait and rest at his house. We left at 10 o'clock, to make up the time at having to cross such a difficult river as Jacques Cartier. I had difficulty climbing to Grandines. The horses slid much as they were not shod for ice. I changed at Ste-Anne, crossing the river in the carriage and arrived at Batiscan at nightfall. I was obliged to wait for horses as they were in the woods. I crossed this river and also Champlain on the ice and arrived at 8 o'clock at Cap de la Madelaine.

13th December

I wished to embark early to cross the three channels, as the river was flowing swiftly. I was obliged to wait until 10 o'clock. The boatmen went to put their canoes to water but they had become trapped in the ice. After they thawed, they came to tell me that it was impossible to cross at our current position. They dragged the bateaux before the house and we loaded them on a *traine* [sometimes spelt *traineau*, essentially a sled] with the *cariolle* and luggage pulling it a quarter of league down river and descending to the river bank. It was very difficult to put the bateau to water because of the fast current. A canoe was able to cross so it was decided. We were able to set off at 11 o'clock and reached the other bank at midday. I sent the grenadier with the boatmen to seek out a *cariolle* and horses, and I stayed to guard the money. A half hour later there arrived a horse which I harnessed to my vehicle and then loaded with the baggage and money. I then followed it on foot and went down to the inn at Trois Rivières, where I stayed until it was time to deliver the letters to the King's Lieutenant which I was carrying for him. I relayed at Massisdon [Grand Omachis]. I went up to the River Loup and passed the coast of Lac St-Pierre. I relayed at Maxkinongai, where I bought over a hundred frozen partridges. (They are kept like this over winter and when one wants to eat, they are thawed in cold water and are as good as if they were killed in the last three days. It is the same for other game, meat and poultry that have been killed when frost is certain. They are left to mortify for a few days and then exposed to the frost and they are preserved until they are to be eaten). We relayed at Berthier, Mauroi, and Autray, and arrived at St-Sulpice at 2 hours after midnight, shivering with cold.

14th December

I left at midday, relayed at Repentinie, 'took the path along the bank to la Prairies, to reach Montréal, where I arrived at 4 o'clock. M. le Marquis de Vaudreuil and those with him were amazed to see me and could not believe that a Frenchman, who had not yet passed a winter in this country, had made in a painful journey in ten days in a season which makes roads impassable.

15th December

I delivered all the letters with which I had been charged. I spent the 16th and 17th making distributions to the regiment of the effects they were to receive before campaigning.

18th December

The river, swiftly flowing, hampered my departure until midday. It was very difficult to put a bateau into the water. I set out with the boxes of money, a portion of the effects stored in the town and twelve soldiers returning to their companies. We took to water at half past midday. After an hour we were opposite the Ormes. I sent a Canadian to go and probe the ice. It seemed strong so we disembarked. I found a sergeant who had come to meet me in a *cariolle* as his guest. I ordered the unloading of the money and then went to sit with my host and gave commands for the sleds to take the money and baggage. I then ordered the sergeant to escort the vehicles up to my lodgings, where I arrived at 4 o'clock, very content to have given good passage to all that I had been charged.

19th, 20th and 21st December

I worked on memorandums and accounts of the companies for the *etat-major* from the 19th of July up until the 1st of January.

22nd December

I went to take the accounts to the five companies at la Prairie and on the 23rd to those at Boucherville. I stayed until the 29th at Longueuil to finish the accounts, being impatient to see the end. As I was able to cross the river, I left here at 1 o'clock, very content to have made up my battalion's accounts before those other officers charged with the details of other battalions had left to seek out theirs. I arrived at Montréal at 2 o'clock.

31st December

M. le marquis de Vaudreuil left for Québec. An interpreter of the Iroquois wanted to spread the alarm around the town, assuring he had heard seven cannon shots within a league of Fort Saint-Frédéric, and shouting that Carillon was under attack. I gave his testimony no credence, finding it lacking and wished to bet that the bangs were the wind and not cannon.

2

The Year 1756

After the celebrated victory over General Braddock at the Monongahela, Governor Vaudreuil wished to go on the offensive. On the south shore of Lake Ontario, Chouaguen, known as Oswego to the British, had long been a thorn in the side of New France. It was established in the 1720s to draw away Native fur traders from French establishments for the better prices of British merchandise. Now with the military might to achieve this, Vaudreuil dispatched Montcalm to capture the post. It was a resounding success, Oswego was left out on a limb with reinforcement too far away to reach it. After the great labours taken to reduce the fort, Montcalm swiftly moved his army back to defend the Lake Champlain frontier after rumours that a British army was assembling for an expedition north. Nothing came of it and British woes increased.

1st January

All over Canada from daybreak to nightfall the New Year was celebrated.

2nd January

An officer detached from Frontenac arrived with two prisoners who had been captured at Chouaguen. They reported that there were four hundred men at the three forts who were beginning to run out of food.

5th January

I went to Longueuil to work and respond to the many letters sent from the detachment at Frontenac.

7th January

Two captains of the regiment, recently married, came with their wives to see the commander and dine with us.

8th and 9th January

I worked on reviewing paperwork.

10th and 11th January

I went to la Prairie and Boucherville to sign paperwork for my fellow officers.

12th January

I went with our commander to Montréal and spent the day with the *commissaire de guerre* for review.

13th January

I went to dine with our commander at la Prairie and the captain of our regiment who commands there. On leaving I saw a fire at a house in the town which I thought was in the quarter I was staying. On arriving at Longueuil, we heard them beat *la généralle.*[1]

14th January

My servant, who had been sick for a few days and stayed in town, arrived to tell me that the house of my host there had been burned down, and that he had not been able to save any furnishings (luckily I did have my sword and a cane. I always believed a stove pipe between a partition caused the fire). After midday I spent a half hour in the town. All those people of my acquaintance attested their great sympathy for my loss.

15th January

The *commissaire de guerre* came to make his review. I followed him to the town where he stopped and I picked him up as his vehicle had broken.

16th January

The marquis de Vaudreuil went back to Québec. He stopped at St-François, to talk to the Abenaki and sing the war song.[2] I stayed at Montréal until the 21st to look after the affairs of the regiment.

22nd January

I went to Longueuil to prepare to make my second journey to Québec.

1 An army drum beat which calls the troops to assemble. *Instruction sur l'exercice de l'Infanterie* (Paris: L'Imprimerie Royale, 1754) p. 22.

2 St-François or St Francis was an Abenaki village between Trois-Rivières and Montréal. It had been populated by migrants from various groups in the late 1600's and was the target of a vicious raid by Roger's Rangers in 1760. Today it is called Odanak. Stephen Brumwell, *White Devil,* (London: Orion, 2004), pp. 31-5.

23rd January

I went with the commander of Pointe au Tremble to dine with the commander of the Guyenne Regiment.[3] I slept at Montréal where I learned that M. le general had received packets from France, carried by two couriers coming from Louisbourg on foot.

25th January

I took the orders for M. le general to Québec. I will not recount the journey having done so above. I arrived there on the 28th at 7 in the evening. I stayed until the 15th of February. On this day the couriers of Louisbourg also left.

16th February

I took the path to Montréal but this time without the trouble of the money chests, the Intendant having obliged the treasurer, after the representations of the regiment, to settle the accounts. I arrived on the 17th in the evening. I stayed until the 22nd to settle the accounts with the treasurer; I worked on preparations and dispositions necessary for a detachment that M. de Vaudreuil wished to send to Chouaguen. Each battalion was to provide twenty men commanded by a sergeant.

23rd February

I left at 8 o'clock to take the regiment's money to Longueuil. I took the Varennes road. Arriving at the Pointe au Tremble, I could not find anyone to guide me. I was afraid of the dangerous crossing. Two men allowed me to use and harness their horses and I promised that nothing would happen to them. I crossed to the end of the Isle Ste-Thérèse and skirted the south the island. I took a Canadian with us for a guide at the last house and to test the ice crossing the water, which was found to be very good opposite Varennes. I stopped for a moment as I could not find any horses. Those from Pointe au Tremble guided me to Boucherville. I dined with my comrades at my arrival at Longueuil, very glad to see the security of the money which had worried me for the last few hours.

Our commander did not wish me to make detailed accounts before Lent, I left to go and see the detachment that was assembling at Lachine. On arriving at la Prairie, I was approached by two men, who came from Sault St-Louis, saying that the river flowed too strongly to cross there.[4] The man who led me from Longueuil suggested

3 This was Lieutenant-Colonel Louis Retauran de Fonbonne. Born in 1705, he died in battle on the Plains of Abraham in 1759.

4 Saulte St-Louis, sometimes simply shortened to the Sault and called Kahnawke/Caughnawaga by its inhabitants. New France had several of these mission villages which had come about in the seventeenth century. Jesuits had sought to convert various tribes of Native people and had been particularly successful at the time when the Iroquois were waging a fierce war against the Hurons and other Algonquin people around the great lakes. Those that sought salvation converted to Catholicism and settled in villages around Montréal, some with their own

I go by canoe to his home. I accepted and arrived there at 11 o'clock. He went to see if the river was flowing and returned to tell me that he would drag the canoe on the ice up to the end of the island where we could cross without obstacle. We set out at midday and disembarked after an hour at the convent of Ste-Marie. We had trouble getting lodgings because of a great quantity of snow. I arrived at 4 o'clock in Montréal, supped with M. le general, who seemed pleased with the detachment he had reviewed at La Chine. It was composed of one hundred and twenty soldiers, two hundred and fifty Canadians and one hundred savages, commanded by M. de Léry, lieutenant of the troops detached from the marines, that I shall call the troops of the colony hereafter, who had sixteen officers of the same companies under him.[5]

26th February

M. le general has learnt that the detachment is on the march and making good time.

27th February

M. de Léry sent an officer from the Cedars, to make it known that the provisions that were given to the detachment were rotten.

4th March

I left at 9 o'clock for Longueuil. I crossed the river on the ice in a *cariolle*. It took all of three days and we got through in the evening.

---

missionary living with them. This caused upset when Catholic Iroquois and their southern tribespeople were called upon by European powers to fight each other. Kahnawake was established in the late 1660's from people of the Iroquois tribes, chiefly Mohawk, who had converted to Catholicism and wished to be closer to the French, feeling ostracised from their communities as a result of their new found faith. The village was a Jesuit mission and as such was not under official control. This resulted in many Montréal and Albany merchants using Mohawk middlemen to transport goods up and down the Lake Champlain corridor, avoiding bans on international trade. See Richter, *Ordeal of the Longhouse*, pp. 105-132 and John Demos, *The Unredeemed Captive*, pp. 120-139 on the founding of Caughnawaga and for the fur trade, Jean Lunn, 'The Illegal Fur Trade out of New France, 1713-60'. *Report of the Annual Meeting of the Canadian Historical Association*, 18, no. 1 (1939): pp. 61–76. Also Peter Moogk, *La Nouvelle France*, pp. 40-50.

5 The journal of de Léry gives 15 officers, 83 soldiers, 166 Canadians, 103 savages. In total 367 men. Chaussegros de Léry, "Journal de la Campagne d'Hiver, du 13 Février au Neuf Avril 1756." *Rapport de l'Archiviste de la province de Québec*, 1926-7 p. 374. Gaspard-Joseph Chaussegros de Léry was the son and grandson of military engineers. He followed in their footsteps, entering the colony troops as a cadet at the age of twelve. He kept detailed notebooks of his expeditions to various parts of the continent and was one of the few Canadian officers held in any respect by Montcalm.

8th and 9th March

I went to la Prairie and to Boucherville carrying the money and accounts for those companies. I returned on the 12th to la Prairie and on the 13th to Boucherville, to learn if they had been working on their arms drill, as I had not been happy with it on the last trip.

15th March

I proposed to go to Varennes, to stay in the town. The man who I took ordinarily to guide me said I could cross next to his house by canoe. I left at 7 in the morning, with two of my comrades, travelling by *cariolle* up to the bottom of Isle Ste-Hélène, where we embarked, disembarking at the base of the Ste-Marie current, where we went into the town on foot, arriving at 9 o'clock. We learnt that M. le general had received a letter from the commander of Acadia, M. Boishébert, informing that the English had attacked and pursued them into the woods, where he counterattacked but was forced to retire with the loss of two hundred men and that the Micmacs captured a merchant vessel bound for Beauséjour, and that they took an officer of artillery prisoner.[6]

18th March

The savages from the mission of St-Regis established on the south of Lake St-François, arrived with eight prisoners they had removed from Chouaguen.[7] They said they spent more than twenty-four hours around the fort without seeing anyone, when they happened to notice a sergeant and eight men who were approaching the spot they had laid their ambush, and who then put down their weapons to smoke, and that they had benefitted from this security to emerge and capture them. The prisoners said there are 300 men in garrison at the fort.

20th March

Some sick officers and men, left at la Présentation by M. de Léry, arrived here.

24th March

I went to Longueuil, where I made arrangements to be carried out to put the regiment into a fit state to begin campaigning.

---

6 Captain Charles Deschamps de Boishébert had been posted out to Acadia in 1754 but the British successes there ended most resistance in the area. He was known to have had friends in high places and was one of the Intendant's associates. He was imprisoned on his return to France in 1760, although acquitted after fifteen months.

7 St. Regis was another Indian mission village which had only recently been settled after land around the Sault/Kahnawake had been exhausted. Today it is an Indian reservation and is called Akwesasne. Darren Bonaparte, *The History of Akwesasne from Pre-Contact to Modern Times.* http://www.wampumchronicles.com/history.html.

28th March

I returned to Montréal and on the 29th distributed the equipment and utensils for the campaign, to which were added other essential items.

I stayed in Montréal until the 5th of April to stop and review the complete accounts with the treasurer.

7th April

We learned that M. de Léry had informed the General that on the 27th of March he had burned down a large storehouse filled with food and ammunition.[8]

10th April

I accompanied our commander, who went to give his compliments to M. le marquis de Vaudreuil on the success of M. de Léry. The general was told that the on the 26th the advance guard of the detachment led by M. Florimond had met six Onoyotès [Oneida] and stopped them on the path with two strings of wampum and asked them to wait there for their 'father' who would follow them at the head of his warriors,[9] and that these savages said they would march and scout for M. de Léry and said to him:

> Does our father not have any older warriors? These he sends are too young.

to which M. de Léry responded:

> I reserve them for more essential operations; the young are more well-suited to these arduous missions.

He then presented them with a wampum collar and asked them about the fort. The Oneida accepted the collar and said that the commander of the fort was on high alert, and that they could take it tomorrow, and that, if he wished they would go to gather information. This was permitted; they caught a bear and spent part of the night getting drunk. They returned at daybreak to inform M. de Léry that the commandant knew nothing of their sortie to the fort and had sent seven sleds loaded with supplies for Chouaguen. Having taken this advice, M. de Léry set to ambush this detachment. As soon as they appeared the savages, mentioned above, took all the drivers apart from a negro whom they could not catch and led the sled

8 This was Fort Bull, between Schenectady and Oswego, located at western end of the strategic portage road between the Mohawk and Oneida rivers. It had a palisade wall and loop holes which served against them as the attackers fired through them into the garrison. None of the garrison survived. René Chartrand, *Montcalm's Crushing Blow: French and Indian Raids along New York's Oswego River 1756*, (Oxford: Osprey, 2014), p. 38.

9 Usually spelt Fleurimont, it appears this could have been Pierre-Phillipe Noyelles de Fleurimont. He was the son of a more notable officer, Nicolas-Joseph. Pierre-Phillip's brother, Charles-Joseph, was commandant at the fort at Toronto at this time.

to their father, who distributed food to the party which was running low. After giving them time to eat, he marched on the fort in three columns, M. de Montigny commanded the right, M. de Portneuf that of the left while he had the centre. At twenty *arpents* from the fort, local workmen learned of the attack and retreated to the fort, barring the door and alerting the garrison which consisted of sixty men and was commanded by a captain. The three columns charged, hatchet in hand. Two French soldiers, one of the colony, and a savage, broke down the door and killed the captain who would not give up and killed a savage. The garrison offered their swords, but the attacking savages wished to give no quarter. The others went to lay in ambush to stop any aid which could arrive from Fort Bull, which was about a league away.[10] M. de Léry had powder and shot thrown into the river and the boats broken. The fire had spread to the nearby woods caused by the black powder. Several barrels fell from a beam which broke the back of a soldier of Guyenne and wounded one of La Reine. The Oneidas advised M. de Léry to change his return route, to avoid meeting Colonel Johnson, who marched with a considerable corps.[11] He took to the Baie de Niaouré where he found bateaux that had been conducted by a piquet from the Béarn Regiment.[12] It is estimated that the English lost thirty thousand pounds of powder and a huge pile of food and goods.

I spent the 11th at Longueuil, the 12th at la Prairie, and the 13th at Boucherville, making inspections of linen, armaments and accounts.

19th April

I stayed at Montréal.

23rd-25th April

I made accounts of the provisions that the Intendant had ordered to be supplied to the officers for each month of the campaign. As the following is not able to be supplied they should be paid in kind as per the following:

a sheep 10 *livres.*,
a pig 8 *livres.*,
3 *livres* of rice 2 *livres.* 5 *sol.*,
2 *livres* of lard 2 *livres.* 4 *sol.*,
2 *livres* of cheese 2 *livres.* 10 *sol.*,

10 This is a misnomer by Malartic. The fort De Léry's force had attacked and set on fire was Fort Bull. At the eastern end of the portage road was Fort Williams and it was from here that possible British reinforcements would arrive. See Chartrand, *Montcalm's Crushing Blow*. pp. 30-40.

11 William Johnson was superintendent of Indian Affairs for the northern British colonies and lived in his house, Mount Johnson, halfway down the Mohawk River, around sixty miles from Fort Bull. He personally enjoyed good relations with the Iroquois most of the time, especially the Mohawk. He spent much of this year trying to gather forces together at short notice at signs of alarm. See William Johnson, *The Papers of Sir William Johnson* (Albany: University of the State of New York, 1921), Vol.IX, pp. 412-504.

12 Baie de Niaouré is today Sackets Harbor, New York.

This totals a sum of 24 *livres*, 19 *sol.* for each officer; for commanders of battalions they receive double and in addition receive a barrel of goose legs paid at 16 *livres*. Naturally a bottle of wine is distributed per day; each month a pot of *eau-de-vie*, 60 *livres* of bread, 15 *livres* of bacon or 30 of fresh beef, 30 pounds of pigs ears, 3 *livres* of apples and of brown sugar, 2 *livres* of salt, 4 *onces* of pepper, 2 of spices, 2 *livres* of gunpowder, 4 of lead shot, one pint of vinegar, a *chopine* of oil and a *livre* of candles.

26th April

I went to Longueuil, there to make accounts of the provisions.

27th April

I received letters from M. Dumas, commandant on the Belle Riviére, who writes that the savages on that frontier ravage Pennsylvania, pushing them on into Virginia, where they continue to spread terror and often take prisoners.

28th April

I went to Montréal. M. le general told me he had great news from the *pays d'en haut*, that all the commanders representing the savages were well disposed to us.

29th April

The habitants of la Prairie say around the market that the Indians of Sault have returned with two officers and nine soldiers taken captive from Fort Lydius.[13]

30th April

The Abenaki accompanying the general took a prisoner given to them by the Iroquois to replace one of their number who had been killed. The Iroquois arrived at 3 o'clock with their captives and asked for council and to give an account of their campaign. M. le general questioned the prisoners, who responded that the English were not yet in force on Lake St-Sacrement and that they are gathering a force of eight thousand men.[14] The officers testified their astonishment at receiving a number of blows with sticks upon arrival at Sault, and the soldiers were very mistreated. M. le marquis de Vaudreuil responded that it is a custom of the savages that he cannot dissuade. (When the savages return with prisoners, the women and young people who have stayed in the village come out, they start by forming a line to receive them which they follow by hitting them with sticks and stones, until they reach the cabins of

13 Fort Lydius, as it was known to the French, was the old post of a trader called Lydius. It was expanded and became the main army staging post before Lake Champlain. Robert Roger's famous ranger company operated from there. The British had changed its name by this time and called it Fort Edward.

14 Lake St-Sacrement was called Lake George by the British.

those who lead them; where they are given shelter from those who abuse them. Then the warriors adopt them for their father, brother, uncle or cousin if they lost any of their relatives, or give them to their comrades where they are treated as follows. The first reception is cruel and there are many nations who practise all kinds of inhumanity on their prisoners, which involve burning them many times. Many have abandoned this cruel practice since many of their own were burned in retaliation.)

1st May

The savages led their prisoners to several houses, so that they would be given shots of eau-de-vie.

3rd May

I went to Longueuil.

7th May

I sent boats to the town from all our quarters to fetch soap which was sold at the Royal Magazine for 10 *sous* per *livre*. There will be 6 *livres* of soap per officer and 2 *livres* per soldier for the duration of the campaign.

8th May

I went to la Prairie where I learned from a woman who came from the town that M. de Rigaud, brother of M. de Vaudreuil, who had been captured the previous year aboard the ship *l'Alcide*, arrived here yesterday.[15] As soon as I had dined I returned to Longueuil to inform our commander, and to see if he had sent for news, being very impatient to have it, I left for Montréal. 3 hours later a grenadier carried me the details of what had been going on in France, of the departure of M. de Rigaud and of the state of the *troupes de terre* who had arrived under the orders of M. le marquis de Montcalm, *maréchal de camp*, M. le chevalier de Lévis, brigadier, and M. de Bourlamaque, colonel.[16]

---

15 François-Pierre de Rigaud de Vaudreuil, whom Canadians called 'Monsieur de Rigaud', was brother to the governor general. He was considered brave but 'shallow-brained.' Firmly part of the Canadian nobility he served in the marines and had become governor of Trois-Rivières in 1749. He was immediately called into active service but was granted the title of Governor of Montréal in 1757. He would sink into obscurity in Paris and died in 1779. *L'Alcide* was 64-gun ship of the line. It was captured near Dunkirk after being raked 'from top to bottom at point blank range' and transferred into British service.

16 Montcalm and his new cadre of officers arrived to replace Dieskau. Lévis and Bourlamaque would take second and third command respectively. Montcalm also had with him his aide, Louis Antoine de Bougainville, who later found fame as a Pacific explorer. He also kept a journal of the war in North America. Captain des Combles and his assistant, Jean Nicolas Desandrouin, arrived to take on engineering duties. Also, there were two new battalions of reinforcements; around 1,200 men of the Royal Roussillon and La Sarre Regiments. William R. Nester, *The French and Indian War and the Conquest of New France* (Norman: Oklahoma University Press, 2014), pp. 196-7.

11th May

M. de Villiers, captain of the colonial troops, made a review of the soldiers that would make up part of a corps of 800 men that M. le general has given him to command. He must go and take up a position in the Baie de Niaouré to worry and harass the convoys destined for Chouaguen. The Canadians and savages make up the rest of this detachment.

12th May

Our commander went to see M. de Vaudreuil who informed him that the La Reine Regiment would leave on the 17th to meet up with that of Languedoc at Carillon, then that Béarn would go the same day to take its place in the town where it would be ready to leave for Frontenac a few days later.[17]

13th May

A courier from Québec came loaded with letters from France which had been carried by a brigantine which left from La Rochelle on the 13th of March, which was wrecked on the tip of l'Isle d'Orleans; however the cargo and equipment were salvaged.

14th May

I went to Longueuil to have the orders of M. le general sent to all our quarters.

15th May

I sent all the equipment and money that we have no need of on campaign, to Montréal.

16th May

I went on a mission with a detachment of soldiers and Canadians to find necessary bateaux to transport the regiment. M. le marquis de Vaudreuil told me that bad weather would delay the departure of La Reine and ourselves by one day. After distributing the bateaux I returned to Longueuil.

17th May

I sent out countermand orders to all our quarters and made recommendations that we will only leave when we have seen that La Reine have departed. I sent word to the

17 Fort Carillon was built further down Lake Champlain to protect the ageing Fort St. Frederick in response to the threat from the British to the south. It was only begun in 1755. Chartrand, *Forts of New France*, pp. 33-5.

town to see if there had been any other changes. We learned of the arrival of M. le marquis de Montcalm at Québec.[18]

18th May

At six in the morning I saw the batteux of La Reine pass by. The five companies from Boucherville met us at Longueuil at midday and we left at 1 o'clock. We crossed the river at the bottom of l'Isle Sainte-Hélène. We disembarked at the bottom of the town. The five companies of the town joined us at the chateau gates where we formed into line in the square.

19th May

The bad weather held up M. le general in making his review of the regiment. The Abbé Piquet arrived with twenty savages of his mission, who had two Englishmen taken from Chouaguen. These prisoners say their commander expects reinforcement.

20th May

M. le general made a review of the regiment and seemed happy.

21st May

I made distributions of equipment for the campaign.

22nd May

Our equipment has been sent by water and land to La Chine. I made up accounts of the pay of the officers who had stayed in the town who were paid at five livres per day for the commander and three livres for the others. The detachment of M. de Villiers has left La Chine in three divisions.[19]

18 Note by Gaffarel – Montcalm left Brest on 3 April with three ships of the line. *Heros*, 74 guns, under Captain Beaussier, *l'Illustre*, 64 guns, under Captain Montalais, *Léopard*, 60 guns, under Captain Germain and 3 frigates of 30 guns. Embarked on the ships were the second battalions of La Sarre and Royal Roussillon, comprising 1,189 men. On the frigates, *Licorne, Sauvage* and *Siréne*, was Montcalm and his staff. He arrived at Québec on 13 May 1756. The voyage had been good. See the letter Montcalm wrote on the occasion to the marquise de Saint-Veran, 11th May 1756.

19 Louis Coulon de Villiers was brother of Ensign Jumonville, killed by George Washington's force of Provincial Virginians in 1754 during the episode which sparked war in North America. Louis quickly took revenge, travelling out from Fort Duquesne in the Ohio valley to catch up with Washington at Great Meadows. De Villiers forced Washington and his men into a humiliating surrender, which acknowledged Washington had 'assassinated' Jumonville. He died in 1757 of smallpox.

23rd May

The first division of Béarn, made up of the first seven companies, left at 10 o'clock for La Chine and arrived at 1. I counted twenty-one bateaux to carry them, designated a number of men for each one and distributed food for fifteen days. They were to leave as soon as possible and the companies pitched camp around the magazine. I had promised to return packages to the general but not being able to leave for the town I sent a grenadier to inform him that I was busier than expected.

24th May

The first division embarked at 6 o'clock. I stayed to wait for the grenadier. I prepared the nineteen bateaux destined for the second division and bales of equipment for the detachment of Frontenac. The grenadier returned at 8 o'clock with packets from M. le general. I left shore immediately. I passed the sand banks at the points of La Chine and landed at the Claire River where I found the lieutenant of grenadiers who was waiting with two boats and two Canadians that the captain of the parish had sought out, to replace two sick men.[20] We left at 1 o'clock despite a wind from the south west which was contrary and violent. After tacking for an hour without making good progress we rested half a league from the church, planning to leave at night if the wind dropped.

25th May

The wind calmed at day break and we left at 4 o'clock and re-joined our division before *la génèralle* was beaten at l'Isle Perrot. I will not repeat the journey having done so in the previous campaign. On the 26th we met twelve laden bark canoes from the Belle Riviére.

4th June

We arrived at Frontenac and found the three piquets in a good state.

5th June

The second division arrived, the boats which had carried our two divisions left for Montréal.

6th June

Many *bateaux du cent* arrived. At 2 o'clock some Canadians made a fire in the barracks that spread to the retrenchments. We had much trouble putting it out.

20 Malartic probably means Pointe Claire.

7th June

A wind rose from the north-west that was hoped to propel the barques. The regiment prepared to embark and unload part of the equipment. At midday the wind shifted to the south west. The boat *le Victor* that had moored at Toronto, and was laden with furs, entered the bay, dropped its cargo ashore and loaded up with food.[21]

8th June

The wind from the north-west returned and calmed at midday. The regiment took supplies and biscuit for eight days and then set off immediately. They then took another supply at midday of fresh bread for six days, and then set out to be ready in a minute. The twelve bark canoes we had met arrived after midday. At 5 o'clock 21 Mississagués [Mississauga] sang the war song with our commander, and danced the dance of the pipe at the fort.

9th June

A great calm. Some *bateaux du cent* arrived at midday. The Guyenne Regiment arrived at 2 o'clock and camped on our right.

10th June

The camp of the Canadians was moved ahead of the Guyenne camp. The Mississagués left to join M. de Villiers. The sergeants took drill.

11th June

The Béarn Regiment performed exercise in detail. The twelve bark canoes left for Niagara with M. de Joncaire.[22]

12th June

Béarn performed exercises. Some *bateaux du cent* arrived.

---

21 Toronto was situated on a strategic water route into Lake Huron from Lake Ontario and the site of first an Iroquois, then a Mississauga village. It had only a very small French presence at Fort Rouille which had been constructed in 1750. See Henry Scadding, *Toronto of Old: Collections and Recollections Illustrative of the Early Settlement and Social Life of the Capital of Ontario* (Toronto: Adam Stevenson & Co., 1873), pp. 5-6.

22 Phillipe-Thomas Chabert de Joncaire was born in 1707 at Montreal and was the son of Louis-Thomas Chabert de Joncaire, the founder of the trading post at Niagara. Phillipe-Thomas lived much of his life amongst the Seneca and was New France's principal Indian agent into the 1740's when he resigned, being replaced by his brother Daniel. He was also a colonial officer and was a captain by 1751. He was involved in diplomacy and trading at Niagara during the Seven Years War. He was almost a counterpart to William Johnson, both of them attempting to influence the Iroquois to their countries interests. Joncaire was captured and shipped to France in 1760.

13th June

The Béarn Regiment was exercised. It rained heavily in the afternoon. The commander of the corvettes advised the commander of Béarn that it seemed there would be a good wind tomorrow and to load all that was not needed on board before nightfall.

14th June

The wind blew from the north-west. The first three companies embarked on the corvette *la Marquise de Vaudreuil*, armed with sixteen 6-pounders; three in the corvette *Hurault*, armed with twelve 6-pounders; two in the *goelette la Louise*, armed with eight three pounders; and two in the boat *le Victor*, armed with four small cannons. The last three companies remained with the piquet that had spent the winter at Frontenac to await the return of the corvettes. This small flotilla set sail at 6 o'clock, passing the point of la Grande Anse and le Petit Cataracoui to the north, then two bays, an islet, then the two islands of Tonoguyon [Toneguignon] and a bay that can accommodate large boats; to the south, those of la Forêt, l'Enfant perdu, Chevreuil and Renard. At one o'clock we passed the islands of de Terre, du Large and of Coui. At 4 o'clock we discovered the point of Quinte [sometimes spelt Kente]. The wind blew from the west which prevented us from going further. It greatly freshened in the evening, raising waves which tormented us all night. At midnight it moved to the southwest and we had to tack often.[23]

15th June

The Captain of *la Marquise* [*de Vaudreuil*], seeing that we were backing up instead of going forward, the wind coming from the southwest and the crew being too tired having manoeuvred through the night, decided to retire to the Isle de Coui, which was a good anchorage. He made the signal and the four vessels anchored at noon below the Isle de Terre on which we descended. Our hunters killed some *tourdes* (a species of pigeon) and some small birds. I walked around the island which I found attractive. It is three quarters of a league in circumference. It is covered in woods and has three fields. There are a lot of cabbages and wild garlic, good to eat. It is surrounded by flats which makes the approach dangerous. You can see the remains of a ship which was lost some years ago.

16th June

Good weather at sunrise. A 6 o'clock a storm blew up which gave us lots of rain with wind coming from the southwest harder than yesterday so we did not give much hope for a change. We descended onto the island and got back aboard at 7 o'clock.

---

23 By following these points on Map 8, it is plain to see the difficulties of navigating on Lake Ontario. The need to steer from island to island to wait for favourable weather is very noticeable here and in subsequent journeys. Historians should note the difficulty of simply crossing the lake in a straight line.

17th June.

Mainly calm. We sent four men per company onto the island to collect herbs and wood.

18th June

The wind changed to the north. We sailed at 4 o'clock, at 6 the wind changed, coming again from the southwest so we tacked. It calmed at the end of the day.

19th June

The wind blew from the east. At daybreak we found ourselves at the point of la Barque. At 7 o'clock the wind changed to the north east and freshened. At 9 o'clock *la Marquise* hove to, to wait for the other vessels, on which we had gained a lot. At 10 o'clock she hoisted the sails, the wind dropped at 11 and it was very calm the rest of the day.

20th June

The wind rose in the southwest, very fresh, raised waves that gave us much bother until sunset when we had calm. At 10 o'clock the wind got up in the northeast and we resumed our journey, discovering by the light of the moon, the River aux Boeufs to the south and to the north the Grandes Accores [Grand Ecort] and the land of Toronto.

21st June

The wind changed to south-southwest. We veered to follow the shore. We met up at the Grandes Accores and its river. We turned north to gain anchorage at Toronto but were prevented by nightfall.

22nd June

At 1 o'clock in the morning, the wind accompanied by a storm and a tempest, which seemed to wish to engulf the boats, blew up and pushed us into the Niagara River where we arrived at 7 o'clock. We disembarked and at 8 we camped in the works.[24]

---

24 Louis-Thomas Chabert de Joncaire (father of the Phillipe-Thomas mentioned previously) first gained permission from the Seneca to erect a trading house here in 1720. Its construction was not begun until 1726 and at the beginning of the war was in a poor state. A lot of work was done on the fort by the Guyenne Regiment during 1755-60. See Dunnigan, *Siege 1759*, pp. 11-15.

23rd June

We established communications in the camp, got rid of the food which had spoiled and separated it from the fresh. The unloading of the *Marquise de Vaudreuil* began. In the evening a very violent storm began which lasted all night.

24th June

The four vessels were unloaded. At 2 o'clock, 24 grenadiers were employed in digging ditches to drain away the water.

25th June

We supplied one hundred and fifty men for the works. They were divided into work groups, those to dig the ditches, form the earthworks, cut the turf, turf the earthworks, cooks and those to transport the earth and turf.

26th June

Work continues as yesterday. M. de Joncaire arrived with the twelve bark canoes. The four companies of the Guyenne Regiment who spent the winter at this fort embarked at midday on the four boats to go and join their regiment at Frontenac.

27th June

Work continued. An officer who arrived yesterday at the portage with eight boats, to load up with provisions for the Belle Rivière, came to the fort and told us that he had left the frontier and it was very peaceful.

28th June

Very bad weather stopped work. At 6 o'clock in the evening, some cannon shots were heard which were judged to be fired by the English barques which were crossing the lake.

29th June

Worked as normal. M. de Chabert arrived with the chief of Five Nations and many savages who came to trade. M. Pouchot marked out a *demie-lune*.[25] The sergeants took exercises.

25 More usually spelt demi-lune: an out-work of the fort shaped like a crescent moon. Pierre Pouchot was a captain in the Guyenne Regiment. He kept his memoirs on his experiences and acted as an engineer, eventually becoming commandant at Fort Niagara. He was successful in negotiation with the Iroquois although his role in events was exaggerated in his own accounts.

30th June

Worked. The ditch of the *demie-lune* was marked out and the covered path of the *ouvrage à corne*.[26] Many savages came to trade.

1st July

The breech in the demi-bastion of the lake was closed by the raising of a platform; there was a little rain. I went to go outside of the fort to examine its position, which I found good. It is located on a high point overlooking the lake and the river basin to the north and the rest to the south, it is 600 feet from the wood, and the land that separates them is a beautiful meadow. It cannot be attacked by land from the front as it is 300 feet between the lake and the river. M. Pouchot has built a large *ouvrage à corne* which takes up the whole of that width, he has also made many redans between the banks of the lake and the river making it very defensible.[27] There are several cannons on barbettes placed on the curtain wall and on the demi-bastions covering the woods,[28] four cannons are positioned at the end of the branch of the demi-bastion of the river, covering the end of the river and a small path. Behind the building is a battery which can fire on the river entrance. This part is unassailable by barques as there are flats up to a quarter league out. The outside of Niagara is beautiful. The woods are lovely and clear, several parts seem to have been planted to form aisles.

2nd July

Ordinary work. M. du Joncaire left at 9 o'clock with his savages. We formed a work group to lift the artillery into the fort.

3rd July

Worked. An officer who arrived from the Belle Rivière, announced that the savages had taken three Englishmen from Fort Cumberland.

4th July

Rain and storms. The prisoners say they expect 500 savages of the southern nations at Fort Cumberland.

26 An outer part of a fort, the head of which is strengthened by two half-bastions, joined by a curtain, and closed on two sides by two wings parallel to each other.

27 Redan: defensive fortification in the shape of a V.

28 Barbette: mound of earth or a platform in a fortification, on which guns are mounted to fire over the parapet.

5th July

Ordinary work. Two *Chaouanons* [Shawnee] who were nominated by their tribe to go to Montréal arrived at 2 o'clock. They were very enthusiastic about our works which they measured. They compared us to the beavers. The sergeants took exercises.

6th and 7th July

Ordinary work. The demi-bastion at the base of the lake was completed. A boat sent to Toronto to carry supplies came back, the pilot said he had seen three prisoners and nine scalps taken by the savages from an English boat which had crossed to the Isle au Galop. The Mississaugués brought us deer.

8th July

Five savages of the Five Nations brought us the scalps of five Englishmen who they had killed on the banks of the Chouaguen River; they had seen a convoy of bateaux coming escorted by a large detachment.

9th July

A courier was sent from the small fort bearing news from five Iroquois who said that the English have eight barques at Chouaguen, a considerable train of artillery and that they wish to attack M. de Villiers.

10th and 11th of July

Ordinary work. At midday a courier came to announce the deputies of the Five Nations. At 6 o'clock, MM. de Joncaire and Chabert arrived with Mississaugués who sang the war song.[29] The deputies who had been announced arrived at the same hour and they camped in a happy family. One of them came to tell us that M. de Villiers attacked a fort which they had surprised and that they were pushed back with the loss of thirty men. That the British had left Chouaguen on the twenty-eighth to go and attack Frontenac, this seemed as though it should merit confirmation. A savage bitten by a small snake ate it in front of us.

12th July

Worked. The Mississaugués left for Chouaguen. The delegates came to the fort, giving the commandant his due compliments. They asked for three days to respond to their words and wampum which they had carried for him over the winter.

29 Joncaire and Chabert were brothers. Phillipe-Thomas Chabert de Joncaire as mentioned above and Daniel-Marie Chabert de Joncaire. Daniel-Marie was the younger brother so possibly he was known as Chabert while Phillipe-Thomas was known as Joncaire.

13th July

A loud noise was heard from afar. We guessed it was made by the boats of Toronto, the workers on the shores of the lake had the idea to cover the barques. Three Mississaugués who had brought us deer said to us that they had met their brothers who had left yesterday.

14th July

Storms and rain suspend the works. The commanders left at 5 o'clock with a sergeant, two soldiers and five Canadians in a bark canoe to carry letters to Frontenac and to find out what is happening in those parts. We received news from the Belle Riviére. Savages have taken scalps there.

15th July

Work. News from la Presque Isle where all is tranquil, the savages brought us a wild turkey which was very good and similar to those of France.[30]

16th July

Letters from Montréal came with orders for the commanders, and news from France where two fleets have left from Rochefort. We learned that our barques attacked two *goelettes* and a skiff but that the wind was lacking so they could not catch the skiff.[31] M. de Bourlamaque who commands at Frontenac ordered our commander to return in the barques with the regiment to Frontenac and to carry the big guns and leave a piquet here.[32] At 4 o'clock we discovered two barques.

17th July

The workers were employed in improving the main body of the place. The two barques were sighted which were running along the shoreline to get here but the

30 Fort Presque Isle was situated on the south shore of Lake Erie and was constructed in 1753. It was the first link in a chain which went on to Fort le Boeuf, Fort Machault and finally Fort Duquesne to reach the Ohio valley.

31 This was the first meeting of the newly built British naval force from Oswego and the French ships based at Frontenac on Lake Ontario. The British ships were poorly built and lacking in cannon. Captain Broadly, Royal Navy, who commanded the British fleet notes this encounter as occurring on 27 of June and on sighting the French fleet decided they could not put up a fight. They left their smaller vessel to its fate as it was reckoned to not be fast enough to outrun the French ships while the two brigs, the *Oswego* and *Ontario*, made their escape back to Oswego. Broadley presumed the smaller vessel had been captured. See Broadley to Admiralty Secretary, 28 June 1756, The National Archives, CO5/47 pp. 123-6.

32 Francois-Charles de Bourlamaque, third in command of the French regular troops, played a prominent role directing siege operations at Oswego and in the next year Fort William-Henry. He was wounded several times and appears to have been a courageous professional officer. After the fall of New France he was appointed governor of Guadeloupe where he died in office in 1764.

wind was contrary. We detached a bateau to go and fetch the letters which arrived back much later without being able to catch them. From 8 until midnight we fired cannon as a signal to prevent the barques from getting lost. At 1 o'clock the wind calmed. The bateau *Victor* entered the river.

18th July

We found the three barques, the wind having changed at 10 o'clock to blow from the north, and they arrived in the river at midday. The regiment received orders to embark as soon as the boats were ready. A courier announced a deputation of the *Loup* [Ohio Delaware] nation of savages.

19th July

Worked. We loaded the barques.

20th July

I went to the falls which is one of the most rare and curious phenomena of nature. It is formed by the waters of Lake Erie, which is very narrow at its mouth. They rush along and are separated by the end of a small island which appears to result from two very high points in the Niagara River. It is one hundred and twenty *pied* high and nearly two hundred *toises* wide. It forms several layers of water infinitely varied in angles as it falls. The spectator is well compensated for the noise caused by the falls by seeing crystal clear water or streams that rise up in all the colours of the rainbow. These falls are often covered with mist and are 6 leagues from Fort Niagara and a half mile from the small fort which is a food storehouse which sits at the end of the great shore. One can set out from this fort very easily. The path that leads to the falls is beautiful and crosses a nice wood. The Niagara River flows into the lake at the point of Niagara. A letter arrived from the marquis de Vaudreuil from Montréal which told us to travel by bateaux if the barques did not arrive.

21st July

Work was suspended and the workers paid. We took food for eight days and embarked with our equipment.

22nd July

The wind was contrary so we remained on land. The *Goyoguans* [Cayugas] had a long meeting with the commandant of the fort.

23rd July

The regiment embarked at 8 o'clock in the four corvettes and barques. They set sail before 9 o'clock out of the river with a wind from south-southwest, at noon the wind shifted to the north and forced us to rest at Toronto where we anchored at 4 o'clock.

24th July

The wind remained from the north-east, so we remained at anchor. We went ashore; I went into the fort which I found to be like those of poor countries and made from wood. It is situated twelve leagues north of the lake and one from the river from which it takes its name.

25th July

The commandant of the flotilla, fearing that we could not leave Toronto if the wind changed, ordered all the boats to raise anchor. We set sail at 8 o'clock, continuing along the coast. The wind continued from the north and we sailed back to Niagara, entering the river at 8 in the evening.

26th July

The *Louise* who had not been able to follow us yesterday came to anchor nearby. We took on food for four days, and took fresh air. We ate on land but returned on board to sleep.

29th July

The wind was variable, the flotilla commandant advised that a good wind was expected tomorrow. The magazine guard was advised to make bread overnight.

30th July

The wind seemed to be set from the north-west. We sent for the bread from the fort which was not ready. So as not to delay departure we took what had already been cooked. We set sail at 7 o'clock and came out of the river immediately, the wind freshened and by 8 o'clock in the evening we found ourselves at the curve of Quinté.

31st July

We came up to the Iles de Coui where we spent a good hour. At 10 o'clock we rounded the point of the petit Cataracoui and Fort Frontenac where we entered the bay at 1 o'clock. We disembarked at the magazine where we went to form a line at the head of the camp to the left of Guyenne,[33] after which we went to see M. le marquis de Montcalm and M. de Bourlamaque.

It is estimated that Lake Ontario is more than eighty leagues long and nearly thirty broad at its widest point.

1st August

We worked on preparations for departure. M. le marquis de Montcalm made a review of the Canadians who were formed into a brigade. There was a general order that they should be given all that was necessary for war.

2nd August

M. le marquis de Montcalm made a review of the Guyenne and Béarn Regiments who then fired at targets. The forty-four boats which would carry the La Sarre Regiment to Niaouré arrived at the fort at 1 o'clock. The general received letters which gave him a mood, because the troops in the camp who had received their supplies for several days were already lacking.

3rd August

Preparations of food and ammunition were made and loaded onto boats.

4th August

The officer who had brought the boats to the bay left with supplies for the camp. The regiment of Guyenne and the Canadians of their division took food for twelve days. M. de Montcalm left at 9 in the evening with the grenadiers of Guyenne, leaving to go to the bay.

5th August

The division of Guyenne, under the orders of M. de Bourlamaque embarked in one hundred and twenty bateaux loaded with provisions and artillery.

6th August

I examined the ninety-nine bateaux designated for the Béarn division and the Canadians who were to pilot them. This division took food for twelve days.

33 'Line' has been used to translate the term '*en bataille*' which literally translates as 'in battle' but in this period denotes the line formation typical of European armies of the 18th Century.

7th August

The division of Béarn under orders of M. de l'Hôpital embarked in their boats which also carried supplies, artillery and horses. All this fleet reached le Large at 10 o'clock. At noon a gale blew up from the south-west which scattered the fleet around the Isle au Chevreuil and forced almost all of the bateaux to land.

8th August

All the bateaux rallied around l'Isle au Chevreuil and at 2 o'clock in the afternoon entered into the Baie de Niaouré and landed ahead of those charged with the artillery. Béarn camped between La Sarre and Guyenne. The corps of M. de Rigaud left in the morning to go by land to Chouaguen and protect the landing of the army.

9th August

The first division composed of La Sarre, Guyenne and many Canadians left to go to disembark above Chouaguen. I delivered equipment to the Canadians of the second division.

10th August

The wind blew up preventing the second division's departure. At 10 o'clock in the evening a courier from the general arrived to hasten our progress. At midnight the wind died down.

11th August

At 1 o'clock in the morning the division pushed off and at 8 o'clock reached the Rive au Sable, where we rested for two hours, arriving at 4 o'clock at the Rivière á la Famine, where we received orders to go in haste to a cove a half-league from Chouaguen where the first division were posted. We set out at 6 o'clock and at midnight were forced to halt behind a point that they could not get around. Being in a bark canoe I was able to round the point and arrived at 1 o'clock to get to M. de Montcalm, where I learned that M. des Combles, our chief engineer, had been killed by one of our savages who taken him for an Englishman because of his jacket with red facings.[34] Two British boats have approached our camp and were forced to withdraw by the cannon balls they received from four of our cannon which we have established on the shore, and on entering the river they suffered lively musketry fire.[35]

34 Note by Gaffarel – The savage who killed him was inconsolable at his clumsiness. He did his best to make it up, taking the scalps of thirty-three English. Pierre Pouchot (trans. Franklin Benjamin Hough), *Memoir upon the late war in North America,* (Roxbury: W. Elliot Woodward, 1866), Vol. I, p. 88.

35 There were three forts, Ontario, on the right bank of the river, Oswego on the left bank, now the town of Oswego, and George on a hill in the same bank. These works were defended by

12th August

The second division landed behind the camp and camped between La Sarre and Guyenne. The bateaux were unloaded and pulled ashore. This division was very tired and ordered to rest. The first division provided the workers to make the path from the camp to the place which had been designated to open a trench, make fascines, *saucissons* and gabions. At 10 o'clock, three English barques came into range of our camp. They were sent a few balls at their approach. A 2 o'clock M. Desandrouins, engineer, went with the officers of Artillery to scout Fort Ontario. At their return one hundred workers per battalion, fifty armed men per battalion and two companies of grenadiers were assembled. These troops left camp at 7 o'clock under the orders of M. Bourlamaque, colonel, l'Hôpital, lieutenant-colonel and Malartic, major. They arrived at 8 o'clock at the depot where they found tools and gabions; at 11 o'clock they marched and by midnight were placed along three sides of a square with the right facing the lake and the left flanked by the right of the fort. Half an hour later the engineers gave the signal to begin breaking ground and the work was begun with great vivacity. At daybreak the workers found shelter.

13th August

One hundred workers went into the trenches to relieve those from the previous night followed by the gunners and Canadians to begin a battery. At 6 o'clock the English began to disrupt the trench with bombs and bullets and redoubled their efforts up to 1 o'clock when they suddenly stopped. After half an hour we saw troops marching along the river and climbing up from old Chouaguen to Fort aux Bœufs.[36] M. de Bourlamaque sent a lieutenant with fifteen grenadiers to reconnoitre. This officer reported that the fort [Ontario] was being evacuated. M. de Bourlamaque sent him some workers and a little later the two companies of grenadiers and the

---

1,130 men from the 50th (Shirley's), and 51st (Pepperell's) Regiments, part of the New Jersey Provincial Regiment and a small company of the Royal Artillery, all under the command of Colonel Mercer. The defences were not considered formidable by their own garrison, who had been poorly supplied since the aborted campaign against Niagara in 1755. The first attack took place on 11 August at daybreak. It was directed against Fort Ontario. This fort was a square of sixty feet wide, whose faces were covered by a redan, which gave it a star shape. It was palisaded, protected by a moat six metres wide, a counterscarp, a glacis and defended by eight cannons, four mortars and two grenade launchers. The engineer des Combles had made the reconnaissance. His report was the basis for the operations that followed. Chartrand, *Montcalm's Crushing Blow*, pp. 14-19; Charles Nicolas Gabriel, *Le Maréchal de Camp Desandrouins, 1729-1792*, (Verdun: Renvé-Lallemant, 1887) pp. 39-40.

36 Although a little unclear from his perspective, Malartic is describing the evacuation of Fort Ontario, which happened at around 4 o'clock that day. Fort Ontario was on the east bank and separated from Old Oswego (Chouaguen) by the river. Its garrison had successfully left the fort by the rear and descended the cliff and crossed the river without alerting the French. After getting back to Old Oswego, the Fort Ontario garrison was sent out to the west fort which Malartic calls Fort aux Bœufs but was known to the British as Fort George and by the British soldiers as Fort Rascal due to its extremely poor construction. It had been used as a glorified sheep pen for much of the spring of 1756. Chartrand, *Montcalm's Crushing Blow*, pp. 6-12.

rest of the workers. M. le marquis de Montcalm arrived along the trench to the fort with M. de Bourlamaque. I accompanied them. We found a star shaped fort built from very thick stakes, surrounded by a ditch twelve feet wide and ten deep. We entered through an opening that the workers had made and planks that served as a bridge. The enemy had left six guns, some mortars and howitzers there. They destroyed the communication bridge with Chouaguen, despite being under heavy fire. We were relieved at 6 o'clock by a company of grenadiers, three piquets and two hundred workers under the orders of M. de Fonbonne, lieutenant-colonel and Mineré, major.[37] The workers made a communication trench up to Fort Ontario, an *epaulement* on the escarpment of the river and transported the necessary artillery and munitions.[38] Two batteries were begun.

14th August

We completed a battery which started firing at 6 o'clock. Despite the superior enemy fire, we had no gunners or soldiers killed. The battalions provided sixty gunners and fifty men to serve the guns. At 9 o'clock the English commander was killed by a cannon ball. At the same hour, M. de Rigaud crossed the river with a body of Canadians and all our savages. A quarter of an hour later the fort raised the white flag. Both sides ceased fire. Two English officers arrived, who proposed on behalf of their commander, to leave if they were granted the honours of war. M. le marquis de Montcalm refused, kept them hostage and sent M. de Bougainville, his aide de camp, and Delapause, *aide-major général*, who drew up the articles of capitulation and the following conditions: that the garrison would be imprisoned until exchanged and that they may take all personal property with them.[39] They accepted and the articles were signed by both sides.[40] At noon, the guards and workers of the trench went to take possession of the forts and the army marched on the right bank of the river to receive the garrison, who were enclosed in Fort Ontario with a guard of one hundred and fifty men who could barely contain the fury of the savages who had been enlivened by liquor which they had found in the cellars of the fort and wanted to kill all the English.[41] The regiments returned to the camp at 6 o'clock, exhausted.

---

37 Fonbonne, as already mentioned, was the commanding officer of Guyenne. Mineré is possibly Jean Dumesnis Simon de Mineray, *aide-major* of La Sarre.

38 An *epaulement* is a barricade of earth like a rough parapet used mainly as cover from flanking fire.

39 Jean-Guillame Plantavit de Lapause de Margon was *aide-major* of the Guyenne Regiment and came to assume general staff duties under Montcalm. A career officer but without much wealth, he continued military service until his death in 1780 at which time he was acting as assistant chief of staff in the building of the Saint-Omer Canal in France.

40 Note by Gaffarel – Montcalm had his own reasons to expedite the signing of the Convention. General Webb was nearby with 2,000 men at some distance from Chouaguen, and expected a notice from Colonel Mercer to come for help. Montcalm had even decided that if he could not take the fort, he would take the offensive against him. 'The need to succeed, he wrote later, for the salvation of the colony, for the honour of arms of the King and myself, has me decided, and it being also a resolution adopted by the principal officers to go to the front and meet the enemy, at a portage three leagues from here to fight'.

41 Note by Gaffarel – Found in the fort; 1,700 soldiers, sailors and workers, 80 officers, hundreds of women and children. 152 men were killed in action. The French lost only 5 dead and 25

15th August

The army rested. Twenty-two boats were loaded with prisoners.

16th August

La généralle was beaten at daybreak. The battalions supplied one hundred and fifty workers each to evacuate and demolish Fort Chouaguen and Fort aux Bœufs. The army took up a new camp with the right at Fort Ontario and the left up to the woods. This was difficult to establish as there were few men with marker flags. Our barques, [for which we had] waited with impatience before the surrender of the fort, arrived at 5 o'clock.

In the three forts taken there were six hundred men of the Shirley's, Pepperell's and New Jersey Regiments. We took four flags, one hundred guns, lots of ammunition, and food for two thousand men for a year. In the great river [the Oswego river] there were six barques of different sizes and a seventh in the dockyard and two hundred barges or bateaux. In the magazines there were trade goods and other specialities. This victory has cost us thirty men killed or wounded against one hundred and fifty Englishmen.

17th August

The battalions supplied two hundred and fifty workers. Twenty bateaux were sent out loaded with prisoners, escorted by thirty-man detachment. The barques were loaded with artillery and supplies.

18th August

The same number of workers. Two barques set sail on the river. They loaded the prisoners and they sailed for Frontenac. Fort aux Bœufs or George was set on fire.

---

injured, including Bourlamaque. Here is the official transcript of ammunition and eatables which fell into our hands: 5 flags, 123 artillery pieces, 23 thousand pounds of powder, 8 thousand of lead, 2,950 bullets, 450 bombs, 1,476 grenades, 130 muskets, 350 barrels of biscuit, 1,386 quarts of bacon and beef, 712 quarts of flour, 200 bags of flour, 11 quarts of rice, 7 quarts of salt, a granary full of peas and flour, 32 cattle, 15 pigs, a large amount of barrels of wine and rum. Gaffrael went on to note that the Indians rushed in to take isolated prisoners who they scalped. At the first sign of this disorder, Montcalm ran in and managed to make them stop with the promise of rich presents for their allies. 'It will cost the King 8 to 10,000 francs', he wrote, 'to prevent the savages violating the capitulation but now more than ever we must retain the affection of these people. There is nothing I would not have given to preserve this process to preserve good faith in the French.' [This quote from Montcalm is interesting as Anglophone historians, such as Francis Jennings, have used it to show that Montcalm did not care much for the prisoners.] The Indians took poorly to this reasoning according to Vaudreuil. In a letter to Machault, the Minister of Marine he wrote; 'All the Indians and even the Abenaki Nipissings and Algonquins, who were always our closest allies, did not hesitate to tell me, after the campaign Chouaguen, that 'they would go wherever I sent them, provided I do not place them under the orders of M. de Montcalm.'

19th August

The battalions supplied three hundred workers. The rest of the barques set out to Frontenac from the river at midday, and after having loaded the prisoners under the orders of M. de l'Hôpital. In the evening, forty-two bateaux loaded with artillery and prisoners left, escorted by two piquets. At 8 o'clock in the evening, the general asked the grenadiers to cut down the stakes of Ontario. They worked all night.

20th August

Almost all the guns had been overturned and were set on fire which consumed the buildings of the fort. M. de Bourlamaque had also taken care of the old fort. His garrison returned after midday and went back to their battalions. Food and bateaux were distributed to the troops. A party of sixty Iroquois arrived to help us with the siege. They were amazed to find only the ruins of the three forts.

21st August

The corps of M. de Rigaud left before *la généralle.* The barrels of bad pork were burnt at the river bank. The army set out at 7 o'clock and marched in divisions. It camped at 3 o'clock on the two banks of the Sable River.

22nd August

The army set out at 8 o'clock and arrived at the Baie de Niaouré. The battalions took up their former camp.

23rd August

The Béarn Regiment left at 9 o'clock to return to La Chine and take 260 prisoners. It was difficult to get around the Isle au Galop and the point of the Ile au Chevreuil because of the violence of the wind. When they reached the main channel, the wind was too strong and they took the opportunity to camp at 7 o'clock at the entrance to the channel.

24th August

They left at 5 o'clock, arriving at La Présentation at 3 o'clock and unloaded the food taken for the fort and went to camp at the Pointe aux Iroquois, where the prisoners found themselves safe from the insults of the savages.

25th August

I left at 5 o'clock in a bark canoe. I reached the Isle au Chats, meeting two bateaux piloted by Canadians, I passed Long Sault, entered Lake Saint-François which I crossed with a good wind in three hours. I reached the other side of the lake reaching the first habitations at 3 o'clock. I went down the le Trou, les Buissons and les Cascades with the help of some men. We were weighed down by grain which kept us heavily anchored. I re-embarked my men at the bottom of the rapids where we went past the Ile Perrot. The canoe was hit and pierced. I was obliged to land and wait until the next day.

26th August

After patching the canoe, I embarked at 6 despite a southwest wind that the Canadians found too strong to go ahead. We crossed Pointe Claire, where we met M. Bougainville at Sault Saint-Louis at 9 o'clock. I asked for a guide from the commander who I found dining with a Jesuit. They promised to give me the most skilful savage in the village if I would help them attack a pie. I did not refuse. After lunch they took me to a church and some cabins which I found very pretty. I took leave of them at 10 o'clock. I crossed the Sault Saint-Louis le Normand easily and reached Montréal at midday.[42] After unloading I went to take orders from M. le marquis de Vaudreuil, who I met at table where he told me that the regiment was to be found at La Chine. MM. de Montcalm and Bourlamaque arrived at 4 o'clock telling me that they had left the regiment at the bottom of the falls and some boats were at La Chine.

27th August

I mounted my horse at 5 and arrived at La Chine by 7. I found six of our bateaux there; the others had arrived by 8 o'clock. They gave our commander the orders of M. de Montcalm and left immediately to inform the general of the regiment's arrival. I then worked to get food to La Chine and to la Prairie where it would be needed it tomorrow.

28th August

After making sure that the commissary and the magazine guard would deliver all that had been asked for, I left from Pointe Saint-Charles.[43] I arrived at la Prairie at 2 o'clock. I found the regiment camped to the left of the fort facing the woods and distributed supplies for four days.

29th August

The regiment remained in place, while providing one hundred and twenty workers to repair the road to Fort Saint-Jean, under M. Pouchot's instruction.

42 Sault Saint Louis was the name given to the falls in the river as well as the Native American village which was founded close to them.

43 Saint-Charles seems to be referring to the old Seigneury of Saint-Charles which is located on the Richelieu near present day Beloil. It seems likely that this area was a military depot and end of a portage from the Richelieu to Varennes.

30th August

The regiment marched at 8 o'clock to camp at la Savanne, less the workers.[44] I left at 9 o'clock to inform the generals of our departure. I left town at 3 and arrived at camp at 7, where we were devoured by mosquitoes.

31st August

The same number of workmen. The regiment decamped at midday, finding a very poor road to take us to Fort Saint-Jean where we set camp at 4 o'clock.[45] The fort is constructed on piles, and is in a very bad state having no means of fire, despite being the depot for supplies from Montréal for Forts Frédéric and Carillon and during the winter has a considerable mass of supplies and ammunition.

1st September

The regiment took provisions for six days and remained here. We took advantage to repair our weapons and I procured twenty-six bateaux to carry the regiment.

2nd September

We embarked at 6 o'clock to set out on Lake Champlain. We stopped at La Prairie à Boilau and them came to camp opposite the mill at Faucault, at 8 o'clock.

3rd September

We embarked at 5 o'clock. A strong contrary wind from the south-west forced us to land after struggling for a league. Canadians warned us they had seen fresh tracks of savages. An officer with eight grenadiers and as many Canadians went out to scout the woods. They returned at 10 o'clock saying that they had come across a place where three men had sat down to smoke. At midday I left with some men and went a league into the woods, to the flank and rear of camp without hearing or seeing anyone.

4th September

We set off at 4 o'clock, benefitting from a wind from the north to travel 30 leagues and camp at l'Isle au Chapon.

44 I have not been able to locate this exact point but it seems to be between Chambly and Saint Jean.

45 Fort Saint-Jean was a post between Montréal and Lake Champlain; between Fort Chambly and Isle aux Noix.

5th September

We decamped at 5 o'clock and arrived at Fort Saint-Frédéric at 3, where we set up camp. The fort is a grand redoubt, constructed on, and clad in stone. It is dominated by a rise a half cannon shot away.

6th September

We left at 6 o'clock and arrived at 2 o'clock at Carillon. M. le chevalier de Lévis commands the army at this frontier, which consists of the regiments of La Reine, Royal Roussillon and Languedoc.[46] The colony troops and Canadians were sent to camp a league ahead on the left bank of the falls into Lake Saint Sacrement.

7th September

We worked on abatis to cover the front, rear and flanks of our camp and protect us from being surprised by the *Agnis* [Mohawks], an Iroquois tribe devoted to the English who often frequent these parts.[47]

8th September

Work continued on the abatis. I went with an escort to reconnoitre the camps of Contrecoeur and la Corne. The first was on the left bank of Lake Saint Sacrement, a league from our camp. The second on the right bank at the end of the portage. Between the two camps there was a strong guard commanded by M. de Saint-Martin and a guard of fifty men between our camp and la Corne's to hold the road to the portage. In the event of attack we had orders to take these two camps.[48]

---

46 François de Lévis was ranked as a brigadier and second in command to Montcalm. He was born into an ancient but impoverished noble family and sought to return to greatness. He had served throughout his youth as a cadet and company commander, rising to staff-officer in the War of the Austrian Succession, however he did not have the resources to supply his own regiment. His service in North America was marked by his character. He managed to get along with Vaudreuil and Montcalm and earned the respect of many, including Malartic who rated his ability much more than Montcalm as we will see later. After Montcalm's death he made sure he was remunerated by the court for his expenses after his tenacious efforts and determination to go out fighting. This secured his reputation despite the outcome of the campaign. After the war his star continued to rise, becoming a guards officer and governor of Arras and later being promoted to marshal of France. His cousin Mirepoix, made a marshal of France in 1751, helped advance his early career but it seemed it was his own merit which caused his later promotions. In 1787 he passed away aged 67.

47 An abatis is a field fortification made by felling trees and arranging them lengthways with the branches facing the direction of the attackers. These can then be sharpened and interlaced with more obstacles.

48 The Contrecoeur and la Corne camps simply referred to the camp sites taken in the previous year at Carillon. See Map 6. St-Martin was a marine captain who was wounded at Sainte Foy in 1760: see E.B. O'Callaghan, John Romeyn Brodhead, and Berthold Fernow (eds.), *Documents Relative to the Colonial History of the State of New York*. Vol. 10. (Albany: Weed, Parsons and Company, 1853), p. 1084.

9th September

We strengthened the communications between the two posts with abatis.

10th September

Work continued. The Guyenne Regiment went to camp on our right at 2 in the afternoon. M. le Marquis de Montcalm arrived at 6 o'clock to the general's quarters.

11th September

The generals went to the camps of Contrecoeur and la Corne to hold council with the savages and then returned to our camp.

12th September

The regiments of Guyenne and Béarn worked to enlarge the approaches to the camp and improve communications.

13th September

I went with M. de Lapause to reconnoitre the mountains which border the right of our camp.[49] We found them practicable for parties and detachments.

14th September

I went to the general's quarters, where I found many savages who were tiring the general with their continual demands for presents. Two piquets which we had left around Frontenac joined us at 5 in the evening. Over the last four days we have sent a guard of two lieutenants and sixty men of the regulars to the lake to reinforce that position. M. le Marquis de Montcalm took with him the grenadier company and piquet of La Sarre, the rest of the regiment worked on the road of La Prairie to Saint-Jean.

15th September

MM. Lapause, Belot and myself went with twenty grenadiers to reconnoitre Mount Pelée which is an hour and a half from the camp of Contrecoeur.[50] We found it very steep and difficult to access, this peak is on the left side of the lake. There is a gorge by the side which is practical to make a road returning to Fort Saint-Frédéric. At the summit we could see a great deal of the lake, l'Isle aux Barques and several others and many peaks.

49 Note the change from Delapause to Lapause, referring to the same officer.

50 Antoine-Joseph Bellot de Segonzac was a captain of Guyenne, born in 1724. He was made a chevalier of St. Louis in 1759 after which he returned to France in 1760 and quit the army.

16th September

M. Laparguière left with six hundred Iroquois, Abenakis and Outaouas [Ottawas] and two hundred Canadians to make a strike against l'Isle du Lac, or close to Fort George.[51] M. de Bougainville and la Rochebeaucourt followed them to reconnoitre the English position.

18th and 19th September

Worked as normal. At 10 o'clock at night many musket shots were heard. The army was on the point of taking up arms but the shots required to announce the coming of the enemy were not fired and it was seen that the party sent out on the 16th were returning.

20th September

M. le marquis de Montcalm made a review of the advanced camps, where he found the returning savages, who said that they had discovered a detachment of one hundred English a league from Fort George, of whom forty marched by land and sixty travelled over the water. Those on land saw the scouts and opened fire on them. The savages did not give them time to recover but descended on them, killing twenty-three and taking their scalps, captured fourteen, after which they withdrew. The sixty on the water were saved by the first shot. Nine Iroquois remained in the field to try and take a prisoner at the fort.

21st September

The savages got drunk and played the devil, killing the officers' sheep. Eighty returned to their villages. The nine Iroquois returned, having approached the English camp and killed a sentry.

22nd September

A convoy of twenty-two boats arrived loaded with supplies and convalescents of the five battalions.

23rd September

The bateaux which arrived yesterday went back carrying almost all of the sick, the general ordered that no guard duty was needed at the hospital and would be restored in a few days.

51 What was known as Fort George to the French was called Fort William Henry by the British. It was constructed in 1755 at the foot of Lake George/Saint Sacrement.

27th September

M. de Florimond left with eighteen Abenakis to go to scout the end of the bay and the surroundings of Lake Lydius.

1st October

M. le Marquis de Montcalm charged M. de Lapause with ensuring that the sawmill at the falls was working as we need three thousand planks for Fort Carillon before the army withdraws.

2nd October

A convoy of bateaux loaded with supplies arrived.

3rd October

M. de Bleury, commanding the convoy, arrived here to inform the general that three savages discovered three barges on Lake Champlain loaded with grape, grenades, powder and ball. M. de Cerifest left with twenty men of the regulars, many Canadians and savages went into the woods to where the barges were sighted by M. de Lusignan, commander of Fort Saint-Frédéric.[52]

6th October

M. de Florimond, returned with the Abenakis, reporting that three scouts had suffered some musket shots, and that two were killed; those of the Nipissingués and *Pouteoutamis* [Potawatomis] who were at the front.

9th October

M. le marquis de Montcalm made a review of the Guyenne and Béarn regiments who were given orders to make eight hundred palisades.

11th October

The general reviewed the La Reine regiment. A soldier of Béarn, who went to fetch a wallet he had lost yesterday while cutting palisades, was taken by three Agnés, who took him while he was occupied. Scarcely had they gone a league when they saw a deer. Two savages ran after it, the third remained in custody of the soldier, who was

52 Lusignan was a captain of the Marines and in July 1749, hosted travelling Swedish botanist Pehr Kalm at Fort Frederick. Lusignan appeared to have shared Kalm's interests and they discussed the natural history of the country. Kalm was impressed with the efforts of the then governor, Galissonière, to reward common soldiers who had investigated 'the discovery and collections of plants and other natural curiosities'. Peter Kalm (trans. John Reinhold Forster), *Travels into North America*, (London: T. Lowndes, 1771), Vol.II, pp. 183-5.

busy collecting wood to light a fire. The soldier threw away the savage's gun and ran back to camp, returning around 9, having received a blow with a club to his hand. M. de Fleury arrived at 3 o'clock with a convoy of bateaux and returned at 9.

12th October

M. le Marquis de Montcalm made a review of the Royal Rousillon Regiment. A soldier of Béarn and a servant were killed carrying letters to Contrecoeur's camp by the Agnés who took their scalps. Some officers, two hundred colony soldiers and some of the sick left for Montréal.

14th October

[The troops at] Contrecoeur's camp withdrew back to la Corne's camp.

18th October

The Nippissingués and Potawatomis brought in a prisoner they had taken on the road to Orange, who said that Lord Loudoun was gathering his army between Forts Lydius and George, to attack in the off-season.[53] He has fortified Orange on the side of the woods. New England has made proposals to make peace to which he responded he would consider them when he had been beaten.

19th October

After the statement of the prisoner, M. le marquis de Montcalm decided to postpone his departure.

20th October

Three Canadians returning from taking food to the falls had left their escort and discovered ten savages or Scots hidden behind trees and fired on them. Their savages responded and wounded two then fled.[54]

53 After the death of General Braddock, command of the British forces devolved to his second, William Shirley, Governor of Massachusetts. By the summer of 1756 John Campbell, 4th Earl of Loudoun had arrived to take the role.

54 A letter sent from Fort Edward on 10 October by General Loudoun to William Shirley states that the general had with him 'three Battalions of the Regular Troops the New York Regt and most of the New Hampshire Men'. See Johnson, *Papers of Sir William Johnson*, vol. 9, p. 553. The 42nd Highlanders were one of the battalions with Loudoun on the New York frontier, alternatively the 'New Hampshire Men' could have been ranging companies who often wore the bonnet as headgear, hence the Canadians mistaking them for Scots.

21st October

An Iroquois interpreter returning from scouting with seven Iroquois and as many Canadians, said he saw a barque of seven men from a distance. A little later another of 8 men and several bateaux making their way to Fort George. They approached the camp which is below the fort. They counted twelve rows of fifty tents. There did not seem to be many people and were surprised to see only thirty, curious at the arrival of the bateaux. A savage and a Canadian, who were making notes by a tree on the road to Fort Lydius, heard the sound of several carriages.

25th October

M. de Bleury, who has been expected for several days, arrived with fifty-six loaded bateaux.[55]

26th October

M. le marquis de Montcalm left with the company of grenadiers and piquet of La Sarre.

27th October

The regiments camped at the falls received orders to make oars for the bateaux.

30th October.

[The troops at] Saint-Martin's post fell back to La Corne's camp.

31st October

The militia and colony soldiers of the government of Québec have left.

1st November

The Guyenne Regiment left for Québec.

2nd November

The Regiment of La Reine have left to spend the winter in the parish of the government of Québec. I left at midday to mark out the camp for the regiment at Fort Saint-Frédéric.

55 Clément de Sabrevois de Bleury was a well-connected trader who managed to amass a small fortune becoming chief of the Intendant 's transport system in the early years of the war. He retired due to ill health in 1757.

3rd November

The companies of the colony and the Canadians from the government of Trois-Rivières departed. The Regiment of Béarn arrived by platoon from 7 in the evening until 10 at Saint-Frédéric. The wind had been contrary so the bateaux could scarcely move and so cold that the tents and equipment were frozen inside the bateaux. We could not get them out and we sheltered as best we could in the barns.

Fort Carillon is located five leagues from Saint-Frédéric on a point of the river mouth from the Falls, which flows into the one that goes to Saint-Frédéric and receives its waters from the bottom of the bay into which flow several smaller rivers. The fort is built from wood, piece by piece, though it sits upon a rock foundation. The wood was on hand when it was begun but now we must go out over half a league and it takes twenty men to drag back each log. The fort is too small and has almost no defence. Better advantage could be taken of this position by keeping the fortified camp which will be needed when we gather a number of troops. Work on Fort Saint-Frédéric is required, which is the gate to Lake Champlain where the two banks could be fortified. Fort Carillon will never be good, costs a lot and will not stop the enemy for long. It would take a year of work. The body of the place is not finished. So many things to say that would require too long a digression in this journal!

4th November

We let the soldiers rest as they were very tired and suffered with the cold yesterday. M. de Bleury arrived at midday with a convoy. We learned of a change in our destination and we were to take the same quarters as last winter.

5th November

Of the two hundred and fifty men we have, one hundred remained at Carillon to work, we sent one hundred and sixty to the left bank to cut wood for the garrison.

6th November

The same number set to work on the right bank. All the Canadians of the government of Montréal, and the companies of the colony destined for that town arrived at midday. One party entered the fort to visit the stores where they asked for some things though they had been well equipped when setting out. Those passing through wished to take what was left for the magazine guard. What the King pays for this consumption is immense. A fire broke out in one of the four chimneys of the fort. This was deeply disturbing as the powder magazine is in the middle of them, but it died without incident.

7th November

A *goelette* arrived yesterday taking the route to Saint-Jean. I left at noon with a man of the company to go and establish lodgings for the regiments quarters. I stopped at 6 o'clock a league from the Rocher Fendu to let the soldiers make supper. We re-embarked at 9 o'clock and disembarked on the 8th of November at 4 in the morning, 3 leagues from l'Isle au Chapon. I was obliged to go in my bateau which took on much water. I caulked it as best I could. We resumed our journey at 7 in the morning, taking advantage of four hours of good wind to reach Saint-Jean, arriving at 5 o'clock.

9th November

I left my bateau to go over the rapids of Chambly and then descend into the Sorel River and re-embarked on the river to carry our equipment to our quarters. I took four soldiers with me on the road to la Prairie. We stopped at the mill which is on the edge of the River of Montréal to rest and dry ourselves. We left at noon, arriving at la Prairie at 2 o'clock, where we found the officers who had left Saint-Frédéric 24 hours before me. We left at 3 and disembarked a quarter-league from Montréal. I was overwhelmed on my return by the bad state of the roads where we had water up to our knees.

10th November

I went to Longueuil, where I found M. de l'Hôpital established. I went to sleep at la Prairie where I had found lodgings for three companies to stay the winter.

11th November

I returned to Longueuil to work on finding lodgings for the three companies of the *etat-major.* I went to Boucherville and established the four companies there and slept at Varennes.

12th November

I travelled the parish of Varennes which I did not know, to find lodging for three companies, then to Boucherville, this parish was the richest of the quarters which we occupy. I returned in the evening to Longueuil.

15th November

I went to Montréal and stayed until the 16th to receive the accounts given for each battalion.

17th November

I carried the money I had received to Longueuil where the three companies sent there arrived at the same time. On the 18th I went to la Prairie on the 19th to Boucherville and on the 20th to Varennes to distribute the money to the companies.

21st November

I returned to Longueuil to make the accounts of the three companies.

22nd November

I went to Montréal. I stayed until the 29th in order to complete the food and other accounts. The ambassadors of the Five Nations arrived on the 28th.

29th November

I went to Longueuil. I spent 15 days on all the accounts I had received.

13th December

I went to Montréal, half of the journey over ice and half by bateau. I remained there until the 24th. Ambassadors of the Five Nations held several councils, where they promised Ononthio to be neutral, and asked for the restoration of the use of an envoy housed with an officer who they would receive at the Riviere aux Ecorces, with the usual ceremonies.[56] They represented that they once made portage at Niagara to do business and prayed Ononthio to provide good stores at Frontenac, Toronto and Niagara so they do not suffer from the destruction of Chouaguen. They warned that Colonel Johnson does not neglect anything to bring them over to the English side but are deaf to his entreaties remembering the destruction of Chouaguen, which purified their lands.

24th December

I went to Longueuil, passing through Varennes, where I crossed the ice of the river which was not passable by boat up to Sault Saint-Louis.

27th December

I returned to Montréal.

28th, 29th and 30th December

The savages demanded many councils that the general gave them which bored him so greatly that he wished he could leave.

31st December

The Marquis de Vaudreuil and M. le chevalier de Lévis left for Québec.

56 Possibly the Riviere a la Grose Ecorces which runs into the south shore of Lake Ontario. See Map 8.

3

The Year 1757

Capitalising on the successes of 1756, French military efforts focussed on the Lake Champlain corridor. The fort at the end of Lake Saint-Sacrement (known as Fort George to the French or Fort William Henry to the English), was the target. This year saw the biggest number of Native warriors from the pays d'en haut *arrive to share in the French endeavours. The New York frontier was vulnerable as the British commander-in-chief in North America, Lord Loudoun, took the bulk of his army to Halifax to await an opportunity to strike at Louisbourg, the French naval base on Cape Breton. If Louisbourg fell the French would be without a naval base to protect the Gulf of St. Lawrence and Québec would be left vulnerable to an amphibious attack. However, a combination of poor weather and French naval vigilance led to inaction and the Royal Navy transport ships remained in port. British efforts against Louisbourg would resume under Jeffrey Amherst the following year.*

1st January

The savages said they could not leave and made some visits, hoping to get some shots of eau-de-vie.

2nd January

Recently a courier left for the *pays d'en haut*. A party of savages went on the route to their villages.

3rd January

A party of twenty Canadians and forty savages under the command of M. Langlade left for Carillon, the rest of the savages returned to their villages.[1]

---

1 Charles-Michel Mouet de Langlade was one of touchstone figures of colonial France. Born in 1729 and son of a fur trader and Domitilde, an Ottawa women and sister of Nissowaquet (Nissowaquet, also known as La Fourche, was an influential Ottawa chief who remained in a position of power well into the 1780's). Langlade's official position as an officer blended with his Indian heritage and he became an influential figure in dealings between New France and the tribes from around his birthplace, Michilimackinac. He traded in furs as did most men in his situation and, after the war, adjusted easily to British rule, working as an employee of the Indian department.

I left at 8 o'clock for Québec with M. le marquis de Montcalm, M. le chevalier de Montreuil, *aide-major général* and M. Maral, aide de camp.[2] We arrived on the 5th of January at 9 in the evening.

6th January

The Intendant Bigot, gave a party for M. Vaudreuil, a supper for sixty people including forty ladies or girls, pretty and kind.

19th January

I left Québec with the *aide-major* of La Reine.[3] We arrived at Montréal on the 21st. I stayed there until the 24th to make up the accounts of the regiment with the treasurer who gave me sixty thousand francs in silver coin. I carried this to Longueuil, where I spent eight days distributing it.

29th January

We heard that M. le marquis de Vaudreuil fell ill at Trois-Riviéres, and that the commissary and surgeon-major were his only rescue.

30th January

I went to La Prairie and returned to Longueuil

31st January

We saw the arrival of the Canadians and savages returning from Carillon, who told us that M. de Rouilly left on the 22nd with sledges, escorted by fifty men to take food from Fort St-Frédéric. They were attacked at Presque Isle by sixty English,[4] to whom he lost seven men taken prisoner, the rest fled to Carillon where M. de Lusignan immediately sent out one hundred soldiers, Canadians and savages in order to cut the retreat of the English; this detachment was not discovered and lay in

2 Pierre-Andre Gohin, comte de Montreuil, remains opaque for a relatively high ranking officer. He was second in command to Dieskau at the Battle of Lake George and was on Montcalm's staff for the entire war. He also was placed second in command at the Battle of Sainte-Foy in 1760 under Lévis. He appears not to have distinguished himself as a staff officer however. Montcalm believed him brave but with no talent for his role. I have found no references to Maral.

3 This was Jean-Pierre-Gaston d'Hert who joined the army as a common soldier in 1736. He was promoted from sergent to lieutenant in January 1747. He died at sea on the return crossing to France in November 1760.

4 Presque Isle translates as 'peninsula' and various sites around New France were given this name, most notably the fort established on Lake Erie which began the chain down to Fort Duquesne. This peninsula is most probably the peninsula on which Fort St-Frédéric is located, called Crown Point by the British.

wait at the appointed place where they heard the English coming, they discharged their muskets when they came in range but the fire was not lively as the moisture prevented several guns firing; the English reached Mount Pelée and defended it well, they were followed close by, and we took three prisoners who were not killed and forty dead who were scalped, we took eight that could not be saved. If our soldiers had snow shoes to stop them sinking and the weapons were in better condition we would have taken more. We had fifteen men killed and eleven wounded.[5]

1st February

I went to Montréal where I heard that M. de Vaudreuil was better.

3rd February

I learned of the arrival of M. le marquis de Montcalm, and went to see him. The General informed me that M. de Vaudreuil proposes to send a considerable force to Carillon for which he has asked for two hundred and fifty men of the regulars.

14th February

M. le marquis de Vaudreuil arrived being fully recovered, he gave the necessary orders to assemble the corps previously mentioned. M. de Rigaud will be its commander, who arrived with M. de Longueuil who would be second in command and M. Dumas who would be *major-général* [chief of staff]; they would pass through Fort St-Frédéric to sing the war song with the Abenakis.[6]

5 The action described here, fought on 21 January 1757, is the first of the two famous 'Battles on Snow Shoes' against Major Robert Rogers' Independent Ranging Company.

6 Rigaud, as already mentioned, was the governor's brother. Paul-Joseph Le Moyne de Longueuil, often called Le Moyne, came from Canadian nobility. His career had started in the regular army in France but by 1726 he was back in Canada and was rapidly promoted to captain thanks to his father's position as governor of Montreal. He spent much of the 1740's as commander of Détroit in the far west and developed good relations with the Indians. (He had spent much of his childhood amongst the Iroquois). He was praised as a capable and intelligent officer. He spent his life after the war in Tours, France. Jean-Daniel Dumas was born in 1721and transferred from the French army into the colonial marines as a captain in 1750. He became a good Indian negotiator and received command of Fort Duquesne after the victory over Braddock in 1755. In the fallout after the loss of Canada, Dumas was lauded as an honest officer. It was said expenses halved when he took command of a post and rose again when he left. After the war he, like Malartic, became governor of Ile de France. It seems either Malartic wished to accompany this raiding party or Montcalm wanted him to keep an eye on it. Vaudreuil denied this request. Montcalm reasoned that Vaudreuil did not want a staff officer of the regulars in the expedition who would be more senior than Dumas. *Journal du marquis de Montcalm Durant ses Campagnes en Canada de 1756 à 1759* (Québec: Demers & Frère, 1895) p. 160.

16th February

M. de Longueuil left to go and sing the war song at Sault Saint-Louis and at the Lac des Deux Montagnes, and invite the Iroquois, Algonkins and Nippisingués to march with M. Rigaud.[7]

18th February

M. le marquis de Montcalm charged me with going to Saint-Jean to equip the detachment of the regulars. I went to La Prairie where I found a considerable number of soldiers of the colony who were greatly exposed for want of lodgings which had not been provided.

19th February

M. le marquis de Montcalm went to La Prairie to review the detachment of regulars, who were composed of a company of grenadiers from the four regiments of La Sarre, Royal Roussillon, Languedoc, Béarn and a piquet from each of those regiments. The general gave a dinner with M. le chevalier de Lévis, and all the officers of the detachment who were commanded by M. de Poularies, captain of grenadiers of Royal Roussillon.

20th February

I arrived at Saint Jean at 10 in the morning. I found the first division in line on the ice ready to depart. It was composed of six companies, each of fifty colony troops or Canadians and commanded by M. de St-Martin, lieutenant of the colony troops. The piquets of La Sarre and Languedoc arrived at 11 o'clock. I delivered them their tarpaulins, bear skins and marmites, so that they would be able to make supper in the woods to the left of the fort. These are arranged very well. They make large holes in the snow and cover it with branches and use the bear skins to lie down warmly and are covered from the rain by the tarpaulins which are big enough for four men. I gave them the rest of their equipment which was issued before 5 o'clock. (This winter issue was more than that of summer which is two pairs of woollen socks, a pair of mittens, a *gilet* [sleeved waistcoat], rags (woollen cloth to stuff in their shoes), deer skin to make shoes, a collar for the sledge, a sledge on runners into which each man would put his food and luggage, a pair of snowshoes and a seal skin to cover everything). The piquets had only one item per two men because the Canadians had received their things before them and taken one each.

7 There was an Indian village at Lac des Deux Montagnes. Its population was not only Iroquois but also included various Algonquin tribes of the Great Lakes.

21st February

I gave out food for eight days to the two piquets, the rations the same as for the summer campaign. The piquets of Béarn and Royal Roussillon arrived at 11 o'clock and occupied the camp of those from La Sarre and Languedoc, which were in line on the ice with three companies of the colony troops to make up the second division under orders of M. Duchat, captain of Languedoc.[8] They set out at 3 o'clock. M. Riguad arrived at 5 o'clock with MM. Longueuil and Dumas. Three officers of the first division brought back their horses and informed M. Rigaud that the ice was not strong. The commander, who was relying on its strength, feared that the first two divisions had not received enough food to reach Carillon and sent orders for them to stop where they were and not leave until receiving a supplement of food which will be sent tomorrow.

22nd February

As it did not freeze last night, we sent a supplement of four days food to the first two divisions. The third division, formed of piquets of Royal Roussillon and Béarn and three companies of colony troops under M. Ducoin, captain of Royal Roussillon, left at noon. The company of grenadiers arrived at midday; I equipped them on the spot and they occupied the camp of the piquets. A courier from M. de Saint-Martin informed M. de Rigaud they discovered only water and M. de Langis went in a bark canoe to see how much navigation is free.[9] M. de Rigaud recently sent a courier to M. de Vaudreuil to tell him of the news.

23rd February

All the divisions returned their horses. M. de Langis arrived and said that he had travelled three hours by canoe, and believes the little ice remaining is fragile. M. de Rigaud sent orders to M. Saint-Martin to go into the woods and take the road. A missionary from the lake arrived with many savages. A volunteer company of the young men from the town of Montréal was formed. A young man arrived from the camp of St-Martin saying they had opened a path. He was named Boileau, and a very experienced guide who comes from Chambly. He assured us that the roads were not bad up to the Pointe aux Fers, where the ice was as strong as could be. We distributed food and equipment to the Canadians and savages, so the rest of the detachment can depart tomorrow.

8 François-Frédéric le Duchat was born in 1719 in Metz. He retired from the army in 1763 after participating in the 1762 expedition to Newfoundland. He later published his memoirs.

9 Jean-Baptiste Levrault de Langis Montegron, often called Langy, was an Ensign in the colonial marines. He acquired a reputation for bravery and daring scouts, being a counter to the activities of Rogers' Rangers. In 1758 Montcalm entrusted him with the command of 130 volunteers to strike against Fort William Henry and then asked for officer volunteers to serve under him. Such was his standing that the number had to be restricted.

24th February

M. de Lotbiniére, the engineer, arrived at 2 in the morning. He carried orders from M. de Vaudreuil for his brother, M. Riguad, to clear the ice from forty-five bateaux (a difficult task because they were not turned over before the frost and are frozen to the ground), to help increase food delivery to the last division who could then supplement the other three.[10] This was an impossibility, as they were already blocked and it was doubtful whether they could meet up before Carillon. M. Rigaud decided to send out envoys to find out exactly where all the divisions were and to inform M. Vaudreuil of this and leave if the rain stopped. He sent a *cariolle* to camp St-Martin to probe the ice and see whether we can get food on sledges and ordered that all the divisions would move tomorrow whatever the weather. M. Saupe has been ordered to spy on some savages suspected of wanting to inform the English; at noon I took the orders of M. Rigaud and left for Montréal, where I arrived at 5:00 to report to M. le marquis de Montcalm.

25th February

M. le marquis de Vaudreuil learned that M. de Rigaud left in the morning with the last division composed of the company of grenadiers, the volunteers of Montréal, three companies of the colony troops and the savages.

26th February

I went to Longueuil.

1st March

I went to Montréal: M. de Bleury, who arrived in the evening, told M. le General that he had carried provisions to the three last divisions at la Pointe aux Pins where he saw them leave and brought back six sick men. M. le general has received news from Acadia, which holds fifteen hundred soldiers and Acadians under M. de Boishébert and has supplies until the 15th of May of fifteen pounds of flour per month and ten pounds of salted beef, if necessary they have in reserve some pounds of cod and bacon and the English have burned the fort at Gasparo.[11]

---

10 Michel Chartier de Lotbiniére was the protégé of ex-governor Galissonière and his father-in-law, de Léry. He had studied engineering in France and hoped to become chief engineer of the colony after serving as assistant to de Léry who held the role until his death in 1756. However, the French court appointed Pontleroy from the French regulars who accused him of all sorts of malpractice and incompetence. He never quite escaped these accusations until years later when the aid of his old commander, Lévis, enabled him to secure a pension. Throughout the war he remained on engineering projects around the defence of Québec.

11 Fort Gaspareaux was constructed on the coast of Green Bay facing the island of Saint Jean in Acadia (See Map 1). Charles Deschamps de Boishébert was an experienced Marine captain. He had served in the west but the bulk of his military experience was in Acadia. During the Seven Years War he made strenuous efforts to prevent the displacement of Acadians by the British although his efforts were not very successful due to a lack of supplies, munitions and

5th March

News from Détroit announced that the savages are better disposed towards the French, that the *Katibas* [Catawba], who had committed acts of hostility against the village of Altigué, have come to recant their crimes and ask to take up the hatchet against the English; the *Sauteurs* have told M. de Mui, commander of Détroit, that they will come in spring to hear the words of Ononthio.[12] M. Pouchot, who commands Niagara, asked the *Loups* to hold a great council with the Five Nations where they would propose that they will fight against the English and threatened to beat them and *mastikoté* them if they remain neutral.[13]

8th March

M. de Vaudreuil received letters from M. de Lignery who found that the Catawba had approached Fort Duquesne.[14] They captured one resident and scalped another. M. Pouchot says the severe cold has prevented work at Niagara and its garrison have put on a comedy play.

10th March

M. de Bourlamaque has arrived from Québec.

12th March

I accompanied M. le marquis de Montcalm, who visited the quarters of Béarn.
I went to make the accounts of our supplies from January to February. We have cut out the suppliers and the habitants are now obliged to feed them for 10 *sol* per day per soldier billeted with them.

15th March

I worked to prepare the equipment and utensils for the coming campaign.

---

men. He managed to bring some Acadian volunteers to assist in the defence of Québec. After the war he attempted to set up a resettlement plan for Acadians to live in Cayenne (French Guiana).

12 *Sauteurs*, meaning the people of the fall: an alternative name for the people more commonly known as the Chippewas.

13 Mastikote could possibly be a varied spelling or transcription error of *maxtikote*, the name of the female form of dress, implying emasculation.

14 Born 1703 in Montréal, François-Marie le Marchand de Lignery was an officer of the Marines. He fought in the Fox Wars in the 1720s and in King George's War, in which he was second in command in an attack on Annapolis Royal, Nova Scotia. He became commander of forces on the Ohio in 1756, having taken part in Braddock's defeat the previous year. He orchestrated the raids from Fort Duquesne until he abandoned it in the face of an advancing British army in 1758. He retired to Fort Machault and was captured with his army while marching to the aid of Fort Niagara. Lignery died of his wounds from that action on 18 July, 1759.

18th March

I went to La Prairie where I left at 9 o'clock with one of my comrades up the Sault Saint-Louis. There was a violent wind and a large amount of snow falling so that the horses would not go forward so we were obliged to return to La Prairie.

21st March

I went to Montréal. I learned from M. le general that he had been informed by courier from Carillon that M. Rigaud left there on the 15th.

25th March

M. de Lorimer arrived with thirty Iroquois from Présentation who asked to hold council. The general gave them 4 hours. After the regular introduction, they testified that Onontio must be angry with them as he had not asked for their warriors to accompany M. Rigaud. They said they had been to a council at Orange where the English wanted to persuade them that all the big canoes of Old England would arrive this summer where they will lay siege to Québec while General Loudoun, after overthrowing Carillon and St-Frédéric, will do the same to Montréal. Onontio thanked them for their willingness and promised them his answers tomorrow.

26th March

I went to Longueuil, the 28th to La Prarie and on the 29th to Boucherville to make inspections. I learned from M. Mercier who had spent last night there that he was informed by the General that M. de Rigaud could not surprise Fort George but he did burn four barques, three hundred bateaux, three storehouses, a large barn, two lime kilns, a sawmill and a large firewood yard.[15] He called on the commander to surrender, who replied that his garrison would not, so he was forced to watch the fire without being able to oppose it.

30th March

I went to Varennes and on the 31st to Montréal. I related to all the account of the corps of M. Rigaud during his five days camped around Fort George.[16]

15 Gaffarel notes that 'On 18 March a reconnaissance was conducted by Captain Poularies. The same evening Captain Dumas advanced onto the ice around the fort; a soldier preceding him hit the ice with his axe to ensure its sturdiness. The noise betrayed them and the English stood their guard.' The subsequent burning of the boats and buildings occurred on the nights of 21 and 22 March. The fort was spared from the fire as the wind was contrary.

16 Note by Gaffarel – Letter of Montcalm to the Minister: 'The Canadians were surprised to see that our officers and soldiers proved themselves in this kind of work to which they were unaccustomed. I must agree that we have no idea in Europe of the fatigues where one is forced to walk for six weeks and almost always sleeping on snow or ice, be reduced to bread and bacon, and often carrying and dragging food for fifteen days. Our troops have carried on

2nd April

Our grenadiers returned from St-Jean, except one who it was believed drowned. M. Poularies, who had burnt his hand in the recent expedition, stopped a while at Longueuil.[17]

4th April

I went to Montréal to make arrangements to send the effects of our piquets to Carillon, where they were staying and did not have winter equipment or their *vestes* [sleeved waistcoats worn under the regimental coat]. The piquets of the other battalions also stayed there.

7th April

The grenadier who we believed drowned, a very brave man named Basin, arrived to see me at 7 o'clock, saying that he had been blinded by snow and cold and had spent two days on the Isle La Motte.[18] He tried to cross the lake five times and would not have made it without the help of the savages.[19]

8th April

The thaw made all communications difficult.

11th April

Vehicles can still travel over the rivers on the ice.

13th April

I left a sergeant and a soldier to escort the equipment for our picquet up to St-Jean.

14th April

I learned that the road to St-Jean was impassable and the equipment could not get there.

---

with much gaiety and without a murmur. I cannot give too much praise to M. Poulariez, who commanded our detachment. He is an officer of great distinction.'

17 François-Médard Poulharies (Poulhariez) was captain of the Royal Roussillon grenadier company. He later took command of the battalion in 1759 and ended his career as a *maréchal de camp* in 1780.

18 Isle La Motte is downriver from Fort Saint-Jean at the mouth of Lake Champlain and was the site of the seventeenth century Fort Ste-Anne.

19 Gaffarel notes that 'Snow-blindness affected around a third of the men on Rigaud's journey back and they were obliged to lead men by the hand. The condition was only temporary and sight returned in a few days'. This was reported by Montcalm in a letter of 26 April 1757.

18th April

I went to Boucherville. The ice in the river began to rise and water reached up to the road which I was obliged to cross at some places.

19th April

The river has receded. It formed several channels and by the evening there was little ice left.

20th April

I sent a grenadier to Montréal who, on his return, said it was possible to cross the river by bateaux. M. le marquis de Montcalm asked me to prepare the regiment to be ready to leave for Carillon when the navigation is free, and to pass the same on to Royal Roussillon, and that M. de Bourlamaque commands on this frontier and that La Sarre is destined to work at Saint-Jean.

21st April

I went to Montréal without hindrance. I heard news yesterday from France, carried from Louisbourg by a ship which came into port on the 20th of February and had left La Rochelle on the 20th of November.

23rd April

I made arrangements for the equipment of the regiment. Abbé Piquet arrived from Présentation.

26th April

M. le marquis de Vaudreuil gave orders and packets to an officer from the garrison at Louisbourg who was returning there. I finished the reviews of the first four months of 1757 with the secretary of the *commissaire*, M. Doreil, who has remained at Québec as he is sick.

27th April

I returned to Longueuil.

30th April

I went to Montréal to make distributions of the regiment's equipment.

1st and 2nd of May

I went to all our quarters to make accounts and announce that we would be ready to leave on the 8th.

3rd May

I went to Montréal on affairs of the regiment.

4th May

I went to Longueuil and sought out a detachment of fifty men who went with me to Montréal.

5th May

I embarked this detachment in six bateaux destined for M. Bourlamaque. They left at 10 o'clock to descend the river up to Sorel and then re-embark at the River Chambly.

6th May

The regiment came to fetch their bateaux and took food for four days.

8th May

MM. Marquis de Vaudreuil and Montcalm sent the Béarn Regiment orders to leave tomorrow from their different quarters to reassemble at Saint-Jean.
M. Bourlamaque left for La Prairie, being designated to perform the role of major-general of his camp. I left with him. We mounted horses at La Prairie, where we went up to the Poteau River where we embarked and arrived at 4 o'clock a half league from the fort at Chambly.[20] We found there the Royal Roussillon Regiment who were busy making a portage of their baggage. The boats of M. de Bourlamaque arrived at 6 o'clock.

9th May

The Royal Roussillon regiment left at 7 o'clock. The equipment from the six bateaux of M. de Bourlamaque was portaged. We left the bateaux that had carried us to Saint-Jean at Sainte-Thérèse.

20 I have not found any reference to the Poteau River on any map but most old maps of Montreal show a river running from La Prairie towards Chambly.

10th May

R. Roussillon left at 8 o'clock, M. de Bourlamaque at 11 o'clock and camped at La Prairie a Boileau at 4 o'clock.

11th May

We embarked at 4 o'clock, landed at Pointe aux Fers to rest the soldiers and Canadians. We went around this point despite a contrary wind. We searched uselessly for a camp between two small bays and were obliged to push up to the Pointe aux Roches. A seventh bateau we had taken from Saint-Jean did not catch up with us.

12th May

We embarked at 5 o'clock. M. de Bourlamaque sent a boat to seek out the one which was lost. We profited from a good wind and went to camp at Gravois.

13th May

We embarked at 4 o'clock, rounding the Rocher Fendu, stopping at l'Isle Pelée, at midday at Saint-Frédéric and we arrived at Carillon at 6 o'clock.[21] M. de Bourlamaque found three prisoners that the Outaouas and Nippisingués had been taken around Fort Lydius. They said that little was going on around the two forts and that at New York they were waiting for troops destined to assemble there.

14th May

M. de Langis arrived at day break with twenty-five Iroquois, and two prisoners taken from around Fort George who confirmed the story of the other prisoners.
M. Bourlamaque made a review of the piquets of the regulars and of the colony. M. de Sabrevois left for Montréal with the Outaouas and Nippisingués. Royal Roussillon arrived at midday and camped between the fort and the redoubt. The Iroquois went exploring to try and find four Agnés they had seen around Fort George.

15th May

The general sent the piquet of La Reine and all the sick to Montréal.[22] M. de Lusignan who had commanded here at Carillon through the winter embarked to go and retake command at Fort St-Frédéric. The piquets of Langeudoc and La Sarre left their barracks to take camp in front of those of Béarn to the left of Royal Roussillon.

21 Both l'Isle Pelée and Pointe au Roches are unknown locations on the journey.
22 From this point until the arrival of M. Montcalm it seems the Malartic is referring to Col. Bourlamaque as 'the general' as he was now in overall command of the Carillon region.

16th May

The general went to reconnoitre the falls and the portage to see where to locate the two camps; he could not find a better position than last year's. Seventy-six workers were provided for works at the fort. Laforce, an interpreter, left with four savages to go and make a scout of the road to Fort Lydius.[23] M. de Gaspé arrived at 6 o'clock with many boats which carried the troops of the colony destined to camp at the falls and the portage and the workers of different professions who will work at the fort.

17th May

Sixty-one men began work at 6 in the morning. Two soldiers of Royal Roussillon, with a Canadian who had gone ahead of them into the woods as an escort, came back to tell the general that the Canadian had been taken prisoner by the English. The general sent out thirty-five men into the field under the orders of M. de Calan, of the Languedoc regiment and some minutes later, two officers with twelve soldier and a savage to follow them and try and cut them off at Mount Pelée. At 8 o'clock there was a review of the colony troops, who were formed into eight companies, five to be sent to the end of the portage and three at the falls. They were found to be in a bad state, most of their weapons were out of service and the soldiers lacking in everything.

At 4 o'clock the detachments that left in the morning were heard, they were shouting so it was thought they had brought back the prisoner. MM. Borgne and Boucherville, who had gone with the first detachment, informed the general that they had gone ahead with five soldiers of the detachment to go beyond Mount Pelée where they saw the English among the trees, who they perceived had abandoned their prisoner, their food and everything they carried but they did not pursue because of their small number.[24]

---

23 Laforce is a confusing name in this period of history. There was a colonial officer known as Laforce, but named as Michel Pépin, who was captured in the Jumonville Glen incident by George Washington's men. It seems he was viewed as an influential figure amongst the Ohio Indians and kept hostage throughout the war. Another Laforce, Réne-Hippolyte, left behind a journal in his capacity as a commander of ships on Lake Ontario so it could be possible this Laforce that Malartic is referring to but we cannot be certain. The *Dictionary of Canadian Biography* conflates these two men but it seems clear that Michel Pépin was kept captive for this period. See Ian K. Steele, *Setting All the Captives Free: Capture, Adjustment and Recollection in Allegeheny Country*, (Quebec: McGill-Queens University Press, 2013), p. 70 and Robert C. Alberts, *The Most Extraordinary Adventures of Major Robert Stobo,* (Boston: Houghton Mifflin, 1965), pp. 326-7.

24 Pierre Boucher de Boucherville was joint seigneur of Boucherville, near Montreal, and captain of Marines. He had led many expeditions in the 1730s and 1740s. This campaign would be his last though, as he retired on 1 January 1758, aged 69.

18th May

The general went to establish M. de Gaspé at the portage and M. de Céloron at the falls, and prescribed what they must do for security.[25]

19th May

Many workers employed in digging up the ramparts and parapet, others to dig out the ditch, several workers making wheelbarrows. Those from last season have been stolen or burned.

20th May

There were many holes in the bateaux which were to carry the Béarn Regiment which delayed them for several days. They disembarked here at 10 o'clock and camped on the left of Royal Roussillon.

21st May

The general sent the bateaux of Béarn with the sick. One of the barques moored in front of the *Hangard*, carrying the munitions of the artillery.[26] Nine Iroquois arrived from Saint-Louis asking to make a strike against Fort Lydius.

22nd May

The general sent a detachment of sixty-six men to Fort St-Frédéric to seek out supplies. He went with an escort of grenadiers to scout around the falls, visit the camp of those at the portage, and see how the works were coming on.[27]

23rd May

The barque set sail. The detachment sent out yesterday returned with ten bateaux loaded with provisions. The interpreter and the four savages returned. They said

---

25 Ignace-Philippe Aubert de Gaspé had a distinguished 33-year career. He spent time in Acadia in the 1740s building and commanding Fort Saint-Jean on the Saint-Jean River. He went to the west in 1753 and took part in the campaign against Fort Necessity in 1754. After a brief stint at Niagara he was on the Lake Champlain front from 1756. He remained in the country until his death at his seigneurial manor house in 1787.

26 The *Hangard* was the name for Fort Carillon's large warehouse, located near the west shore of Lake Champlain below the fort. Hereafter referred to as the warehouse. Céloron is probably Pierre-Joseph Céloron, son of Pierre-Joseph Céloron de Blainville. Pierre-Joseph senior was famous for the Céloron expedition down the Ohio valley in 1749. He led 213 men into unknown territory to bury lead plates pronouncing the region to fall under the dominion of the King of France. His mission also uncovered an alarming amount of Native support for the British in the region. Pierre-Joseph Junior ended the war as a poor captain on half-pay.

27 The falls refers to the falls of La Chute River (literally the Falls River) which was also the location of the saw mill. The portage refers to the camp at the end of the portage.

they had approached Fort George where they saw some men come out, but did not see any tents or bateaux, and they then went on to set ambush on the road to Fort Lydius, and there they saw wagons pass by with two hundred men, so being too many to take any prisoner, they then went up to Korlack where they killed one man.[28]

24th May

The number of workers was increased to help the miners clear stones from the two demi-lunes. The savages called a council and expressed a great discontent that they had not been given more *eau-de-vie*. M. Lotbiniére, who has been expected for several days, arrived with three bateaux loaded with drink and provisions for the canteen. He had no news of France. The letters from Fort Duquesne and Niagara announced that the English would make an attempt against the Belle Riviére.

25th May

The general sent a detachment of one hundred and twelve men to make an abatis on the right bank of the Chute River to guarantee the navigation will not be surprised by the Agnés. The savages got drunk and stole from the camp and were sentenced to leave. Thirty men went to fish in the R. de Pendu, where they caught one hundred and twenty excellent carp.

26th May

Work continued on the abatis. A road was opened to the warehouse of the fort to help the artillery up. The wooden barracks were demolished. A canoe loaded with fish arrived from Fort St-Frédéric.

27th May

The work on the abatis continued. A detachment was sent fishing, who did well. A building was begun for the bakery.
The general, who looked over the works whenever he was free, visited the abatis. The barque constructed recently at Saint-Jean moored at 7 o'clock in front of the warehouse.

28th May

Work continued as normal on the fort and abatis. The boat was unloaded and seven cannon mounted on the fort.

---

28 Malartic makes several references to 'Korlack' or 'Korlak'. It seems he is referring to the town of Schnectady, close to Albany. The name is probably a derivation of the original Dutch landowner, Arent van Curler (later Corlaer). He had a reputation for fair dealing amongst the Iroquois and 'Corlaer' was used as a title for the Governor of New York during the later seventeenth and early eighteenth centuries.

30th May

The general went to the abatis where he had sent twenty-six men who would finish it that day and then cut wood for the lime kilns. He then returned to the portage at the falls to visit the works and scout out the path that the Agnés took to reach the falls. It proved a chore to carry the wood and instruments of the mill and take up the wood for the lime kilns to the falls.

31st May

We sent out a detachment of thirty men to cut down some trees which blocked the view from the fort on the left bank of the Chute River. We doubled all the naval gun carriages. The cannons were placed behind embrasures in the fort. The Iroquois returned at 2 o'clock and said they had been on the road from Fort George to Lydius; they discovered a camp half-way with troops coming out of it. They asked to go back to take prisoners.

1st June

Increase in workers to go and drag the *diables* for the logs necessary for the parapets and demi-lunes.[29] The general held council with the savages. Those of the Sault promised to make a path to Fort George, and those of Présentation told him they want to go to Montréal. A detachment was sent to clear up the point of the River Chute and take wood for the lime kilns. The Iroquois left at 2 o'clock with an officer and a cadet.

2nd June

Increase of workers for felling trees on a rise which was around twenty toise [1 toise equalled 6 french feet or *pied*] in front of the demi-lune of the plateau.
At 7 o'clock six savages of various nations arrived conducted by M. Langlade. They asked to go towards Orange.

3rd June

A detachment of forty-four men were sent to Fort St-Frédéric to fetch food. The general held council with the savages who testified he was very glad to see them, they asked him lots of things and he said that he wishes them to go against the two forts; they were willing to subscribe to his wishes even though M. de Vaudreuil has engaged them to take prisoners around Orange. The savages who left on the 1st arrived at 2 o'clock to inform that they approached Fort George and saw a barge loaded with thirty men who they believed went towards the Maltaches woods. The general sent M. de Langlade with the savages to attempt to remove it.

---

29 Malartic here adds a note to explain that the *diables*, or devils, were two small carts with low drag wheels to carry very large pieces of wood.

4th June

The general went with M. le chevalier de Bernetzs, commander of Royal Roussillon, and several officers of the two battalions to reconnoitre the road to the posts they should occupy in case of an enemy attack and that post at the La Chute. He found it to be well marked.[30] The detachment which left here returned with ten bateaux loaded with food. M. Langlade returned at 3 o'clock, reporting they had found the trail of the English but subsequently lost it without being able to pick it up; they guessed that twelve men had probably gone up Mount Peleé, where they were seen to arrive at the camp of Gaspé and rested there as they were far ahead of them. The savages were given food for twelve days so they could leave tomorrow at a good hour.

5th June

The savages asked again for certain things. They wished to take with them a sergeant and seven soldiers who they knew were good walkers to the bottom of the bay where they would hide their canoes. Masons were sent to St-Frédéric to repair their chimneys and kilns.

6th June

An increase in the workers to fell many of the trees at the entrance to the woods on the slope which leads to the falls. The surgeon major arrived with two boats.

7th June

While the workers assembled several gunshots and bangs where heard from the portage at La Chute which announced the arrival of the enemy. *La générale* was beaten. At this moment, the general left with two companies of grenadiers and the piquet from the small camp. The battalions left each of their piquets and all their guards to hold the fort under orders of M. de l'Hôpital. Royal Roussillon took the new path up to the heights of the left bank of La Chute which linked to the Agnés path and ended at an impassable ravine. Béarn, at the falls, went from their former camp and followed the old road. The general went from La Chute and marched a company of grenadiers, some minutes after the other, and two picquets of Béarn, to secure or support M. de Gaspé from whom he had received no news. He asked for another piquet from Béarn to guard the road and then carry on to the end of the portage where he learned that before they had set out, a sentinel had glimpsed something in the woods and fired with his musket, upon which a troop came out and fired many volleys by platoon into the camp and then seemed to turn back to retreat into the woods when they heard the bangs; a detachment sent in pursuit saw them re-embark on eleven barges. The general sent out two detachments to follow

30 Paths through the woods were marked by cutting into the trees at intervals, after which the path was said to be *plaqué* – literally plated or veneered – which is the term that Malartic uses in the original French text.

the two shores of the lake and observe the movements of the enemy, and sent the battalions back, and at midday came back with the piquets to discover the arrival of twenty-two bateaux loaded with food and supplies for the hospital. The detachments returned at two o'clock and said they had seen the barges taking the route back to Fort Saint-George [sic.] around the Pain de Sucre.[31] A detachment of forty men of the regulars was sent to the camp at the Portage. At 4 o'clock, the workers returned to the works and began an épaulement to cover the bakery, shops and stables that are all below the fort on the edge of the river.

8th June

Work as normal. The detachment sent to the camp at the portage returned at 8 o'clock. M. Jacob, lieutenant of artillery, arrived with twenty-eight boats loaded with supplies for the artillery.[32] Another ten loaded with food came from Fort St-Frédéric. The savages that we wished to send to the portage refused to march.

9th June

Work as normal. Eighteen bateaux left for Saint-Jean. The savages finally set out for the Portage. A detachment was sent out to look for the wood of the *sapinette,* which is one of the best remedies for scurvy.[33] The general went to the portage to bind the savages together with six strings of wampum and engage them to go up to Fort George. An artillery park was begun on the right of Royal Roussillon.

10th June

Increased the number of workers. A detachment was sent into the wood to make fascines. Twenty-two bateaux left for Saint-Jean and two for St-Frédéric to take utensils for the hospital. The general made a trip to the stores to satisfy the troops of the colony.

11th June

Work continued with the ordinary detachments but was suspended at 4 o'clock by a very violent storm.

31 Pain de Sucre literally translates as sugar loaf and was the name given to a large hill on the east side of Lake George. See Map 6.

32 Louis-Thomas Jacau de Fiedmont, (1712-1788) also often called Jacob, was second in command of the artillery under Mercier. He commanded the second company of *Cannoniers-Bombardiers* which was raised in this year. He was later captured by the English and returned to France after the capture of Québec. He ended his career as *maréchal de camp,* having been promoted in 1780.

33 *Picea glauca,* known in English as the White or Canadian Spruce. M.M. Grandtner, *Elseviers Dictionary of Trees vol. 1: North America* (Amsterdam: Elsevier, 2005), p. 632.

12th June

There is a mist in the air which has made all the powder very damp. At 10 o'clock ten Nippisingués arrived in a canoe, saying that M. Langlade's party attacked yesterday, took four men and four scalps, and been pressed by the English who marched towards their canoes; a quarter of an hour later, several musket shots were heard from Cap au Diamant. Eight bateaux were sent there which brought back seventy savages and five soldiers. M. Langlade added to the report by the Nippisingués that he had been forced to return very quickly, abandoning their canoes and leaving behind a wounded savage, a sergeant and two soldiers who could not walk as fast as them. The testimony of the prisoners taken was that there were two thousand men at Fort George and fifteen hundred at Lydius, the greatest part of which are militia who are waiting for reinforcements, that there is much small pox at Orange, they are working on the fortifications of the two forts, that Lord Loudoun is embarking in three days with the regular troops to besiege Louisbourg. The savages held council with the general who recommended they go to pick up the wounded. This they refused saying that it was recommended that they should be used to carry news. M. Langis arrived at 7 o'clock to give an account to the general that he had approached very near to Fort George and seen twenty tents outside, that his savages had wanted to take the two sentinels but on being discovered sixty men came out of the fort and forced them to retreat. A detachment has gone to reconnoitre the other side of Mount Serpent Sonnet which borders the path of the portage.

13th June

Ordinary work. The general made great efforts to persuade the savages to go and seek out the wounded. They finally sent five who were taken in a bateau by eight soldiers, who disembarked a league from camp. The Iroquois who had returned with M. de Langis left for Montréal. At 3 o'clock, three musket shots were heard from Cap au Diamant. A bateau was sent who brought back one of the savages who had left that morning, who had been lost. At 4 o'clock we heard more musket shots from the same place. The Iroquois went there in their canoes and brought back the other savages who said they had found fresh tracks and they believe a considerable detachment of the enemy was lurking in the vicinity. The general suggested that the savages go and scout for them. They asked to hold council and asked him to give them one hundred Frenchmen. He replied to them that he would but only so that they were posted somewhere appropriate to fight or to cover their retreat: the Outaouas, Nippisingués and Sauters refused to go. The Iroquois promised to leave tomorrow and asked for a sergeant and eight men to conduct a bateau for a certain distance. A habitant left in the morning for the small swamp but did not return.[34]

34 Habitant was the term used to describe the French settlers of Canada and Louisiana.

14th June

The Sergeant and eight soldiers left in the night with the savages and returned at daybreak after having dropped the Iroquois on land three leagues from camp. The Outaouas left for Montréal. M. de Gaspé summoned the general who had seen five men in the former camp of Contrecoeur.

At one o'clock, a musket shot was heard from Cap au Diamant. Three bateaux were sent and brought back the Iroquois who reported that they had seen two hundred Englishmen pass by with two prisoners but did not dare attack them, recognizing some of the savages with them. At 2 o'clock a small canoe was seen rounding Cap au Diamant. We were pleasantly surprised to see the sergeant and two soldiers who had been abandoned in the woods. The sergeant gave his account to the general and said that the canoes and baggage of the savages were still where they had hidden them; the English had not approached the boats so he took one of them. The small barque arrived loaded with straw for the hospital and equipment for the troops. Fifteen Iroquois left for Montréal.

15th June

A detachment of seventy men left to go and get supplies from Fort St-Frédéric. The general held several councils with the savages who promised him they would leave tomorrow. The sick who were in the hospital at the fort were transported to the one in the redoubt.

16th June

Increase in workers to drag the two *diables*. A path was made to go from the hospital down to the bottom of the rocks where water could be drawn which is less bad than elsewhere. In the afternoon, the bad weather suspended works.

18th June

Normal work detachments. The *goelette* arrived at 11 o'clock. The Outaouas who had remained to guard their wounded arrived in the canoe of the habitant who had recently been taken. They asked that we should go and look for their comrades who they left a league from here. A detachment of twelve men were sent who brought them back. At 2 o'clock the general held council with the Iroquois who asked to leave tomorrow to go to the fort at Couarinet near which they hope to take prisoners.[35] Two bateaux arrived from Fort St-Frédéric.

35 This could possibly be the old fort, sometimes called Fort Ann, near to Fort Edward. See Map 6. The French called it Fort La Reine (Fort of the Queen). It was ruined at this time but the roads were still used.

19th June

Worked unceasingly. A detachment went to make a fire at the abatis of the River Chute; another to go and look for hemlock and sapinette. Two bateaux left for Fort St-Frédéric. Ten savages who left with M. Langis returned in four canoes abandoned by the Outaouas. The general went to reconnoitre the reverse slope of Mount Serpent Sonnet and then round to the portage following the reverse, and on his return marked a new location for the hospital. The sawmill began work.

20th June

Ordinary work. The savages left for the fort at Couarinet. An officer from the portage camp returned an account that he had seen two English barges coming under full sail, they had change course when they saw us, one of them capsized. The *goelette* set sail. M. de Lusignan told the general that a soldier of the garrison, who went stealthily hunting yesterday, had been taken. The savages we wanted to go to the portage refused to go and loan their canoes.

21st June

A detachment of twelve men left with four savages to try and discover the trail of the English lurking around Fort St-Frédéric. A canoe of Mississagués arrived and forty bateaux carrying two hundred troops of the colony. News from France arrived at Québec on the 5th and Montréal on the 8th.

22nd June

The general made a review of the detachments that have arrived here and sent them to the falls and the portage to reinforce those two camps. M. de Gaspé reported that he observed the two English barges which landed some troops who fired on his camp; he sent a detachment of sixty men to remove them. The forty bateaux left with an escort of eight men.

23rd June

The new hospital was begun; the carpenters were given an escort which was necessary when they went to cut wood on the left bank of the falls river. A bateau and a detachment was sent to bring planks from the sawmill. Increase of workmen for the artillery and engineers. The detachment sent from the portage camp returned.

24th June

The general went to the portage by the mountains. This road was found to be longer and less practicable than the other. He was told that the English barges have been seen again. A clerk arrived from the Marines to function as a commissary; he brought with him bakers and armourers. The camp of the La Reine Regiment was marked out ahead of the camp of the piquets.

25th June

Ten bateaux loaded with bricks to repair Saint-Jean's furnaces left today. M. Jacob made a trial of a twelve-pound cannon which he mounted on the front of a bateau. It fired well and [could be] dismounted easily. Six Abenaki arrived who said they were followed by two hundred other savages. The bad weather suspended work.

26th June

Much rain. A small detachment was sent to cut down big timber for earth kilns at the portage camp; since yesterday five soldiers have gone missing from this camp. The general went to visit the two camps and ordered a scout by land to see if the English had posts on any of the islands of the lake with an officer and five savages.

27th June

An hour after midnight, the sergeant of the guard of the small camp sent a report that a sentinel and corporal of the guard had heard barges going along the banks of Cap au Diamant. The general went into the field at the edge of the hospital to question the sentry. The piquet of Béarn and the corporal told him they could hear the sound of oars crashing against the rocks. He sent an officer and eight soldiers in a bark canoe to go and probe the coves and bays and if not finding the enemy to push on to Fort St-Frédérick to give notice to M. Lusignan and the barque. He asked M. de Gaspé for some soldiers practised in the woods to go out onto the road to Fort St-Frédéric on both banks to see if they had landed on either one. He posted a corporal and four men in front of the woods to the rear to discover all the barges and boats which came from Fort St-Frédéric and ordered that several bateaux should be prepared. At 2 o'clock we heard several musket shots that were a signal from the corporal that he had seen the barges. As they were not followed by any others, they were judged to have been from the woods. At 3 o'clock the officer sent out to Fort St-Frédéric returned to report that he saw nothing going out or returning; more than 500 savages who came here yesterday from Fort St-Frédéric beat through the woods from north to south. The Outaouas arrived at 6 o'clock following the old trail. M. Langis arrived at 11 o'clock leading two prisoners taken from the banks of the River Orange, two horses and the rest of the canoes and equipment from the Langlade party.[36] The prisoners say that militia are assembled in two small camps under the forts of the R. Orange for the safety of the convoys.

29th June

Ordinary work. The Iroquois who returned with M. de Langis left for Montréal. The Outaouas killed several sheep in the camp saying that all the beasts of the earth belonged to them and they were for the common good of all; they were restrained.

36 Malartic is referring to the Albany River. Orange was also the French name given to the town of Albany.

In council they asked for muskets, equipment and fresh meat. The general gave them two of the sheep. Three officers and seven cadets went with them to the portage to go and fight alongside them. The guard on the artillery park was increased as it was now a considerable size. At 7 in the evening seven soldiers arrived from Fort St-Frédéric to inform us that two English prisoners who had deserted from Montréal gave themselves up there yesterday, greatly fatigued and hungry. They said they left in a party of four from Montréal five days ago; these two had preferred to come into the fort rather than face starvation; the others continued their journey to Fort George. The scouting party from the south arrived in the evening from Fort St-Frédéric.

29th June

Two bateaux left with an escort of twelve men to go and fetch oxen from Fort St-Frédéric. A guard was put on the bakery to protect the biscuit, of which there was a great quantity which could be squandered. The general sent one hundred workers to begin a road to go from the falls to the portage for the artillery and spent a great part of the day in council with the savages who wearied him with their continuous demands. At the end of the council they killed a bull. Some of the Iroquois and Outaouas got drunk and fought.

30th June

Work as normal. The savages left at nine o'clock to go to the bottom of the bay. Planks and boards were brought from the mill. The general went to see the new road which he found to be good and well advanced.

1st July

Ordinary work. We sent a bateau to meet up with the *goelette* which we believed to be at La Presque Isle.[37] M. de Lusignan wrote that the Agnés lifted the scalps of two soldiers who had gone fishing; killing one, the other still lived; that the Iroquois searched for them in vain. Crusts were fetched from the sawmill (These are the first and last planks from a log). At 6 o'clock some musket shots were heard from beyond Cap au Diamant. A quarter of an hour later, we could see many canoes rounding the point. They landed at daybreak. The officers came to tell the general that yesterday evening, at 10 o'clock, they wished to go into the River Chicot where they could hide their canoes on the banks;[38] they were driven off by several volleys of musketry; they could not approach the shore because of the rocks and were forced to land on the other back and spent the night there very tired. The English withdrew before daylight; the savages who followed them found a dead Moraignan and one who they captured as well as an Englishman; they returned to fetch their wounded, two of

37 Most likely Crown Point peninsula, near Fort St-Frédéric.

38 The river which flowed into Lake Champlain, now forming the New York/Vermont state line, near Dresden, NY.

whom died as did a cadet. They promised to leave soon to go and eat. The bateau sent out to the *goelette* left Fort St- Frédéric where it [the *goelette*] was moored.

2nd July

Fifty men were sent to Fort St- Frédéric to fetch provisions. The two dead savages and cadet were interred with full military honours. The Sauters came to see their father [the general], to tell him how angry they are at having been surprised at night and fired on and asked him to take pity on them and give them eau-de-vie so that they could cry and then laugh; their father recompensed for the dead and wounded with a capot, a shirt and a pair of mittens, he gave them strings of wampum to wipe away their tears and something to drink, then the other nations came to ask for the same. The general interrogated the Englishman and the Moraignan who said that they had come from Fort Lydius where two thousand seven hundred militiamen camped outside; inside the fort were five hundred regular troops; that General Webb was coming with three thousand veteran troops; that there were two thousand at Fort George; that Colonel Aldyman [sic.] had been detached with three hundred men and spent eight days around the bottom of the bay to find out if we had formed some position; that the detachment which had fired on the canoes was sixty men strong; that when they had been discovered, two men were detached to give notice to the fort and send help; they retired after the forth volley and had been sent to cut off the retreat of one of our party who had been taking prisoners on the edge of the River Orange; that they had been directed to the left bank of the Chicot, where they had discovered the hidden canoes. They did not know if Lord Loudoun has already left; however they had heard that he is set to embark.[39]

At midday thirty-eight bateaux arrived carrying supplies, seventy-two oxen, some horses and munitions. At 9 in the evening, the savages thought they saw a barge around Cap au Diamant, heard cries of death and beating drums. The general proposed they go to look. They refused because he would not give them any soldiers to go with them; they began to prime their weapons and stationed themselves behind tree stumps as if the enemy were coming. We sent a sergeant and eight soldiers in a bateau to be set down on the point between the front of Cap au Diamant and the camp of l'Hôpital to observe the approach of bateaux or barges. At 11 o'clock, a sentinel thought he heard two death cries and thuds that he mistook for gunshots, and the other for the crash of oars. The guard at the warehouse was increased.

39 The French knew that Loudoun was planning on attacking Louisbourg. Colonel Webb was commander at Fort Edward/Lydius and was expecting attack, desperately calling for the colonies to supply him with militia men. The report seems quite exaggerated. There were only five companies of the 35th Regiment of Foot at Fort George along with Colonel Parker's New Jersey Provincial Regiment. The presence of Aldyman [Lt.Col Frederick Haldimand] is probably confused. Haldimand was in command of a battalion of the 60th Royal Americans, some companies of which were sent to the New York frontier, but Haldimand was not amongst them. Brenton C. Kemmer, *Redcoats, Yankees and Allies: A History of the Uniforms, Clothing and Gear of the British Army in the Lake George-Lake Champlain Corridor 1755-1760* (Bowie: Heritage Books, 1998) pp. 16-19.

3rd July

The sergeant detached in the bateau returned at 4 o'clock and said he had seen nothing of note. The savages went to scout, returning at midday saying they found the tracks of two Englishmen. The bateaux [those carrying supplies that had arrived the previous day] left for Saint-Jean with an escort of a sergeant and eight men, and the barque with a corporal and eight men.
The oxen and sheep were taken to the right bank as there is no good grass around Carillon. At five o'clock there was a clap of thunder, which the sentinels thought was Fort St-Frédéric firing the cannon which signalled an enemy party in the field. The general ordered some savages with M. Langis to the portage to take the road to Fort St-Frédéric up Lake Saint-Sacrement to cut off the retreat of the enemy. It rained heavily.

4th July

An escort of fifteen men was given to the foragers. Sixty savages travelled to the portage at 4 o'clock to scout this area. They returned at noon saying they found no trails. The timber piles of the mill were searched. The workers were increased with the artillery and engineers.

5th July

Ordinary work. Those with the artillery began a ramp from the river to the warehouse to ascend more easily when we land them using the crane. Rain interrupted the work. Two canoes of savages arrived who said they had left the La Reine and La Sarre Regiments at Fort St-Frédéric. The general went to mark their camp on the two banks of La Chute.

6th July

The general changed the position of the camp to take the right bank and the left of the road. On returning to camp he found he learned that instead of three canoes, seven canoes of savages were enroute for Montréal. The two regiments arrived at 10 o'clock and went together to their camp. We sent fifty men to Fort St-Frédéric to unload the *goelette*. The troops of the colony who were camped at La Chute went to join the camp at the Portage.

7th July

The general sent out fifty bateaux, conducted by one hundred and fifty Canadians and escorted by a sergeant and ten soldiers. M. le chevalier de Lévis arrived at 10 o'clock with the grenadier company of Languedoc who went to occupy the redoubt at La Chute. M. Mercier, commander of the artillery, came accompanied by two bateaux brought for the transport of the artillery. M. le chevalier de Lévis sent a detachment of forty men to go in ten bateaux to Saint-Jean where they are lacking. The general went with M. de Bourlamaque to La Chute to visit the camps and made a portage of a bateau that thirty men dragged on a *diable*. The detachment that left yesterday reported that the cargo of the goelette was at Fort St-Frédéric. Three bateaux arrived with a detachment of cannoniers arrived from France.[40]

8th July

Two bateaux sent to Fort St-Frédéric. The Languedoc Regiment arrived at 7 o'clock and went to occupy the old camp of the Guyenne Regiment. The general held council with the savages to go out and take prisoners, they promised them they would leave at 10 o'clock. Few workers are needed for the fortifications but many for the artillery. The general went to camp at La Chute to hasten the portage. The piquets that were camped in the small camp went to join their respective regiments. The supplies for the troops of the colony were taken to La Chute where they checked the milled timber. The savages have left a small black flag near their cabins to amuse the *manitou*, which is what they call an evil spirit.

9th July

Five bateaux were portaged. Those sent here from Frédéric made a report of the necessary provisions. The Iroquois, Abenakis and Outaouas have gone to reconnoitre the road from the portage up to Fort George.
M. de Bourlamaque went to La Chute where he found M. le chevalier de Lévis established with three battalions. M. de Raymond arrived with one hundred and sixty-six soldiers of the colony who camped in the small camp. M. de Lusignan said that a corporal of his garrison had been captured from there and taken south.
The savages believed they had seen and heard the barges pass by the left side of the camp of Béarn but went to clarify and realised they were mistaken.

10th July

A bateau escorted by fifteen men left for Fort St-Frédéric. M. le chevalier de Lévis told M. de Bourlamaque that the savages that went out yesterday returned to him at 11 in the evening with eight prisoners and two scalps, and that they had set an ambush with many of their number to take the officer and seven soldiers, that the prisoners said they had come to scout the fort at Carillon. M. de Raymond passed by La Chute with his detachment. Work with the wagons of the artillery. The Outaouas arrived at midday with three prisoners saying they did not wish to kill the officer, who had not been able to escape and was accompanied by a soldier and a Mohawk. The Iroquois left with their prisoner and promised to return after a few days. Two hundred and fifty Canadians arrived in twenty boats with munitions.

40 It seems that these gunners were from the *Corps Royal de l'Artillerie* of the Army who were then mixed in with the *Cannoniers-Bombardiers*.

11th July

Some of the Outaouas went to Montréal with their prisoners, others have promised to stay if they were given a barrel of wine, which was presented to them within a minute. M. de Vergon has arrived with one hundred and sixty-seven soldiers of the colony,[41] and M. de Bailleul with two hundred and ninety-nine Canadians, they both went to La Chute. A detachment of forty men was sent to the mill.

12th July

All serviceable boats were sent to La Chute. M. de Cabanac arrived with one hundred and eleven Canadians and were sent to La Chute. Fifty men and some bateaux went to fetch oats from Fort St-Frédéric. M. de l'Hôpital, *lieutenant-colonel* of Béarn, has died while hunting, he had long complained of an internal pain.

13th July

All bateaux which remained at Carillon were sent to La Chute. M. Marin arrived with two hundred and fifty savages, Folle Avoines [Menominee], Renards [Fox], Crys [Cree], Pous, and Cicachas [Comanche] and M. Laparguière with four hundred soldiers of the colony in forty bateaux of munitions which were unloaded and returned. The detachment which was sent to Fort St-Frédéric yesterday, returned and sent their bateaux to La Chute. At one o'clock a musket shot was heard which was fired from the right bank opposite the camp of Béarn and two men were seen jumping into the water. A bateau and canoe were sent there. Two savages were brought back who said they had found five hundred English at Deux Rochers, who had pursued them, and that they had been sent by their leader to give notice to us.

14th July

M. Marin left in the morning with six hundred savages. M. le chevalier de Lévis went to the fort to hold council with the other savages, to engage them to go between the two forts, which was agreed. The Mississagués who were in the same party as those who returned by swimming [the two picked up by boat the previous day], denied their report. The general sent one hundred Canadians to accompany the savages to La Chute. Twenty Canadians were established at Carillon to prepare deerskins to be

41 Probably Louis Du Pont Duchambon de Vergor. An associate of Bigot, his pimp as some claimed, he has been damned for his conduct as commander of Fort Beausejour, accused of enriching himself and was described as incapable, stupid, unsuited to command and barely literate. He had served since his youth, enlisting as a cadet and becoming a Captain in 1750. He was also in the unfortunate circumstance of commanding the guard post at the top of the Anse au Foulon. This was the path which General Wolfe led his troops up to secure the heights of Abraham outside the city of Québec. Vergor's post was quickly overrun and he was shot in the leg.

made into shoes. The chief of the Mississagués came to say they had heard the sound of several *caisses.*[42] A soldier was killed in the night by a savage.

15th July

Several officers with nine hundred colony soldiers and Canadians arrived, who left to go to the Chute where they began a portage of their bateaux. In the afternoon, rain stopped the portage and carts.

Several musket shots were fired during the night at La Chute; the sentinels heard noise which they judged was made by enemy savages, our savages came to tell their father that the master of life had sent the rain to prevent them from setting out and so avoiding the bad shots.

16th July

Bad weather. The savages refused to leave, saying that there are three thousand men at the bottom of the bay, and that they would be sent to the slaughter. M. de Sable asked to go scouting with six savages, promising to push as far as possible. A cadet of the colony drowned at the portage. Those at the camp of Saint-Martin discharged their weapons without prior warning. *La générale* was beaten and a part of the army took up arms.

17th July

The roads are very bad, and no portages can be made. The pontoons have carried some guns and ammunition; the savages went to scout the left bank of Lake Saint-Sacrement where they fired on the barge which they believed were the English, having seen men embark as soon as they were seen. M. de Sable returned saying that they had been up to Deux Rocher and seen nothing new.

18th July

A detachment of thirty men went to Fort St-Frédéric to fetch rigging and gear for the artillery. M. Marin set out with forty-five soldiers and Canadians and four hundred savages to scout between the two forts.[43] The escorts of the different convoys which have been away for the past several days have returned. M. le marquis de Montcalm

42 This word is a name used for a drum. The usual army drums however are called tambour by Malartic so this word could perhaps indicate an Indian drum. In modern French, the word is used is to describe larger tom-tom type drums.

43 Joseph Marin de la Malgue, son of the better-known Paul Marin de la Malgue. He spent his youth in the *pays d'en haut* before being recalled to fight in Acadia in the 1740s. He spent the early 1750s involved with diplomacy and exploration of present day Minnesota. He received some grudging praise from Montcalm (Marin was related to Vaudreuil which always soured Montcalm's opinion) and led mixed groups of Native and Canadian raiders during the Seven Years War. He remained in the military after the fall of New France and died of a fever in 1774 during an attempt to retake Madagascar.

has arrived with M. de Rigaud, many officers of the colony, the company of grenadiers of the Guyenne Regiment and three hundred savages of thirty-three different nations. M. de Postuaine disembarked at La Chute with five hundred and fifty-seven Canadians.

19th July

A detachment of forty men went to fetch their effects from the barque, which has returned to Fort St-Frédéric due to contrary winds. The Marquis de Montcalm held council with the savages, then went to La Chute and the portage. It was reported to him that eight English barges had been discovered on the lake. The militia from Montréal arrived numbering four hundred, as did nine canoes of savages and munitions with two canoes of good weapons. The detachment which left this morning returned.

20th July

The militia of Montréal went to La Chute. The artillery has been furnished with many workers to hasten their work transporting and portaging. M. le marquis de Montcalm has been informed that M. de St-Ours had been sent with eight Canadians to scout the Isle à la Barque,[44] and had been attacked by five barges, he raked them with fire and also a troop which they landed to the north, and forced the enemy to let him re-embark and return to port by his good defence by waiting to discharge until at almost point blank range. He was slightly wounded in the hand, a cadet dangerously wounded and three Canadians only slightly.[45]
A convoy of thirty-six bateaux arrived.

21st July

Twenty-five boats were taken from the route of Saint-Jean and eleven of those at Fort St-Frédéric to carry biscuit. The wounded cadet died. M. de St-Ours came to Carillon to add to yesterday's report. After re-embarking he was followed by a barge which he allowed to approach, then fired some bullets which drove it away and changed its course, and he reckoned by their appearance that the English had been out for quite some time as they had very long beards. The general went to the falls, the savages accompanied him and stayed there. Ordinary work.

---

44 François-Xavier de Saint-Ours came from a military family and served in Acadia, upper New York and the far west by the 1750's. He had commanded one of the M. Rigaud's columns in the earlier raid on William Henry in 1757. He received praise in September 1757 for repulsing over 100 British soldiers with only ten men at Fort Carillon. He was killed on the Plains of Abraham in 1759.

45 Note by Gaffarel – This small detachment was sent out to scout by Rigaud. Lieutenant Saint-Ours managed to defeat the English by ordering his men not to fire until close range and put three bullets in each gun. Frustratingly, this detailed footnote is not credited to Malartic, nor referenced by Gaffarel.

22nd July

A lot of food was moved to La Chute. Thirty of the savages who had left with M. Marin returned this morning who reported that their advance guard had fallen on an enemy post of thirty men killing some and others being taken captive or fleeing, that they were sent back by M. Marin because they had become barefoot and lacked food, while he continued on his way. M. de Saint-Luc arrived at midday with several officers and the Abbé Piquet with two hundred savages.[46] The general went to La Chute and the portage. He learned from here that the savages had seen the barges on the lake and left with three hundred, including Canadians, to lay an ambush and take the men who disembarked. Forty other savages of M. Marin came in at 7 o'clock. A courier from M. Vaudreuil came to inform M. de Montcalm that two ships of the line and several merchantmen have carried two battalions of the Berry regiment to the port of Louisbourg and that they are waiting for a considerable squadron from Toulon which has spread joy through Québec as they are lacking many things.

23rd July

Transportation continued. The *munitionaire* left for Saint-Jean. A detachment of the *corps royal de artillerie* composed of six officers and twenty gunners who had left France at the beginning of May, has arrived. The general was informed that the savages who left this morning have been fired on at daybreak without making a scout and that one was injured. The bateau sent to Saint-Jean has returned. M. le chevalier de Lévis told the general that a grenadier of Languedoc was killed and two others injured while returning to camp, by a party of fifteen Agnés and that he had sent twenty grenadiers in pursuit and detachments from all the camps.

24th July

M. le marquis de Montcalm was informed that the Canadians and savages have seized the three barges which carried thirty men, that M.M. de Corbière and Langlade had pursued twenty others, that the prisoners said they were from this detachment and had gone by land and that they were followed by land to report if they were approached. The Abenaki led their prisoners to the general at 10 o'clock.

M. Marin arrived at the same time and gave an account that his men took a post of thirty men and had approached Fort Lydius; that the English had made a sortie in great number and followed them for over a league, that they had killed one hundred and fifty men and taken a prisoner, that the savages took thirty-two scalps and they lost a single man who died of fatigue; he had a lot of praise for the Folle Avoines.

An escort of the fifty men was given to the reapers. M. le chevalier de Lévis

46 Luc de la Corne (also known as Saint-Luc or sometimes Chaptes) like many others used his military career to further his trading enterprises. A shrewd merchant, he ended up amongst the richest Canadians with a fortune of 1.2 million *livres*. He spoke multiple Indian languages fluently and fought on the Lake Champlain frontier throughout the war. After the surrender, he remained in Canada and hoped for a re-conquest by the French. He was accused of stirring up tensions with the Indians during the Pontiac Rebellion.

informed the general that all the barges have now been taken along with one hundred and twenty men, that one hundred and eighty have been killed and we have had just one savage wounded in the two actions. The prisoners said that the detachment was of three hundred and fifty men, commanded by M. Parker of the New Jersey Regiment; that he had gone out with three barges and was ordered to attack our outposts and stay a few days to take prisoners from Carillon; they were locked in the new hospital.[47] Two hundred savages arrived at midday with their missionaries and interpreters.

25th July

Bateaux loaded with artillery have arrived; the savages have led their prisoners to the portage where they are guarded. Some Outaouas have left for Montréal, the general had difficulties in retaining them. We have received many convalescents and Volontaires Étrangers who will form new colony companies.[48] The general went to the portage to make a review of the battalion formed from colony troops, the brigades composed of Canadians and the *compagnies franches*.[49] He ordered that the prisoners should leave tomorrow but the savages opposed this and threatened to go with them. M. de Bougie (?) was obliged to go and confer with M. de Saint-Luc and harangue the chiefs of the nations, who finally agreed to the departure of the prisoners, provided that M. de Vaudreuil will give them white bread, shoes and will take care of them.[50]

26th July

Work and transport as normal. The prisoners left at 9 o'clock, escorted by a lieutenant and forty men who will embark a party in the barque at Fort St-Frédéric.

---

47 This engagement was on the edge of Lake Saint-Sacrement. M. Corbière commanded the advance guard of 50 French troops and over 400 Canadians and Indians. This action was the Sabbath Day point massacre where a party of around 150 of Parker's New Jersey Provincials were captured. The episode was made infamous by reports of the ritual cooking and eating of some prisoners. Ian Castle, *Fort William Henry 1755-57* (Oxford: Osprey 2013) pp. 53-5.

48 The Volontaires Étrangers that Malartic here refers to was a small body of part of the regiment of the same name. One hundred and fifty men led by Saint-Rome volunteered to come to Canada and set sail on 8 April 1757 in the *Robuste* with six eight-pound cannon and eighteen six-pound cannon. Their uniform was the same style white coat of the regular infantry but they had green collar and cuffs. In 1758 a whole battalion of the Volontaires Étrangers would be sent out to Louisbourg. Fournier, *Combattre*, p. 88.

49 Gaffarel notes that on this date from a report of Bougainville, 8,013 men in total comprising of 7 battalions of regular troops (3,081 soldiers), 7 brigades of militia (2,946 soldiers), 188 gunners, 820 domestic savages with 10 French officers, 6 interpreters and 3 missionaries, and 986 savages of the *pays d'en haut* with 7 officers and 5 interpreters. There were 33 different nations represented by the savages. Malartic's use here of the term *compagnies franches*, literally 'free companies', is interesting. The term is usually used to describe the companies of Canadian Marines, but as Malartic uses the term Marines and troops of the colony, he could be referring to the volunteer companies he describes earlier.

50 The name of M. de Bougie is question-marked in Gaffarel's text: presumably as it was unclear. I have found no reference to a Bougie.

Fifty bateaux sent back from Frédéric, half of the detachment and all the Canadians. The general sent three prisoners away at 10 o'clock in a bateau who were wanted by the savages. The Volontaires Étrangers were sent to the portage. The general fixed the date of the 28th for the departure of the corps under the orders of M. le chevalier de Lévis, which was composed of six companies of grenadiers, eight piquets, a company of volunteers of three hundred men, three brigades of Canadians of four hundred men each and seven or eight hundred savages. He went to La Chute to hold council with all the nations and on his return he held back the departure of M. le chevalier de Lévis by a day; the number of prisoners requested by the savages has been reduced.[51]

27th July

A convoy of eighteen bateaux have arrived. The general went to the falls to establish a great council with all the nations to make the arrangements for their departure and the march of the army.[52]

51 Note by Gaffarel – These councils were very important. Bougainville, in a letter to Minister of War, dated 19 April, 1757, has kept the details of what happened in the assembly of Nippissing warriors. Kisenseck, the chief, began by praising past achievements and encouraged the Indians of other nations to persevere with the French alliance. Montcalm then spoke. 'My children, I am delighted to see you all gathered in such large numbers on this important matter. As long as this union is held, the English cannot resist you. I cannot say better things than my brother Kisenseck. He has found in you the secret of your strength. Our great King has without doubt sent me to protect and defend you, but he ordered me especially to make you happy and invincible. You will be happy and invincible if you keep concord and union between yourselves, and if you help one another in these enterprises that are for the common good.' He then presented them with a wampum collars, six thousand beads, as a token of good intelligence and union, and tossed them into the middle of the meeting. The Iroquois picked them up. The chief Pennahouel gave the same presentation to the nations of the West, beseeching them to focus on the fortunes of France. The collars belonged by right to the nation that had provided the largest number of warriors, the Iroquois of Sault St. Louis and Lake of Two Mountains, but they gave the honour to the nations of the West.

52 Note by Gaffarel – Two days earlier, on 25 July, Montcalm had sent instructions to each commander. They contain interesting details, and are testament to the wisdom of the general. 'You are not ignorant of the nature of the expedition we endeavour. Your experience in the art of war says to you that speed is the principal means of success..... You also know what the difficulties are, obstacles and consequently the slow transport in this country. We have few boats; but munitions of war and food are important for such a large party, such it is that we are forced to send a large division of the army by land. Does it not do justice to your zeal and that of your officers to be convinced that they will, with good grace and joy, do all that is asked of them that may hasten the end of our business? They will see themselves that what might normally be regarded as something of necessity, would, on this occasion, become a luxury detrimental to the good of the service.' Following this are various prescriptions to alleviate the running of the baggage train: Here is a curiosity; 'The blanket and a bearskin is the bed of a man of war in such an expedition. I will not defend a mattress. Age and disability can make it necessary for some people. I will not carry one, and do not doubt that all will willingly do as I do. They are provided only for the sick and wounded of the army.'

28th July

Forty-nine soldiers of the Volontaires Étrangers arrived, several Canadians and savages and many convalescents that M. Bourlamaque sent immediately to their corps. He formed a guard of the Volontaires Étrangers to form a garrison at the fort. Supplies of food and munitions were carried over the portage.

29th July

The baggage of the army has been deposited at Carillon in several of the designated magazines. The companies of grenadiers and piquets of R. Roussillon and Béarn went to Contrecoeur's camp, where the corps of M. le chevalier de Lévis is assembling which will march tomorrow to go by land to Ganaouské Bay, where it will wait for the army. The garrison of the fort took possession of it at midday, under the orders of M. Dalquier, captain of grenadiers of Béarn, and is composed of forty-two regular soldiers and forty-nine Volontaires Étrangers.[53] The brigade of R. Roussillon provided several labourers to conduct the loaded bateaux over La Chute. Malartic, major of this brigade, left at 6 o'clock from the portage to take the orders from the general for this brigade's camp.[54]

The savages killed several oxen, stole wine and other effects from some officers and made a din all night. We were obliged to leave behind those that remained.

30th July

M. le chevalier de Lévis left at daybreak. The brigade of R. Roussillon went to camp at the front of the portage, the right facing the lake and the left towards the mountain.[55] The general held council with the Indians to scold them. The brigades of La Sarre and the Marine occupied the Brûlé camp, each soldier carrying a traine or oars. Worked all day to portage the munitions. One brigade was commanded to sleep during the day and take over from the other at night. A fire from the camp of the savages spread and reached the portage; all brigades sent detachments to extinguish it.

31st July

The Royal Roussillon brigade and one of Canadians went to the falls to pick up all the effects that remained there. M. de Bourlamaque, who followed, sent a detachment of thirty men to Carillon to fetch food and many utensils; the brigades of La Reine

---

53 Jean d'Alquier de Servian became acting *lieutenant-colonel* of Béarn in September 1757 after the illness and death of its commander, de L'Hôpital. Malartic later records how he made a significant contribution to the Battle of Sainte-Foy where he commanded a brigade. See below (p. 265).

54 Malartic referring to himself in the third person could indicate that he used these journal entries in official reports in which this was standard practice.

55 Note by Gaffarel – The fixed point for the first stage was Ganaouské Bay, 40 km from the portage, 16 from Fort George. The Iroquois chief Ganactagon had himself given this valuable information.

and La Sarre provided two hundred to make the portage, the savages left at 4 o'clock in the morning to go four leagues ahead and wait for the army. The fire from their camp has caused almost the whole army to stop and has impeded the artillery. M.M. Wolff, lately detached from M. le chevalier de Lévis, arrived at 2 o'clock to inform M. de Montcalm that they camped five leagues from the Brûlé camp yesterday after going over some very bad roads, that all the troops are in good form, except for two sick officers who he has sent back. The brigade of R. Roussillon, a battalion of Marines and the Canadians have taken bateaux and food for eight days.

1st August

The brigades staying at the Brûlé camp have taken their rations. The troops have embarked their equipment. Several sick were sent back to Carillon. M. le marquis de Montcalm has recently sent a courier to inform M. de Vaudreuil of the departure of the army which set out at midday, in the following order: the brigade of La Reine, formed of one battalion of this regiment, one of Languedoc and one of the Marine, the brigade of La Sarre, from one of that battalion and one of Guyenne, and that of Courte-Manche, formed from soldiers of the colony and Canadians; one hundred and ten bateaux loaded with artillery which carried the brigade of Royal Roussillon, formed of one battalion of the same name, and one of Béarn; that of Saint-Ours, composed of Canadians and all the gunners, bombardiers and engineers attached to the artillery; thirty two bateaux loaded with food and carrying the brigade of Gaspé, formed of Canadians; and two bateaux carrying a piquet of Royal Roussillon, as a rearguard.[56] They passed the Brûlé camp, Mount Pelée and the Maltaches woods, despite heavy rain which lasted until 7 o'clock. A short stop was made opposite Pain de Sucre and arrived,[57] on the 2nd of August at day break, at Ganaouské Bay where they found M. le chevalier de Lévis, who left at 10 o'clock with his corps.[58] The general put the army in motion at noon, travelling by land. It stopped at nightfall at l'Anse au Sable. The bateaux joined us there; the savages captured an English barge from around there which they discovered.[59] The army

56 According to Bougainville, the pontoons which carried artillery were 'made of two bateaux fastened together with a platform on top. These pontoons carry the cannon and mortars, mounted on their carriages. They are very well conceived for a lake with high shores like Lake St-Sacrement.' Bougainville, *Adventure in the Wilderness*, p. 156

57 A note in the French edition records that this was to visit the battlefield which had been reported by Corbière. The traces were fresh. Some bodies were still floating on the water. Others were lying in the woods, but horribly mutilated and chopped to pieces by the savages. It is unclear as to whether this note was added by Malartic or by his editor Gaffarel.

58 Note by Gaffarel – Lévis' march through the woods was very painful, even for the savages due to excessive heat, and obstacles such as fallen trees. The Indians came to admire their French chief. 'I have the confidence of all troops, even Canadians and Indians who say I am a man like themselves; it is the last march that I made for our expedition, where this praise originated, which is great among the savages.' Letter from Lévis to Marshal Mirepoix.

59 A note in the French edition records that the French were not expected. A sheep that was carried by the army began to bleat, and the cry revealed the ambush; but the savages rushed in pursuit of English uttering horrible cries, and managed to seize the boats and three prisoners. Again, this point is not noted as Malartic's own nor is it referenced by Gaffarel.

rested for an hour and then set out again to reach the camp of M. le chevalier de Lévis at 10 o'clock. The artillery did not arrive here until daybreak of the 3rd. Necessary guards were set for the bateaux.

3rd August

The army was formed *en bataille* at 5 o'clock; M. le chevalier de Lévis, his corps being the advance guard, marched together to take position on the road to Fort Lydius and prevent any aid reaching these parts: the army followed in three columns and arrived in this order until within sight of Fort George; the brigade of R. Roussillon received orders to line the crest of a ravine which is opposite the fort, 1 hour later, they were to join the army on a plateau which is on the left of the fort. It remained in position until 5 o'clock in the evening. The savages have put a lot of fire against the fort and repelled several small sorties, killing around one hundred men and taking four prisoners. They have killed or captured one hundred oxen, one hundred and fifty sheep and twenty horses.

At 6 o'clock the general sent word to the brigades of La Sarre and R. Roussillon to go and establish a camp as designated by M. de Bourlamaque and the rest to go with the La Reine Brigade and spend the night in bivouacs with M. le chevalier de Lévis. M. de Bourlamaque made camp with the brigade of La Sarre at the edge of the ravine, the left going up to a small bay where the artillery would be disembarked, and R. Roussillon on the right. There would be a guard of fifty men in front of the ravine and the same number in the bay, the entrance of which was lit at night to show the way to the bateaux. At 7 o'clock M. de Bourlamaque received a note from the general relating that our scouts around [Fort] Lydius have seen troops going through the mountains. The piquets of this camp slept in bivouac. A mortar and two howitzers, a lot of ammunition and tools were unloaded. The prisoners taken yesterday and today agreed that on the 1st they had 1,200 men in the fort and fortified camp, and that on the night of the 1st and the 2nd and the day of the 2nd this had grown to 3,300 men.

4th August

The brigade of La Sarre went to camp at the right of R. Roussillon, that of Gaspé a little to the rear and the right of La Reine, that of Saint-Ours to the rear of La Sarre. The general arrived in camp at 7 o'clock and went with M. Bourlamaque, the engineers, and officers of the artillery to reconnoitre the fort and decided to open a trench and establish the batteries.[60] On his return he wrote to M. de Lévis to return a portion of his detachments and to occupy the heights which border the right of the camp with four brigades of the colony, independent companies and the savages.

60 Fort William Henry formed a square flanked by four bastions and protected by a moat. The scarp and counterscarp were made of loose earth. Twenty-three cannon, four mortars and swivel guns lined the walls; also there was a ravelin on the south side. The fort was not large enough to house all the soldiers so a large fortified camp had been constructed to the east behind the fort. Castle, *Fort William Henry*, p. 57.

Tools were given to the troops who were ordered to make fascines and *saucissons*. At 1 o'clock one hundred and fifty workers were commanded to open a road from the depot to the beginning of the trench. The hospital was established on the left of the small bay where a guard was posted. M. de Bourlamaque, who was charged with the direction of the siege, ordered four hundred and fifty workers and three hundred guards to rest during the day. These troops would return at 9 o'clock to rendezvous and be posted together to open a trench one thousand *toises* from the fort;[61] and begin two batteries. The *cannoniers* who were to mark out the right battery did not respond to a '*qui vive?*' [who goes there?] from the guards and suffered a few musket shots which made them and some labourers quit the works; they returned some minutes later. The six piquets were placed in front of the left battery and one on its left, two in front of the right battery and one on its right. Work continued with great vivacity until 4 o'clock in the morning when the piquets entered the trench. The workers of the night were relieved by two hundred men who finished off the work and greatly lengthened the communication trench. The enemy gave us some shells and bullets but did little harm to the trench. Several dropped in the camps of the brigades of La Sarre and R. Roussillon, the general ordered them to move back four hundred *toises* immediately and establish communications. The brigade of La Reine was ordered, in case of attack, to take the right of the *batterie royale*,[62] La Sarre to take the end of the trench, R. Roussillon to take the head and M. le chevalier de Lévis would descend the heights to take the enemy in the flank. Around 4 o'clock, scouts came in and said a reinforcement had arrived from Fort Lydius. The general sent three companies of grenadiers to M. le chevalier de Lévis with orders to go and meet this reinforcement. After this followed a party of the army who had been given a prisoner taken by one of the savages and brought the jacket of a man they had killed, in which was found a letter from General Webb, commander of this frontier, which gave the position of Fort Lydius and that he did not think it prudent to march on Fort George. That he had heard the news from Frenchman recently captured. The troops who had been set to march returned. At nightfall, three companies of grenadiers and two piquets were sent into the trench as yesterday, under the orders of M. de Fonbonne, *lieutenant-colonel*, and Dhert [sic.], major, and six hundred workers employed on the batteries and communications.[63]

6th August

At daybreak the general went to see the trench and open up the *batterie royale* composed of nine cannons and a mortar.[64] The night workers were replaced by

61 Note by Gaffarel – The trench was opened at seven o'clock in the evening, at seven hundred yards from the point of attack, under the protection of soldiers commanded by Roquemaure and Sermonville.
62 The name perhaps indicates a battery manned by the *Royal Artillerie* troops.
63 This was Jean-Pierre-Gaston d'Hert, previously noted was the *aide-major* of La Reine.
64 Note by Gaffarel – The left battery had eight guns and a mortar, and was opened on the night of the 5th to the 6th. It was placed to defend the lake front, the west and the harbour for the boats. The right battery, of eight guns, two howitzers and mortar, was opened on the night of the 6th to the 7th. This was placed to attack the fort, and, by extension, the entrenched camp.

three hundred to finish the works. Enemy fire was not lively. Several of our bombs and balls went into the fort. The guard of the trenches were relieved at 4 o'clock by three companies of grenadiers and three piquets under the orders of M. de Privas, *lieutenant-colonel* and Malartic, major.[65] Four hundred workers were employed in perfecting the royal battery and opening a channel to the gardens of the fort. The fire of the enemy, though lively has not killed or injured a single person.

7th August

The workmen who had been going since daybreak were replaced by three hundred more who continued through the night. The general went to the batteries at 6 o'clock and was greeted by a general gun salute.[66] They continued to fire one shot per minute. The savages shouted with joy when they saw a ball hit the fort and the shells fall into it. About 3 o'clock the English tried to make a sortie to establish a post on the way to Fort Lydius. M. de Villiers, commander of the *compagnies franches*, attacked them with his troops and savages, killing fifty men, taking four prisoners and forcing the rest back to the fort.[67] The brigades provided seventy-two servants to the artillery.[68] The lieutenant who had led the prisoners from Carillon to Montréal returned to join us bringing many letters from France. The troops made a lot of gabions, fascines and *saucissons*, and the Canadians chopped logs to establish a path over the small marsh and ravine that must be crossed in order to reach the gardens.[69] The guard of the trenches were relieved by three companies of grenadiers and six piquets under the orders of M. de Senezergues, lieutenant colonel and Joannès, major.[70] We provided two hundred and fifty workers, one hundred for the two batteries and to

---

At six o'clock in the morning a double gun salute from both batteries greeted the visiting Montcalm in the trench.

65 Marc-Antoine de Privat was *lieutenant-colonel* of the Languedoc Regiment. He was born in 1710 and entered the military in 1726 as an ensign. While in Canada he received permission to marry and retired at the end of the Seven Years War in 1763.

66 Note by Gaffarel – Montcalm had received the news that he had been appointed Commander of the Order of St. Louis and letters from France announced this as an award for the capturing of Oswego. As such morale was high with the besiegers. See the letter he [Montcalm] wrote about it, 15 April 1757, to de Paulmy, minister of war.

67 Note by Gaffarel – This raid took place on the night of the 7th and 8th according to Bougainville's report.

68 'Gun servants' refers to infantrymen used to perform the non-technical roles of the gun crew such as fetching ammunition.

69 Note by Gaffarel – This marsh was partly covered by a hill, but had an opening twenty metres wide. Montcalm, to avoid delay completed this difficult task during daylight, despite fire from the ramparts. Before night the marsh was crossed by a road capable of bearing artillery.

70 Étienne-Guillaume de Senezergues was a career officer and *lieutenant-colonel* of La Sarre. He was oft praised as the most fit and able battalion commander of the regular army and he was rewarded with a promotion to brigadier in February 1759. He fell in battle on the Plains of Abraham, charging the British left. Égide-Armand Joannès began his military career as a lieutenant in the Languedoc Regiment in 1747 and the age of 12. He seemed to be a jack-of-all-trades as his record shows he was promoted to *aide-major* but holding the rank of captain. He was also employed as the engineer of Québec from 1757-9. After the war he became a *maréchal de camp* in 1790. He died in January 1814.

start building a third, one hundred yards front and centre of the other two, the rest were to go with the engineers and lengthen the passage down to the ravine and construct a bridge. At ten o'clock in the evening, some savages stationed in front of the piquet fired on two Englishmen who declared they were deserters. They gave one to the general and kept the other.

8th August

The piquets and workers were relieved at daybreak. They were replaced by three hundred more and were employed at the new battery to make a rampart to cover the port, and a ramp leading to the gardens which was planned to be completed by the next night, during this work there were two men killed and five wounded. It took a lot of gabions, fascines and *saucissons*. Several bombs were dropped into the fort where one among them went into a bastion and blew up a powder keg. At three o'clock in the afternoon, we saw gleaming guns and men on the mountain. The Indians made their cry to assemble, the discoverers warning that relief had arrived.[71] The General sent three companies of grenadiers with M. chevalier de Lévis, followed by the brigades of La Reine and Gaspé. Brigade R. Roussillon was focused on the heights, in case they needed to follow the general or come to the aid of the trench. Then La Sarre reinforced the trench and Saint-Ours remained to guard the bateaux. M. Bourlamaque made dispositions to repel sorties, and ordered the officers to shoot at random on the entrenched camp, where we saw a lot of movement and the English in line of battle. At 4 o'clock we heard several shots, followed by cries from the savages, half an hour later, an aide of the General came to inform M. Bourlamaque that the relief was overcome and the troops would return. The guards and workers were relieved at 5 o'clock by three companies of grenadiers and six piquets under the orders of M.M. Lévis, Bernetz, lieutenant colonel, and Bellecombe, major, and by five hundred and fifty workers, including one hundred for the battery, and others to complete the bridge and build a post on the outer edge of the ravine.[72] A deserter arrived at 10 o'clock saying there are five hundred men in the fort, and fifteen hundred in the entrenched camp, and that they were very worried by our bullets and our bombs. The enemy's fire was lively, in the trench two men were killed and eight wounded.

9th August

The workers found cover having established themselves in the gardens. They were relieved by three hundred more who were busied perfecting shelters. Our batteries were firing briskly. At 7 o'clock the fort raised the white flag, seeing this the guards

71 Note by Gaffarel – This turned out to be a false alarm from the savages. According to Bougainville, 'the readiness of our movement at least served to further increase the confidence that the savages have in us, and shows how they rely so much on the vigilance and valour of the French troops who they call their supporting wall.'

72 Félicien de Bernetz was the *lieutenant-colonel* of Royal Roussillon.

sent a detachment to scout.[73] The officer commanding said he was followed by a wounded lieutenant colonel who was responsible for proposals of capitulation, M. Bourlamaque sent a report to the general who came to the trenches, we kept the detachment and lieutenant colonel, and sent two of our officers to the fort as hostages. The general met with Lieutenant Colonel Young and agreed the surrender of the fort and fortified camp with the following conditions, that the garrison of two thousand two hundred men would be let out of the fort and camp with weapons and luggage and a single gun, they will not serve against France and her allies for eighteen months, food and ammunition will be left in the stores as they are, that all the French prisoners taken in North America are to be released within four months, that the garrison evacuate the fort this afternoon and leave tomorrow at dawn, escorted by a company of grenadiers and a piquet.[74] The articles were signed by both sides at noon and at 2 in the afternoon, the guards took possession of the gates of the fort and camp. At the same time, M. Lévis was posted with the brigade of La Reine and the four of the colony on the path to [Fort] Lydius, where he established his camp. The general kept L. C. Young as hostage. He was forced to go and scold and harangue the savages who wanted to kill and kidnap the English. He allowed them, as well as the Canadians, to plunder the goods that were in the fort. The English officers gave them money which guaranteed their fury.[75] The general could not return to sleep till nine. It was left to M. de Bougainville to carry the news of the surrender of the fort to M. de Vaudreuil.

10th August

The garrison was roused at 6 o'clock to march to Fort Lydius under escort as proscribed. The savages followed, kidnapping and robbing several officers and soldiers.[76] The General ran after them, accompanied by several officers, to stop them. He brought those he could reach and that the savages wanted to capture into the fort and the fortified camp [for their protection]. The greater part of the savages resembled mad men who no longer recognised their father and nothing could make them remember, they took English officers and soldiers, their women and children by force. Their rage had subsided a little by 10 o'clock.[77] Some nations went to Montréal

---

73 This was at 9 o'clock according to Bougainville, *Adventure in the Wilderness*, p. 169.

74 Lt. Colonel Young was an officer in the 60th Royal American Regiment who had been wounded in the siege. He was accompanied by one of his captains, Swiss-born Rudolphus Faesch. See Ian K. Steele, *Betrayals: Fort William Henry & the "Massacre"* (Oxford: Oxford University Press, 1990), pp. 109-10.

75 Malartic was of the same opinion as most other French officers, in that the British should have resisted giving away their goods to the Indians as their passivity only made matters worse for them. See Bougainville, *Adventure in the Wilderness*, p. 171.

76 The events were reported hysterically back in the British colonies but the ensuing chaos covered up reality. There were far fewer casualties than reported but the legend was seared into public consciousness by Fennimore Cooper's *Last of the Mohicans*. The most in-depth and balanced study to date is Steele, *Betrayals*.

77 Note by Gaffarel – Montcalm later admitted he had run more dangers in trying to stop the fury of the savages than by taking the fort. Without the help of the French, no Englishman would have escaped. Nearly fifty of them were nevertheless massacred. There was an

with their prisoners.[78] Others came to the General and told him they had no spirit and recognised their fault, then brought their prisoners who were immediately taken from the field to the fort.[79] The brigades of La Sarre and Royal Roussillon decamped at noon to go to camp on the plateau which is to the left of the fort. The Saint-Ours Brigade on the banks of the lake and Gaspé in the gardens. The commander of the escort of prisoners returned at 2 o'clock, informing the general that he was unable to stop the fury of the savages, who wounded two of his soldiers, that he lost a sergeant, who, according to witnesses, led the English who had escaped the savages to Fort Lydius.[80] The general has removed all those who remained and they have been put into the fort and the fortified camp which has doubled their guard. He kept Colonel Monroe, a lieutenant-colonel, and two other officers with him. M.M. the officers, following his example, took responsibility for all the others. We started clearing the artillery and ammunition from the fort. It consists of eighty guns, fifteen thousand balls, two hundred bombs, thirty thousand pounds of gunpowder, twenty carriages or *crapaux*,[81] three thousand three hundred barrels of flour and bacon, and a few barrels of salt and peas. The general has sent a letter to inform the Marquis de Vaudreuil of the savages conduct.

They [unclear from the original, possibly meaning the French's allied Indians] were ordered not to depart because Agnés roam around the camp. A courier was killed yesterday and an enemy savage captured who had got into the camp. A letter from General Webb which he [the courier] carried said he had received a reinforcement of two thousand men, they will rest on the 9th, and then he will send one thousand men to the camp with one hundred and fifty savages, led by Colonel Johnson, this help would have been too late to help those forces at the fort. The British officers complain loudly.

---

outrageous travesty by the novelist Cooper in his *Last of the Mohicans*. Did he not argue that 1,500 English had been the victims of perfidy of the savages! This figure is contradicted by the official reports of Vaudreuil, Bougainville, and the detailed account of the campaign by the missionary of the Abenakis, probably Father Roubaud.

78 Note by Gaffarel – From Desandrouins: 'Three or four hundred paces from the camp, I saw a savage quietly leading an Englishman, following our trench. Thinking he probably sought to rob his coin and maybe even kill him, I boldly went to meet them, and, having caught them, I seized both of the savage's wrists before he could challenge me. Holding him so I cried to the frightened Englishman, and signalled he should flee to our camp. But this man, taller than me by four inches, remained motionless and petrified.'

79 Note by Gaffarel – Desandrouins reports that nearly 400 British were swept away by the savages to Montreal. 'The Marquis de Vaudreuil, could not use force that he did not have but by much trouble was able to get them to release some of their prisoners, yet rather by their desire for strong drink, rather than by persuasion or regard... I do not know if those they took beyond Montreal, have ever found a way to return to their homeland.'

80 Of the 2,308 men who were paroled at Fort William Henry, 1,783 were safe by the end of August. Another 217 were returned by the end of the year leaving 308 still unaccounted for. Over the next few years more returned leaving the number of killed or missing at 174. Steele, *Betrayals*, pp. 135-9.

81 *Crapaux* (lit. toads) were gun carriages; from the inference, maybe mortar type or naval trails.

11th, 12th, 13th and 14th of August

This time was spent employing 1,500 workers, who excavated artillery and food that was taken to the port, and the demolition of the fort. Some time was spent unnecessarily seeking a cache in the fort where an Englishman said we could find two million. A convoy arrived at the portage. The Regiment La Sarre and piquets of the army took up arms for the execution of a soldier who had insulted an officer of the colony. In the evening we set fire to all buildings and wood remaining in the fort. A detachment of thirty men, commanded by a lieutenant, went to carry letters to Fort Lydius.[82]

15th August

A few bateaux arrived at the portage. The commander of the detachment that left yesterday returned from Fort Lydius. It is said that he was well received by the English, though they are very angry we did not foresee the breach in the capitulation made by the savages. The general sent back all the English we removed from the savages at 10 in the morning. They were escorted by two companies of grenadiers, and the *compagnies franches*. The foundations of the fort were filled in.

16th August

The Regiments R. Roussillon and Béarn left at 6 o'clock in the boats of the La Sarre Brigade to camp at Isle Longue and waited with the boats. The army embarked at noon, the chevalier de Lévis commanding the vanguard. Nine English deserters arrived, who say that the militias are going back to their provinces.

17th August

The regiments have received twenty-three bateaux [each]. We sent a courier to request a supplement, twelve more arrived in the evening.

---

82 Note by Gaffarel – One of these letters was addressed to General Webb from Montcalm : 'After the honourable defence of Colonel Monro I was determined to give him and his garrison an honourable capitulation. This would have occurred if your soldiers had not given rum to the Indians, and if they had gone out with more order to execute what I had prescribed to them, and if the Abenaki idolaters of *Penaskessé* in Acadia were not believed in complaining about some abuse. You know what it is to contain two hundred savages of thirty-three different nations. I feared greatly, as such I did not let my summons to the fort commander be ignored. I feel happy that the disorder has not been followed by any more tragedy which I rightly feared. I am grateful, for I exposed myself personally as did my officers, in defence of yours, who do justice to all that I have done on this occasion.' He also wrote to the commander in chief Lord Loudoun to pray to enforce the capitulation strictly, and to inform that he could not stop part of the massacre. These two letters are a testimony of righteousness and humanity of Montcalm. They were published in L. Dussieux, *Le Canada sous la Domination Française d'apres les Archives de la Marine et de la Guerre* (Paris: Jacque Lecoffre, 1862), pp. 310-4.

18th August

The regiments embarked at 6 o'clock, halted opposite the Isle à la Barque and arrived at 3 o'clock at the portage. R. Roussillon made camp at the post to the right of La Reine and Béarn up to the Petit Rapide. M. le marquis de Montcalm was established at the Portage and the chevalier de Lévis at La Chute. M. de Rigaud left yesterday with all the Canadians who arrived at the portage, they thought only of returning to their homes without shouldering the burden of the considerable work which remains to be done.

19th August

Béarn went to occupy the old camp at Carillon, and provided workers required for interior work on the fort, digging in the artillery and supplies. We sang the *Te Deum* in the three camps in thanksgiving for the capture of Fort George.[83]

20th August

Bad weather made the portage difficult. Three musket shots were heard from Cap au Diamant. We sent a bateau which brought back four Nippisingués with two English prisoners, taken from around Orange.

21st and 22nd August

Bad weather. The general made a review of troops camped at the Portage and La Chute.

23rd August

Good weather. We were able to portage a great deal of food. The general went to Carillon to make a review of Béarn.

24th August

Bad Weather. Workers were given to the artillery for the fortifications.

25th August

Good weather. Much work at the portage. M. de Bougainville arrived at midday carrying many letters from France.

83 Note by Gaffarel – The news of this victory was announced to Louis XV on 11 October and on 22 November, Bernis, the then minister of foreign affairs wrote to Montcalm; 'I saw with pleasure the success that you have had and am happy to read the details in the letters you did the honour of writing to me on the 20th April last. Everything is due to the wisdom of your conduct and your combined skills. You referenced justice here. I admire, personally, those that you are pleased with: those officers who have assisted you in your operations. All they hope for they can have. I count on them a lot, and congratulate you with all my heart.'

26th August

Good weather. The portaging is greatly advanced. M. le marquis de Montcalm has gone with the engineer to oversee the works adjacent to the fort.

27th August

We profited from the continued good weather by being able to accelerate the pace of transport through the portage.

28th August

Bad weather. The general left with four bateaux conducted by soldiers of the colony. The *munitionnaire* arrived at 10 o'clock.[84]

29th August

Good weather. Two deserters arrived from Fort Lydius saying that the English are still on their guard and rarely leave their entrenchments, and that they have sent out a detachment to scout Fort George. M. le chevalier de Lévis has sent a detachment to these parts and another to the bottom of the bay.

30th August

The detachment from the bottom of the bay returned as they had seen a barge which went to ground as soon as they were spotted and that the men leading them made a lot of noise as they went into the woods.

31st August

Royal Roussillon went to camp on the right of Béarn. M. de Bourlamaque has gone to take command of this camp. The Languedoc Regiment has gone to camp below the fort on the left bank of La Chute River.

At 10 o'clock something was seen coming around the point of Cap au Diamant. A bateau was sent which returned towing a raft carrying three Canadians who had been captured at different times by the English. They had come from New York where they had escaped. M. le chevalier de Lévis went to camp at Carillon with the Regiment of La Reine and the battalion of the Marine.

84 The *munitionnaire* was Joseph-Michel Cadet (1719-1781). His role as *munitionnaire du Roi*, roughly purveyor-general, gave him the responsibility of supplying the material goods and victuals for the army. He amassed a great fortune through contracting and was accused of profiteering in the trials which followed the fall of New France. In the enquiry into the loss of Canada, he was tried for corruption in 1763, banished from Paris and fined 3 million *livres*. Malartic also refers to *comissaires de munition*. It is assumed that they are local assistants of Cadet's office.

1st September

The regiments of La Reine, La Sarre, Languedoc, Guyenne and the battalion of the Marine will leave in succession to camp at Fort St-Frédéric and cut wood for the garrison. M. le chevalier de Lévis left at 10 o'clock with six companies of grenadiers, six piquets and one hundred Canadians for the bottom of the bay. M. de Bourlamaque went to the portage to give the order for the retiring battalion of Marines and told them to remain here.

2nd September

Workers sent for the fortifications and artillery. The battalion of the Marine went to camp beneath the fort.

3rd September

M. le chevalier de Lévis, returning, was content with the reconnaissance that he had made from the bottom of the bay and the banks of the R. Chicot. He destroyed the entrenchments that he found. The general left at midday for Montréal.

4th September

Two bateaux loaded with sick men left today. M. de Raymond has gone with a detachment to the portage, to hide six bateaux in the small bays under branches.

5th September

M. de Bourlamaque went to the portage to see that the bateaux were well hidden, take several barges out of the water and bury the bateau with a cannon.[85] Work was done on the battlements of the fort, putting across the necessary beams to cover and mount cannon on the warehouse of the fort.

6th September

Ordinary work. Canadians were sent to the portage to fetch the barges and burn those which were out of service.

7th September

Ordinary work. The reapers have been employed over the last fifteen days making hay and there is much to carry. The regiments were to put up palisades, and obliged to supply five hundred each.

85 This was done at the end of the campaign season so they did not have to be transported and could not be burned by enemy raiding parties.

8th September

Bateaux arrived from Saint-Jean and Fort St-Frédéric.

9th September

Bad weather suspended work. Bateaux arrived loaded with food and refreshments. They left after being loaded with bacon for Fort St-Frédéric.

10th September

Bad weather continued. An officer and seventeen soldiers of the companies of the Marines left, being asked for by Vaudreuil for a council of war which he ordered to be assembled to examine the conduct of the commandant who had defended and lost the fort of Beau Sejour.[86]

11th September

Good weather. One hundred and eighty sick departed.

12th September

Ordinary work. Wood cutters were sent out for cedar which is used for shingles and laid like slates to cover buildings.

13th September

Increased number of workers to embark the artillery which must come down and to load seventeen bateaux with bacon.

14th September

Again the number of workers was increased. All the bateaux have left. A soldier of the Marine deserted with an English soldier.

15th September

M. de Sabrevois has left with fifty Canadians to go after the deserters and if they do not catch them will go up to Fort George to see if the English have made any establishment there. Bateaux from Fort St-Frédéric arrived.

86 Note by Gaffarel – This officer was called Vergor. He was a protégé of the Intendant, Bigot, who, on giving him command of Fort Beauséjour, gave him odious council. 'Enjoy your place. Reap from it: you have all the power, so that soon we can go back to France and you can by property next to me.' Vergor surrendered the place assigned to him with little resistance. He deserved death. His high protection saved him from this infamy. See above (p. 124).

16th September

Ordinary work. An escort was provided for the reapers who had gone out around Deux Rochers and said on their return that they had seen a barge and fresh tracks.

17th September

Ordinary work. The carpenters have begun the left casemate. M. de Sabrevois has returned with his detachment saying that he could not find any fresh tracks, nor any small establishments at Fort George.

18th September

The carpenters and renderers worked; the other workers rested. The reapers went out to the different places where the hay lay. Fishermen sent out but were not successful.

19th September

Ordinary work. Three regular soldiers deserted.

20th September

M. de Bourlamaque sent M. de Mazerac, captain of Béarn, with a detachment of sixty men to go and camp this evening at Deux-Rochers and tomorrow scout around the end of the bay and the River Chicot.

21st September

Work. The commander of Fort St-Frédéric wrote that two English who had escaped from Montréal had come in exhausted and starving, they said that there had been four of them and the two others continued their route. Some were sent to go into the woods and bring them to the general.

22nd September

Ordinary work. M. de Mazerac returned at midday and gave his account to the general that he made a tour of the bottom of the bay; that he went up the Chicot River and it appeared that the English would not be coming for a long time.

23rd September

Nothing of interest.

24th September

Two colony soldiers deserted.

25th September

The general embarked a detachment of Canadians from the end of portage with orders to go to Ganaouské Bay to lay an ambush on the road to Fort George to stop the deserters.

26th September

Worked. Foragers and cedar wood cutters went out. The flank angle of the powder magazine which links to the épaulement was marked out, a small ditch with palisades encircled this part.

27th September

Worked. We began raising the frames for the battlements to the left and putting in palisades.

28th September

Fifty boats arrived loaded with provisions.

29th September

The rest of the artillery went down and was shipped off.

30th September

The sick left.

1st October

Each battalion was ordered to make three hundred more palisades.

2nd October

The savages brought in a lot of game which they sold dearly.

3rd, 4th and 5th October

Ordinary work. The embrasures have started to be cut out.

6th October

At 6 o'clock in the evening several musket shots were heard fired from La Chute. M. de Barraute, captain of Béarn, commanded the guard and went to inform the general that the advance guard had been fired on by the Agnés who had wounded two sentinels. The general took to the field and reinforced the bivouac of the grenadiers with twenty more.

7th October

The grenadiers of the bivouac went to scout around La Chute. The general went there at 8 o'clock and learned that yesterday evening that eight musket shots had been fired on the forward post, who returned fire immediately from the entrenchment; that two men had been killed and their scalps taken. From the tracks, it was judged there were eight savages.

8th October

The number of workers was increased. M. de Raymond went to the end of the portage and put four bateaux into the water.

9th October

M. d'Oreillan [sic.], captain of Royal Roussillon, went with a detachment of fifty men to embark on Lake Saint-Sacrement to conduct an English captain, a woman and three soldiers who had been taken by the savages and who were recovering from their wounds.[87]

10th and 11th October

Ordinary work. The number of workers increased to four hundred. The battalions have received orders to make one hundred bundles of firewood each for the garrison.

12th October

M. d'Oreillan, returning with his detachment, reported that he had left the English [the wounded party mentioned on the 9th October] with a detachment from Fort Lydius and they immediately went their separate ways. The soldiers reported that there were a great number of vegetables in the gardens of the Fort George where there was still no English established.

87 Antoine Aureillan de Pradines was born in 1733 at Béziers and had been made a lieutenant in 1744 at only 11 years old. He was promoted captain in 1756 on coming to New France and was captured after the siege of Québec in 1759, indicating he was probably one of the wounded left behind in the city's hospitals. He retired from the army in 1768 and died in France in 1788.

13th October

The general went to the portage with a detachment of grenadiers, and ordered the removal of the bateaux and the guard which is posted there all day at the portage. The brick makers went back to Québec in two bateaux loaded with many effects.

14th October

The Agnés appeared three times last night in front of the post at La Chute. They tried to capture the sentinels but were received with musket fire. The general went to this post at 8 o'clock to reinforce it with some guns and increased the guard by twelve men. The Canadians went to the portage to fetch joists and beams.

15th October

The engineer charged with the direction of the works left for Québec. Four piquets of the regiments of La Reine, La Sarre and Languedoc, designated to form part of the garrison of the fort, arrived at 4 o'clock and camped on the plateau of the fort.

16th October

Bad weather suspended all work.

17th October

Ordinary work.

18th October

The patrol of grenadiers was fired on at the entrance to the woods by the Agnés who killed four and took their scalps and wounded three who retired. A large detachment was sent after them but could not find them. The second patrol brought back an Englishman who had been found in the woods coming from Montréal.

20th October

The general sent back the battalion of the Marine and Canadians of the three governments. At midday a company of grenadiers, three piquets and sixty Canadians embarked at midday to go to Deux Rochers and the bottom of the bay. The battalions worked at the fort and carried palisades and necessary wood.

21st October

The Béarn Regiment did not supply a guard. The general returned at 9 in the evening with a party of his detachment, very content with the reconnaissance of the bottom of the bay.

22nd October

The Béarn Regiment embarked in seventeen bateaux and left a piquet for the fort garrison. I left a half-hour after the regiment; I made a stop before Fort St-Frédéric and, hampered by a violent north east wind, I camped on the Pointe á la Peur, eight leagues from Carillon.

23rd October

I embarked at 7 o'clock. We had trouble rounding Rocher Fendu, where we had lunch. We stopped at 7 o'clock on the R. Sable to have supper. The wind calmed at 9 o'clock, we had re-embarked having rounded the islands of Quatre-Vents, au Chapon and de Velcourt.

24th October

We landed on the island of La Motte at 3 in the morning, and left at 4, having had a little sleep, rounding the Pointe au Fers, the Faucault Mill and arrived at Saint-Jean at 7 o'clock. I found the regiments of La Sarre and Languedoc, that of La Reine having left for Québec.

25th October

I left my boat to descend the rapids of Chambly and remounted it to go up to Montréal. I took up with a small detachment on the road to La Prairie by land which was very poor as almost all the grassland is flooded. I stopped a while at the mill on the Montréal River. I arrived at 3 o'clock at La Prairie and 4 at Montréal, where M. le chevalier de Lévis commanded in the absence of M. de Vaudreuil who is at Québec.

26th October

I worked on lodging the regiment.

27th October

I have been to La Prairie to see if the regiment has arrived there. I found two officers, to whom I gave the orders of M. de Lévis and I returned immediately to the town.

28th October

The regiment disembarked at 9 o'clock at the Pointe Saint-Charles, six companies left for Pointe Claire, Sainte-Anne and Sainte-Geneviève, the others have gone into the town and suburbs where they will be lodged.

29th and 30th October

Nothing of interest.

1st November

The ration of the soldiers has been reduced to a half-*livre* of bread, a *livre* of meat and a *quarteron* of peas [each]. M. le chevalier de Lévis has learned of an English fleet, which has come before Louisbourg, On the 22nd of September they were hit by a storm which flung them on the rocks, two hundred men escaped and were taken prisoner at Louisbourg.

5th November

I left to go and make a visit to our quarters which I found passable. They are stretched over half the island. Royal Roussillon is in quarters at La Prairie, Boucherville and Varennes. Guyenne occupies Chambly, Saint-Charles, Saint-Antoine, Saint-Denis; Saint-Ours, Sorel and Contrecœur; Languedoc in Trois-Rivières and some parishes of that township. The troops of the colony, the others; La Sarre, l'Ile Jesus, Terre-Bonne and l'Assomption; La Reine, Québec and Berry in its surrounding parishes.

7th November

M. le marquis de Vaudreuil arrived at Québec.

11th November

M. de Fleury received orders to go to Saint-Jean and take six bateaux to go and fetch flour from Carillon.

15th November

News from the *pays d'en haut*. The commandant of the Belle Riviére wrote that he had sent a party towards Fort Cumberland which was discovered because of a deserter. The commander of this fort sent out one hundred and fifty men to cut off their retreat and they lost a man killed and two wounded. The commandant of Détroit said his son, who was sent out commanding a war party, has been lost.

18th November

M. de Beletre, who left at the end of September with three hundred soldiers and Canadians has returned from an expedition against the borders of the Agnés with one hundred and fifty prisoners.[88] He reported that he had seized three forts and

88 The raid was to the upper part of the Hudson river, inhabited by the Agnés/Mohawk Indians. François-Marie Picoté de Belestre was born in 1716 and had been in the colony troops since at least 1738. He fought in Acadia but seemed to enjoy a position of respect in the far west, becoming commandant of Fort Saint-Joseph (Niles, Michigan). From 1749 to 1759 he also ran a fur trade business along with his military responsibilities. During the 1750's he was very active, first being commissioned to undertake a report on British incursion into the Ohio in 1751 around Pickawillaney. In 1756 he was raiding with Miami and Shawnee warriors into

burnt the village of Palatin, where his detachment took considerable booty and killed four hundred men.[89]

22nd November

M. de Fleury arrived from Carillon reported that around three hundred English had come with the aim of burning them out.[90] They could not overcome a guard of fifteen men, who were in a small retrenchment, commanded by a sergeant of Béarn named Aymet, that they only managed to burn the charcoal furnace, after which they retired, and that a soldier of Béarn was killed.

The soldiers ration was reduced to a half-*livre* of beef or otherwise horse although there is no lack of cattle, I cannot fathom what knavery caused this;[91] letters from Québec say that there they play ruinous games.[92]

Carolina taking some 300 prisoners. He was also present at the siege of William Henry in 1757. After this raid, he was promoted to command Fort Détroit. He remained there until surrendering it to Robert Rogers after the peace of 1760. After a brief spell in Europe he returned to Canada, pledging himself to the new regime and taking an active role in politics.

89 Palatin referrs to the village of Herkimer or German Flats, New York. The name Palatine comes from the middle Rhine area of Germany which is where the majority of the town had emigrated from. It always had a large store of merchandise and provisions as it was one of the most western points on the Mohawk River after the fall of Oswego. According to one report there was plenty of merchandise to be taken in the raid. Hamilton Child, 'History of German Flats, NY' in *Gazeteer and Business Directory of Herkimer County, NY* (Syracuse: H. Child, 1869).

90 Note by Gaffarel – A riot broke out at Fort Carillon following the shameless stealing of military subsistence. See the journal of Desandrouins: 'The exasperated soldiers resolved to kill their officers and deliver the fort to the English'. The riot was appeased by the energetic intervention of the commandant d'Hébécourt.

91 Note by Gaffarel – During September, the ration reduction was already exciting murmurs of discontent. By December, rebellion was threatening. Without Lévis, who harangued his grenadiers to set an example as if caught in a besieged city, serious disturbances could have erupted. See letter of Montcalm to Saint-Veran: 'Our troops have been and still live on, a half-pound of bread, three pounds of horse meat and one pound of cod. The people have only a quarteron of bread. At my house and those who dine there daily the bread ration is the same. There is trouble brewing with the people and the troops.... You can see that we are not without concern.' Also, see the journal of Desandrouins.

92 Note by Gaffarel – See this letter from Montcalm to the Minister of War (24 April 1757) 'I have found our officers indulging in games of chance. They did not play these in Montreal or Québec until the arrival of M. de Vaudreuil to Québec. M. Bigot loves gaming. M. de Vaudreuil has seen fit to allow M. Bigot to be a banker for the games. I say what I must but do not offer a defence. M. Maron, a captain in the regiment of La Reine, lost 12,000 Francs. This tolerance of the house of M. Bigot would have meant he would have continued to play, if I had not put the captain under arrest. I have not written to M. de Machault [Minister of Marine] as this would only serve to destroy the peace between M. de Vaudreuil, Bigot and myself; but I write to my minister to give account of my conduct.' A letter from commissary Doreil (28 February 1758): 'We played here in Québec, with the Intendant, up to Ash Wednesday, games to shake the bravest players. Bigot has lost more than 200,000 *livres*, at *quinze* [A precursor to 'vingt-et-un' or 'blackjack'], *passe-dix* [known as 'Passage' in English. A dice game], and *trente et quarante* [A card game in English 'thirty and forty' or sometimes 'Red and Black'].' Montcalm writing to the minister of war: 'Gambling is carried to excess with the Intendant, I have not written to the Minister of the Marine as I would avoid anything that

20th December

M. Vaudreuil sent out a detachment of one hundred Canadians and Savages.

looks like a complaint or reproach. The King has sent the ordnance of the 6th of August to M. de Vaudreuil which is reminiscent of the one from 1744 which warns off gambling and the requiring the colony to work together.' Journal of Desandrouins: 'The games were pushed above all to the last excess. I have seen bets of between 15 to 1,800 louis with loss and gain. The Intendant has lost 204,000 *livres* over the winter. Several officers have won prodigiously; others are lost and thoroughly ruined.'

4

The Year 1758

1758 saw the beginning of the end for New France. William Pitt was ascendant in British politics. He appointed a new commander in chief, General Amherst and unlocked the treasury, allowing large reinforcements to be sent to America. The capture of Louisbourg was still top priority and newly appointed Major General Jeffrey Amherst was sent to lead this expedition. General Abercromby would push up the Lake Champlain corridor towards Montreal, while Brigadier Forbes was to lead a third force against the Ohio. Despite the odds, Montcalm still managed to triumph in the miraculous defence of Fort Carillon against Abercromby, causing his army to retreat. Relations between Vaudreuil and Montcalm deteriorated to the point where both sent their own representatives to Versailles during the Autumn of this year. Vaudreuil sent Michel Péan to ask for Montcalm's recall.[1] *Montcalm sent Bougainville and Doreil asking for reinforcement and to petition for his promotion to supreme command of the armed forces, citing Vaudreuil's incompetence. Montcalm received his promotion in time for the 1759 campaign but received only four hundred new recruits.*

2nd January

A courier from Carillon informed us that the English, around the number of one hundred and fifty, had reappeared on the 24th of December and tried to set fire to the houses under the fort but were prevented from doing so by cannon fire; they spent 24 hours in the woods, killed fifteen cows and attached a letter to the head of one which read: 'I am obliged to you sir for the stay that you have let me make and the fresh meat you have sent me. I will take care of your prisoners. My compliments to M. de Montcalm. Signed: Roger, Commander of the Independent Companies'.[2]

1 See above (p. 56) for Péan's biography.

2 'Roger' was of course Robert Rogers. Born in 1731, Rogers garnered great renown during the Seven Years War but sealed his reputation with historians in the publication of his Journals in the 1760s. His reputation for the success of his company of Rangers seems to be over-exaggerated when looked at in balance. Undoubtedly a tough soldier, Rogers was not the originator of the ranging company idea although he did publish his 'Rules of Ranging' which was used as a staple of light infantry training. Rogers ended his life in poverty in London after running up debts.

18th January

A commissary of the *munitionnaire* left to go and make a visit to the magazines of [Forts St-] Frédéric and Carillon. A detachment of twenty-two men of the regular troops and some Canadians chosen from the populace were sent out to reinforce the Carillon garrison, as the commandant was not content.[3] He complained that the food was bad and he had not received the equipment promised. M. de Vaudreuil charged a captain of the colonial troops and the lieutenant-general of Montréal police to go and conduct a census of all wheat and other grain belonging to the government. The courier from Fort Duquesne said that all is tranquil on that frontier, that the savages baulk at going to war as they have not received many presents, the stores being empty.[4]

9th February

M. de Vaudreuil received letters from France by way of Louisbourg. The governor of that Isle informed him that he awaits the English to come early this year. The men charged with the letters have been on the road for two months. They passed over l'Ile Saint-Jean,[5] crossed Acadia, then re-embarked on part of the Saint-Jean River where they went up to Kamouraska, 40 leagues from Québec. They crossed all the rivers over ice.[6]

3 Note by Gaffarel – The soldiers were badly treated. A letter from Bougainville, 20 January 1758: Expatriates, lacking everything, not imagining this type of glory which one acquires by steeling oneself against all types of difficulties, hated, envied, always suffering from the climate, the country and habitants, we learn here to be patient.' Letter of Doreil from 26 February 1758: 'The people perish in misery; the Acadian refugees have eaten nothing but horse and hake for the past four months. Three hundred have died already. The people of Québec are always reduced, as are we, to a *quarteron* of bread per day and for meat are obliged to take half horse for six sols. Our soldiers have been on a half livre of bread per day since the 1st of November. They are given three livres of horse, three of beef, two livres of bread and two livres of hake for eight days, they take this with patience'.

4 Note by Gaffarel – The savages had been badly mistreated. See the journal of Desandrouin: 'Great agitation in the spirit of the savages of the upper country. All those people who had descended last year to besiege fort George have reported that small pox in their country has ravaged them. These suspicious people imagine that the French attracted them to fight just to spread the disease amongst them. On top of this is the bad feeling on the part of those fur traders and commanders of posts who find it impossible to give presents as they do ordinarily.' – 'The Choctaws, a powerful nation, seem very unhappy' – 'With a good commander in that country we could impose on the savages with our forces and content them with rich presents'.

5 Ile Saint-Jean was the French name for what is now Prince Edward Island, situated north of Acadia and west of the island of Cape Breton.

6 Note by Gaffarel – The winter of 1757/58 was very bad. The temperature fell to twenty-eight degrees below zero several times. From the journal of Desandrouins: 'We found eight or ten Acadiens, old and sick, frozen stiff in their beds due to a lack of wood, despite there being a contractor paid for by the King to supply it to them!'

14th February

The *commissaire* returned from Carillon saying he had found the food supplies in a good state in the two forts, that the English would not be coming for some time, that a great quantity of snow around the woods hampered all enterprises.

24th February

M. le marquis de Montcalm arrived at Québec with M. de Pontleroy, chief engineer, who came from Louisbourg.[7]

30th February[8]

A courier from Carillon apprised us that M. de Langis with the Iroquois had attacked two hundred men at the foot of Fort Lydius, who were screened by a detachment; he scattered them all, killing twenty-two men whose scalps were taken by the savages without losing a single man. M. de Vaudreuil has ordered a party of two hundred Canadians and savages to depart in the first days of March for Carillon, where they will try to capture some of the convoys which move between Sarastou [Saratoga] and Fort Lydius.

15th March

News from Carillon, telling the general of the return of M. Wolff who brought word of Fort Lydius.[9] This officer had been civilly received there. He saw Captain Rogers who jested that it was the last fresh meat he would eat before he returned. He responded that he should be on his guard because we had recently had our news from M. Langis. Four Outaouas attacked a small convoy then dispersed, killing four men, taking and plundering several sledges.

7 Nicolas Sarrebource de Pontleroy had been sent to serve as engineer at Louisbourg in 1755 after a nineteen-year career in Europe. After the death of Chaussegros de Léry in 1756 he was appointed chief engineer for the whole of New France over the governor's preferred candidate, Lotbinière. He immediately joined Montcalm's faction of metropolitan officers and as such encountered resistance from Lotbinière and Vaudreuil. They in turn complained of Pontleroy's conduct. One of his most significant reports must be that of his assessments of the upper town of Québec which he regarded as extremely poorly defended and not capable of withstanding a siege. His opinion could have been an influence on Montcalm's decision to march out with his army onto the Plains of Abraham in 1759.

8 The date is curious. 30 February does appear in Julian calendars but the French had been using the Gregorian calendar since the 16th Century. In the 18th Century the Swedes changed their calendar to have 30 days in February but it did not last. I have found no other reference to calendars used in New France. It could simply be a transcription error.

9 Note by Gaffarel – Lieutenant Wolff had been sent by Montcalm to General Loudoun to negotiate exchange of prisoners. The negotiation did not take place because of the pretext of unjust crimes committed by the savages after the taking of Fort William Henry.

19th March

A cadet detached from Carillon came to inform the general that two hundred men who recently arrived there left on the 12th; that same day an old *jongleur* announced that we would soon see the English;[10] that on the 13th, five savages who were scouting said they had seen the tracks of a detachment of two hundred men; the chiefs immediately gave out cries and left with all the savages and some of the French; they went close to three leagues without meeting anyone; doubting the English were coming up the road to la Chute, they retraced their steps to follow the same road as M. Durantaye, who, with the advance guard, met the enemy at Mount Pelée;[11] he was caught up in the first discharge which made his troops recoil a little; then M. Langis, who had returned with the greater part of the savages fell upon them and totally defeated them. The savages found a scalp in the road from an Englishman who would not give quarter and altogether took one hundred and forty-four scalps and we believe out of all this detachment only twelve men survived.[12]

23rd March

Some Abenakis left for Carillon.

28th March

The Iroquois arrived at Sault Saint-Louis. M. de Durantaye went to see the general and told him of the details of the affair of the 13th.

29th March

The wounded savages arrived at the Sault. M. le general sent for the surgeons.

31st March

The great chiefs at Sault came to hold council and speak of their afflictions with Onontio from the affair on the 13th when seven of their warriors had been killed and fifteen wounded. The general opened their ears and throats and wiped away their tears with many presents.[13]

10 A *jongleur* is a wandering minstrel, juggler or jester. Malartic uses the term here as a derisory noun for a Native American medicine man or shaman.

11 Durantaye was a colonial ensign under the orders of Langis during the Battle on Snowshoes. Bob Bearor, *The Battle on Snowshoes* (Bowie: Heritage Books, 2005), p. 22.

12 This became known as the 'Battle on Snowshoes', the second and more famous of two actions accorded that title. The British forces were under the command of Robert Rogers. Their retreat back to Fort Edward was one of great privation and on his return he assembled a rescue party to retrieve the wounded who could not make their own way back in the harsh wintery conditions. Bearor, *Battle on Snowshoes*, *passim*, & Stephen Brumwell, *White Devil*, (London: Orion, 2004), pp. 112-18.

13 Note by Gaffarel – Montcalm boasted to Moras, the Minister of the Marine, of how he had befriended the savages, 'Regarding the savages, I think I have entered into their thinking and

1st April

The savages were bored. At 9 o'clock in the evening we saw a great and extraordinary cloud, very white, which ran from east to north and took an hour to pass. We learned that the Acadians captured two hundred oxen and a bateau led by five Englishmen and missed a *chaloupe* loaded with food.[14]

2nd April

An officer of artillery charged with recording the state of the train which is at Saint-Jean, came here to return the account of his work.

3rd April

Two couriers from Carillon informed M. le general that M. Wolff had been with the Abenaki in the Boston area, but that he could not take any prisoners. He burnt two houses down and killed forty oxen. An English captain and lieutenant from the Blacney [sic.] regiment came into Carillon on the 19th, exhausted by hunger and fatigue, they had roamed for seven days in the woods without finding the road they had taken with Captain Rogers.[15] These officers believed that Lord Loudoun had left for London.[16]

5th April

The general dined with some savages, one of them assured him he had killed Captain Rogers, who gave him his writing case and a medal, which he left for the commandant of Carillon.

9th April

News from Niagara and Cataracoui where all is quiet.[17] It seems that the English are planning a great movement to break our alliance with the Five Nations and the Loups. The government of Philadelphia have held them at great councils, where they have given many pipes of peace, and forty *hausse-cols* of silver.[18] A chief of the Five

their manners. Maybe I should have more confidence in my success to my feeble talents; but at this moment, I venture to affirm that even in the *pays d'en haut*, my name alone gives the impression of an idol to those people. They consider me to be the war chief and chief of their cabins.' Letter of 19 February 1758.

14 Chaloupe is the French name for a sloop. 'A small vessel with one mast.' Falconer, *An Universal Dictionary of the Marine*, p. 290.

15 These were Captain-Lieutenant Henry Pringle and Lieutenant Boyle Roche of Blakeney's 27th Regiment of Foot. They were part of a group of eight who had volunteered from the 27th to go with Roger's raiding party. Brumwell, *White Devil*, p. 116.

16 Loudoun had been recalled by William Pitt and command passed to Abercromby, his second.

17 When writing of Cataracoui, Malartic is referring to the north shore Lake Ontario posts, including Fort Frontenac.

18 The hausse-col, or gorget, was the crescent shaped metal badge which denoted an officer in

Nations carried one of these *hausse-cols* to the commandant at Niagara. On it was a sun, a savage man and woman looking after a fire, and a savage smoking with an Englishman under a tree of peace. The chief went to go and lay an ambush with a party and eat the fresh meat of a convoy of cattle that the English were sending to the Loups of Thioga.

13th April

Some Iroquois went to see the general.

14th April

The rivers thawed and the main channel is flowing.

15th April

Some canoes arrived from the south.

17th April

Fifty pounds of beef for fifteen days was given to the soldiers and salt for preserving it. We killed many for this great quantity, there will be a lot wasted. It would have been better to give the troops horse meat.

18th April

News from Niagara announced that Colonel Johnson has held a great council with the Five Nations and said that the British were very sensitive to the loss of Palatine where matters were poor, that they had found a way to reduce Canada preventing food and aid from reaching there, that we will die of hunger, because although last autumn they captured many ships loaded with relief, this would not compensate them for the losses before Louisbourg. At the end of the council, the colonel wished to go to all the villages to give presents but he was deterred by two Onontaguès [Onondagas] who persuaded him that Ononthio came with his warriors. The Agnès sent their responses of necklaces that the Iroquois there had given, they promised to observe and exact neutrality, and invited to come to a grand council to be held at the Grande Cabanne.[19]

---

most eighteenth century European armies. The name and shape derived from the old collar piece of armour to protect the neck. Native Americans liked these badges and they were popular trade items and gifts.

19 Likely to be Onondaga which was the village of the central tribe of the Iroquois and their seat of government. See Francis Jennings, *The History and Culture of Iroquois Diplomacy: An Interdisciplinary Guide to the Treaties of the Six Nations and Their League*, (New York: Syracuse University Press, 1985), p. 221.

22nd April

M. le general sent a courier by *goelette* to France. Some Iroquois, Nippisingués and Algonkins set out to avenge the death of a savage recently killed.

24th April

M. de Chabert left with some officers for Niagara, where he will be ambassador with the Five Nations; he is followed by a commissary of the *munitionnaire* charged with visiting the magazines of all the forts to see the state of them and their supplies.[20]

26th April

A detachment of workers left for Carillon.

27th April

News from Saint-Jean. The barque which was constructed over winter has been launched onto the water. She will be continually responsible for carrying effects for Carillon.

2nd May

News from Cataracoui and from Carillon. The former told of an Onontaguè who came from Orange and met a party of English that wanted to kill him, he was saved by someone in the party, who assured [him] that he was from the Five Nations, that he complained to the commandant of Orange who responded that the English are determined to avenge the daily betrayals by the Five Nations. News from Carillon announced the return of M. Langis, who came down the road driving a convoy of two hundred carts but he had not been able to capture a single prisoner.

20 Note by Gaffarel – This investigation, though necessary, was not taken seriously because it was led by the very people who had an interest in hiding all wrongdoing, Intendant Bigot and his accomplices Péan, Breard, Varni, Estèbe, Cadet. From their trial instituted in 1763, Bigot and his associates were revealed to be part of several societies organized to steal from the state; such as the Gradis house of Bordeaux (act of 10 July, 1748), and the house of Claverie Québec, known as the Friponne. In addition, they exaggerated their memories, and duplicated the numbers of the states of rations; as they gained falsely from these 250 per 100. See also the letter from Montcalm dated 4 November 1757 addressed to Belle-Isle, minister of war. 'Greed won over the officers, storekeepers and clerks around Ohio or who go to the savages in the upper country. They make astonishing fortunes. An officer engaged here for twenty years as a soldier made 700,000 livres. False certificates are also accepted. If the savages had a quarter of what we spent on them I would assume the King would hold all of America, and the English.... I believe would all hasten to make their fortune before the loss of their colonies, several welcoming it as an impenetrable veil to their conduct.'

3rd May

The courier from Québec told us that on his departure he was not aware of any ships on the river. An officer of artillery left with twenty-five bateaux loaded with food, munitions and merchandise for the forts of Frontenac, Niagara, and Belle Riviére. This officer is responsible for reinforcing the fortifications at Niagara.

5th May

A courier was sent carrying orders for the regiments of La Reine and Berry to form piquets from their soldiers as the habitants can no longer feed and send them to Carillon.

7th May

The courier from Québec informed us that in the town they are running short of many things.[21]

10th May

News from Présentation, this told of eighty-four savages from the village who had been around Korlak and taken forty-six scalps and three prisoners, that one of the Iroquois was killed and an Onontaguè wounded. The prisoners said that a fort is being built at the Palatine village.

12th May

The courier from Québec told us they were in great misery.[22]

15th May

The savages of Présentation arrived here with their prisoner. A courier recently sent from Fort St-Frédéric by the commander informed the general that four men of this

21 Note by Gaffarel – Fragment of a letter to the Minister by M. Daine, in the first days of May. 'There is nothing sadder and more distressing than the current situation of the colony. Having spent part of the autumn and last winter on a quarter livre of bread a day for each person, we have been reduced to two *onces* for the last six weeks. All resources are exhausted, and we are on the verge of being wiped out by the cruellest starvation if help does not arrive in a fortnight. Words fail me to describe our misfortunes. Animals begin to fail; butchers cannot provide a quarter of the beef necessary for the subsistence of the habitants of the city; we are without poultry, without sheep, without calves and without vegetables.'

22 Note by Gaffarel – A Letter from Lévis to Marshal Mirepoix (26 June): 'We just spent a miserable winter due to lack of food. The colony was reduced to only having half a livre of bread a day and eating horse. We had great difficulty in restraining the people to reduce them to this kind of life. In my own case, it took a great deal of firmness with the troops to prevent a revolt.'

garrison were taken by the Agnés and a party of English and defeated seventeen men from Carillon, who were in a bateau.

16th May

A cadet detached from Carillon to conduct two English prisoners that M. de Langis had taken on the Boston road, told us that the commandant of Carillon being in need of wood to cover a warehouse, had scouted the banks of the River Pendu, the next day he sent out a detachment of forty-five men in three bateaux. One of the three, carrying seventeen men, was fired on while approaching land by forty English and savages. The two others were badly placed to return fire and received orders to return to the fort. A worker and soldier of the colony who were out hunting were taken prisoner, despite their precautions.

News from all the posts of the country. All remain tranquil. At Fort Duquesne supplies for Illinois are waiting. The commandant of Détroit is dying. The Five Nations are rarely at Niagara, not finding the commander agreeable to them. There are stirrings of discontent against us with the savages of St-Jospeh,[23] the Miamis and the Ouias. The Folle Avoines have killed eleven Frenchmen at the bay but missed the commander and pillaged the magazine. The commandant died at Michillimakinak, many of the savages had small pox. The English do what they can to persuade them that we have given them this disease to destroy them. The commandant of Louisiana tells that he has had no news from France for two years, he is very troubled to satisfy the savage nations having nothing to give to them.

18th May

A courier was sent with orders for the *pays d'en haut*. A negotiator left with four canoes for Détroit. The general sent orders to remain at St-Jean.

19th May

Thirty Nippisingués who were going to leave for Carillon, went to see the general to sing the war song with him.

20th May

Some savages of Présentation and the Five Nations held council with the general. They warned that half of their brothers were in favour of us while the other half the English; that it would be easy to win them back with gifts of food and goods. There is a rumour that four English barges entered Lake Champlain. The Nippisingués and Algonkins crossed the river to meet them.

23 The mission of Saint-Joseph was at the extreme meridian of Lake Michigan.

22nd May

News from France. We learned that a frigate and eight merchant vessels moored on the 19th before Québec; they set out with twelve ships from Bordeaux; they were separated by a great sandbank; they captured an English ship who told them they had been scouting M. de Boissier [sic. Beaussier] with five ships of the line a league from Louisbourg.

24th May

The La Reine Regiment arrived at Chambly and received orders to return to Carillon.

25th May

A courier from Québec told us that two ships from Louisbourg had arrived loaded with food. The letters from that place said that a battalion of the Cambis Regiment and one of the Volontaires Étrangers had arrived;[24] that M. Desgouttes is in port with five ships and three frigates; that the next day eight English vessels appeared in sight of the island.[25]

26th May

A courier from Québec announced the arrival of two vessels. One was from the first division, the other of the second. The one from the first was sent out from Brest but the ship which accompanied it was forced to stop to resupply. That of the second reported that its division was attacked by five corsairs;[26] that the frigate charged with escort duty gave the signal '*sauve-qui-peut*' [every man for himself], and went in to attack the biggest; that he saw the sailors of the other three ships ignore the plight of the others.

27th May

A courier from Carillon carried to the general dispatches from Alberkombrik [Abercromby]. They were given to M. d'Hébécourt, commandant at Carillon, by a detachment of fifty Englishmen who said that their commander had an army at

24 The Cambis Regiment had been engaged in seizing Minorca from the British in 1756 and after a brief respite in Brittany the second battalion was sent out to Louisbourg at a strength of 599 officers and men. After the fall of Louisbourg the soldiers and officers were held prisoner in Tavistock, Devon. The second battalion of Volontaires Étrangers, or Foreign Volunteers, embarked with Cambis for Louisbourg under the command of Henri-Valentin Jacquot d'Anthonay. They were mainly composed of German recruits and had an initial strength of 708 men. Fournier, *Combattre*, pp. 68-9 & 88-9.

25 Jean-Antoine Charry, marquis Desgouttes, was Captain of the *Prudent* and commander of the French naval squadron stationed at Louisbourg since 24 April. He would remain naval commander during the siege of Louisbourg in this year. Johnathan R. Dull, *The French Navy and the Seven Years War* (Lincoln and London: University of Nebraska Press, 2005), pp. 105-6.

26 Used here in the sense of a privateer.

Halifax;[27] a normal garrison at Fort Lydius with a Scottish regiment; that Captain Rogers had not been killed and that it was he who took four men of Fort St-Frédéric; that the seventeen from Carillon were taken by the Five Nations, who killed seven and led ten to Fort Lydius, two of whom were wounded. The English general proposed an exchange of Colonel Schuler and M. Martin for six cadets or Canadians.[28]

29th May

News from the Belle Riviére. The commandant of Fort Duquesne says that the Katibas have killed a man and taken two prisoners from the garrison; that the Loups have retaliated by bringing him one hundred and forty scalps of prisoners and then sent out more than one hundred savages to war in different parties.

30th May

The courier from Québec tells us that the vessel *Le Lion* is wrecked on l'Isle aux Barques and that smaller boats have been sent out to save her cargo of flour and bacon.

1st June

M. de Langis, who arrived from Carillon, said he was not able to take a prisoner on his last scout. That the English had a small camp at Fort Lydius and around the river at Orange for the security of the convoys.

2nd June

We learnt from Carillon that M. Outelas,[29] with thirty Algonkins and Nippisingués, discovered the tracks of an English detachment which had come up the right bank of Lake Champlain; that they came caught up with them and killed two English, two savages, took nine prisoners and had no one killed or injured. The news from Québec announced that the vessel *Zélindor* has grounded at Sault de Cochon, it

---

27 The army at Halifax was under the command of Jeffrey Amherst and included James Wolfe amongst the men who would go on to besiege Louisbourg. Abercromby was assembling an army much larger than any America had seen before to strike against Fort Carillon: the dispatches mentioned here could have been deliberately leaked to reassure the French that there would be no great effort to strike up the Lake Champlain corridor. d'Hébécourt was a captain of La Reine and had been commandant at Carillon since 1756. Born in 1724 he resigned in 1765.

28 Colonel Peter Schuyler was the officer of the New Jersey provincial regiment and had been held by the French since his capture at the siege of Oswego in 1756. He was a well-liked commander and concerned himself with looking after fellow prisoners and gathering military intelligence.

29 Outelas was an ensign in the colony troops. Archives National d'Outre-mer, *Officiers Militaires et Civils en Service au Canada: Matricules (1692/1776)*, R ANOM COL D2C 59, Folio 54.

touched the bottom several times and lost its rudder. Fifty sailors have been sent out to retrieve its cargo.

3rd June

We learnt of the arrival of the frigate *Judith* which had taken two English ships at the Grand Bank.[30] The sailors said that a large French ship loaded with troops was lost with all hands on *Terre-Neuve* [Newfoundland].[31]

4th June

The general held a council with the Algonquin and the Nippisingués, urging them to go and strike some blows against the Fort Lydius frontier and return in twenty-five days, telling them he will need them for an important expedition. M. Outelas arrived with his prisoners; the Iroquois would have killed them had they not been prevented. The general warmly embraced Kisentsk, a famous chief savage.[32]

5th June

Seven companies of Béarn who had been in the town went to go into camp, four at Saint-Gabriel with a piquet of the Marine and three around the mill at La Chine to work on the road which is very bad. M. de Bourlamaque has arrived from Québec.

6th, 7th, 8th and 9th June

Was spent working on the roads which employed two hundred men.

10th June

I was at La Chine. I found too much work for the number of workers.

---

30 Johnathan Dull notes that a frigate *le Bizarre* had set sail from Brest on 21 April accompanied by two other frigates and become separated. After reaching Louisbourg and finding the British fleet in the area she went to Quebec instead, returning to France that autumn and capturing a dozen prizes on the return trip, including a British frigate. There seems to be no reference to a ship called the *Judith* and so perhaps Malartic was misinformed and this was the vessel but it cannot be certain. Dull, *French Navy*, p. 106.

31 The Grand Banks of Newfoundland mark the underwater plateaus of the continental shelf.

32 More commonly called Kisensik, he was a chief of the Nipissings of the Lac des Deux Montagnes/Kanesetake. He referred to himself as a 'domiciled' Indian in a speech he delivered to tribes from the *pays d'en haut*. His village was located at the confluence of the Ottawa and Saint-Lawrence rivers near Montreal. Originally a Sulpician mission, it housed Mohawks as well as Nipissings and other Algonquians. From limited evidence it seems clear that Kisensik took part in the French campaigns of 1756-58. See D. Peter MacLeod, *The Canadian Iroquois and the Seven Years War*, (Toronto: Dundern, 2012), pp. 99-100.

13th June

Savages of different nations have come to see the general who engaged them to go out to take prisoners from Fort Lydius.

14th June

Some voyageurs arrived from Cèdres saying they had found tracks of a party of thirty men.[33] Some officers have left to go up the Sault des Sauvages and search for this party.

16th June

We learned of the arrival of the vessel *Le Rhinocheros* which left a three-mast ship at Kamouraska.[34]

17th June

The courier from Carillon said that a detachment had been sent out in pursuit of a deserter and reconnoitre an English party. M. de Lusignan [commander of Fort St-Frédéric] informed that this party had fired some musket shots against his fort.

18th June

The La Sarre Regiment left for Carillon; the seven companies of Béarn camped at La Chine and at Saint-Gabriel returned to occupy their lodgings. The six companies housed on the island came to camp under the town.

19th June

Worked on the embarkation of Béarn. The news from Carillon was that Captain Rogers approached the Falls with a detachment of thirty-five men, that the savages sent to intercept him killed half of them and took two prisoners. The preparations and movements necessary for the departure of M. le chevalier de Lévis were hurried along as he must go with a considerable body of the Five Nations and together make an important expedition.[35] From Fort Duquesne we learned that the Katawbas

33 Voyageurs were those who transported furs along the rivers of the *pays d'en haut* from Indian suppliers back to the fur trade hub of Montreal. The term also infers that the voyageur is an employee of a licensed fur trading company rather than the entrepreneurial, independent, *coureur de bois*. See Carolyn Podruchny, *Making the Voyageur World: Travellers and Traders in the North American Fur Trade*, (Lincoln: University of Nebraska Press, 2006).

34 The *Rhinoceros* was a *flûte*, carrying 12 guns. Constructed in 1751 it was captured in October 1758 by the *Isis*.

35 Note by Gaffarel – Vaudreuil concluded that the English would attack Carillon and wanted to make a diversionary attack on Lake Ontario. Lévis was responsible for this delicate operation, which had the triple purposes of bringing the Iroquois into closer alliance [this land belonged to the Iroquois and would mean the French could claim to be liberating them from

surprised some Canadians while they were cutting wood, mortally wounding one who did however break the leg of a savage who was trying to take the scalp of one of the other Canadians, those who had fled returned at their cries and took the scalp of a savage and brought the wounded back to the fort; a convoy from Illinois escorted by six hundred men arrived there [Duquesne]. The testimony of prisoners say that the English have left for Louisbourg with a considerable fleet, that they have five thousand at Fort Lydius and they have three hundred waiting to go and camp at the edge of Lake Saint-Sacrement.

20th June

A courier from Québec told us of the arrival of the ship, *La Valeur* which had left another at the entrance of the river.[36]

The Béarn Regiment embarked in twenty bateaux to go to Carillon and up the River Chambly. They left a detachment of sixty-one men for M. le chevalier de Lévis' expedition who was camped at Vercher seven leagues away.[37]

21st June

Bad weather. The regiment embarked at eight o'clock suffering several thunderstorms before entering the River Chambly and camping before Sorel, eight leagues away.

22nd June

We embarked at 5 o'clock, made a halt at Saint-Ours and camped at Saint-Antoine at 5 o'clock.

23rd June

We passed before Saint-Charles-Bel-Œil and camped at the entrance of the basin of Chambly, making eight leagues.

English interference], it would prevent the restoration of Fort Oswego and worry the flank of Abercromby's army. 800 soldiers and 2,200 Canadians were entrusted with this but were rapidly recalled with the news that the English were already in our lines. – Letters of Lévis to comte d'Argenson (2 July) and comte de Belle-Isle (4 July).

36 *La Valeur* was a sixth-rate frigate of 24 guns. Constructed at Rochefort, it was captured by the *Lively* in 1759 and brought into British service where it fought in an action off Cuba in 1760.

37 This journey (which took until the 24 of June to reach the rapids at Fort Chambly) shows the importance of using bateaux to transport troops and material and the dependence on good navigable rivers. Boats had to travel north up the Saint-Lawrence to Sorel and then double back to enter the Richelieu River (which Malartic calls Chambly River here) to be able to travel south to Chambly. See Map 5.

24th June

Despite very bad weather, we came to Chambly at 6 o'clock in the morning, making a portage of the equipment, leaving those bateaux at Chambly and taking others at Sainte-Thérèse and arrived at Saint-Jean at 4 o'clock.

25th June

We took supplies for six days, blessed the *drapeaux* and embarked at noon in twenty-seven bateaux and camped on the prairie at Boileau at 4 o'clock.[38]

26th June

We embarked at day break, made a halt at Faucault Mill and camped in the bay of Roches-Noires. We passed many bateaux coming from Carillon, the pilots urged us to be diligent as we await the enemy.

27th June

Embarked at day break and rounded the Isle au Chapon despite a great wind and camped at l'Anse aux Gravois at 11 o'clock.

28th June

A strong south-west wind delayed our departure until midday. We could not camp at Rocher Fendu because the bateaux would not have been safe there. At 6 o'clock we entered l'Anse à la Bouteille [Isle aux Boiteux on Map 3] on the right bank at 7 o'clock.

29th June

Some bateaux which we left behind caught up at six o'clock at l'Anse a la Barque, made a stop at the first houses of Fort St-Frédéric and despite a contrary wind rounded the peninsula at half past six.[39]

30th June

Left at daybreak, arriving at Carillon at 8 o'clock and camped at the edge of the River Chute. M. le marquis de Montcalm arrived at 2 o'clock with the officers of the *Corps Royal de Artillerie.*

38 *Drapeaux*: the colours or flags of the battalion.

39 I have been unable to locate either Roches-Noires, Gravois or l'Anse a la Barque on the route to Fort St-Frédéric.

1st July

The army was mobilised at 5 o'clock, the regiments of La Reine, Guyenne and Béarn went to camp at the head of the portage, La Sarre and Languedoc on the left bank of the River Chute, and [Royal] Rousillon and the 2nd battalion of Berry, between Fort Carillon and the redoubt and the 1st battalion of Berry inside the fort.[40] The troops were occupied throughout the day establishing the camps and portaging equipment. Some savages who arrived from scouting said that the English are making a road which links to that [road] of the Agnés which goes around the reverse of Mount Pelée. M de Langis who came by the same route, reported to the contrary. A detachment of thirty men were embarked in two barges to scout out the lake.

2nd July

Some musket shots fired in front of Béarn's camp caused them to take up arms and make ready to march forward; when the captain of the guard was called for, he sent a report that his lieutenant, detached with six men, discovered a feather while searching for his sabre. When a musket was fired at him by a savage, the lieutenant promptly retired behind a tree, the savage was ready to pounce on him. The officer could not stop him as a blow from the musket caused him to fall to the ground, the savage then proceeded to take him prisoner when he heard cries: 'To me, volunteers!' who rushed to him on hearing the savage's cries. M. Bourlamaque came to camp behind the La Reine Regiment and went to scout the mountains which border the left of the camp. Ammunition was carted and there was much portaging of artillery equipment. M. de Montcalm established himself at the La Chute camp. Two companies of volunteers were formed of one hundred men, from each of the eight battalions, one was commanded by M. Bernard, of Béarn, and the other by M. Duprat of the La Sarre Regiment.[41]

3rd July

The barge sent out scouting returned seeing nothing new. The large guard post between the lake and mountain was reduced to seventy men. Food was fetched for Carillon. Wood was collected to build a bakery. M. Raymond arrived with one hundred and eighteen Canadians and colony soldiers. M. Mercier arriving from Montréal, told us that M. le chevalier de Lévis was on the march to join us, that there are some warships and merchantmen on the river, come out of Louisbourg since the British landing.[42] A drunk Abenaki has slain a comrade and left.

---

40 The Berry regiment had sent its 2nd and 3rd battalions to New France the previous year (see entry of 22 July 1757, p. 128). Malartic's numbering probably refers to their seniority i.e. he terms the 2nd battalion as the 1st and the 3rd battalion as the 2nd.

41 Jean-Baptiste Duprat had risen from the ranks. Born in 1718, he first volunteered in the Regiment du Roi in 1736. He was made an officer in 1745 and received his company in 1754. He died, presumably of wounds sustained during the battle of Sainte-Foy, in the General Hospital of Québec on 28 April 1760.

42 Louisbourg had been besieged for over a month. An unstoppable British fleet left Halifax on

4th July

M. Bernard went to scout with a party of his company on the right bank of the lake, but found no tracks. A small retrenchment was begun to cover the head of the bridge of the Petit Rapide. M. de Montcalm went to the camp at the portage. M. de Raymond camped beyond the bridge. M. de Langis embarked with one hundred and twenty-eight volunteers at 7 o'clock to find out what is happening at Fort George.

5th July

Ordinary service. Some munitions were portaged. At 3 o'clock in the afternoon, a musket shot was heard from the mountains on the left of the camp and a white flag was seen rising and falling, which is the signal given by the lieutenant of the guard to warn of a sighting of barges or bateaux on the lake. A 4 o'clock a party of M. Langis' detachment returned. The officer commanding reported that they had left that morning from Ganaouské Bay and had been spotted at Fort George, sixty barges were sent out after them, initially pursuing them quickly but then slowing; then M. de Langis stopped with some of his canoes to observe. M. de Bourlamaque immediately sent out M. de Trepézac, captain of Béarn, with three piquets and one hundred volunteers to go to Mount Pelée to discover the movements of the enemy and prevent them from landing in these parts. M. de Langis arrived and then followed them. M. Germain, captain of La Reine, was sent out at 5 o'clock with three piquets between the mountain and the lake to support our outposts and impede the enemy establishing these parts.[43] All the troops were ordered to be very alert and be ready at first notice. Three barges were sent out scouting.

6th July

At one o'clock in the morning, a dozen musket shots were heard from the outposts. The troops ran to their arms. A quarter of an hour later, they received orders to return [to camp]. We learned that the enemy savages had fired on a corporal, named Parisien, of Béarn and his men who they wished to capture; they were repulsed with musketry but had already collared the corporal and sentinel. Today we saw the signal flag fall and rise and we perceived many barges travelling north to south searching out a place to land. The scouting barge came back reporting the same. M. Germain returned at 7 o'clock. M. de Bourlamaque ordered work on portaging equipment, having received no news from M. de Trepézac; he gave the order to be on the defensive and burn any equipment which could not be taken away and he put the brigade in a reverse column of march; the grenadiers and volunteers to be the rear-guard who pulled back after receiving a few shots from the approaching barges. The brigade arrived at the La Chute at 9 o'clock and went ahead of the two brigades who

28 May and reached Louisbourg by 2 June. A beachhead was established by 8 June. By this time the town was under regular bombardment and would resist until the end of July. René Chartrand, *Louisbourg 1758: Wolfe's First Siege,* (Oxford: Osprey, 2000), pp. 48-65.

43 François-Joseph de Germain was born in Montpellier, 1717. He had served as the commandant of Port-Louis and Lorient in Brittany. After the war he was made a baron.

were in line on the two banks of the river and stopped at the right of La Sarre, at the foot of the heights where they rested. Bateaux from Carillon were sent for to take the baggage which was wearisome to the soldiers. At 4 o'clock we heard gunfire which we judged came from the detachment of Trepézac and the English. The general was tempted to march to his rescue. A quarter of an hour later, some soldiers from that detachment arrived saying that M. de Langis, who guided them, was lost and had not been able to find the right road for 3 hours. They then endeavoured to cross the Chute River, by way of a small island, but the first who attempted it found the water too deep so went ahead to find a better crossing. When the re-entered the woods they came under several volleys of musketry from a considerable enemy detachment; nearly fifty men fled in all directions;[44] M. de Trepézac was mortally wounded, and from that number two other officers, all the others were killed or captured. At half past 5 o'clock, the army moved out to return to Carillon, where it arrived at 7 o'clock and formed a line at the start of the desert and spent the night in bivouac.[45] The English army disembarked at the Portage with 1,500 barges.

7th July

The *généralle* was beaten on this day. Some regiments went to take their food. The three brigades went to hold the entrance to the woods. They began an abatis and worked throughout the day with incredible energy. This abatis covered all the land between the River Chute and goes up to the woods to the rear which border Lake Champlain.[46] At 5 o'clock in the evening, M. de Bourlamaque spaced seven battal-

44 This action was particularly confused on both sides. The British army under General Abercromby was extremely close to Trepézac's advance party of 350 men. His second in command, Viscount Howe, resolved to sweep the French away with his advance guard of Rangers who had managed to cut off the retreat of the French. However, despite the British successes in killing and capturing most of the French forces, the popular Lord Howe was killed in the action which seeded confusion amongst the army as they imagined the whole of the French army surrounding them. George Augustus Viscount Howe had come to America as colonel of the 60th Royal Americans in 1757. By the end of that year he was appointed to the 55th Foot and made brigadier general. He perceived the value in training light infantry skills to the regulars and was popular with both men and officers. René Chartrand, *Ticonderoga 1758: Montcalm's Victory Against all Odds*, (Oxford: Osprey, 2000), pp. 18 & 37-45.

45 By 'desert' Malartic is probably referring to the wide expanse of clear ground that had been cut down to allow a good field of fire from the defences.

46 Note by Gaffarel – The importance of this position was signalled by a young officer of the Carillon garrison, d'Hugues. On 1 May 1758 he prepared a detailed memorandum for the engineers who were charged by Montcalm to organise the defence and had the good sense to follow the instructions. He wrote, 'To take Carillon the enemy must first seize the heights. It is therefore essential to defend them, and a general wishing to prevent a siege must make a good entrenchment. This entrenchment should be made of stacked tree trunks and staked with sharpened seasoned branches, well pruned and interlaced. All approaches should be impeded by abatis of wood to a distance of 100 *toises*. This retrenchment should be able to be perfected in two times 24 hours and can be well guarded by 6000 men. It will cost a lot of men to overcome it and if it is well defended would not be overcome by an army three times larger than the besieged.' From the journal of Desandrouins, 'these entrenchments were made of logs laid one on top of the other parallel to the ditch. The earth of the ditch was made into a parapet and arranged in such a manner that musket shots could pass over the traverse. On

ions equally along the abatis and they were each given one hundred and twenty seven paces to guard; he permitted some tents to be held at the rear for lighting cooking fires; he ordered them to sleep in camp, the guards at the edge of the abatis to make frequent patrols outside and light great fires there. 300 soldiers of the colony and Canadians were posted to the woods of the reserve. The piquets who had remained at Montréal to embark with M. le chevalier de Lévis arrived at 5 o'clock and at 7 were placed at the rear of their battalions with the volunteers.[47]

8th July

The *généralle* was beaten long before daylight. M. le chevalier de Lévis arrived with M. de Senezergues at 5 in the morning.[48] Each battalion worked on their ground. The guards and grenadiers were posted at one hundred and fifty paces in front of the abatis to cover the workers. At 9 o'clock we discovered many on the summit and bottom of the mountain which is on the right bank of the Chute River, where they fired on our left flank. The volunteers of Bernard posted in the woods on the left bank responded similarly.[49] We guessed that the enemy general used them to scout our position. The chevalier Darenis, lieutenant of the volunteers, suffered a broken arm. Our generals visited the abatis and found it to be in a good state of defence. At midday the regiments of La Reine and Béarn began to build up some epaulements, to provide cover to enfilade some of the heights, when we began to hear a lot of shots fired from our left. A moment later, on the centre and then on our right. A cannon fired from the fort signalled us to convene for the beginning of the attack and sent each man to their post. The grenadiers and guard retired without losing a single man. The battalions lined the abatis three deep, with their grenadiers and piquet behind them to shore up places which needed support.[50] The La Sarre Brigade responded with a good discharge on a column which presented itself in front of them. Those of Royal Roussillon fired at two who came at the centre and La Reine and Béarn at

front of the entrenchment was a great quantity of tree branches, sharpened at their ends and interlaced in the manner of a *chevaux de frise*.'

47 Gaffarel notes that these piquets were 400 elite men of the Béarn Regiment under the orders of Captain Pouchot. However, 400 men would imply almost the whole battalion so this statement should be treated with scepticism.

48 The French army numbered around 4,200 men. Only fifteen natives remained with the army, in stark contrast to the 1757 campaign. The British army vastly outnumbered them with 5,825 regulars and 11,775 auxiliaries and provincials, also including 400 Mohawks under Sir William Johnson bringing the total to around 17,600 men. Chartrand, *Ticonderoga 1758*, p. 29.

49 Malartic forgot to mention the volunteers of Duprat. They defended the left with the regiments of La Sarre and Languedoc.

50 Note by Gaffarel – The entrenchments were worked on until the last minute. See the journal of Desandrouins, 'Throughout the day I was occupied in animating the soldiers work, explaining how to arrange the trees and branches, and especially to give the old soldiers the impression of the excellence of our position as both flanks are supported by two escarpments and despite the contours of the works have only 300 *toises* of frontage to cover. They listened attentively to these points and took much confidence.'

a fourth which came of the right.[51] Many barges came up the Chute River to land troops to turn our left. M. de Poularies, captain of grenadiers of Royal Roussillon, went down with his company and volunteers of Béarn to the river banks to fire on them. Some volleys of cannon were fired from the fort which sank two barges. The others went back down the river and did not return.[52] Fire was lively from both sides. Our soldiers were so fixed to their places that I could not find two to fetch cartridges when we began to run low.[53] I was obliged to order two sergeants of distinction named Radurel and Saint-Antoine to follow me to fetch a case of cartridges I had set aside. We carried it between the three of us, distributing them around the field. We were fortunate enough to not be struck by many of the musket balls which hit the ground in abundance as we travelled. Two minutes after we had finished the distribution, I carried an order from the general to M. le chevalier de Lévis and while at his side was hit by a shot which pierced the bend of my left knee. I tried in vain to get up; I had to be lifted and carried to the hospital. The attack and defence continued with equal valour; the enemy columns, though refreshed with reinforcements and frequently coming together to make joint efforts, sometimes on the right, the centre or the left, could not advance more than ten paces, finding in all parts vigorous resistance by the soldiers who fired while aiming and with speed and the general posting the piquets and grenadiers where they were needed.[54] M. le chevalier de Lévis moved the La Reine Regiment behind that of Guyenne, where the enemy seemed to be making more progress;[55] He stopped and ordered the Canadians in to make a sortie out into the woods behind the fort, to worry the left flank of the enemy. At half past five, their fire began to slow down. We sent out some soldiers who took some prisoners. At 6 o'clock they made a new attempt which failed worse than the first. They began their retreat at 7 o'clock, leaving their best troops behind

---

51 A battalion of the Berry regiment was also posted in the centre, though not mentioned here. See Chartrand, *Ticonderoga 1758*, pp. 78-9.

52 Note by Gaffarel – These boats were transports which had come up Lake George the night before by force of arms. They were intended to make a diversion on the left of the hillock and support the assault columns.

53 Note by Gaffarel – The orders of the day, prepared by Montcalm before the battle, specifically address that, 'When there is some order to be passed on during the attack, or any request to be made, they will only be carried by one officer of each battalion that the battalion commander will send for.'

54 Note by Gaffarel – Abercromby, unable to be persuaded that an enemy so inferior in numbers could put up so much resistance, repeated his attack six times. They were all repulsed with losses. From the Journal of Desandrouins: 'I have never witnessed more coolness and bravery in my life than on this day by those soldiers. I witnessed no one firing without first aiming at his man and most waited, often quite a long time to see a marksman appear, stationed behind a tree stump so as not to miss, though bullets rained down as thick as hail.' The savages said later that the French were "all guns." In fact, says Desandrouins, each soldier fired between 70 and 80 shots. 'So we were forced to change a quantity of guns during the action.'

55 Note by Gaffarel – A strange incident almost compromised all of this. Captain Bassignal, of Royal Rousillon, amused himself by floating a red handkerchief on the end of a musket. The English took the sign for a flag of truce and ran to the entrenchment holding their muskets above their heads and crying for quarter. The French believing the English wanted to retreat, went up on the parapet to receive them. Fortunately Captain Pouchot realised this wrong move and ordered a firing line that repulsed nearly three hundred attackers.

to protect them; fatigue and our small number of troops prevented our generals giving them any trouble. They made a firing retreat, and we saw that sweeping fire came from some hidden behind trees, who waited for nightfall to retire.

It is believed the loss of the English was very significant from this day and from the 6th.[56] Five hundred men killed or wounded including thirty-eight officers. From the regiment of Béarn, M. Pons, a lieutenant, and Doué, an ensign, killed; Montgay, captain and Malartic, captain *aide-major*, wounded.[57] M. le marquis de Montcalm took wine and beer to the troops who were in great need. The general went with M. le chevalier de Lévis before all the battalions and they testified to their great satisfaction with them. We worked through the night cleaning weapons and raising some of the right epaulements. The troops slept along the abatis, very alert and keeping watch for the enemy again tomorrow.

The *généralle* was beaten an hour before daylight.[58] At 5 o'clock we sent out some soldiers who killed some Englishmen who offered resistance. We saw a very thick fire coming from the falls. M. Bernard went to scout and sent back a report that all the retrenchments along the road to the falls were set on fire. The general sent him orders. Some savages and Canadians went forth to plunder and came back to tell us that the enemy were re-embarking and had no other projects. We buried our dead.[59]

---

56 In his report Abercromby stated that 2,987 men were incapacitated including 628 killed or missing. It seems he understated the number of fatalities with Chartrand estimating around 2,600 being lost in the whole campaign. Chartrand, *Ticonderoga 1758*, pp. 87-8.

57 The French lost 12 officers and 92 soldiers killed on the battlefield, 25 officers and 248 soldiers wounded according to the official returns. However when looking at the overall campaign the figure should be brought up to around 550 to include those lost at the engagement outside the fort on 6 July. Chartrand, *Ticonderoga 1758*, p. 88. Note by Gaffarel – Bourlamaque had his clavicle and scapula broken.

58 Note by Gaffarel – On this same day of the 9th, Montcalm sent Vaudreuil an abstract battle report. While telling him 'he put the army in formation again if the English wanted to come on,' he did justice to his comrades: 'I have been very fortunate to be general of troops who are so brave.' See his letters to the minister: 'The success of this event is due to the incredible valour of the officers and the soldiers. The officers who make up this army gave such great examples of courage that everyone deserves special commendation.' – Letter dated 12 July: 'If ever there was a body of troops worthy of offerings, is that those that I have the honour to command. So I beg you, my lord, to satisfy this. For me I do not ask anything other than to pass on my return to the King.' Letter to the Minister from Doreil (18 July): 'What can we say about M. de Montcalm who is above all praise, conqueror of Chouaguen and Fort George, constantly victorious since his arrival in Canada, he did without his glory to save the colony at the decisive moment.'

59 Note by Gaffarel – The dead were buried on the battlefield. At the top of the mausoleum a large cross was erected with the inscription:

Quid dux? Quid miles? quid strata ingentia ligna?
Ensignum ! En victor ! Deus hic, Deus ipse triumphat.
[Roughly, What use is a general or a soldier, or great timber walls?
The Cross: that is the victor! Here is God; it is God himself who triumphs]

The general himself composed this quatrain;

Christians! It was not Montcalm and his prudence,
These fallen trees, these heroes and their exploits,
Who confused the English and broke their hope,
It is the arm of thy God, who won on the cross.

The Abbé Piquet composed another more fiery inscription: *'Non plus ultra qui jam a Gallis*

M. Wolff arrived at 8 o'clock in the evening with his detachment. This officer told the general that they landed at Fort George but found no-one; but a half-league from the fort they scouted a considerable body of troops, commanded by milord Hauw [Viscount Howe], who had been killed in the affair of the 6th, that this corps camped in battalion square, in the centre being the barges, bateaux and ammunition, that the general had asked him what his orders were, and had treated him honestly and the next day conducted him to Fort Lydius, where General Abercromby detained him, telling him that Vaudreuil's letters demanded long answers and he would give them [to him] in a few days. M. Wolff doubted this and thought the real reason was to prevent him coming back to inform us of their movements. Abercromby asked him about news of the party commanded by Captain Rogers, who had had a bad spell, that after his response, Captain Rogers was scolded. He [Wolff] was then detained at Fort George with their army, which he judged to be of 20,000 men ready to embark in 2,000 barges or bateaux, with 1,500 for the transport of troops and the rest for the artillery. This army was ready in a moment and took the Portage Road as if conquest was assured. He followed them and when they marched to the falls he was conducted to Mount Pelée where he spent three unhappy days; Colonel Johnson arrived on the 7th, with four hundred savages of the Five Nations, Loups or Moraygnans; that same day a courier passed through and announced the taking of Louisbourg, that on the 9th in the evening, he saw a line of many barges pass by loaded with wounded.[60] The officer who guarded him called out to them several times but gave up. On the 9th all their army took the road to [Fort] George where he was taken until he complained to the major general, whereby that officer ordered that he should be let go with his boat.

The troops slept along the abatis. The prisoners left for Montréal.

10th July

M. le chevalier de Lévis went to the portage with the companies of grenadiers and piquets of the army. He found that along the banks of La Chute to the portage and Camp Brûlé, the entrenchments had been destroyed. He sent twenty barrels of flour. The English threw a lot into the lake as they embarked. The soldiers and Canadians returned laden with booty and many shoes with their buckles.[61] M. le chevalier de Lévis returned at 5 o'clock. The English dead were buried on the battlefield.

---

coesi, victi, fugatique fuistus Angli, anno 1758, die vero 8 julii, septem contra unum.' [Roughly, 'Now more than ever the united the French, defeated and drove to flight the English, in the year 1758 on 8 July, who outnumbered them seven to one.]

60 The news of the fall of Louisbourg was premature; the fortress did not capitulate until 26 July. The pessimism reflected the thoughts of the senior army officers in New France who recognised that their situation was desperate.

61 Note by Gaffarel – They found over five hundred pairs. These were lost by the soldiers as they crossed the swamps which bordered the banks of the lake.

11th July

The regiments of La Reine, La Sarre, R. Roussillon, Languedoc, Guyenne and Béarn went to camp in front of the fort. The two battalions of Berry between the fort and the redoubt.

12th July

We began to re-work the abatis and make entrenchments. M. de Rigaud arrived with three hundred Canadians and also savages of the Iroquois, Nippisingués, Algonkin and Abenaki tribes.

13th July

The *goelette* left for Saint-Jean. MM. de la Valtrie and le chevalier de la Corne, arrived with one thousand soldiers of the colony and Canadians.[62] Two workers found an English sergeant in the woods who said he was a deserter. He was led to M. le marquis de Montcalm for interrogation. He said that the English lost around six thousand men in the attack on the abatis and retired very frightened. They lost several officers of distinction. That colonels Johnson and Brostrik [possibly Bradstreet] left yesterday from Fort George with all the savages and seven thousand men for Korlack, to oppose any projects we may have on that frontier. There are eleven thousand more men at Fort George who are entrenched. They portage some heavy artillery and barges. They have four officers and one hundred and ten soldiers of Trepézac's detachment held prisoner.

14th July

The general formed two battalions with the soldiers of the colony and the Canadians.

15th July

The general sent orders to M. de Saint-Luc, who is six leagues from here with many savages, to not arrive back here too late so as not to delay the departure of the savages, which he decided yesterday to send to see what is occurring at Fort George.

16th July

M. de Courtemanche left with three hundred savages and two hundred Canadians to go and embark between forts George and Lydius, disrupt the portages of the

62 Louis de la Corne was known as the Chevalier de la Corne to distinguish him from his brother, Saint-Luc de la Corne. Older brother to Luc, Louis was born in 1703 and had a long career in the colony troops, rising to commandant of the far west in 1752. Here he established forts as far out as present day Saskatchewan. He returned to the heart of the colony for the duration of the war when he ran patrols along the St. Lawrence from Montreal to Lake Ontario. He died in a shipwreck enroute for France, just off the coast of Brittany in 1761.

English and intercept their convoys. M. Saint-Luc arrived at 3 o'clock after midday with two hundred savages and some Canadians.

17th July

M. de Rigaud went to camp at La Chute with the first battalion of the colony, composed of one thousand two hundred soldiers and Canadians. Two musket shots were fired from Cap au Diamant. A canoe was sent out that brought back two Abenaki who had sore feet.

18th July

M. le chevalier de la Corne went to camp at the portage with the second battalion of the colony, composed as the first. M. de Saint-Luc left with a cadet, a Canadian and six savages for Fort George.

19th July

Three English deserters, sent from the portage, confirmed the report of the sergeant and added that six thousand men were missing after the attack at the abatis but that it was forbidden to say they had lost more than one thousand nine hundred.

20th July

M. de Saint-Luc went to establish himself at the portage with the savages. Five hundred men from the town of Montréal arrived under the orders of M. Prudhomme.[63] The savages who left on the 18th have returned. They said they had been to Ganaouské Bay. They saw several fires which prevented them from going further.

21st July

M. le chevalier de Lévis went to the portage with a company of grenadiers. A convoy of bateaux arrived loaded with food. Two shots were heard from Cap au Diamant. The canoe sent out reported three Abenaki.

At 3 o'clock the canoes of M. Courtemanche were seen, who came in to land at 7 o'clock. This officer informed the general that the savages had been too eager to capture a patrol of eight men, sent out behind an entrenchment of three hundred men, who, when they saw the savages and Canadians made ready to pounce on them. He has brought back thirty-five prisoners and scalps. A savage was killed and three wounded, two mortally. The savages made an Oneida they have captured dance and sing.

---

63 Although there is little record of Louis Prud'homme himself, it seems he was grandson of one of the first settlers of Montreal, another Louis Prud'homme. Prud'homme junior was made *lieutenant colonel* of Montreal's militia in 1751 and commanded them in battle at Sainte-Foy in 1760.

22nd July

M. le marquis de Montcalm has held many councils with the savages, to engage them to remain with him. He barred the path to Montréal with a wampum collar and assured that he had nothing against them in his heart but would be very glad to keep them and for many of them to follow M. de Saint-Luc who must go to war with the Nippisingués. They promised the general they would respond tomorrow.

23rd July

The Iroquois responded to the general that they believed he was angry as they had been reproached, but that he has opened his heart they will leave him some of their warriors. Bad weather prevented M. de Saint-Luc from leaving. At 5 o'clock, the general was informed that an English detachment had arrived at the l'Isle au Mouton, led by Lieutenant Colonel Schuyler and an artillery officer, who M. de Vaudreuil had given parole to go and spend six months in New England, and with him a captain of Québec Militia, who general Abercromby had given permission to accompany and spend some time with him. The savages taking him to be an Englishmen wanted to mistreat him.[64] The Marquis de Montcalm and M. le chevalier de Lévis embarked for the Sault. They returned the English officer and left him with M. de Rigaud, to avoid any accident. The militia captain said that when he arrived in Orange, everyone said they had taken Carillon, and then three hours later there was consternation at the first news of the defeat of the English army.

24th July

Some savages have left for Montréal. the English officer asked for news of several officers who he believed had been captured. M. le chevalier de Lévis went to reconnoitre the swamp to the right of the ravine. M. de Saint-Luc embarked with five hundred Canadians and savages to take or impede convoys on the Fort Lydius road. M. de Montcalm sent the English officer to Fort George to respond to the English general at 6 o'clock.

25th July

Abbé Piquet with other missionaries returned from Deux Rochers where they saw M. de Saint-Luc depart this morning. Some savages returning from hunting say the found more than four hundred English who had died from their wounds near Mount Pelée.

64 It is unclear where Isle au Mouton is from this story. There is an Isle au Mouton in the Saint-Lawrence on the approach to Montreal but it would seem unusual to transmit this story across to the Lake Champlain frontier. It is possible that there is another Isle au Mouton somewhere before Fort Carillon.

26th July

M. Mercier left for Montréal. An officer of the colony embarked with eight Canadians and eight savages for Ganaouské Bay.

27th July

Some wounded were sent to Montréal. M. Jacob exercised the gunners in firing the 12 pounders which were mounted on a bateau.[65] An officer left to fetch recruits in Québec. The small barque moored at the warehouse, the large one set sail for Saint-Jean. A company of grenadiers went to guard the workers cutting wood on the right bank opposite the lake.

29th July

MM. de Montcalm and de Lévis went to visit the camp at the falls and stir up some war-parties. At 9 o'clock in the evening we heard the cries of savages. The Canadians and savages, conducting a canoe, approached the camp, they said that M. de Saint-Luc had made a good strike and would arrive tomorrow.

30th July

M. de Saint-Martin left with two hundred men for Fort George but returned at 1 o'clock and reported that he discovered fifteen barges who wished to engage but he did not wish to hazard this, knowing the islands were well guarded. M. de Saint-Luc arrived at 8 o'clock and reported that on the 28th he had attacked a convoy of forty-four wagons, led by one hundred carters, sutlers and merchants, and escorted by one hundred men. He took eighty prisoners and the savages took eleven scalps. He wrecked all the barrels of flour and bacon and barrels of wine and eau-de-vie. He killed the oxen and let the rest be plundered. After this he retired with the loss of a savage and three wounded. All the musicians of general Abercromby were amongst the prisoners. The barque and two bateaux left for Saint-Jean.

31st July

A convoy of bateaux arrived. Many savages got drunk. We saw some English barges on Lake Saint-Sacrement.

65 Montcalm and Bourlamaque were both interested in Jacau's (Jacob's) idea to mount cannon on small boats or rafts. He carried out this project at Carillon and one of his creations went down to Fort William Henry accompanying the army for the siege. This design was used many times during the Seven Years War and came to be known as 'jacobites', presumably after their inventor.

1st August

A deserter from Fort George said that there were fifteen thousand men, five hundred in the fort and a thousand at Fort Lydius. That General Abercromby wished to re-embark the army to come and take revenge but the militia refused to march so he decided to wait for seven thousand men to return from Louisbourg. They occupy the two largest islands on the lake and guard each with four hundred men; there is a detachment of two hundred men on the mountain on the right bank; that Captain Rogers is constantly out scouting, sometimes north sometimes south; that Fort George is being entrenched with logs but there are no cannons on the entrenchment; some small cannon have been placed in the small fort built on the site of the one we burnt down last summer; that he had sent for some cannon, mortars and two hundred barges from Fort Lydius; they put the rest in the swamp between the fort and entrenchment.

M. le chevalier de Lévis went to the portage; bateaux loaded with wounded departed. Forty-two Mississagués arrived. Those soldiers who can swim and dive received orders to go to the portage and claim any artillery and ammunition that the English have thrown in the lake.

2nd August

The general visited the works.

3rd August

M. Pouchot, captain of Béarn, was charged with constructing a redoubt to protect the right of the entrenchment. The savages who set out enroute for Fort George returned saying they would rather go to the bottom of the bay.

4th August

M. Marin left with four hundred Canadians and savages to go and take some convoys on the road to Fort Lydius. We heard a few cannon shots from Fort George.

5th August

Some savages who had not yet left went out to join M. Marin. M. le Borgne embarked from the end of the portage with seventeen chosen men, to disembark at Pain de Sucre and approach Fort George by land.

6th August

The general sent some savages to scout. M. de Boucherville, who arrived from Montréal, gave us news of Louisbourg.[66]

66 Boucherville had supposedly retired as of 1 January. Perhaps he was acting unofficially or working as a contractor. Alternatively this could be a relative.

7th August

M. de Bougainville left for Montréal, where he will communicate certain dispatches with M. de Vaudreuil. A fire started at the entrenchments was extinguished immediately. An English deserter who had arrived yesterday evening said that Captain Rogers had been detached with nine hundred men to oppose the retreat of M. de Saint-Luc.

8th August

Two savages arrived from Deux Rochers saying that they had seen the remains of a camp. At 3 o'clock a violent storm arose.

9th August

Two colony soldiers who had deserted were arrested; two savages from M. Marin's party arrived with two prisoners.

10th August

M. Marin arrived with his detachment and gave his account to the general that he had decided to go and lay an ambush on a busy road not far from Fort Lydius. On his way there, he heard some musket shots and discovered they were a signal and that they had been discovered by a party of one hundred Englishmen who pressed them closely. He immediately ambushed these people; they gave them two volleys and scattered the English behind trees, where they kept up a very lively fire. The English were soon reinforced by a relief of five hundred men and shortly afterwards another two hundred. Realising that having several wounded, and that the British were so many in number as to force them to retire, he pulled back in good order, bringing his wounded and five prisoners. He left thirteen dead on the battlefield. He was not pursued. Some savages returned to the battlefield during the night and found the English drinking and singing.

Twelve bateaux arrived here loaded with food. A detachment of two hundred Canadians went to cut wood for the garrison of Fort St-Frédéric.

11th August

M. Wolff has left to take the responses of our general to Fort George. The bateaux that arrived yesterday have left loaded with wounded.

12th August

Two hundred Canadians have left to relieve those at Fort St-Frédéric, who have been given permission to return home.

13th August

M. Bougainville, who came in from Montréal, told us of the arrival of several merchant ships.

14th August

The two hundred Canadians sent to relieve those at [Fort St.] Frédéric were sent home. M. de Bougainville left at daybreak for Fort George. The surgeons ordered a change of air to help heal my wound and I was embarked at 10 o'clock. My bateau rounded the peninsula and stopped a while at Fort St-Frédéric, where I learned that the English captured a man who had gone south from there to look over the harvest. We finished supper at Rocher Fendu. We left at midnight and arrived at daybreak on the 15th of August at l'Isle au Chapon where we rested for two hours. We dined at Pointe aux Fers and supped at the Faucault Mill. We found some Mississaguéss who were without food so I gave them some. We arrived at daybreak on the 16th at Saint-Jean. We immediately descended to Sainte-Thérèse; I disembarked some men and equipment to lighten the load so we could pass more easily over the rapids at Chambly. I arrived at the fort at 10 o'clock. They carried me on a stretcher to La Prairie, where we arrived at 5 o'clock.

17th August

I embarked at 8 o'clock and disembarked at 9 o'clock at Montréal. I went at once to the general.

19th August

A courier carried the responses of the English from M. Bougainville to the general.

21st August

M. Montigny arrived from Québec and told us of a vessel from Marseilles, which had been captured while travelling to Canada.[67]

67 In his youth, Jean-Baptiste-Philippe Testard de Montigny learned Indian languages, probably at Michilimackinac which his father commanded in the 1730s. He became a cadet in the colonial Marines and served under Paul Marin in the War of the Austrian Succession. After taking part on the raid on Fort Bull in 1756 he spent most of 1757 and 58 at Détroit. He was part of the force attempting to relieve Niagara in 1759 but was captured and sent to England. After the Seven Years War he received a pension and brought his family over to France, retiring to Blois.

23rd August

News from the Mississippi and several outposts. Some letters announced that the English have marched on Fort Duquesne and were well received.[68]

24th August

A courier from Québec announced the arrival of two vessels from La Rochelle who came out with others from the same port, escorted by two war ships. The news from Louisbourg said they were attacked and defended themselves vigorously; that the English had lost five hundred men in a sortie on the 9th, commanded by M. Marin, lieutenant-colonel of Bourgogne Regiment, who had seventy men killed or wounded.[69]

26th August

At one in the morning, a courier lately arrived from Frontenac told us that the savages who had gone to war on the Chouaguen frontier came to tell M. de Noyan that they had seen many barges come into Baie de Niaouré carrying a considerable body of troops, with the appearance of moving against Fort Frontenac and on to Présentation. M. de Vaudreuil gave commands to the militia of the town and area.

27th August

M. Duplessis, who was nominated commander for the relief of Frontenac, went to La Chine with all the officers of the colony, militia and four hundred Canadians.

28th August

M. Duplessis is still at La Chine. The embarkation of the men is slow and they are wanting a thousand things through lack of foresight, which holds them back.

29th August

The rest of the Canadians went to La Chine led by M. de Contrecoeur. News from Frontenac said that the English began crossing to the Grande Isle. M. de Noyan has sent notice that all necessary precautions were being taken for a good defence, that they have armed the barques and put a traverse across the entrance of the bay so they can bombard any landing attempt.[70]

---

68 The small army of General Forbes was pushing through Pennsylvania with the objective of neutralising Fort Duquesne and gaining control over the Ohio valley.

69 Michel du Bouzet de Marin was the commander of the second battalion of Bourgogne, stationed in Louisbourg. He was born in 1706 and retired from the army in 1766. He was captured but freed on parole and dropped at Dunkirk in December 1758.

70 Note by Gaffarel – Noyan commanded Frontenac, but the fort, like most in Canada, was poorly constructed without *terre-plein*, fosses nor covered way. 'This is called a fort in this

30th August

We learned that Fort Frontenac capitulated on the 27th in the evening, 48 hours after trenches were opened. M. de Noyan and the garrison were made prisoners of war.[71] M. de Noyan returned on parole. The English seized the two barques, they capsized one and burnt the other and they worked to ship the food, ammunition, artillery and goods which they found in large quantity. M. de Noyan noted the very good treatment he received. It would have been easy to avoid this considerable loss by sending a corps of troops to this frontier when M. de Montcalm informed M. Vaudreuil that the English, after having retreated from the portage, were moving troops to these parts.[72]

31st August

The garrison from Frontenac arrived, the courier from Québec announced the taking of Louisbourg.[73] News from Cèdres which told us of the arrival of M. Duplessis at Pointe au Diable. M. Benoit has left with the 1st division. M. de Vaudreuil ordered to prepare thirty bark canoes to send to Présentation where they will carry five hundred men to Niagara.

---

country,' wrote the engineer Pontleroy to the minister of war on 18 October 1758, 'enough to hold against the savages or parties without artillery; but today the great amount of British forces and their artillery will change the system of war and therefore the defence of the frontiers.'

71 Note by Gaffarel – Frontenac was the depot of the French navy on the lakes. It was almost deserted since troops had been concentrated on Lake Champlain. The English Colonel Bradstreet with a detachment of three thousand men and eleven guns had no difficulty in the encounter after three days of resistance. He found two million of goods, two thousand quarts of flour and five hundred quarts of bacon. Here is how this misfortune was announced to the Minister by Montcalm; 'The enemy has captured Fort Frontenac, which in truth was worthless, but more unfortunately, they took a lot of food, goods and eighty small and large cannons and the navy was destroyed which was owed to my taking of Chouaguen, burning five and taking two away... I asked for my recall after the glorious day of 8 July, but since the colonies affairs go wrong, it is for me to try and repair or delay the loss as much as it is possible for me. I hope that my intentions are seconded: I dare not reply.

72 Note by Gaffarel – Vaudreuil had indeed taken no precautions to ensure Frontenac, whose commander, Noyan, he did not like. It seems that his last request for reinforcements sent by the unfortunate commander was replied to with an insulting tone, 'this officer must be afraid.' It was already too late when he decided to send Duplessis, major of Montreal, with one thousand five hundred Canadians and all the savages he could gather. They advanced by forced march and had arrived at Présentation when they heard of Frontenac's capitulation. Noyan had seventy men under him. Montcalm, writing to the Minister of War, Belle-Isle, did not hesitate to hit back at Vaudreuil on his responsibility for the taking of Frontenac. 'The savages had warned him three weeks ago. They had told him: You sleep! Where is our war chief?'

73 This time the news was correct. General Amherst's terms were that the garrison should become prisoners of war. The military were outraged that they should not be granted the honours of war and be allowed to keep their arms and colours. However, Amherst was adamant and the French administration persuaded most of the French troops that the civilian population needed to secure a peaceful end to the siege. The men of the Artois Regiment mutinied and destroyed their own arms and colours. Chartrand, *Louisbourg*, pp. 80-2.

1st September

We sent out several canoes loaded with food and ammunition necessary for Présentation. Some savages of the Five Nations came to see the general, who assured him that the British were only amusing themselves by seizing the islands on Lake Saint-Sacrement and that they thought only to restore Chouaguen and the forts on that river. Having learned that we had a small garrison in Frontenac, they had sent a body of two thousand men to take it. They sent them there again when they heard cannon fire; they then passed around the islands opposite. They advised him to send young men to Niagara to avoid the same fate. They warned that the Cayugas complain bitterly that they received no part of the presents carried by M. de Longueuil and that a few have left Présentation. They said to the commandant that, knowing he would be attacked by the English, they would come to help defend, die with him, with their father, the *robe noire*, and their brothers in the village.[74] Vaudreuil has sent them with many presents and urged them to leave tomorrow for Présentation. Several canoes from Michillimakinak have arrived. We stopped the pilots and sent them to Présentation. News from Carillon said that the English are well entrenched in Fort George and are building a galley.

2nd September

The general [Vaudreuil] sent a courier to M. le marquis de Montcalm to engage him to come and spend some days with him. The rest of the bark canoes left for La Chine.

3rd September

It was learned that all the canoes are enroute for Cèdres.

4th September

The savages assured us that the English have abandoned Frontenac, that M. Duplessis must have arrived at Présentation and that the other divisions will arrived there tomorrow.

5th September

M. de Sacépée reported to M. de Vaudreuil from Saint-Jean, that he was informed yesterday of an enemy detachment five leagues from his fort.[75] He sent the militia of Trois-Rivières and the Abenaki for security and to scout out the enemy.

74 The natives called the Jesuits 'black robes'. Here they are referring to Abbé Piquet from Présentation.

75 The only reference I have found to Sacépée is regarding an Indian captive called Jemima Sawtelle (her biography is written in the Dictionary of Canadian Biography). Jemima had been captured from Bridgman's Fort in New Hampshire in 1755. She had been adopted and lived in Saint François/Odanak with the Abanaki. She was sold to Sacépée at Fort St. Jean in 1756 who was described as a gentleman and possibly the commander of that fort. Jemima was

6th September

We learnt that the pilots of a bateau loaded with provisions out of Saint-Jean, saw tents around Faucault Mill of one hundred and fifty English and savages and did not dare continue their journey. M. de Charly, who arrived from Carillon, said he did not see anything on the lake and reported that M. de Sabrevois, who had been scouting around Fort George, believed the English camp was only half the size of our camp and there are less bateaux than last month. General Abercromby's aide-de-camp wrote to M. de Bougainville to inform him of the capture of Louisbourg.

7th September

The Canadians and savages returned from Saint-Jean saying that Canadians who had deserted from Carillon had caused the alarm over the last few days.

9th September

M. le marquis de Montcalm has arrived from Carillon with M. de Bougainville, *aide marechal des logis génèral de l'armée*, and Pontleroy, chief engineer of the colony. They conferred with M. le general [Vaudreuil] on the affairs and state of the colony. A courier was sent to Québec to give the six warships there permission to leave. M. le general received many savages of different nations. He proposed to send one to Carillon and the others to Présentation.

11th September

The courier from Présentation announced the arrival of all the canoes and that M. de Montigné had left yesterday.[76]

12th September

The courier from Québec told us of the arrival of two vessels from La Rochelle. M. de Godefroi came from Détroit with six bark canoes saying that he had left Niagara on the 6th of this month; that he had left the commandant of that post very nervous on account of the barques which were long overdue; he was ignorant of the taking of Frontenac and only learned of it from some Mississagués when he reached the Coui Islands. M. le general received letters from M. de Boishébert that informed of his return from Miramichi with all of his detachment and he sent his relation of the campaign on Île Royale.

later bought and freed by Peter Schuyler and lived at Vernon, not far from where she had been taken prisoner, until 1805, aged 82.

76 Presumably Montigny.

13th September

M. le marquis de Montcalm worked this day on his memoirs on the part he had taken in the present circumstances, handed them over to M. de Vaudreuil and left for Carillon with M. Bougainville.[77] Many canoes from Michillimakinac and other outposts arrived transporting a considerable amount of food and merchandise to La Chine.

14th September

M. de la Colombière has arrived with a detachment of Canadians from the government of Québec. He informed us of the arrival of a ship.

16th September

A courier from Carillon told us that eight English barges had approached the Isle au Mouton; that M. le chevalier de Repentigny went in pursuit.[78] The Abenaki arrived from Korlack brought a prisoner to M. le general who said that the English have ten thousand men at Fort George; six thousand men have been disembarked at New

77 Note by Gaffarel – There was disagreement between Vaudreuil and Montcalm on the direction of military operations. Here is the letter written by Montcalm on his proposals to the minister of war (28 July): 'Since the 8th, Vaudreuil, was filled with helpful ideas of the experience of war and knowledge of a frontier that he has never seen, and he is about to lose, and never ceases in writing to me that it is possible with large detachments to make the enemy quit their position on the edge of Lake Saint-Sacrement. I have reason to believe that this idea presented is chimerical and is impossible without compromising myself... You can assure S.M. [Sa Majeste – His Majesty the King] that diversity of opinions never hurt, and do not offend me in my service. Indeed it was diversity of opinion and respectful submission which I always observed and delivered in the enterprise against Chouaguen. The marquis de Vaudreuil, having done what he wished, was close to surrender and I brought him back with these memories.' From another letter from 4 August: 'It is hard for a well-meaning general to be located 1500 leagues from his country, serve outside of his department and always fear the need to justify his action … I cannot refrain from informing the Minister of my sad situation. My health is wearing; work is motivated by worry and grief. In the midst of success, I fear that my conduct is disapproved of.' Vaudreuil had in effect asked for Montcalm to be recalled. 'Montcalm can be used very successfully in Europe. No one can be more just than myself on his excellent qualities; but these are not needed for war in this country. It takes a lot of sweetness and patience to order Canadians and savages. The King has given me this colony, I cannot help to prevent the bad consequences that could occur with a long stay by M. de Montcalm.' Montcalm on his side had asked for the recall of Vaudreuil, and Doreil, his confident, worked during his stay in France to immediately change governor and replace him with Montcalm. See the letter cited by Garneau, *Histoire du Canada depuis sa découverte jusqu'à nos jours,* Vol. II, p. 292: 'If the war continues or not, if we wish to save or establish Canada firmly, that S.M. entrusts command with M. de Montcalm. He is a man of practicality and detail, just, selfless, scrupulous, perceptive, active and has a good vision; in a word, he is a man of universal virtue. Where Vaudreuil shares parts of these talents he still has one original defect, he is Canadian.'

78 Louis Legardeur de Repentigny was born in 1721 and joined the colony troops as a cadet aged 13. He served mostly around Michilimackinac. He was present at the siege of William Henry and the defence of Carillon. As commander of the army reserve he defeated the attempted landing of General Wolfe on the Beauport shore in 1759. He ended his career as governor of Senegal.

York, returning from Louisbourg; they have six thousand men on the Chouaguen frontier occupying the portage; it is believed they have not re-established the forts there.

17th September

M. de Fleury, arriving from Présentation, informed M. le general that he has been to Frontenac with M. de Contrecoeur; that they found the fort easy to repair; that the ovens and buildings were not destroyed; they found six 12-pound guns which were not spiked. M. d'Hugues has left for Présentation with a detachment of troops of the colony.

18th September

M. de Langis, who arrived in the night, gave an account to M. le general about his journey to Chouaguen with some savages; that he found it abandoned; that he saw one of our barques burnt; the other was wrecked with several barges; he judged this by the amount of material and rigging floating in the water. M. le general ordered the officers destined for Présentation return to Carillon, where he also sent the news from M. Langis.

19th September

M. de Pontleroy left to go and reconnoitre the frontier of Lake Ontario and find a good position to construct a fort. The Abbé Piquet, who returned triumphantly from Présentation, will accompany him.

21st September

News from Carillon where all is peaceful. M. de Repentigny went out on ambush for three days and found no occasion to take a prisoner.

23rd September

A considerable convoy was sent for Présentation, and thirty canoes of merchandise for the Belle Riviére.

24th September

We learned from the Québec courier that a large merchant ship has arrived.

25th September

We learned of the return of the pilot who conducted the war ship up the river.[79]

79 Malartic seems to mean a different ship than the one in the previous entry, perhaps the *Aigle*, referred to below in the entry for 8 October.

News from Belle Riviére where all is tranquil. The English have sent wampum collars out with an envoy to the Loups to engage their neutrality. The Loups took these collars to M. de Lignery, commandant of Fort Duquesne. M. de Montigny returned after seven days at Niagara. The commandant of this fort learned of the taking of Frontenac eight hours before his arrival and prepared all his garrison of one hundred men to defend it as best he could and burnt the outer fort.

26th September

M. de Saint-Luc, arriving from Carillon, said that there is no news of the enemy, [and] that two parties were out on campaign, one towards Fort George and the other against Fort Lydius.

28th September

The Superior of Saint-Sulpice, arriving from Québec, told that while he was leaving, the Lieutenant of the King was questioning an Acadian, who had heard word of a ship's captain he had seen around Gaspé of twenty sails on seven warships.[80]

29th September

News from Carillon announced that a deserter from Fort George said that they had left seven thousand men in the entrenchments, eight hundred in the fort warehouse and one thousand five hundred at Fort Lydius, where they have a considerable artillery train and are awaiting five regiments that have come from Louisbourg.[81] They

80 Note by Gaffarel – After the capture of Louisbourg, the British fleet took the island of Saint-Jean and destroyed the settlements of Gaspé and St. Louis established by the Acadians. They also made an attempt against Miramichi and retired in mid-October.

81 Note by Gaffarel – The situation was indeed desperate. Montcalm was not ignorant of this. On 1 September after the taking of Frontenac and Louisbourg, he had written to the minister of war: ' The situation in the colony is most critical, peace is necessary. The English, without counting the army of Louisbourg, have thirty thousand men to act against Canada. We only have eight battalions, twelve hundred colony soldiers; the surplus are in the forts of the Ohio.... I write the truth, as a citizen, without being discouraged, resolving to bury myself under the ruins of the colony. Peace is necessary or Canada is lost.' This was also the impression of Doreil: 'Peace must be made this winter, otherwise Canada is irretrievably lost. Besides the outside pressures, internally evil machinations are rising and it is ready to crumble. But there is little hope despite the care and talents of the Marquis de Montcalm. I would not be surprised if the enemy were masters of the colony before the arrival of the first aid in spring.' See the same of Doreil in a confidential letter of 31 July 1758, addressed to the minister of war Belle-Isle at the department of war vol. 3498 piece 191: 'The folly, intrigue, deceit and greed causes great loss in this little colony, and costs the King so much. If it escapes this year, which is not certain, the enemy can return with greater forces and preparations. It is absolutely necessary to make peace this winter, or it will be in English hands next year... Peace, peace no matter at what price limits; we will gain it back through work when it is concluded.' He finishes by requesting the replacement of Vaudreuil with Montcalm. Another letter from Doreil to Belle-Isle (12 August and 31 August 1758) where he emphasises the need to conclude peace. (Department of War, Vol 3499, pp. 28,43). Letter from Lévis to the Minister

are doubling the number of barges and bateaux and it is believed they will return to Carillon when they are reinforced. A savage arriving from Fort Bull, said there are eight thousand men in those parts, that many of the Five Nations joined with three hundred of our allies to make war on that frontier.

30th September

A courier from Québec carried to M. le general that confirmed the report of the Acadian given above. M. le general gave the command for the Canadians to be in a state to march, to go to Carillon, and prepared the savages to make ready.

1st October

The savages of the Sault and of the Lake, went to see M. le general, saying to him they had ninety-five warriors in their villages who awaited his orders. That the others were at war or out hunting.

2nd October

The Canadians who were destined for Frontenac were sent to La Chine.

3rd and 4th October

Some officers left for Carillon with many Canadians.

5th October

Guides were sent to La Chine who would travel in front and behind the bateaux destined for Niagara. M. de Saint-Luc left for Carillon with some savages he had assembled.

6th October

Lots of munitions and food went to supply the fort which was to be constructed on the frontier of Présentation.

7th October

A courier from Carillon carried dispatches from General Abercromby, who wished to reclaim the prisoners to be returned to him in exchange for the garrison of Frontenac. The news from the Belle Riviére announced that an army of seven thousand English were a dozen leagues from Fort Duquesne on the 15th of September.

---

of the Marine Berryer (17 May 1759): 'I think it will, if necessary, be more useful to the King's service that we perish sword in hand rather than capitulate which will cause the colony to be forever lost to His Majesty.'

8th October

M. Doreil, *commissaire de guerre*, arrived from Québec. We learned that the *Aigle*, a vessel of fifty cannon was wrecked near Mécatinat, by the fault of the pilot.[82] That two hundred and eighty crew were saved with some of their things. That the English are establishing themselves in Gaspé Bay, they have brought in logs to build their houses.

9th October

A courier from Présentation announced that a savage returning from Fort Bull said that Colonel Brakstreck [sic. Bradstreet] is returning to Frontenac with a considerable body to prevent us from recovering it. News from Carillon where it is quiet.

11th October

Deputies of Présentation announced that the ambassadors of the Five Nations request that M. de Longueuil arrives there on the 16th when they will also arrive as they can only stay for four days.

12th October

A courier from Carillon says that much work is being done and they await the enemy with calmness.

13th October

Many bateaux set out for Présentation.

14th October

The Abbé Piquet arrived with the ambassadors of the Five Nations, who say that the English are always at Fort Bull and they are constructing two forts at the ends of the portage there.[83] They go out to the mouth of the Chouaguen River and they assure them they will take Carillon. Thirty savages who set out to war have returned having killed an Onazote [Oneida] dressed as an Englishman. The courier from Québec tells us that the English have ravaged the habitations of Montlouis,[84] that they are well established at Gaspé where they have built two forts.

---

82 The *Aigle* was a fifty-gun ship of the line, launched in 1750 at Rochefort. Mécatinat was to the far north of the Gulf of Saint-Lawrence on the north shore and is today called Petit Mécatina.

83 Fort Bull was the British supply point on the Mohawk River that had been raided and destroyed by de Léry in March 1756 as a precursor to the taking of Oswego that summer. The portage, known as the Great Carrying Place, was a most important strategic point. This reconstructed fort became known as Fort Stanwix, site of the famous treaty, and is situated in present day Rome, New York.

84 Present day Mont-Louis, near Gaspé.

15th October

I embarked in a *goelette* to travel to Québec. We passed Longueuil, Longue Pointe, Pointe au Tremble, the end of the island, Varennes, Repantinie [Repentigny], Vercher, Saint-Sulpice, Contrecoeur, Lavalterie, Saint-Ours, Aultray, la Noray [Lanoraye], Sorel and Berthier and moored between the islands.

17th October

We sailed at daybreak and entered Lake Saint-Pierre and passed through Maxkinongé, Maxa [Bay d'Yamaska], Saint-François, Riviere du Loup, Massis, l'Abbadie [?], Trois-Rivières, Cap de la Madelène [Madelaine], Champlain, Batiscan; then descended the Richelieu [Islands], rounded la Platon and moored at Cap Santé.

18th October

During the night we slipped our anchor and were forced to sail before daylight and arrived in Québec at 8 in the morning. We learnt that the two hundred and eighty crew of the *Aigle* were at Mécatinat. That the English have returned half the crew of a merchant vessel which they captured in the Bay of Gaspé.

22nd October

News from Carillon where everything is quiet.

23rd October

A courier from Montréal told us of a detachment of eight hundred English who went to Fort Duquesne to take it, burn the buildings outside and kill those who opposed them. They were defeated by the Canadians who sortied out of the fort and captured Major Grant, commander of this detachment, three officers, fifty soldiers and they killed or wounded four hundred and scattered the rest into the woods. The savages did not join the Canadians at the beginning of the battle, wishing to preserve their effects, and only joined in when they saw victory was assured. So they took their scalps and the next day returned to their villages.[85]

I left by land with Colonel Schuyler and another English officer that the Intendant asked me to lead to Montréal. We passed through Sainte-Foi, Cap Rouge, la Pointe au Tremble, les Ecureuils, la Riviere Jacquartier, Cap Santé, and came to sleep at Deschambault.

85 Major Grant had persuaded Colonel Bouquet, Forbes' second-in-command, that he should be allowed to make an attempt on the fort with a party of around 800 men. Forbes, laid low by illness, was unaware of this authorisation. The raid was a disaster. Grant only expected the French to have around 200 men, however they had around 700. The 77th Highlanders and provincials making up the force were gradually encircled by the French sallying out of the fort and Indians crossing the river. The encounter occurred on 14 September. René Chartrand, *Tomahawk and Musket: French and Indian Raids in the Ohio Valley 1758*, (Oxford: Osprey, 2012) pp. 49-59.

26th October

We left at 6 o'clock and passed over Grandines, la Riviere Sainte-Anne, Batiscan, Champlain and met an artillery officer at Cap la Madelaine who told us we had abandoned Frontenac. We passed the Trois Chevaux [maybe a group of islands nearby] and slept at Trois-Rivières.

27th October

We left at 6 o'clock passing Labadie [this was a seigneury near Trois-Rivières], Riviere du Loup, Maxkinongai, la Baye des Atokas [?], le Chenail du Nord [?], Riviere au Chicot, then Berthier and slept there.

28th October

We left at 6 o'clock passing through Lanoraye, Autray, la Valtrie [Lavalterie], Saint-Sulpice, Repantinie, la Riviere de l'Assomption and the end of the island, Pointe au Tremble, Longue Pointe, and arrived in Montréal at 2 o'clock. I gave M. le general the two English officers and received nothing but praise.

29th October

News from Carillon and Niagara. The first says that the English army is beginning to march through the area.

30th October

An officer arriving from Carillon reported that the English have abandoned the banks of Saint-Sacrement; that they have left a thousand regular troops at Fort Lydius and two hundred and fifty militiamen.

31st October

Several officers and many colony soldiers have arrived.

2nd November

The English officers left for Carillon. I have been from Longue Point up to Pointe au Tremble and la Riviere des Prairies to establish lodgings for the companies that will spend the winter here.

3rd November

I have been to do the same at Saint-Sulpice and Valtrie [Lavalterie]. I saw M. Bougainville who conducted the prisoners from the Belle Riviére to Québec.

4th November

I returned to Montréal where I learned that the English have abandoned Gaspé.

5th November

Several officers of the regulars arrived to work on lodgings for their battalions.

6th November

It has become extremely cold.

8th November

M. le chevalier de Montreuil, *aide-major général*, arrived from Carillon saying that the great cold was causing the troops to suffer.

9th November

M. le general sent a courier with yesterday's dispatches for France. M. le marquis de Montcalm arrived at 10 o'clock in the morning and M. le chevalier de Lévis at 7 in the evening, very fatigued from the bad weather.

11th November

I went to await the regiment at Point au Tremble.

12th November

I learned that the regiment had gone down the River Champlain where they were forced to leave their bateaux which became trapped in the ice and go by land to Longueuil, where they crossed the river on the 12th in the evening and the 13th in the morning.

15th November

I went to Pointe au Tremble, la Riviere des Prairies and Sault des Recollets to oversee the lodgings of the companies. I met the courier who carried news of the departure of the ships.

16th November

I did the same as yesterday at Repantinie, Saint-Sulpice and Lavalterie.

17th November

I returned to Longue Pointe, where the regiment's staff are. I learned from M. de Saint-Ours, who arrived from the Belle Riviére, that M. de Lignery had sent a body of four hundred men against the entrenched camp of the English which was twenty leagues from Fort Duquesne.[86] They dispersed the advance guard of one hundred and fifty men, killed or took four hundred horses and many oxen, and that nobody made a sortie from the entrenched camp.

19th November

I sent forty men to go and fetch the regiment's equipment from Chambly.

20th November

I went to Montréal. There I learned that all the troops had gone into quarters as follows; La Reine and Berry around Québec; Languedoc with the troops of the colony around Trois-Rivières; La Sarre, Royal Roussillon in Montréal; Guyenne and Béarn with the colony companies in Montréal. Three hundred men were sent to Présentation and a courier charged with orders for the departure of a ship which had not followed the others.

22nd November

Some officers arrived with many Canadians from Niagara.

23rd November

The officers who arrived yesterday said they heard several musket shots when passing Quinte [on the north shore of Lake Ontario]; they found they had come from several helpless bateaux who asked for aid.

26th, 27th and 28th November

Different couriers announced the departure of the last ship and the arrival of a *goelette* which left from Bordeaux in August. The two vessels have been sent to the Mecatinat coast. The crew of the *Aigle* is thirty leagues from Québec. M. Wolff arrived from Fort Lydius where he said he had been well treated. He said that General Abercromby has been recalled and replaced by General Amherst who commanded the siege of Louisbourg.

---

86 Captain d'Aubry launched a counter-raid on 12 October against Fort Ligonier, the British forward post. The 1,500 defenders abandoned cattle and horses outside the fort for the safety of their defences allowing the French raiders to ride back to Fort Duquesne in triumph laden with supplies. Chartrand, *Tomahawk and Musket*, pp. 60-9.

30th November

A courier was send to tell the *goelette* which landed yesterday to depart. Several bateaux from Niagara arrived.

1st December

News from Carillon. The barque finally arrived. A party of sixty savages is on campaign and a detachment in pursuit of three deserters. An officer from Fort Duquesne arrived with two English deserters who assured that they lost much in the attack on their outpost; they [the English] are reduced to salted meat, disease has taken around fifteen hundred men; three thousand are left in the entrenched camp where they await the general who is staying at Williamsburg.

8th December

News from Fort St-Frédéric. Four Canadians who had escaped from New York say that in November some French frigates appeared along the coast of New England where they captured some corsairs and held the merchant vessels in port; that the English have two thousand men at Louisbourg; that they are demolishing the fortifications and plan to come and have their revenge at Carillon next spring with twenty thousand men; that they will besiege Québec with an army by land and by sea; that the people are tired of war and want peace.

10th December

News from Présentation where work is pushed on quickly. Sites for the construction of two barques have been established and the wood is ready.

22nd December

M. le marquis de Montcalm has left for Québec despite the blizzard of thick snow.

5

The Year 1759

New France was on the back foot. Supplies were short and it now seemed only a matter of time as to when the British would capitalise on their success at Louisbourg. After Abercromby's disastrous campaign against Carillon he was recalled and Jeffrey Amherst was rewarded for his successes at Louisbourg with promotion to commander-in-chief in North America. Amherst sent out three armies. One, commanded by himself, would work up the Lake Champlain corridor from the south. Fort Duquesne had been abandoned the previous year and the route was now open from there to strike at Fort Niagara; this second army was entrusted to General Prideaux and William Johnson. Finally, an amphibious force under General Wolfe and Admiral Saunders would sail from Louisbourg to besiege Québec. According to Commissaire Doreil, 'England currently has more troops moving into the continent than Canada contains habitants, including old men, women and children. Who is able to resist this multitude?'[1] Although this statement was an exaggeration, almost thirty thousand British soldiers assembled to invade New France. New France could call on just over five thousand soldiers and around fifteen thousand able-bodied militia. The noose was tightening and hope was dwindling for the French.

10th January

At ten o'clock two officers who arrived from Fort Duquesne told us that on the 23rd of November M. de Lignery was obliged to burn down this fort before the approaching English army; that he sent the munitions and sick to Illinois and he retired with his garrison to Fort Machault, followed by some savages, the others having returned to their villages well disposed towards the French; some days before the retreat, one of his party defeated some English and took five prisoners carrying letters written to the English general by an officer who was going to the village of the Loups.[2] This officer wrote that he knew he risked his life but was happy to sacrifice it

1 Doreil quoted in Abbé Brasseur de Bourbourg, *Histoire du Canada: de son Église de Ses Mission,* (Paris: Société de Saint Victor pour les Propagation des Bon Livres, 1852), Vol. 1, p. 302.

2 Forbes decided to winter at Loyal-Hanna but when an escaped captive described the pitiful state of Fort Duquesne he decided to take advantage of his numerical superiority and move against it. The Indians had left; supplies were short and the garrison numbered around 200 men. Lignery could not resist and agreed that they should burn the fort. He embarked his artillery up the Ohio and retired to Fort Machault which was situated south of Lake Erie, not

for his country and hoped to join the general again in a few days at Fort Duquesne if he returns unharmed.

An artillery officer who had gone with these two officers was lost to them between Toronto and Frontenac. There has been no news of him. These officers say that there are few savages at Niagara; they wish M. Pouchot to return there. The courier from Québec says that the habitants of the lower river assure us that a brigantine that left France at the end of summer is harboured at Saint-Nicolas.

15th January

News from Carillon. The savages stopped two deserters from the Berry Regiment close to Fort Lydius. They cut off the head of one and forced his comrade to hold it on the end of a stick up to the fort; they went to put him in prison where he hoped to obtain grace from the fort commander who questioned him. He went to trial and was executed before the open gates.

17th January

A commissary of the *munitionnaire* was sent to Presque Isle and, a courier to take orders to all the upper posts.

18th January

The lost officer of the artillery arrived here, eleven days after his departure from Toronto. He had to turn back to find his way again. He said he met a courier from Détroit who heard rumours that the English were holding a grand council with the savages of the Belle Riviére to ask to make an alliance with them.[3] They have promised on the condition that their border is the Appalachian Mountains. The river froze on the 10th and by the 15th we could cross on the ice.

25th January

A courier from Québec announced there was great misery in the town.[4] The Intendant requests wheat for this government and promises to pay twelve *livres*

---

far from Venango in the Allegheny valley. On the morning of 23 November 1758, Forbes' army heard the explosion of Duquesne's powder magazine through the forest. By the time Forbes got there, there was nothing but charred ruins. He gave this heap of ashes the name Pittsburgh after William Pitt the Elder. Forbes had been seriously ill during the campaign and died in March 1759. Chartrand, *Tomahawk and Musket*, pp. 71-2.

3 A reference to the Easton Treaty, concluded by William Johnson and several governors with the Indian tribes of the Ohio.

4 Note by Gaffarel – According to Garneau (Canada II. 289), a portion of the population had been torn from agriculture to the exigencies of war, and the land was left without labourers, requiring imports of cereals even greater than in previous years, on this front, hostilities at sea made importing very difficult, and it was necessary to manage the farmers and adjust military operations in order to be able to free the largest possible number for sowing and harvesting.

per *minot* [equivalent to an English bushel or 8 gallons]. A public order was issued cancelling all contracts that people have made to supply grain to private individuals. The savages of Sault ask for grain and merchandise and threaten to go elsewhere to establish a living.

29th January

Two colony captains left with a secretary of M. le general to go and make a general census of the militia of this government and organise the roles of those who are fit for service.[5] These reviews are being carried out in the other governments. Several trains of flour have left for Québec. The lieutenant-general of Montréal police was instructed to go with a commissary of the *munitionnaire* to find the quantity of wheat that each parish can supply.

2nd February

The courier from Québec told us of the arrival of three prisoners who had been taken from Miramichi, who say that if there is no peace they will attack Canada with a hundred thousand men from different borders, and that they have never seen such great preparations. The commandant of Miramichi says the Acadians under his command are always indolent and too lazy to do what they are ordered; that the English entered Deux Rivières and wreaked havoc on the banks, killing and capturing some men, the cold stopped them. He sent a party of fifty men to the new fort; that they have received food which puts them in a state to wait for the spring relief; that he sent the courier back by a path which he believes to be the shortest of fifty leagues and that he ordered the courier to mark it on his return. The Intendant wrote that Saint-Castin, a chief of the Mic-Macs, has been killed by an habitant of Kamouraska, that the savages are furious and wish revenge for the death and will be difficult to calm.

As war and culture wounded each other both walked together towards a common ruin. Also, we understand from their correspondence that Montcalm, Doreil and even Bigot himself, insisted on the need to conclude peace.

5 Note by Gaffarel – From a letter of Montcalm to Belle-Isle, Minister of War (12 April 1759): 'The general census of Canada; although a copy has not been sent to me, I think I am sure in saying that there are no more than eighty-two thousand souls, of which no more than twelve thousand are men capable of fighting, and of these, removing those needed to work and transport vessels in the upper country, we will never have more than seven thousand Canadians, and if they do not have time to sow the crops the land will be barren, famine will follow; our eight battalions make up three thousand two hundred men, of the colony, more than fifteen hundred men are in the field. What are these against at least fifty thousand Englishmen?'

5th February

A courier from Détroit informed us that M. de Beletre [sic. Belestre, as previously noted], commandant in those parts, is re-established.[6] The savages are well disposed, and learned of the evacuation of Fort Duquesne a long time after. The courier said that there are no enemy tracks around Cataracoui. Barques are being constructed at Pointe au Baril where we have a party of our savages on campaign.

11th February

News from Presque Isle. The English have constructed a fort on the Malengeulée [Monongahela] river. They have left four hundred men there. Their heavy artillery has been sent to Royal Haneau,[7] and the troops returned to their provinces.

Courier from Carillon. The commandant writes that the savages have taken a scalp and two prisoners from around Fort Lydius. It is reported that a battalion of Royal Americans are in the fort and that they will shortly be relieved by another of the same regiment. That Colonel Priovt, who commands on this frontier, left for Orange where a great quantity of barges and bateaux are being constructed;[8] that General Amherst is at New York, where he is holding the levy for the troops and subsidies that the people find enormous; that their regiments are in quarters around Orange, Korlak and in Pennsylvania; they have three thousand men in Louisbourg where they work to re-establish this place; they have three ships of the line in port; they have a body of troops on the Saint-Jean River; they have not received recruits from old England, rather the regiments recruit from New England; they say they will take Canada or perish; that at Fort Lydius, two savages came to inform them of what is happening at Carillon, and they have two parties of fifty men each in the field campaigning.

A part of the gathered wheat was sent to Québec. The savages brought four Iroquois of the Five Nations to the general, who they had met while hunting around Pointe au Baril where they had come to scout and take prisoners; they were diverted and committed to come to Montréal to see Onontio. They told him that the English are stockpiling provisions at Fort Bull to come and burn down the constructions at Pointe au Baril, they have gathered all the equipment and ammunition needed for a winter expedition; at this fort they have six hundred bateaux and three thousand men in quarters between the fort and Korlak, where, as well as in Orange, they have many bateaux. These savages pressed M. le general to quickly secure Pointe au Baril, to preserve this post. Those of Présentation represented to him that it would expose their village to being burnt and they would lose everything they owned. He

6 Belestre was appointed commandant at Detroit in May 1758 so this entry would seem to indicate he had got back there safely after being away from his command. He was made captain and chevalier of St. Louis in January 1759, so it is likely that he had been to Quebec to receive the promotion.

7 Loyal-Hanna, a fortified base built by General Forbes for his campaign against Lignery at Fort Duquesne. The new fort was Fort Pitt.

8 This was Brigadier General John Prideaux. He had been tasked by his commander, Amherst, to re-establish Fort Oswego and then proceed west to attack Fort Niagara.

promised not to abandon them and has treated with those of the Five Nations, who engaged to spend some time with him, and gave commands to four officers and one hundred and fifty soldiers of the colony to go and reinforce the garrisons at Présentation and Pointe au Baril.

1st March

A commissary of the *munitionnaire* left with twenty-three men, destined for Niagara, Détroit and other outposts.

2nd March

M. de Céloron left with the officers and soldiers ordered to Pointe au Baril, where he would command. M. de Benoit will command at Présentation.

3rd March

M. le general held council all day with our domiciled savages and those of the Five Nations, who he has given dinner to every day and asked if they would stay with him a few more days to give M. de Céloron time to make his way. The *munitionnaire* also gave them a sumptuous meal, they showed great astonishment and asked if there were some higher leader than Vaudreuil, and that the English are not as good at their hosting.[9] They promised to make it known to their nation and their allies.

The artillery and munitions have been sent up to Cèdres, necessary for arming the barques and troops who will leave for Niagara on the first navigation, and held in readiness. The corn gathered did not supply half of what was asked for. It is believed that the census has been done badly, and there is talk of making a second. We have sent MM. the priests as emissaries to induce them to provide everything they have. The habitants sell it [corn] all day for gold or white silver.

7th March

M. le marquis de Montcalm arrived from Québec.

10th March

A detachment was sent to guard the artillery, rigging and munitions at Cèdres.

12th March

Four Mississaguéss arrived from Toronto carrying the letters of the commanders of this and other posts. They said to Onontio that they came to offer the services of

9 The *munitionnaire* was the aforementioned Cadet. See 28th August 1757 (p. 141).

their nation, and find out which parts they are destined; they found M. de Céloron at Présentation, where there is no news.

14th March

News from Louisiana and all outposts of the upper country. M. de Plevet telling M. le general that he did not receive any merchandise from France. That he had been very embarrassed and the savages had found means through the Spanish and from New England. M. Macastin, commandant of Illinois, wrote that he had been very surprised to see the arrival of the artillery from Fort Duquesne, that the *Serokis* [Cherokee] had attacked the convoy and two men killed and three wounded. M. de Lignery wrote from Presque Isle that the English have reinforced the Belle Riviére [frontier] and were constructing bateaux; they have roused the savages to war and have merchandise and ammunition to give them. The commandants of the other posts say the savages are in the best dispositions. The Hurons of Détroit went for a council which they were invited to by the Loups and Shawnee.

15th March

A savage of the Five Nations came to tell M. le general that the English are swarming around Fort Bull and the Chouaguen River, they march in divisions of five hundred men with food and supplies for two months. That the divisions are preceded by detachments of militia armed with their own tools for breaking the ice, that it is believed that they are enroute to come and burn our barques, that he saw them go by and to him they seemed in good spirit. Colonel Bradstreet said to them that he was going to kill Onontio, that he asked that they not interfere in their quarrel, but come to see.[10] He recommended that they engage their brothers to retire, so they do not soak their hands in their blood; he has sent five thousand men to Niagara while a naval force will take Québec, and another army will penetrate Canada by Lake Champlain; that Ononthio is done for; they see his death incessantly, and that they will not be like the French, who have done nothing to speak of since the taking of Chouaguen.[11]

10 John Bradstreet was born in Nova Scotia and came to prominence in the 1745 campaign against Louisbourg. There he gained the attention of William Shirley, a powerful player and sometime governor of Massachusetts. When war came round again Shirley was initially made second-in-command of British forces under Braddock and took on responsibility to campaign against Niagara in 1755. Bradstreet received a commission in the army and became fixed in the business of keeping supplies running up the Mohawk to Fort Oswego. A political player, he managed to distance himself from Shirley when he fell out of favour and the new commander Loudoun was appointed. Bradstreet wasted no time in ingratiating himself into Loudoun's circle. He remained an important operator within the army, often undertaking the role of quartermaster general. His most successful exploit was a daring raid during 1759 launched from Oswego to destroy the vulnerable Fort Frontenac. Bradstreet was a successful self-publicist but never quite managed to attain the higher offices he desired.

11 Note by Gaffarel – Montcalm had perceived the intentions of the British. Here is a fragment of a beautiful letter addressed to Marshal de Belle-Isle, Minister of War from 12 April 1759: Regarding Québec, the enemy can get here if we do not have a fleet and if Québec is taken,

M. Benoit says that Présentation is safe from a strike, and that his garrison is determined to defend well. The courier from Québec told us that some prisoners, taken by M. de Monteroille from the fort the English have on the Saint-Jean River, speak only of preparations they are making at Chibouton [French name for Halifax, Nova Scotia] and at Louisbourg, for the siege of Carillon.

16th March

News from Carillon saying that on the 9th, two savages came back from scouting to inform the commandant that they had found the tracks of a considerable party. Immediately a cannon was fired to call in the fifteen men who were cutting wood on the right bank opposite the hospital; those workers, who thought the sound of the cannon was that of a mining explosion, remained in the woods and were attacked a quarter of an hour later by sixty men, who captured or killed eleven; four escaped back to the fort. Some savages went out in pursuit of this party and took one prisoner. In the pursuit an Abenaki was killed and two wounded. The prisoner said that his party was of three hundred and fifty men who had the objective of burning the warehouses and vessels of the lower buildings and to take a plan of the fort. That the garrison of Fort Lydius had been reinforced, and that each day more troops were expected; that they were delivering lots of hay, that the artillery train was doubled; that General Amherst is in New York; that the provincial assemblies for militia have been completed, that Boston is supplying five thousand; that Captain Rogers commands the last party and is waiting to be given hundred men to augment his rangers. The commandant of Carillon told the Abenaki that they are wrong to complain that the Iroquois spoke to the Agnés during the pursuit and calling for them to be executed.[12]

19th March

Abbé Piquet wrote from Présentation that all was peaceful and they remain on their guard.

---

the colony is lost. However no precautions are made; what I have written I have said to M. de Pontleroy, engineer and an excellent subject, and sieur Pellegrin, captain of the port of Québec and an excellent sailor, to make provision to prevent any poor manoeuvres at the last alarm. I offered to give the orders but the response was; "There is still time." I know nothing of the projects of M. de Vaudreuil, even less of what can be put in the field in a campaign in Canada, likewise with food and ammunition; the public tells me we are wrong in one paper and another, and still believe that the food ration is badly governed. I should consider myself lucky in the circumstances not to be consulted, but devoted as I am to the service of His Majesty, I have given a written notice for the better, and the Chevalier de Lévis, M. Bourlamaque and myself will delay the loss of Canada with courage and zeal.

12 The Canadian Iroquois, although not part of the Five Nations, were closely related to the Mohawks and numerous instances are recorded of their reluctance to fight one another. See Macleod, *The Canadian Iroquois*, *passim*.

22nd March

M. le chevalier de Repentigny has arrived with five hundred men destined for Belle Riviere. They will leave on the 24th for Cèdres, where they will go on to Présentation by land. M. Marin arrived from Québec with another detachment.

27th March

M. Pouchot left for Présentation, where he will command until the barques can sail to Niagara.

28th March

M. le general has heard that ice is threatened and so ordered the piquets destined for Niagara to return to Montréal.

31st March

The piquets of Royal Roussillon and Guyenne have left with a detachment of two hundred Canadians. We learned from an envoy sent over the ice on the lake that M. Pouchot left Cèdres today.

1st April

The piquets of La Sarre and Béarn have left with two hundred Canadians.

2nd April

The last detachment destined for Niagara left for Cèdres. M. le general received a letter from M. Pouchot, saying that the lake is clear. The river has begun to flow.

4th April

The river has cleared, and was a curious spectacle. The ice broke with such violence, that the ice along the banks was pushed out above it forming several mountains and knocking down a house.

7th April

A courier came from Fort Machault. M. de Lignery says that he is still in control, that the English have built forts at Altigné and Loyal Hanna;[13] that the savages are

13 The fort at Loyal Hanna is more commonly known as Fort Ligonier, named in honour of Britain's commander-in-chief, Sir John Ligonier. Today the fort has been reconstructed and located at Ligonier, PA. Altigné is presumably Fort Bedford, located at present-day Bedford, PA, which was the central supply depot for Forbes' campaign.

becoming familiar with them but they still seem attached to us and he hopes to commit them to a strike, if he receives aid he can impose upon them, he has several parties out at war.

M. Pouchot wrote that he arrived at Présentation on the 5th, where he scouted the surrounding area, that he could not find any good position, there is no case for new entrenchments to be made, that the best recourse is to keep under arms and be ready to strike at the enemy while they disembark.[14] All that is precious from Présentation has been stockpiled on the Isle au Galop. This island can be defended by two hundred men. That the barques are to be launched onto the water as soon as possible. They are working on the best possible entrenchments at the Pointe au Baril, once they received the necessary tools, that M. Daillebout has returned from Cataracoui, and has seen nothing interesting on his route. A party of savages who left with M. de Labourladerie has returned, and that this officer continued the route by land. Six Loups have gone to see what is happening at Chouaguen.

11th April

A Canadian, lately from Acadia, informed M. le general that the English have entered the Saint-Jean River; they have destroyed some settlements, killed six habitants and captured others; that our troops are lacking food; the commander prepares to go and scout the English as soon as they make a move; that M. de Boishébert had not yet arrived.

14th April

A courier from Carillon told us that the party of M. Hertel came in lacking food, having been around Boston for the last forty days where they took one of the poor habitants killing his wife and burning their house.[15] This man assured that the militia are not yet assembled. An Iroquois captured a soldier who is American from the fort between Orange and Sarastou [Saratoga] who had come out to make a patrol. This soldier says that General Amherst is in New York; he expects seven regiments to arrive from old England, and prides himself on taking the campaign to Canada, which he proposes to attack on different fronts. The major of his [the prisoners] regiment commands at Orange, Colonel Haldiman at Fort Lydius, where he awaits Colonel Privot;[16] that the garrison of the fort is composed of eight companies

14 Note by Gaffarel – Vaudreuil wrongly distrusted this excellent officer. Montcalm on the other hand wrote highly of him on 17 April 1759 to Marshal de Belle-Isle, 'Finally M. Pouchot has gone to command at Niagara, where he was recalled from last Autumn; he was capable and agreeable to the savages; ... but it was determined he would be relieved by a Canadian officer, though not as capable and less agreeable to the savages'.

15 Joseph-Hippolyte Hertel de Saint-François was one of five brothers in the colonial marines. In 1755 he had been present at the Monongahela as a cadet. He had previously been serving at Fort Carillon and was an able interpreter. He was thus sent out with Indian raiding parties such as this one. He remained as an Indian agent after the conquest of Canada.

16 The British officers referred to here are Frederick Haldimand and Jacques Prevost, The latter was commander of the 4th battalion of the 60th Foot which had wintered at Fort Edward with

of the Royal Scots, four of the Royal Americans and Rogers' troops. Another savage had captured two men on the road between Orange and Lydius where he led them tied together. One became detached and he fired is musket at him and took the scalp of the other.

15th April

A courier arrived from Québec today having taken six days because the roads are very bad.

18th April

News from Présentation. Several savages came in saying have returned from a meeting with M. de la Boularderie and the Onontaguès a league from Fort Bull.[17] There, saying they had come to find out the news, they were presented with four wampum belts; an Onontaguè there proposed to take them to their village, where they will go on to a great council at la Fourche, where they have been invited by Colonel Johnson, telling them they will learn the news.[18] That the English will treat them well; that they can follow them in safety; that they will seek out the French in neighbouring villages to explain to them what they have to say; M. la Boularderie has taken his party to follow them; the barques are gathered ready and waiting to sail.

22nd April

News from Presque Isle, Niagara and Présentation. Nothing has been seen of enemy movements around these posts.

28th April

News from Présentation. M. Benoit wrote that the barques have been out since the 25th and M. Montigny with thirty bateaux since the 24th and is entrenched on the Pointe au Baril; that his depot is on the Isle au Galop; that they are working on a third barque; that M. La Boularderie has returned, after having travelled with many

---

Haldimand. Both he and his battalion had been assigned to Brigadier General John Prideaux who was to command the expedition to destroy Fort Niagara. Haldimand was appointed second-in-command but General Amherst, who was now commander-in-chief, ordered him and the battalion to keep communications open at Oswego and reconstruct the old British fortifications there.

17 Antoine Le Poupet de La Boularderie was a somewhat impoverished nobleman. He had started off his life in the regular army and then as a courtier in France before returning to North America to lands granted on Île Royale. After the capture of Louisbourg in 1745 and then the subsequent taking of it in 1758 all his investments had come to naught. He was a colony officer during the Seven Years War and remarked upon as capable and brave. He died in misery and poverty in France in 1768.

18 La Fourche, literally The Forks. This would be the old site of Fort Duquesne, now rebuilt by the British as Pittsburgh and the starting point of the British corps which would move against Niagara.

Oneida to the village of Sonontacans, where his arrival was announced by the beat of a drum.[19] A savage warned him that he had been given away to the English, he went along the river far enough to avoid a large detachment which he saw after half a league. That the Five Nations seem determined to remain neutral, despite a few betrayals; that the English have built a fort at the portage and the garrison including that of Fort Bull are not numerous.

1st May

M. Mercier,[20] arriving from Québec, told us that the *goelette la Sérieuse,* which left there on the 22nd of November, was lost on Cap Nord[?] and the crew was saved. The commandant of Miramichi says they lack food; that this dearth prevented him doing much harm to the English over winter. One named Beausoleil proposed to capture the first vessel that comes into Beauséjour.

2nd May

M. Outelas arrived with two men who he had taken prisoner around the River d'Orange [the Hudson river around Albany] from a small detachment come from Fort Lydius which were scouting the travelling canoes of the savages. The rest of this detachment fled or were killed. It is seen, from the dispositions of these prisoners, that the battalion of Royal Americans, which is at Fort Lydius, has been relieved by a regiment of Hanover;[21] that the companies of Royal Scots and Rogers' troops are still there, composing four hundred men, which will be increased shortly by one hundred men and several Moraignans; that General Amherst is making a tour of Pennsylvania and is expected in Boston; that this general will not come up to Canada; that they will attack Canada from the top of the river [St. Lawrence] to the bottom. In Halifax they have twelve ships of the line and expect others from old England; the militia will be transported from the ports in New England where they are commanded, but they are not yet assembled. The five provinces neighbouring

19 Possibly the village of Seneca (also Sonontoen, Sonnotouan, St. Jacques) located a mile south of present day Victor, NY. The Jesuit mission of St. Jacques was in this village. See Jennings, *History and Culture of Iroquois Diplomacy*, p. 224. Alternatively it could be a badly spelled version of Onondaga which was the central place of Iroquois government.

20 Mercier was commander of the *Cannoniers-Bombardiers*, although he also held a commission in the regular army, and one of Bigot's accomplices. Montcalm speaks of him in derogatory terms in a confidential letter to Marshal de Belle-Isle, 'M. Mercier, who commands the artillery, is an entrepreneur under other names. Everything is made badly and is expensive. This officer came here as a simple soldier twenty years ago, will soon be worth around 6 or 700,000 *livres*, perhaps a million, if he continues.' (12 April 1759). A more balanced view would conclude that he carried out his duties and was one of the few formally trained artillery officers in the colony. He was acquitted in the subsequent trials after the fall of New France.

21 As noted above, the 4th battalion of the 60th went to join Prideaux's campaign against Niagara, meanwhile Amherst assembled a force at Fort Edward to strike at Carillon. This did include the 77th and 42nd, both Highland regiments, but there were no forces from Hanover. Most of the battalions were veterans of the previous year's campaign against Louisbourg.

Orange will each provide eight thousand men; the remainder will supply the Belle Riviére where a small army will be assembled. The troops will be assembling at Orange and New York, where the depots are; that the buildings made at Fort Lydius are barracks; and they are working on refitting the artillery, barges and bateaux.

3rd May

M. Bourlamaquė has arrived from Québec.

6th May

A courier from Québec apprised us that M. Stolbo [Robert Stobo] has fled the prison of this town with a militia officer and an Irish family; they have gone the river in a bateau of the king which they stole. Pursuit has been sent.[22]

7th May

Many Canadians were ordered to load up thirty bateaux at La Chine. All day they carried munitions and merchandise to be sent out to Présentation.

8th May

Permission was given for the Canadians to go out [to trade] to the Strait of the Ouias and other posts.[23] These men are the best and strongest in the country. A letter from Québec said some habitants have seen the bateau of M. Stolbo [Robert Stobo] slip along l'Isle à la Gráce.[24] The La Reine Regiment arrived yesterday at Chambly.

---

22 Robert Stobo had been a hostage taken after the defeat of George Washington's Virginia Provincials at Fort Necessity in 1754. Stobo felt the terms of the Virginians' surrender had been breached by the French and so determined that he should embark on a course of espionage. He set out passing details of Fort Duquesne, where he was held, to Indian messengers who delivered it back to the Virginians. Stobo was discovered in 1755 when letters he had sent were discovered in the baggage of General Braddock. Held in Québec he attempted escape many times and was placed on trial. Finally managing to break free he made his way over land and water to Louisbourg where he was received by General Amherst and immediately pressed back into service to help guide General Wolfe in his campaign against Québec. His exploits seem more dramatic than fiction. For an account of his life see Robert C. Alberts, *The Most Extraordinary Adventures of Major Robert Stobo*, (Boston: Houghton Mifflin, 1965).

23 The most likely place for this seems to be the post called Fort Ouianton, on the Wabash near present day West Lafayette, Indiana. It was used as a depot to trade with the surrounding Wea people and was near the rough boundary between Louisiana and New France. Carl Ekberg, *French Roots in the Illinois Country: The Mississippi Frontier in Colonial Times* (Champaign: University of Illinois Press, 2000), p. 32.

24 These small islands were in the St. Lawrence between Montréal and Québec just by the Island of St. Ignace, opposite Sorel.

10th May[25]

M. de Bourlamaque left to go to command the frontier of Carillon.

11th May

The thirty bateaux have left for Présentation. M. de Vassan, arriving at 9 in the evening, carried us news from Niagara of the 4th, Forts Machault and Détroit from last month, and Saint-Joseph from the 10th of March. Here is an extract: The barques carry well with sail. They carried him from Niagara to Frontenac in seventeen hours, where he had trouble finding a bateau to land. The savages seem to favour us; the Hurons and Outaouas of Détroit defeated a detachment of fifty men who were conducting sick from Fort Duquesne to Loyal-Hanna. The Chouanons and the Loups routed the vanguard of a corps which marched on Fort Machault. M. Belstre must return to Presque Isle. Détroit is not in a state to provide food, the last harvest was lost for the want of anyone to do it. The English wish to establish three hundred German families in Belle Riviére country. This news divulged made talk among the savages that they want to usurp their land. It is believed M. Langlade left with lots of savages of Michillimakinak for Fort Machault. Two *Tetes Plattes* [Flatheads] came to see M. Hertel at Chatacouin, who carried good words for their nation and for the Loups who seem willing to take up the hatchet for their father the French. They complain about the betrayals of the English and he testified to be surprised to have received no response from their father since they had sent a necklace in 1756. M. Pouchot said he had learned from the Sononthacans [Seneca] who had arrived with those of Colonel Johnson that the objects of this campaign are to attack Québec and Carillon and to hold Fort Bull and Belle Riviére on the defensive. He [Pouchot] intends to flush out the English, if a party he sends to Chouaguen with orders to push onto Fort Bull can confirm this report. M. Verrier says of Saint-Joseph that the savages are hunting; that, when they return he will send them to a destination that he prescribes.[26] All the posts are in need of food.

13th May

We learn from a courier from Saint-Jean that M. de Bourlamaque left there on the 11th with the bateaux for the artillery and the La Reine Regiment left on the 12th. The second battalion of Berry arrived today and the third tomorrow; that two schebeks have been launched on the water; the third one will be ready next week and the fourth a few days later, and the barques are ready to set sail.[27]

25 Note by Gaffarel – On this date, governor Vaudreuil sent instructions to all heads of office to demand that all men from sixteen to sixty years old would be held in readiness to take up arms. At the same time there were public prayers to God, asking for victory.

26 It is unclear who this Verrier is but he should not be confused with Étienne Verrier, the engineer officer of Louisbourg.

27 A schebeck, more commonly spelt chebec in French or xebec in English, is a small three-masted vessel built for speed. Built with a cambered deck and great breadth to run off the water and avoid tipping due to its low profile.

14th May

M. Bougainville, who had left for France last autumn, and set out from Bordeaux on the 28th of March, arrived at 10 o'clock in the morning loaded with letters from the Court.[28] He announced a fleet of eighteen merchant vessels of four hundred tons each, carrying food and ammunition.[29] His arrival filled all the colony with joy, especially the regular troops.[30] They have not had much luck for a long time and are heavily burdened.[31]

15th May

An officer of the fleet came to inform M. le general that they landed at La Prairie, that they were missing three vessels, which had been separated from the fleet for a long time, that they believed they had trouble with the bottom of the river.

---

28 Bougainville had left on 12 November 1758. He did the rounds to try and garner more resources but met with the same answer. France could not afford to protect its North American colony. Berryer, Minister of Marine, said to him, 'when the fire is at home, we do not look after the stables'. Four hundred new recruits were all that was added to the usual supply fleet. Promotions and honours were forthcoming however. William R. Nester, *The French and Indian War and the Conquest of New France* (Norman: University of Oklahoma Press, 2012), pp. 305-10.

29 Note by Gaffarel – These vessels carried three hundred and twenty-six recruits; a paltry relief, but, as Montcalm wrote to the Minister on the arrival of the convoy; 'The little is valuable to those who have nothing... I dare reply to you that I have a complete devotion to saving this unfortunate colony or perish.' From Bigot in a letter to the Minister, 22 May 1759: 'There will be provisions for eighty days of food for the soldier at the rate of half a *livre* of flour and a half-*livre* of bacon per head; This is not by a long way the ration due. Once this is consumed, we will be reduced to salt meat until harvest. We asked for three times as much food.'

30 Note by Gaffarel – Bougainville, before leaving France, was appointed colonel and knight of St. Louis. He brought rewards requested by Montcalm, which gave him the brevet of *lieutenant general* with flattering letters, but he had no illusions about the outcome of the campaign. As he had written, before leaving France, to the Marquise de Saint-Veran [Montcalm's mother]: 'Almost all favours asked by your son for the troops are granted. Their treatment is bettered, and M. de Montcalm will on the part of the Court have all the things that can make his occupation more agreeable, and I trust he will have all the facilities to do good without being barred in his operations. Unfortunately it is very late, and I think it is the case of calling the physician after death. At least it is a satisfying thing to M. de Montcalm and his parents that his glory will be preserved, and that the court, although informed of the position of Canada, and of the helplessness where he can establish even a slightly less monstrous inferiority they will be grateful to their general who at all times will resist the loss of this new colony.' Montcalm, on his side, could not keep hope, as seen from the letter that he sent to the minster of war, 19 February 1759; ' Besides that reinforcement would only increase the scarcity of food which you can see proven only too well up until now, it would be feared that they would be intercepted by the English in the passage; and, as the King would never send relief proportionate to the forces the English are able to oppose, efforts made here would have no other effect than to excite the ministers in London to do more to conserve the considerable superiority which they have acquired in this part of the continent.'

31 Note by Gaffarel – Vaudreuil was awarded the Grand Cross of St. Louis and Montcalm, commander of the same order; Lévis, *maréchal de camp*, and Bourlamaque and Senezergues, brigadiers; Dumas, *major-général* and Inspector of marine troops. Crosses and grades were also given to many officers. The letter of thanks is retained, sent by Montcalm to the minister of war. (Dépôt de la guerre, vol. IO-35, Exhibit 60).

17th May

The Iroquois led in a prisoner they had taken around Orange who assured us that the troops are still in their quarters.

19th May

News from Carillon. M. de Langis brought in several prisoners from around Fort Lydius. After their testimonies were heard, M. le marquis de Montcalm decided that M. le general [Vaudreuil] should go to Québec.

20th May

Couriers were sent out to all the posts.

21st May

M. le marquis de Montcalm embarked for Québec with MM. Bougainville and Malartic.

22nd May

We disembarked at Cap la Madeléne and from there arrived at Québec at 7 o'clock in the evening.

23rd May

Five vessels arrived here that joined the others. The captains who moored today said they had seen ten vessels moored at Bic, but that the bad weather and fog prevented them from finding out if they were ships of war or merchants. M. le marquis de Montcalm has sent orders for the Languedoc Regiment to return here as soon as possible. At midnight, the signals came that the vessels were English. Two couriers were sent to inform M. de Vaudreuil to bring down all troops who are in the government of Montréal as soon as possible.

24th May

Two couriers confirmed the signals. M. de Vaudreuil arrived at four in the morning with several officers. M. de Montcalm made a reconnaissance with MM. De Bougainville and Malartic of good positions to site camps and work to arrange for the defence on this front.[32]

32 Montcalm wanted to establish a battery at Pointe Lévis, before Québec. He also wanted to retain control of the river with heavy batteries defending the plateau of Cap Tourmente, which commanded the pass at the eastern tip of the Isle d'Orleans, and the high point of the bay facing the western tip of Isle au Coudres but these plans were not approved by Vaudreuil. Only defences at Beauport were carried out and they were not begun until June

25th May

MM. Bougainville and Pontleroi went to reconnoitre l'Isle d'Orleans. Malartic was ordered to reconnoitre the parts around Cap Rouge.[33] Several sailors have sounded the traverse to see if it can be barred.[34]

26th May

M. de Montcalm went to Cap Rouge. M. Bougainville and Pontleroi gave him their account that the Isle d'Orleans is not suitable for defence. M. de Levy wrote that a savage had told him that he had counted six sails at l'Isle Verte and fifty at Bic. All the officers of the colony left to go to both sides of the river to remove all the cattle and drive them to the rear or into the woods and cantons out of reach of the enemy. A courier was sent to hasten the progress of M. de Lévis and the regular troops with the Canadians who were to come down. The sailors found the traverse too wide to be barred.

27th May

M. de Bougainville and Malartic scouted the banks of the River Saint-Charles, Beauport and Montmorency, they found it easy to defend at certain points but in others too extensive to be held by a small number of troops. the English are in the same places. L'Isle aux Coudres could not be defended by a corps of four thousand men. M. de Vaudreuil sent orders to evacuate, and to burn the *Cazeux* which are good for nothing, though the King has paid greatly for them.[35]

28th May

The courier from Montréal told us that M. le chevalier de Lévis was descending with great diligence and was followed by his troops.

29th May

M. le chevalier de Lévis arrived at 10 o'clock in the morning saying that his battalions followed closely behind. Malartic received orders to go and stop at Cap Rouge

---

1759. C.P. Stacey, *Québec, 1759: The Siege and the Battle,* (Montreal: Robin Brass Studio, 2002), p. 42.

33 On the right bank of the Saint-Lawrence downriver from Québec, just after l'Isle d'Orleans. There is another Cap Rouge upriver, not far from Québec, near Sillery, mentioned above.

34 The traverse was a river channel in the Saint-Lawrence that ships had to pass by. Montcalm had hoped to have a battery to overlook it but it was not to be. Both Montcalm and Bigot complained that the pilots and seafarers of Québec placed far too much confidence in the dangers of the river to stop British ships. During the summer James Cook, later famous as an explorer, spent much effort surveying the river in detail. See Stacey, *Québec, 1759,* pp. 38 & 46-7.

35 *Cazeux* or *cayeux* were rafts, or rather trains of wood, designed to carry either troops or sometimes even artillery. John Francis McDermott, *A Glossary of Mississippi Valley French, 1673-1850* (St Louis: Washington University, 1941) p. 41.

to make camp; he arrived at 3 o'clock. He learnt that some bateaux had already passed by, there were more than twenty gone onto the river. They were obliged to climb to camp, when they received orders which arrived at 10 o'clock that the battalions were to be sent to Québec. They slept in their bateaux which was terrible, being worn out with fatigue and swept with rain all day.

30th May

M. le chevalier de Lévis has gone to reconnoitre a camp on the right bank of the Saint-Charles River and has established it a half-league above the general hospital, in beautiful grounds, a little sandy, bordered by woods behind and surrounded with water. He sent orders to the troops to enter into the river at high tide to reach the camp, where the battalions arrived successively from 10 o'clock until midday. The first division of the colony troops arrived at 3 o'clock.

31st May

Several battalions have been to fetch food from the town. The news from below is that the English have seventy-six vessels at l'Isle au Coudres.[36]

1st June

Several platoons of colony soldiers arrived with Canadians of the governments of Montréal and Trois-Rivières. They camped to the left of the regulars.

2nd June

The battalions have sent their bateaux to the town. They have each supplied one hundred workers to begin a bridge on the Saint-Charles River and works to cover it. The Canadians of the government of Québec were given permission to return home. M. le chevalier de Lévis went to scout the land irrigated by the Rivers Beauport and Montmorency.[37]

3rd June

An officer detached from Carillon has arrived with a prisoner, that M.de Langis had taken from Orange. This man said that the English march for Fort George with a large artillery train. That five battalions of regular troops will be embarked at

36 This was the fleet of Admiral Saunders, albeit overstated. It was composed of 22 ships of the line, 13 frigates, 4 sloops, 3 bomb ships, 3 fire ships and 4 auxiliary vessels. Stacey, *Québec*, Appendix F – The Royal Navy at Quebec, pp. 231-7.

37 Montcalm decided not to defend Québec, whose fortifications were sketchy and could not be completed quickly. It was resolved to construct a fortified camp ahead of the town, on the bank of the Saint-Charles, and soon, when Lévis had arrived, to continue a line of defensive works up to the Montmorency River which was easier to defend.

New York and Boston for the expedition against Québec. That they are waiting on General Wolfe who is in charge with three regiments from old England, and detachments of other regiments. That they have four thousand men destined for Korlak and six thousand for the Ohio.

4th June

M. le marquis de Montcalm came to visit the camp.

5th June

We have been apprised of the arrival of five large vessels. It is very busy in the lower town with the movement and evacuation of the houses as well as some in the upper town.[38] M. Niguerville [sic. Niverville] left with the Canadians and savages for the Isle au Coudres.[39]

6th June

Firelight in the south makes us believe that part of the fleet is on that half of the river. Several cannon shots were heard.

7th June

M. de Niguerville returned very angry at the savages who did not want to go to the island. He greatly praised seven Canadians, who they taunted, who followed him and captured three marine guards. These young people assure that there are seven ships of the line at l'Isle au Coudres. That the others are frigates or captured ships; that they left from Halifax on the 7th of March; that the army and navy was assembled [at Halifax] and was ready to leave at the end of this month [March].

38 Note by Gaffarel – From the report of Joannès, 'the Marquis de Vaudreuil sent several colony officers with orders to evacuate the homes at the edge of the river and to hide the women, children and livestock some leagues into the woods; but the enemy discovered them in the most part, and did not go without beef during the whole campaign, this convinced us that is was quite unnecessary that we had gone on eating the horses of the troops throughout the winter.'

39 Joseph Boucher de Niverville, born on 22 November 1715 at Chambly, was a marine officer who began his career in 1734 as a cadet in the Fox Wars. He spent time in Detroit, at garrison in Fort Chambly and fighting the Chickasaws in Louisiana. Promoted to ensign at the beginning of the War of the Austrian Succession, he led many raids into Massachusetts. Despite this service he was only promoted to his lieutenancy in 1756. After a brief disappointing stay in France after the fall of New France, he returned to Canada and took an active role in its defence against the American invasion force during 1775-6, despite his advanced years. He remained a colonel of the militia of Trois-Rivières until his retirement in 1803. He died in August 1804.

8th June

A blaze started on a fire-ship while it was being prepared. It was far from the other vessels. News from Carillon where everything is quiet.

9th June

A letter arrived from the Isle d'Orleans sent by a sailor, that gave account that eight English vessels were at the bottom of the traverse. They wish to take a sounding [of the depth of the river]. The works at the port were pressed. Redans and redoubts were raised in different locations.

10th June

M. de Courtemanche has left with five hundred Canadians and savages for the Isle d'Orleans, and M. de Repentigny with two hundred men for Saint-Joachim.[40]

11th June

We began a second bridge on the right and very close to the other. News from Montréal.

12th June

We learned of the arrival of eight vessels that had advanced past Bic. All the generals and M. de Vaudreuil have made a visit to the camp and all the posts, and dined with M. de Bougainville, who commands the camp of Beauport formed of all the grenadier companies and twelve hundred Canadians.

13th June

Over the last few days the troops have provided two thousand four hundred labourers for the works of the town, the bridges, the fords and the Canardière.[41] Several vessels were loaded with food, ammunition and merchandise for Trois-Rivières and Montréal. The Bishop has abandoned his palace, which is to be fortified to defend the way up from the lower to the upper town.

14th June

Ordinary work. We learned that a vessel has crossed the traverse and is followed by seven others. The evacuation of the lower town was hurried along as was the departure of the vessels. Each battalion has received one hundred and eight Canadians

40 On the northern shore of the Saint-Lawrence just beyond the end of the Isle d'Orleans.

41 The Canardière was a small settlement on the Beauport shore. A battery of three 12-pdr cannons was installed. Chartrand, *French Fortresses in North America 1535-1763*, p. 26.

who will be attached to them for the whole campaign and will perform the same service as the soldiers.

15th June

M. Mercier has gone to the Isle d'Orleans with M. Courval to reconnoitre the English fleet.[42] At 4 o'clock in the evening, we learned that four vessels have come past the traverse. A fire-ship was sent out to try and burn some of them. A detachment of the *Corps de Cavalerie*, which was formed at the camp at Charlesbourg, has gone to fetch arms and equipment from the town.[43] M. de la Rochebeaucourt, aide de camp of M. de Montcalm, commands this corps.

16th June

M. Mercier, who had returned from the Isle d'Orleans, said that the English vessels are anchored near Saint-François and number seven. He returned with four twelve pounders to try and keep them away from the coast. We unleashed a fire-ship and a few [fire]rafts which had no success. News from Belle Riviére says that the English have few troops on that border. Word from Niagara says the savages have come from all over to see M. Pouchot; he is campaigning with several parties of savages and Canadians who will take back parts of the Belle Riviére. Letters from Présentation say that the English are assembling an army of ten thousand men at Korlak. Some believe they plan to re-establish Chouaguen, the others that it will just be a depot; that they will separate in two; one division to march on Niagara, the other to descend on Présentation.

17th June

The troops were ordered to embark equipment to send to Deschambault and to keep only what is absolutely necessary. We learned from the Isle d'Orleans that twenty-seven barges, detached to remove our fire-ship, were stopped by several cannon-balls from M. Mercier; that the savages who saw them going back to their vessels took to their canoes and followed them and seized a chaloupe [sloop] conducted by seven men which they have brought to M. Vaudreuil. These prisoners said that the ships were moored further than cannon shot away from the Isle d'Orleans; that their army is composed of twenty-two ships of the line, thirty frigates and two hundred transport boats; that they have fifteen thousand men landing; they believe

---

42 François-Louis Poulin de Courval was a naval officer, born in Québec in 1728. He studied pilotage at the Jesuit college in Québec and in 1747 began sailing between Québec and Île Royale.

43 This hastily-raised unit was the first cavalry unit to serve in Canada. 'It was organised during June 1759 with 200 Canadians led by five French army officers. It patrolled, skirmished with enemy outposts and delivered dispatches until it was disbanded following the surrender of French forces... Its uniform was blue with red collar and cuffs, and probably a bearskin cap although the officers apparently kept the white uniforms of their respective regiments'. Chartrand, *The French Soldier in Colonial America*, p. 36.

that everything will be in the river within fifteen days; that on board these vessels opposite the Isle d'Orleans they have seventeen thousand regular troops and two hundred coureurs des bois;[44] they expect that we have two thousand regular troops and three thousand Canadian troops to oppose them. The Battalion of Montréal has gone to camp at Beauport.

19th June

Violent wind from the north accompanied by rain. The artillery which had been carried to the Isle d'Orleans was brought back; several platoons of Canadians from the government of Montréal arrived; several vessels loaded with diverse effects of the town have set sail to go up river.

20th June

We learned that M. Aubert has become aware of an increase of fourteen vessels [to the British force downriver]; the mist prevented counting any more. The Intendant prayed that MM. the officers, particularly those with coin, to give them in to him for bills of exchange for the royal treasury, of which he is banker. He needs it to find corn.

21st June

A courier from down river told us of the arrival of the rest of the fleet composed of one hundred and thirty sails which were at Bic. Several couriers were sent out to hasten the retreat of the women, children and livestock from the most exposed parishes and recommend to the officers at the front to have the greatest vigilance. A floating battery of twelve cannon was launched. It was named the *Diable*. It was decided to disarm two frigates to use their equipment on land. It was ordered that all houses under the fire arc of the upper batteries have their roofs removed.

22nd June

The courier from down river says that eighty-four sails have passed l'Isle Verte. The works of the town and elsewhere were pressed.

23rd June

M. Aubert informed that he had withdrawn; that the first vessels of the second division were at Pont à l'Eau-de-Vie. I have seen the state of our army which, when it is assembled, is of fifteen thousand men.[45]

---

44 Malartic is probably referring to British Rangers or Provincial soldiers.

45 Note by Gaffarel – Letter from an eyewitness quoted by Garneau (Canada, II, 303). 'We had not counted on such a strong army, because we had not expected to have a large number of Canadians; it had been the intention to assemble only the men capable of supporting the

It is as follows:

Troupes de Terre	2,200
Government of Montréal	4,800
Government of Trois-Rivières	1,100
Government of Québec	4,400
Town of Québec	840
Royal Syntaxe or the College[46]	35
Acadiens	150
Savages	300
Cavalry	200
Artillery	200
The Bay [La rade][47]	1,460
Total	15,685

The troops of the colony are included with the governments; from this must be deducted the sick, the garrison of the city who will remain around Sainte-Foi, the guards of the bridges, the redoubts and the other works necessary to serve the artillery.

24th June

A courier from Montréal announced the arrival of the savages. One from down river reported that twelve vessels had crossed the traverse and thirty more were waiting to undertake it.

25th June

A courier from Montréal came with responses from General Amherst to M. de Vaudreuil. M. de Bourlamaque said that the English army had begun the portage, that General Amherst is camped at Fort Edouard and is apparently ready for immediate operations.[48] Montréal writes that they [i.e. the people of Montréal] will send what help they can to Carillon.

---

fatigues of war; but there reigned among the people such emulation that we saw 80 year olds and children of 12 to 13 years arrive at camp who did not wish to take advantage of the exemption to their age; never were subjects more worthy of the kindness of their sovereign, by their patience in the troubles and miseries in this country which have been extreme, either by their constancy in work: as in the army they were exposed to all chores.'

46 These were schoolboys of the Jesuit College that 'some wag' had given this grand appellation. Stacey, *Quebec*, p. 70.

47 Presumably this refers to the militia of those small settlements north of Quebec along the Gulf of Saint Lawrence.

48 This is the first time the Malartic refers to Fort Edward instead of 'Lydius'.

27th June

The regiments of Royal Roussillon and Guyenne are camped on the two banks of the Beauport River. M. de Vaudreuil has left for Montréal with several ladies. Three vessels presented themselves at 8 o'clock at the entrance to the river basin and stayed until 11 o'clock. In the evening we had a violent storm.

29th June

The Regiments of La Sarre and Béarn and the battalion of Trois-Rivières are camped between that of Guyenne and the Canardière, near the river, in order to block those places where the enemy would wish to disembark. The fire-ships went downstream to try to burn some of the enemy vessels. Those who commanded them were too eager to set them on fire. They did not reach any vessel and were grounded on the tip of the Isle d'Orleans. The English mocked them, laughing a lot.[49]

29th June

The [militia] of the government of Québec came to camp on the right of Trois-Rivières. The generals made visits to all the posts. The *Diable* went to anchor with several chaloupes armed with cannon between the Beauport River and the Canardière.

30th June

Eight vessels entered the river basin early in the morning; several chaloupes presented themselves to probe in front of the Isle d'Orleans. Two bateaux armed with cannon sent several volleys which sent them back behind their ships. These ships put away to the south, where it is assumed they will make a raid. The Intendant, treasurer and *munitionnaire* came to establish themselves at headquarters. M. Langlade arrived with two hundred Indians. MM. Courtemanche and Repentigny have withdrawn their troops camped around the falls of Montmorency. We saw a column above the Pointe de Lévis. It seems they are working on entrenchments; several savages who approached killed eight men and took a prisoner who said that we were to be attacked this night between the rivers of Beauport and Saint-Charles; that the biggest vessels remained at the Isle au Coudres; that Admiral Saunders is on a frigate; that three thousand men had disembarked on the Pointe de Lévis, and a great number on the Isle d'Orleans. At 8 o'clock in the evening, the troops received orders to go to the posts that they were assigned to be on alert all night.

49 The hopes the French pinned on fireships was misplaced. The men of the Royal Navy were able to simply tow them out of harm's way. Stacey, *Québec 1759*, p. 51.

1st July

The troops returned this day. A great fusillade was made by the Canadians who believed that the enemy had penetrated part of our defences. Worked to build epaulements and facilitate communications with different points. We saw an encampment on the Isle d'Orleans and on the Pointe de Lévis, near to which several vessels were moored. The bateaux gunners fired some shot against the barges who tried to probe, and the *Diable* fired on a frigate which approached it.

2nd July

The troops were ready armed an hour before daylight and returned [to camp] after sunrise. It seemed that the position of the camp on the Isle d'Orleans had changed and the camp at Pointe Lévis was reinforced. At 3 o'clock after midday, one could see from the town, on the plateau opposite, two detachments who looked to all appearances to be reconnoitring. The savages as well as the volunteers of Repentigny went to establish themselves at the camp of M. le chevalier de Lévis, at the Montmorency Falls. At 10 o'clock in the evening, we saw and heard a signal party from the fleet. The troops were brought immediately to their posts. A loud noise made in front of the place guarded by Béarn hastened the march of that regiment who learned it had been made by a bateau, which was hit by a wave which filled it. M le marquis de Montcalm rushed there with his staff. The Royal Roussillon Regiment fired on a bateau which did not respond to the '*Qui vive*!'

3rd July

The troops returned at broad daylight. Bad weather impeded work. The camp of the Isle d'Orleans has been enlarged.

4th July

The troops were ready on their arms an hour before day and stood down after the return of the patrols by land and water. It rained heavily through the day. At midday a barge was sighted making its way towards the town carrying a flag of truce. A bateau gunner was sent to meet it, who stopped it and took a letter from Admiral Saunders for M. de Vaudreuil, who sent him his response a half-hour later with M. Mercier, who was stopped by the first frigate. At the beginning of the night, we heard a lot of noise and different drum beats from the camp at Pointe Lévis.

5th July

The troops were on their arms as normal. The [English] Admiral returned the captured women as he had announced yesterday. They report that the English have ten thousand regular troops, but they wish to persuade us that they have eighteen thousand; they count on joining with two thousand sailors to attack us imminently, they believe we have few people and that Carillon had been taken on the 12th of June. A courier from Montréal carried the news of the *pays d'en haut*. A corps of fifteen hundred has left from Niagara for the Ohio. A party of Agnés attacked M. de la Miltière who had just come from the Five Nations and took him prisoner.[50] M. de la Corne is on the march with one thousand two hundred men, to go to the right bank of the Chouaguen River, which the English have not yet taken. M. de la Veranderie,[51] arriving at Montréal with some savages, said that the Christinaux did not dare come down because of the small pox of which they are very concerned.[52]

6th July

Under arms as normal. The Outaouas pursued a barge which approached the falls to scout, and caught up with them near the Isle d'Orleans, they captured two men who they killed because they did not want to walk. They made several discharges on a column which came at them, and re-embarked under cover from fire from their comrades, who went down to the shore to secure their retreat. One of the batteries of M. de Lévis camp fired on the column. Two balls were seen to hit it.

7th July

A party of Micmacs went to disembark to the south, opposite an enemy post which they harassed. A deserter who arrived assured that we will be attacked very soon on three different points, namely the Falls, the River Beauport and the Canardière. In the evening we saw much movement in the enemy camp.

8th July

At 2 o'clock in the morning, our patrols saw two vessels sails and made a signal. The army was brought forward within a minute and stood down at daytime. A 2 o'clock, two frigates entered the channel to the north of the Isle d'Orleans, followed by two vessels. They bombarded the camp of M. de Lévis until sunset. The batteries of the town sent some bombs and balls to those of the enemy at Pointe de Lévis. At 4 o'clock, we saw many barges file along the Isle d'Orleans. The army came under arms at sunset and went to their posts.

50 Probably Honoré Dubois de la Miltière, a captain in the Languedoc Regiment. He married in Montréal 1757 and remained in America until his death in New York around 1788. He had a brother in the French Navy at Quebec who was known as Dubois and who commanded one of the futile fire-ships, *l'Embassadeur*, launched to try and disrupt the Royal Navy. Dubois died aboard his vessel. 'Journal du siège de Québec du 10 mai au 18 septembre 1759, annoté par Aegidius Fauteux, bibliothécaire de Saint-Sulpice', *Rapport de l'Archiviste de la Province de Québec* (Quebec, 1920-21), p. 224 and Stacey, *Quebec*, p. 252.

51 Note by Gaffarel – De la Vèrandrye belonged to the family of heroic explorers who came to prominence by their travels and adventures in the western regions.

52 Note by Gaffarel – The Christinaux lived beyond the great lakes of the Saint-Lawrence, being of the Nippissing and Winnipeg.

9th July

The army stood down at daylight. We learned that the English had disembarked at l'Ange-Gardien, and they approached the Falls.[53] The Canadians, Outaouas and Micmacs went to attack the vanguard, and pushed on a corps of the army who they shot at, after which they retired. They say they have killed eighty to one hundred men, they had twenty of their own killed or wounded. A company of volunteers was formed, drawn from the five battalions of regular troops. The army took up arms at the end of the day.

10th July

The army stood down at day. An English deserter who came to us said that he wanted to see Québec where he had lived for some years, and which he enjoyed greatly. He reported that the English have three thousand men at Pointe Lévis, where there is a battery of thirty mortars and six 32lb cannon; they have seven thousand men at the falls; that the general reported to the Admiral that he had lost no-one disembarking; that fifty men had been killed in a small ambush. The batteries of the town fire on those of the enemy. Our volunteers and savages shoot at the English across the banks of the [Montmorency] Falls River. Another deserter arrived. The soldiers slept clothed in their tents.

11th July

The batteries of the town fired on those of the enemy. The reserve of Repentigny has gone to the camp of M. de Lévis. News came from Carillon from the 3rd [of July] which told of the prisoners that M. de Langis had taken from in front of the camp of Fort George. They [the prisoners] said that the English army is not yet assembled and will not be ready until about the 15th. That General Amherst will come to Carillon by land and water. The news from Niagara announced that M. Pouchot recalled all the detachments that were out and the enemy arrives before him. That from Présentation says that M. le chevalier de la Corne is on the Chouaguen with one thousand two hundred men; that our savages have, before Korlak, taken prisoners who they were obliged to kill, before they were attacked on their return by the Agnés. That from Montréal, six thousand *minots* of corn was picked; that the rolls, made by the priests, of the men who have stayed in their parishes and in a state to bear arms number one thousand two hundred. Our volunteers and savages have been shooting against the English. We have had a captain of militia and a savage killed and a soldier wounded. The Regiment of Royal Roussillon has gone to camp at the right of the camp of Lévis. Those of La Sarre, Guyenne and Béarn and the battalion of Trois-Rivières took their camp a quarter league away, to be able to strengthen that of Lévis, at their former sites, at the lookouts or the Canardière. The grenadiers and piquets slept in bivouac.

---

53 Wolfe and the grenadiers of the army had landed on the night of the 8th and 9th. Once established, Townshend's brigade joined them on the 9th. Murray joined them on the 10th making a force of around 4,000 men at the Montmorency falls. Stacey, *Quebec*, p. 69.

12th July

The battalions have provided workers for two batteries, to be constructed at the camp of Lévis. Those of the town fired on those of the enemy. We saw many barges file along the Isle d'Orleans. A detachment of Canadians from the Baye Saint-Paul arrived, who avoided the camp of the enemy who were not aware of this party.[54] Our volunteers and the English kept up firing. We had a soldier wounded. At nightfall, a frigate and a *goelette* approached the town which they bombarded and shelled. The battery on Pointe Lévis also made a very lively fire all night. M. Dumas left with two thousand men to try and seize this battery.[55]

13th July

The detachment which left last night could not achieve its objective. Bateaux from the falls, point Lévis and the galliots fired on the camp of Lévis and on the town, into which lots of bombs fell. There was a Canadian killed in the camp of M. de Lévis. The general has raised up several epaulements to cover the troops from the batteries of the English on the left bank of the falls, which enfilade the said camp. Our scouts gave notice that the enemy had made a road from his camp to the winter ford.[56] M. de Lévis reinforced this post and ordered it to closely observe all that happens in the area. M. de Montcalm went to the city to reassure the bourgeois who were very afraid of the effects of the bombs. We are obliged to send twenty men per battalion to reinforce and encourage the garrison; these will be rotated every two days. M. Hertel arrived with one hundred savages, Scious [Sioux], Aouias [Wea] and other nations. A violent storm has silenced the batteries.

14th July

The camp at the falls gave a lively bombardment to Lévis' camp where work continued on the epaulements. M. Duprat has gone to the winter ford with the volunteers and one hundred Canadians. Around midday, the enemy fire relented. M. le chevalier de Lévis made a visit to all the posts and fords. M. le marquis de Montcalm went to all the lookouts. We carried a cannon to the camp of Lévis. Our bateaux gunners pursued a barge which escaped them and ran aground. We learnt that the enemy are forming other batteries at Pointe Lévis and the falls. All the communication paths to the outposts have been completed.

---

54 Baie Saint-Paul (modern spelling) is a small village on the north bank of the Saint-Lawrence opposite the Isle au Coudres.

55 The townspeople of Québec asked to be allowed to help in their own defence. After initially rejecting the scheme, Montcalm and Vaudreuil allowed a force of around 1,600 men under Jean-Daniel Dumas to attempt to knock out the batteries on Pointe Lévis. The night attack was too difficult for the capabilities of tradesmen and college students. Confusion reigned in the dark and two were shot by their own side. Nothing was achieved and all had retreated to the north shore by morning. The British were totally unaware the action had taken place until news came from a deserter five days later. Stacey, *Quebec*, pp. 70-1.

56 The passable crossing of the Montmorency River, some miles inland.

15th July

The English have warmed up the camp of Lévis and the town.[57] We drove several cannon up to the said camp.

16th July

A party of Canadians and savages passed over the River of the [Montmorency] Falls. The fire on the camp of Lévis and the town was lively. In the camp three Canadians were wounded who were helping to drag a mortar; a pot of fire engulfed a house in the town which was, with four others, reduced to cinders. The courier from Montréal told us that the chevalier de la Corne, who went to Chouaguen, had found the English entrenched in the old Fort Ontario, that he probed these entrenchments; he fired at them for an hour when he retired with the loss of twenty men and as many wounded to the Isle au Galop. M. Pouchot said that three thousand English would arrive on the 16th three leagues from Niagara and that he awaited all the detachments sent to the Ohio.

17th July

The savages brought three prisoners, and carried nine scalps from a patrol of twelve men who they had captured, although they were supported by several companies of grenadiers. The depositions of the prisoners told that General Wolfe is at the camp at the Falls, where he often speaks of attacking us, giving orders to attack yesterday but countermanding the order at the end of the day. They intend to cross the falls on bridges which they have been working on for a week. The light troops will come along the banks; they have lots of mortars and canon at the camp of the Falls where they have ten thousand men and six thousand at Pointe Lévis. They have thirty flat bottomed bateaux capable of carrying one hundred men each. Five hundred coureurs de bois come out all night up to the lookout posts, sometimes accompanied by their general.[58] They believe that we have five thousand men and three thousand savages. That the rumour in their camp is that we wish to abandon this bank of the Falls; they expect that General Amherst is ten leagues from here; that seven or eight women and an old man often carry refreshments to their general; but that it is forbidden to question them.

The Regiment of Royal Roussillon and the [militia of the] government of Montréal are too exposed and have been camped behind the house of M. de Lévis. They have been replaced by the La Sarre Regiment and the detachment of the three governments. These troops have been stood-to every day. This post is as dangerous as one in a trench.

---

57 Malartic uses the word *chauffer* which translates as 'to heat'. This is used frequently to describe heavy artillery bombardment.

58 The term *coureur de bois,* literally woods runner, has become used to describe Canadian auxiliaries of the western frontier so it is interesting to see it being used to refer to woodsmen/rangers/fur trappers on the British side.

18th July

Much work in the camp of Lévis. The troops of the camp of Montréal have carried many gabions, fascines and *saucissons*. Seven hundred savages who crossed the Falls returned this evening, saying that the Outawas barred the way for the other nations because they did not have all of their warriors and prayed that they wait until tomorrow to make the best strike. The fleet made lots of signals. We have seen several barges and chaloupes come and go, one amongst the others seemed to have several officers of distinction who went to address the Admiral. Some ships have set sail and gone downriver. Our bateaux gunners bombarded several barges. M. de Montcalm made a visit to several posts. News from Carillon is that all is peaceful and parties had left to get information on the movement of the enemy. At 11 o'clock at night, four vessels or frigates passed beyond the town, which were given free passage.

19th July

M. Dumas has been detached with six hundred men, to go and seek out the vessels which passed above the town. They set fire to the only remaining fire-ship in Sillery. The commanders of the frigates left to go up the Richelieu. M. de Boishébert arrived with one hundred and ten men exhausted by famine and fatigue.[59] The vessels fired a great deal into Sillery. A column was discovered in the south marching to the same location. The troops were under orders to sleep clothed and be ready to march. M. le chevalier de Lévis, on making a visit to his posts, came to be facing General Wolfe on the other side of the river, who was doing the same. A deserter said that the general was, at 5 o'clock in the evening, at Pointe Lévis with five hundred grenadiers.

20th July

Several discharges of muskets coming from Sillery went on for a long time during the day. All were close to their arms from 2 o'clock in the morning and remained at the head of the camp. La Sarre went up to la Boulangerie, and Béarn to the great road, opposite the house of Duchenai [Duchesnay], and all stood down at sunrise.[60] The English camps appeared tranquil. We learned that the discharges from Sillery had been made against the barges that tried to put men ashore. M. Dumas followed the ships by land.

News from Niagara which told of trenches being opened, that the enemy made a lively fire, and is an army composed of 3,500 men, that the Five Nations asked for a council with M. Pouchot, to which he agreed, and asked to be forgiven for giving passage to the English and guiding them over their lands. They offered to stay with him but he refused. He demanded that they take the road back to their villages;

59 Boishébert was the commander of the last Acadians who stayed loyal and marched overland to participate in the defence of the colony.

60 The great road (*grand chemin*) was the road that led out of the city, over the Plains of Abraham towards Sillery.

the detachments from Belle Riviére were expected on the 16th. M. de Vaudreuil dispatched a courier to carry orders to Niagara and the Isle au Galop. The batteries of the Falls and the tip of the Isle d'Orleans kept up a lively fire to support the return of General Wolfe. A corporal of the colony, who had been sent to pursue M. Stobo and was captured by the English, returned to join us. The volunteers of Duprat opened fire on 11 o'clock on the enemy who were working at the first ford. They continued through the night. They responded with grenades. Our workers continued on the boyau on the left of the right bank of the Falls River.[61] The batteries on the Pointe de Lévis fired vigorously on the town. The Béarn Regiment mounted guard on the left with five hundred men of the government of Montréal and fifty of Trois-Rivières. Two hundred men were placed on the heights, eighty in the first redoubt which is on the left, and sixty in the second redoubt, where it provides small outposts on the edge of the river and Falls. The rest were distributed to stand for the time needed for points at risk.

21st July

We saw stretchers loaded with wounded going from the left down to camp. The curious among us received some volleys from the cannon and several bombs. Three fell in the ground around the Béarn Regiment but killed no-one. We have learned that three hundred English disembarked yesterday at Pointe aux Trembles; that three hundred Canadians or savages were sent to force them to re-embark; they took several women. It rained all day.

22nd July

The bad weather continued. The cavalry left for Pointe aux Trembles. The commander of the vessels which went above the town wrote to M. de Vaudreuil that he would return the women and old men his troops had captured from the Pointe aux Trembles tomorrow, and requested permission to let him send down a bateau loaded with sick. The priest of Cap Santé said that he saw a chaloupe in which were many people approaching Platon.[62] At 11 o'clock at night, the batteries of Pointe Lévis began a vigorous fire on the town. They threw fire pots which reduced the cathedral to cinders. We reduced the guard on the left to a company of grenadiers and fifty men of Trois-Rivières.

61 A boyau is defined as 'a Moat border'd with a parapet, which is drawn from one Trench to another for better Communication' in William Allingham, *The New Method of Fortification, As Practised by Monsieur de Vauban, Engineer-General of France. Together with a new Treatise of Geometry* (London: A. Bettesworth, 1722), p. 70.

62 In the French edition, this passage is given as '...approaching *du platon* (?)', the question mark seemingly indicating that Gaffrael was unsure of the meaning. Since Platon and Cap Santé are opposite one and other, the interpretation given here seems most likely.

23rd July

We learned that fifteen houses burnt down with the cathedral. Two frigates attempted to pass under the town at daybreak. Our batteries forced them to change course. The Regiments of Guyenne and Béarn went to occupy their old camp near the Canardière. The women and elderly announced their arrival. They said they had been well treated on board; but that their homes had been pillaged; that General Wolfe and M. Stobo were on the vessels.[63] At seven o'clock in the evening, a vessel fired eleven guns. After the sun set, the batteries on Pointe Lévis threw many bombs and fire pots into the town.

24th July

News from Carillon where all is tranquil. General Amherst is known to be at Fort George. An English officer came to the Anse des Mers demanding that we comply to the prisoner exchange. M. de Bougainville gave him the response of the general. The priest of l'Ange-Gardien said that a detachment of two hundred English went inland and captured the livestock. M. le chevalier de Lévis agreed that two hundred savages should cross the Falls River. The batteries at the Falls and Pointe Lévis made a lively fire. One house has been burned. The troops of the camp sent one hundred workers to the town for the artillery.

25th July

Many workers were supplied for the artillery. On our right the *généralle* was beaten after a general opinion that the enemy had landed their forces at Saint-Michel.[64] M. de Bougainville marched there within the minute with three companies of grenadiers and the piquets. At 7 o'clock, M. de Vaudreuil received a letter from M. de Saint-Martin which informed that he had followed eight barges which were attempting to put men ashore, and that he hoped to oppose them. We learned that a frigate and eight barges which appeared before Sillery, had found five of our chaloupes and several bateaux abandoned by their guards, who went to ground rather than defend them; they took one chaloupe and one bateau, but were forced to abandon a third which they had towed away. The troops of the right remained under arms until 9 o'clock. M. de Bougainville returned at 2 o'clock. Five Canadians of l'Ange-Gardien took a prisoner from a small party that they dispersed. This prisoner said that they had constructed another battery in the Falls camp; that the general could not find an easy passage to attack.

---

63 After his escape from Quebec, Robert Stobo managed to steal a boat and made his way to Louisbourg, reaching it on the 6th of June. The newly installed British Governor of Louisbourg, Whitmore, lost no time in forwarding Stobo's eyewitness accounts of French numbers and defences to William Pitt and General Amherst. Stobo volunteered to assist General Wolfe's army and so set sail back to Québec on June the 12th, reaching the British army in early July. Alberts, *The Most Extraordinary Adventures of Major Robert Stobo,* pp. 237-245.

64 Just above Québec, near Sillery.

26th July

The batteries on the Pointe Lévis have greatly worried the town. At daybreak we discovered new ones which aimed towards our great road and several barges and bateaux behind the frigate. An hour after midday, we heard several discharges. We were informed, from 2 o'clock, that the savages attacked a column which came up to the winter ford; they initially repulsed it and then they in their turn were pushed back by a second column which came to the aid of the first; they were forced to cross over the Falls just at the moment that M. de Repentigny wished to cross to support them; Repentigny's men lined the entrenchments, giving a fire so intense that the English columns were forced to retreat. We had eighteen killed or wounded. The English losses are not known but we have seen several stretchers descend to their camp. M. de Lévis marched with a party of his camp to aid M. de Repentigny and M. de Montcalm who moved with all the grenadiers and the Royal Roussillon Regiment up to the house of M. de Lévis. The generals returned at 4 o'clock with their troops. The Acadians led in three prisoners of a small party they had routed to the south; these prisoners said they were from the five regiments at Pointe de Lévis, at the River Etchemins three hundred men are entrenched, and in front of them one hundred coureur des bois; in the camp there are four hundred men always under arms to give aid to these two posts; that the general visits often; on the vessels above the city they have thirteen hundred men with flat bottomed boats which can each carry one hundred men; they are making rafts for six canon and one hundred and fifty men. The rumour in their camp is that there will be an order to attack, which will be perilous, and that they will move four vessels in front of the town.

27th July

A very great fire on the town, quite slow on the left. The savages have crossed the Falls to lift scalps from the men they killed yesterday. They reported 12. They found an Outaoua pierced several times with bayonets and his ears and nose cut off. Thirty grenadiers and sixty volunteers embarked at nightfall to help those conducting the *caïeux*.[65] They ignited close enough to the vessels but could not approach them as they were diverted on the current and hooked by the barges sent to divert them; the enemy took revenge by making a terrible bombardment on the town.

28th July

A fierce fire on the town; the left [flank] has been spared. A barge approached the city with a flag of truce. The boat sent to meet it carried a letter from General Wolfe who cautioned all Canadians to realise that from the 10th of August, he will treat with the utmost rigour, all those captured bearing arms.[66] At 9 o'clock, M. de Repentigny

---

65 The literal translation of this term is 'bulbs' in the botanical sense. I can find no archaic etymology but from the following description it seems to describe some other sort of fire-ship.

66 Note by Gaffarel – Here is the manifesto of Wolfe: 'His Excellency, stung by the small regard that the people of Canada were in, the cabinet of June 29th last is determined not to listen to humanitarian sentiment that carried to spare the blind people of their own interest. The

gave notice that he had seen a corps of four thousand men opposite. All the troops took arms to the field. Two hours later, he sent word that this was a patrol which was much stronger than ordinary. The troops stood down after this. Courier from Montréal; nothing transpires in his dispatches.

29th July

Fire is intense as normal. Workers were sent to Sillery. The regiments have made gabions and fascines for the town. All the carts attached to the corps and others left at 9 in the evening to go and fetch grain from Pointe aux Trembles. The town asked for them [the carts] as they fear an escalade by the rear of the lower town. A mortar from the camp sent some bombs at a vessel which tried to approach.

30th July

A great deal of firing on the town, almost none on the camp of Lévis. M. de Montcalm has gone to the town to try and reconcile the engineering and artillery. The Béarn Regiment mounted guard on the left.

31st July

Fire on the town as normal. Since yesterday evening at 10 o'clock, there has not been a single cannon shot against the left. Béarn supplied three hundred workers to continue the zig-zag. At 10 o'clock in the morning, I went to visit the works. On the plateau of the left bank of the Falls, I perceived a dozen officers examining our position. At 11 o'clock, two frigates sailed and came on to press opposite the two redoubts guarded by MM. de Mazerac and Laparguière, captains of Béarn. They were followed by a vessel of sixty guns which pushed ahead of them. All three began to fire vigorously on the two redoubts and the entrenchments that we had lined at that moment. The three batteries of the falls began firing at the same time battering our rear and continued, along with the three ships, from noon until 7 o'clock. Several bombs and bullets fell into the entrenchments and redoubts, where they killed or wounded sixty men and burned some tents. At 3 o'clock we saw many barges and bateaux carrying troops assembling behind the ships, some proceeding towards the falls, and some towards Pointe de l'Essai [Pointe Lessay] We had seen much of the movement in the camp of the Falls and a column sent out to wait on the shore; M.

Canadians, by their conduct, have shown themselves unworthy of the great offers that have been made to them. This is why he gave orders to the commanders of the light troops and other officers to move into the country to seize and take the habitants and their herds, and to destroy and overthrow that which they judge proper. Besides, though he is sorry that it has come to these barbaric ends it is the Canadians and the Indians their allies who have set the example, he proposed to defer until next April the 10th, the decision on the prisoners, who he will use for retaliation, unless during that interval, the Canadians come to submit to those terms which were proposed in the cabinet, and by their submission he will reach clemency and bring with it tenderness. Given at *Saint-Henri*, 25th July 1759. Joseph Dallin, major of light troops.'

le chevalier de Lévis came immediately behind the centre of the Regiment of Béarn, where he observed the enemy. Then he went to visit some posts and returned to the regiment where he engaged in conversation, which was inspiring to us, being exposed to a hail of bullets and shells. He gave his orders with an admirable tranquillity and coolness.

At 5 o'clock the column that had descended from the Falls began to cross the river along the shore and formed up after crossing. At the same time, the barges emerged from behind the ships; the men which they carried disembarked, formed in column and marched, as did the column from the falls, at our entrenchments and were forced between the two redoubts. They came under fire from the redoubt guarded by M. Mazerac which forced them to give a lot of ground on their left. The other redoubt, not being capable of defence, was abandoned by its guard, who retired on the heights occupied by the government of Montréal. M. le chevalier de Lévis went there and by his presence animated the Canadians. He found the regiments of La Sarre and Guyenne, sent by M. le marquis de Montcalm who was at the centre of the army: the enemy seized the abandoned redoubt and attempted to climb up the heights. The Canadians fed them with fire which lasted for less than half an hour when they were forced to retire, abandoning the redoubt and returned to their barges and their camp. A violent thunderstorm sprang up and great rain which prevented us from descending from our entrenchments to disrupt their retreat. The crews of the frigates came out and set them [the frigates] on fire. It appeared that the English had five hundred men killed or wounded. They only suffered from the fire of the redoubts and a party of the government of Montréal, having passed out of reach of the other troops. Some volunteers who were let out captured a Scottish captain and several wounded soldiers. Béarn was relieved at 10 o'clock in the evening and did not arrive back to their camp until midnight due to the bad roads, very happy to have only lost thirteen men killed in the bombardment and shelling it sustained for eight hours. A sergeant, deserted from the Royal Americans, reported that the English had lost two captains, two lieutenants and forty-five soldiers, they had a lot of injured, amongst them the major general who had a broken arm, in the action of the 26th.[67]

The courier from Montréal told us that the enemy was, on the 20th, thirty *toises* from the covered way at Niagara, where no new detachments have arrived from Belle Riviere.[68] M. Bourlamaque has retired behind the Barbue River, and Carillon has been besieged since the 25th.

67 This day marked what was to become known as the Battle of Montmorency. Wolfe was attempting a landing and intended to seize the redoubts and strengthen them as a base to push inland. He overestimated how far away from the shore they were though and as the two frigates (actually armed transports) went in, covered by the guns of the *Centurion*, it became clear that the redoubts were within range of the shore and could not be held. Wolfe resolved for a full-on attack but his grenadiers set off too quickly without awaiting reinforcements and his transports found it difficult to land. The transports were damaged beyond salvation and Wolfe lost 210 killed and 230 wounded. The French losses were 60 killed and wounded: the majority of these coming from the battery at Montmorency Falls which raked them throughout the day. Stacey, *Quebec*, pp. 85-91.

68 Niagara had been under siege by Prideaux since 6 July. Captain Pierre Pouchot was commanding the French garrison. Prideaux was killed when stepping in front of his own

1st August

The troops have been rested. The savages returned with some prisoners they took overnight. The batteries at the falls fired on the Canadians and soldiers who went up to the frigates so they could not burn the hulls. There was a report on the works and tools. Sixty-eight English were buried who had been found dead on the battleground. Workers were supplied for the town and to take a *crapaud* to the left. The convoy from Pointe aux Trembles arrived at midday. M. Dumas returned with the cavalry and a piquet.

2nd August

Workers were sent to Sillery, employed under the direction of M. Joannès, major of Languedoc. The English bombarded the town and occasionally volleyed those who approached the frigates. The generals have written to Admiral Saunders, after the insistence of the Scottish captain.[69] Workers were sent to the town to clear debris and repair the streets that the bombs have rendered impracticable. We have seen much movement in the camp of Pointe Lévis and barges around the area of the falls. The regiments took gabions and *saucissons* to the city.

3rd August

Before sunrise the English towed the vessel which had been in the channel of the Isle d'Orleans and then came out. They fired fiercely on the town, very little on the left. At 8 o'clock, our generals were informed that the enemy was making signs of movement opposite the post of Repentigny. M. le marquis de Montcalm quickly ran at that instant up to the left. He ordered the troops to take up arms and advanced Royal Roussillon to carry and secure the parts which were threatened. They returned at midday and the troops were stood down; they said to us that they believed that Admiral Saunders had come with a large detachment scouting the banks of the Falls River. M. de Blot, captain of the Guyenne Regiment, went to replace M. Dumas. M. de Lévis informed M. de Montcalm that he knows that the enemy has taken a corps of one thousand two hundred men to the winter ford.

4th August

Fire on the town as normal. M. de Boishébert, who was in front of the town said that he had five English deserters at his post. We had seen the passage of munitions for the camp of the Falls. At 2 o'clock, the batteries of Pointe de Lévis raised the French and English flag, and we saw an officer arrive in a barge, charged with the responses of the Admiral and General Wolfe. They complained about the cruelties

artillery on 20 July, command passing to William Johnson. However by the 26th the Fort had already surrendered with Pouchot being commended for a tenacious defence. See Dunnigan, *Siege 1759, passim.*

69 It is unknown as to which Scottish captain Malartic is referring to here but as can be seen the next day, letters were exchanged under a flag of truce.

of the savages, and announced that they cannot follow certain articles of the agreement, and that we must have some prisoners from the last action; that they will keep the women until we return those who we hold in the colony, and it is the intention to retaliate for all the barbarities of the savages. The Regiment of Béarn and all the piquets took up their arms for the execution of a deserter. This regiment had stood guard on the left and were working around Cayeux;[70] a soldier who was on duty on the shore deserted and provided the guard who was posted there with a shower of grenades.

5th August

Terrible firing on the town. Barges came to the camp of the Falls which unloaded munitions and loaded many cattle. At 2 o'clock a bateau of twenty tonnes entered the north channel past the Isle d'Orleans and met the frigate. Three English deserters have been brought in from the post of Repentigny. The Béarn Regiment employed three hundred men on the works of la Crète.[71] The volunteers came to fetch tools for a new boyau and the Canadians raised the epaulements in the areas which they are guarding. At 4 o'clock, we saw a detachment of four hundred men descend from the camp of the Falls and embarked taking the route to Pointe de Lévis. At 7 o'clock, a vessel set sail and went down the south channel. Our batteries fired several shots on the barges, which was responded to by their batteries of the Falls who responded with a hot fire.[72] It rained heavily in the evening. M. de Vaudreuil sent responses to the Admiral.

6th August

Rapellé [call to assemble] was beaten throughout the night in the town to assemble the garrison to be on high alert due to the passage of some barges. The troops on the right took up their arms an hour before daylight and stood down after sunrise. The deserters arrived here and said that the enemy lost five hundred men in the attack of the 31st, that they attacked without the orders of the general, they attacked again immediately by the fords and moored four ships by the burnt frigates; that the general assembled the grenadiers there two days ago and asked if it was their opinion they should attack and take their revenge, and they responded yes, he had expressed regret at the loss of the 31st, and raised their hopes that the next action would be happier, that generals Monkton [sic.] and Murray were wounded on the 31st. Our deserters said to them that we have fourteen thousand men and eight hundred savages, that we have no lack of bread, but of meat, and that General Lévis has been on horseback ten hours on the 31st going from one post to another. It has

70 The location is unclear but could be Cariere, a small habitation around the Beauport River and south of Beauport village. Robert de Villeneuve, *Carte des Environs de Quebec en La Nouvelle France Mesuree tres exactements en 1688 par le Sr de Villeneuve Ing.* (1688).

71 Unknown location.

72 The batteries referred to here are those of Wolfe's camp on the north bank of the Montmorency River.

been rumoured for several days in their camp that General Amherst is five leagues from here with many prisoners.

M. de Saint-Martin said that he had seen thirty barges opposite Sillery. At 2 o'clock we saw sight of movement in the fleet and a vessel under sail. All the army was held ready on their arms. The vessel cannonaded two of our bateaux who were observing it. At 5 o'clock, a *senault* came to join the vessels which were at the Falls.[73] At 8 o'clock in the evening, M. de Montcalm received notice from M. d'Hastrel that he had seen 27 barges loaded with troops before the vessels which were opposite Cap Rouge, there were twenty behind a frigate which was carrying people. M. Bougainville left at 10 o'clock with the grenadiers of Béarn to go to observe. He was followed by a detachment of Canadians.

7th August

Fire of the utmost fury on the town. At 8 o'clock, enemy movement was seen opposite the post of Repentigny. The troops were held ready to march. M de Montcalm went there with M. de Lévis. M. de Bougainville wrote from Pointe aux Trembles that four vessels were moored in front of the church, that he believes that they have nine hundred men landing, the same number as he, and that he will make war with his eyes;[74] that five barges, which wanted run a line past to the south were pushed away by a volley from some Canadians; that the ships wish to seek out our frigates or want to ravage the south. Courier from Montréal, nothing has transpired from his despatches.

8th August

Ordinary fire on the town, quite keen on the left. M. Bougainville says that the enemy are moving in his area. We have learned that our frigates, which went up the Richelieu, are safe.

9th August

The enemy have thrown a great quantity of bombs and incendiaries into the town, such that almost all the lower town is burned down, but it was possible to put out the fire; on the left they sent many bombs and grenades. M. de Vaudreuil received a courier from M. de Bougainville who gave an account that the English landed at Pointe aux Trembles at 9 o'clock yesterday, he marched immediately against them with four hundred men and forced them to re-embark.[75] Towards 2 o'clock they

73 A senault was the French term for a snow which is defined by Falconer as, 'generally the largest of all two-masted vessels used by Europeans, and the most convenient for navigation.' Falconer, *An Universal Dictionary of the Marine*, p. 291.

74 By this turn of phrase, Bougainville is describing his task which was to shadow the British landing craft up and down the Saint Lawrence to prevent their landing. He had to be constantly vigilant to any attempt and respond before Wolfe's troops could establish themselves in any meaningful way.

75 Wolfe had ordered Murray to force the passage to Trois-Rivières on 3 August by river to try and block communications and shipping. He tried to land twice at Pointe aux Trembles, the

hoped to take their revenge, the barges came down three quarters of a league lower than they had been in the morning; as soon as he was informed of this he sent thither six hundred men, posting the Canadians in a small clump of trees, the grenadiers of Béarn on the right, a piquet of Languedoc to the left and the rest of the Canadians in the centre. The barges approached in good order, and the troops gave four volleys as appropriate and gained the open water. M. de Bougainville praised the officers and troops in general and said that the cavalry and several detachments made an incredible effort to join up with his force.

At 10 o'clock, I accompanied M. de Montcalm to the town. Along the way we met five prisoners taken in the south by the Mic-Mac. I have not seen a spectacle more horrific than the appearance of the town; from the building of the Jesuits to the part of the river which runs through the lower town, there is not a house which is not holed; there are two hundred which have been entirely burnt. The general, whom I had not left, descended to the lower town. We found the ground and walls burning. He visited all the posts, ordered the necessary repairs in all of the destroyed field works. At 2 o'clock, the courier from Montréal told us that the English are in possession of Niagara, that the garrison are prisoners and are being conducted to New York; that the detachments of the Belle Riviére have been defeated and most captured. M. le chevalier de Lévis left at nightfall, with M. de Lapause, for Montréal. All the army views the departure of this general with regret.[76] Two companies of grenadiers have been sent with munitions to Pointe aux Trembles.

10th August

The enemy fire was relentless. At 6 o'clock, six barges or chaloupes, heavily laden with troops, left from the Falls. They came down the north channel. A carriage drawn by six horses made several trips from the top of the falls to the bottom, loaded with barrels and shells. The batteries of the falls unleashed several volleys on the men who went to burn the vessels. Four hundred Canadians were sent to Montréal. M. de Montcalm is established in the house which was occupied by M. de Lévis.

11th August

One hundred volunteers from the regulars and four hundred Canadians have been sent to Montréal, and ammunition passed to Pointe aux Trembles for the projected expedition. In the camp and fleet much movement has been seen and troops have been spotted embarking into vessels. At 9 o'clock in the evening, four vessels set sail. Scouting canoes warned that they wished to come up river. The batteries of the town fire against them was so great that they were forced to return to the fleet; the troops of the right took up their arms and lined the entrenchments and the port

first time repulsed by rocks as the tide had not risen high enough, the second by Bougainville's men. Stacey, *Quebec*, pp. 93-4.

76 At the news of the loss of Niagara, Lévis was detached to shore up defences on the Montréal front towards Lake Ontario.

guards were reinforced. During the morning, M. de Repentigny attacked the enemy workers and would have captured them all, if the Outaouas had followed the good example of the Canadians and Abenaki.

12th August

Very strong wind and rain. We learned that the cannons of Sillery fired yesterday on a *goelette* which was trying to come up river, and which then ran aground to the south. The commandant of the town gave us an alert, which kept us under arms all night.

13th August

Movement, work, bombardment and cannonade as normal.

14th August

M. de Montcalm sent M. de Bougainville a reinforcement of two hundred men. We learned that the English have burnt and ravaged three parishes of the south, but spared the churches. M. de Privat, *lieutenant-colonel*, and Joannès, major, of Languedoc, went to the town to replace the Lieutenant of the King and the major who are sick. The habitants coming in from the Baye Saint-Paul say that the English ravaged those parts and have burnt twenty-two houses.

15th August

The guard of the left will henceforth be composed of six piquets. M. de Bougainville reports that the enemy are reinforcing the position opposite his.

16th August

M. de Montcalm saw a corps of six hundred English coming from l'Ange-Gardien, and sent five hundred men to the left bank of the Falls. A firepot burned down a house in the town last night. Prompt aid secured the houses that surrounded it. The equipment of the grenadiers and piquets who were sent to Pointe aux Trembles was sent to them. It rained so much that the guard of the left had difficulty getting to their post.

17th August

All the carts of the army went with a considerable escort to fetch food. English deserters say that there are many sick in their army, that they believe they will not attack again and will embark after burning the crops. A party of savages who passed over the Falls River returned; they report that the Abenaki went to attack a house occupied by the English, who killed one savage and wounded another.

The courier from Montréal told us of the return of M. le chevalier de Lévis, who had been to Présentation, and reassured those of the town who were in consternation. The Canadians who escaped from Chouaguen reported that there were only two thousand [British] troops; part of which is the army of Niagara who are busy pulling down the defences of said fort, and the other part who are conducting the [French] garrison to Orange. Sixty men were sent out to fetch the bateaux from Cap Rouge and a detachment to retrieve all the bateaux which are drifting and bring them into the Saint-Charles River. The guard on the left saw six guns embarked at the bottom of the camp of the falls.

18th August

The troops on the right took up their arms at 2 o'clock but were stood down at half past. Three vessels were seen setting sail. The detachments which left here yesterday have returned. M. de Repentigny returned at midday and was greatly saddened that the savages, who abandoned him, prevented him from capturing a considerable detachment. The carts have returned loaded with food. The guard on the bakery was increased to prevent losses. The guard of the left saw artillery embarking.

19th August

Bombardment and cannonade as normal. A detachment of sixty men left to assemble and bring back all the carts and wagons which they find around Charlesbourg.

At 3 o'clock, a courier from Pointe aux Trembles told us that the enemy had disembarked that morning at Deschambault and that M. Bougainville marched towards them. On learning of this M. de Montcalm went to see M. de Vaudreuil. He left after a few minutes and ordered three companies of grenadiers and eighty of Repentigny's men to join Bougainville with the utmost haste.[77]

At 9 o'clock in the evening, a courier sent by the *munitionnaire*, informed M. de Vaudreuil that he had loaded up much of the food and reported that the English had set fire to three houses and were preparing to re-embark as our cavalry detachments had arrived.

At 10 o'clock several musket shots were heard, we believed to have been fired by some one of our scouts. La Sarre, Languedoc and [the militia of] the government of Québec took up arms and returned when they were assured there was nothing new. The guard of the left saw guns and munitions being embarked.

77 This force was Murray's brigade again. He enjoyed more success here and managed to hold off the Canadian defenders whilst destroying the spare equipment and baggage of the French regulars which was stored there. Wolfe, however, was frustrated by not being able to bring the French to battle and recalled Murray to the main army a few days later. Stacey, *Quebec*, pp. 94-5.

20th August

All the carts in the camp have left for Pointe aux Trembles.[78] M. le marquis de Montcalm told us that at his arrival there yesterday he found M. Bougainville who had returned there and informed him that the enemy had re-embarked with haste when they saw his advance guard, having already burnt down the house that contained the equipment of five battalions of the regular troops and two others. The general gave six *livres* and a shirt to each soldier in compensation for that which was lost at Deschambault. The grenadiers and detachments which left here yesterday returned at midday. The enemy fired several volleys on the left and many into the town.

21st August

Bombardment, cannonade and ravaging fire from the enemy as usual. A courier from below [downriver, north of Québec] said he counted one hundred and thirty-eight vessels, of whom twenty-eight of this force are between Kamouraska up to Sainte-Anne, where in these areas they send out barges to burn and ravage the country side on the banks. A savage that the English had captured and held aboard a frigate was rescued through a gun port. He recounted that he was led from one camp to another all day then in the evening confined to the frigate where he was shackled and guarded by three sentinels.

22nd August

The bad weather tempered the fire of the enemy. Two Germans who had deserted the day that the enemy landed at Deschambault said that they were followed by several others who feared the savages.

23rd August

The carts have returned loaded with food. We learned that the English tried to return to Deschambault, but that forty cavalrymen prevented them. A courier from Montréal told us that there was no news from the Isle aux Noix, where M. Bourlamaque had withdrawn to, or from above the rapids [meaning the St. Lawrence rapids leading to Lake Ontario].[79] That the harvest has begun and is plentiful. I was in Québec, where I found the town completely destroyed in several quarters. At 11 o'clock in the evening, a few bateaux arrived to us loaded with supplies. M. de Montcalm sent several detachments to the left bank of the Falls.

78 Note by Gaffarel – There was no water supply to Québec since the English were masters of the Saint Lawrence. All supplies were thus transported by land and as only women and children were available, it was they who performed this hard task.

79 It had been decided that holding Carillon and Fort St. Frederick was not possible on the Lake Champlain frontier. Isle aux Noix, an island much closer to Montreal was chosen to be fortified to hold back the advancing British forces. See Map 3.

24th August

The carts of the army left for Saint-Augustin. M. de Saint-Laurent went to carry the letters of M. de Vaudreuil and return the effects of the Scottish officer, dead of his wounds, to the first frigate. The right was supplied with one hundred workers from the town. Fire on the town less severe than normal. the English have burnt the houses of l'Ange-Gardien. A convoy of boats loaded with food and necessary effects arrived.

25th August

The enemy fire was as yesterday. The commandant of the town said that a frigate and a *goelette* descended to l'Anse des Mers. M. de Ganes, *aide-major* of Trois-Rivières, arrived at 4 o'clock, charged with packets which were found on two English officers, who had been led by the Loups through the woods and entrusted to the Abenaki who took them to Trois-Rivières where they were transferred aboard a frigate. These packets contained the letters of General Amherst in which he told General Wolfe that our lines at Carillon would have cost him dearly to force if we had had enough people to dispute them. They lost seventy men there; two general officers have been killed at the siege of Niagara, they believe that the French have good defences on the Saint-Jean River, and are in a good condition to attack and that they will wait for news of the success of these operations. The guard of the left saw artillery, planks and other effects embarked aboard ship.

26th August

The frigate and *goelette* which descended the river have come back. M. Bougainville said that the English have burnt their camp at Saint-Antoine, and have gone to camp further up. The courier from Montréal told us that three English deserters, coming from Fort St-Frédéric, told M. de Bourlamaque that General Amherst recently dispatched several officers to General Wolfe to inform him that he intends to come to join him without delay. That he has constructed a galley and several floating batteries to come and attack the Isle aux Noix. The *munitionnaire* left for the fleet with several merchant officers and many sailors. Volunteers have arrested a deserter of the colony and killed one who did not wish to return. An English deserter sergeant assured that they had begun evacuating the camp at the Falls. The heavy artillery has already been embarked and in three or four days the troops will move onto the Isle d'Orleans; that in five days the army will return; that the three decker vessels are ordered to descend; that those above the city will soon descend; Murray's brigade has called for reinforcements, but they are not yet sent to him, and that General Wolfe has had a fever for two days.

27th August

Cannonade, bombardment and movements as normal on the part of the English. M. Bougainville said that the troops who have been camped at Saint-Antoine, have embarked; that the Canadians and savages, who were sent into the south, forced the rear guard back into the water promptly and the vessels still remain in the lower river. At 5 o'clock two large ships were seen going from the Isle d'Orleans to Pointe de Lévis. One of the two sailed at 9 o'clock. The batteries of the town and those of the Anse des Mers made several discharges on the vessels which held their course. At 11 o'clock, we learned that five more passed. The right took up arms and stood down at midnight. M. de Montcalm has sent two companies of grenadiers and two piquets into the area around Sillery and Samos, and ordered all the army to take up their arms an hour before daybreak.

28th August

Bad weather. We learned that the ships passing in the night were three frigates and two senaults, which moored opposite Sillery. Tents and equipment were sent to the troops in those parts. The bread ration has been reduced to three *quarterons*, and is given to the soldiers, Canadians and savages every morning along with a paltry eau-de-vie ration.[80]

29th August

Little fire on the town, the vessels which were above have moored between Cap Rouge up to Saint-Augustin, where M. Bougainville is supporting. Several officers said that the last vessels passing were sorely mistreated. Out batteries at the Falls fired several volleys on a *goelette*, which ran aground in the channel of the Isle d'Orleans. A habitant who came from the south said that the English have abandoned the camps which they have in the area and loaded up a lot of wood. The savages who live eight hundred leagues from here have asked M. Vaudreuil permission to return home. Much movement was seen in the fleet and two columns came out from the camp at Pointe de Lévis. At 11 o'clock at night, a considerable cannonade was heard from around Saint-Augustin.

30th August

We learned by decree from post to post, that the enemy tried to land last night at Saint-Augustin and was repulsed. The fire on the city was stronger than usual. The batteries of the Falls sent shrapnel into our volunteers. Our guards in those parts witnessed much equipment being embarked. The generals received letters at noon from M. de Bougainville who said that the vessels of yesterday fired musketry and artillery very heavily on a small island opposite Saint-Augustin; that two soldiers and a Canadian who were on the lookout were wounded. A detachment of one hundred and ten volunteers went to camp at the Saint-Jean gate.

80 Note by Gaffarel – According Bigot (Letter to the Minister of War, of 15 October 1759), 'It was not without infinite pains I had managed to preserve our army in Québec, which consumed at least 20,000 rations per day, including the families of the savages. I supplied a further 4 or 5,000 rations of a *quateron* of bread to women and children of the city. Besides this, I had to preserve our army at Lake Champlain and the Rapides.'

31st August

Much movement was witnessed in the camp at Pointe de Lévis. It appears that troops have been embarked on transport ships and the enemy has abandoned the camp at the Falls.[81] M. de Bougainville said that the vessels which were opposite him have lifted anchor and he has followed them. The *munitionnaire* told us that the frigate *Manon* of 26 guns has run aground on the flats of the Grandines and that the English vessels are moored at Pointe aux Trembles.[82] At 11 o'clock in the evening, several musket shots were fired on the edge of the town and the batteries made some discharges on five boats which were passing. The army took up arms and was stood down at midnight.

1st September

M. le marquis de Montcalm said to us that the English have burnt the area around the camp at the Falls. A courier from Montréal told us that all is peaceful at l'Isle aux Noix, as it is on the frontier at Présentation, and that the savages are well disposed. M. de Bougainville said that there are twelve ships or frigates opposite Pointe aux Trembles. M. de Montcalm went with M. de Vaudreuil to assist in a grand council demanded by the Outaouas who wish to return home. This general [unclear if Malartic means Montcalm or Vaudreuil but seems more likely to be Montcalm], who honoured me with his friendship, testified to me that he was very occupied with the different movements of the English and had unpleasant forebodings. The fire on the town was more intense than yesterday. A courier from Montréal carried the testimony of two prisoners taken before Fort St-Frédéric who said that the militia are asking General Amherst for permission to return to their homes; that they were promised this when they have cut the necessary wood for two forts; that there are two parties on campaign around Chambly; that our savages sent to scout found tracks and took an engineer on the lake. At 10 o'clock in the evening, M. Bougainville said that the vessels descended the river.[83]

2nd September

Firing on the town has not been as heavy. The English continue to embark the artillery and equipment at the Falls camp. A frigate passed under our batteries at noon into which we sent some volleys. A ball sank a barge from which two men escaped.

---

81 Over the previous few days Wolfe had recovered from his illness and decided that he should change tack and bring the ships above Québec to get the British army between the city and its lines of communication with the interior of the colony. Stacey, *Quebec*, pp. 109-111.

82 The *Manon* was a private frigate which had arrived at Quebec just before the Royal Navy in a convoy of eight vessels (2 royal frigates and 6 private ships). See Stacey, *Quebec*, p. 252.

83 Note by Gaffarel – These comings and goings exhausted Bougainville's troops. According to Joannès, the English were masters of the manoeuvres of landing: 'The enemy was attentive to our approaches and had the idea to first fatigue the body which was observing them; therefore, using the tide, they were sometimes six leagues or more above Québec, and the ebbing tide allowed them to drift back to within a quarter league of the said town. The corps of observation followed these movements with great pain and extraordinary fatigue.'

M. de Montcalm has changed his dispositions in case of an attack. The general went with M. de Vaudreuil, and said that the English are always on the move in the camp of the Falls, where there are no more than one thousand men. M. Bougainville said that he followed the vessels which were opposite Saint-Michel. The army received orders to be on the alert. The English have placed several buoys overnight between the River Beauport and the Canardière. Our canoes have removed these under fire from their frigates. These buoys have been a well-placed diversion of their plans. It is not apparent that they want [to attack] these parts, and they are not as occupied as the others.

3rd September

A *goelette* passed during the night from the Falls to Pointe de Lévis. At daybreak, eighty barges were seen loaded with troops, assembled behind the frigate in front of the Falls. M. de Montcalm detached an *aide-major* with twelve grenadiers to go and reconnoitre the enemy camp and fire some musket shots into it. The men who had stayed behind at the camp went at full speed behind the entrenchments. They stood at the approach of our detachment, set fire to the camp and took off to embark. There was a lot of movement seen in the camp at Pointe de Lévis, the troops embarked in barges which went behind the ships. The troops took up arms and were stood down at midday. M. de Montcalm remained in the entrenchments with six hundred men on the left to watch the retreat of the English who, after about an hour, filed away in their barges and put them away onto land on the Isle d'Orleans. We fired over two hundred cannon shots; several of which carried true. At 3 o'clock, we saw a camp of two battalions on the Isle d'Orleans and one of three battalions behind the batteries of Pointe de Lévis. Canadians and savages crossed the Falls River and entered the English camp. They reported several barrels of flour and rice left behind. The companies of grenadiers and piquets who were separated from their corps have re-joined them. There are ships opposite Saint-Michel. Six hundred men of the government of Montréal went to camp at the right of those from Québec. The garrison of the town was reinforced.

4th September

M. de Montcalm went to visit the English camp which he found to be well fortified. On his return, he sent the Guyenne Regiment to the right, very close to the bridges, the reserve of Repentigny into the camp just vacated by Guyenne, Royal Roussillon on the plateau of the Beauport church, four hundred men of the government of Montréal to the left and one hundred and eighty men to the watchtowers, and he installed himself in the house of Salaberrie, after which he formed a chain of posts from the Falls up to the town.[84] M. de Bougainville, who went to spend an hour in the

84 This was the house of Michel de Salaberry, an active member of New France's commercial maritime community. He sailed merchantmen during the War of the Austrian Succession and became a ship owner. He joined the Navy in the 1750's, cruising off Louisbourg as captain of the frigate *Fidéle*. He was the grandfather of the celebrated Charles-Michel d'Irumberry de Salaberry who fought in the War of 1812.

quarters of the general, said that the vessels indicate by their manoeuvres that they mean to descend [the river]. The courier from Montréal told us that all is peaceful above the Rapids and at the Isle aux Noix. The prisoners say that General Amherst is building barques and bateaux able to carry cannon, and a fort on the foundations of Fort St-Frédéric to hold two thousand men, and that he has completed Carillon; a large fort will be built on the Chouaguen River.

5th September

The commandant of the town said that during the night forty barges were heard passing by. Fire on the town very vigorous. M. de Bougainville said that there was much movement in the fleet; that there are many barges behind the ships which are coming and going. M. de Montcalm at that moment with M. de Vaudreuil, sent M. de Bougainville the company of grenadiers and piquet of Guyenne, and ordered that all news should be brought to him according to the circumstances. At 2 o'clock, a column judged to be around two thousand men was seen taking the heights of the Pointe de Lévis and the road of the Etchemin River. Four piquets were sent immediately to Cap Rouge, and *la générale* was beaten to assemble the soldiers. Guyenne received orders to post piquets on the Heights of Abraham.[85] Wagons were seen arriving at the camp of which the enemy was moving out, and were loaded up with tents. At 6 o'clock, we heard them beat the assembly in the Pointe de Lévis camp. A ship fired four cannon shots. We saw and heard many barges go from the Isle d'Orleans to Pointe de Lévis. A courier from M. Bougainville said that the column passed the river at 5 o'clock; that nine ships were well placed to the south; that many of the barges entered the River of the Chaudière Falls. At 11 o'clock, the reserve of Repentigny went to the post near the gate of Saint-Jean. It rained all night.

6th September

The rain continued. The troops were on high alert and had worked on several entrenchments. M. de Bougainville reported that the ships were opposite Sillery; there are no troops above there and no more have been seen on the ground. It became apparent that they returned to their camp during the night. The Regiment of Guyenne returned, as did the reserve of Repentigny. A new camp was perceived on the left of the batteries of Pointe de Lévis. At 3 o'clock, a column of twelve hundred men was spotted. M. de Bougainville gave warning of movement within the fleet, that troops were in barges and that he continued to observe. At 6 o'clock a skiff left from Pointe de Lévis and passed under our batteries of the town which sent after it several volleys, but did not make it change course. At 7 o'clock, four companies of grenadiers were ordered to take post at the fork in the road to Samos and Sillery. The English burned many houses on the Isle d'Orleans. Fire on the town was less fierce than yesterday.

85 The Heights of Abraham were to the west of Québec and were not fortified.

7th September

M. Bougainville said that several vessels were redirected at the end of the tide and the others are opposite Sillery. Carts were sent out loaded with tools for Saint-Augustin and also companies of grenadiers and piquets with their marmites [cooking vessels]. At midday we saw that the vessels that had come up were opposite Cap Rouge. At 6 o'clock, we saw many barges cross from the Isle d'Orleans to Pointe de Lévis. At 9 o'clock we heard the English cry, "Hurrah!" on the ships and we saw a great number of barges ahead of the ships. The patrols on the water gave this notice. All the troops were brought to the entrenchments. M. de Bougainville reported that a frigate and a senault presented themselves at the entry of the Cap Rouge River and that our gunboats forced them to move away; that the barges made the pretence of wishing to land and that he was disposed to receive them.

M. de Rumigny, captain of the La Sarre [Regiment], reported from Sillery that he had gone to the south with his lieutenant and thirty men who brought back seven horses from a troop of fifty who they met; that the English have no establishment between the Etchemin River and the Chaudière Falls; that in those parts the posts are manned by eighty men each.

8th September

M. de Montcalm had ordered the troops to be stood down at 2 o'clock in the morning, but the river patrols did not agree on the state of the [enemy] barges and so he decided that they would remain behind the entrenchments until day light. It rained throughout the night. At 3 o'clock, the town gave a great fire to the vessels which tried to go upriver under cover of fog. At 8 o'clock four had made their way to Cap Rouge. M. de Bougainville wrote that they were all anchored in those parts. The fire on the town was very fierce.

9th September

It rained throughout the day. M. de Bougainville reported that three vessels and eight barges had gone up past Pointe aux Trembles; one other, with several barges, had descended to Sillery, and that the others remained opposite his position; that they manoeuvred to persuade him that they wished to make a landing and then changed tack to put detachments onto the southern shore where they are wreaking havoc.

10th September

Cannonade and bombardment as normal. M. de Bougainville reports that the English have a camp at Saint-Nicolas which is not considerable. It rained all day.

11th September

The enemy compensated for the bad weather by redoubling their fire on the town; they burnt many houses and barns on the Isle d'Orleans. M. de Bougainville wrote that the ships are in the same position at Cap Rouge; that those which went up to Pointe aux Trembles have descended the river. Many of the savages have left to return to their homes. The courier from Montréal told us that M. le chevalier de Lévis has gone to the Isle aux Noix, and that the harvest will be taken in soon in that government.

12th September

Cannonade and bombardment as normal. M. de Bougainville wrote that the vessels have descended the river. There was a warning order that loaded bateaux will pass under several of our posts; they must be recognised so as not to give notice to the enemy. A few buoys were removed that had been left by the English between the River Beauport and the Canardière.

13th September

An hour after midnight, the patrols on the water warned that they had heard many of the barges filing along the coast of the town. At 2 o'clock, the troops received orders to go to the entrenchments. At daybreak we heard the cannon of Samos and several discharges of musketry around l'Anse des Mers. The Guyenne Regiment received orders to send two piquets to [The Plains of] Abraham and a half hour later to patrol around it.

M. de Montcalm was established at the Canardière. An account was given to him that the enemy had disembarked between the Foulon and l'Anse des Mers.[86] The general ordered that a piquet from each battalion and 600 men of Montréal be sent there. He followed shortly after, leaving M. de Senezergues, brigadier, *lieutenant-colonel* of La Sarre, in the Beauport area. He ordered the militia of Trois-Rivières and 100 of Québec to follow and to send the La Sarre Regiment when the 400 men of M. Leborgne arrived there.[87] He sent orders to the bridge to march the regiments of La Sarre and Languedoc and the 400 men of M. Leborgne without delay. Two minutes after this, another order was carried to Béarn to march, who, on the road were met by the *major-général* who told them that the English were drawn up in line opposite the town, that he was going to fetch Royal Roussillon and the other troops,

86 Note by Gaffarel – The officer in command of the Anse au Foulon was Vergor Duchambon, captain of the troops of the marine, a close friend of Bigot, the same who had already given up Fort Beauséjour without a fight. Bigot in his letter to the minister of war, sought to excuse him (15 October 1759), 'The English were let past without being recognised. The officer who commanded these posts did so in the belief that they were the flat bateaux loaded with food, that the commandant of this place had ordered this evening to let pass...The English having been able to scale the steep slope... which without doubt they knew would not be guarded, climbed up and attacked from behind one of our posts, which guarded a ramped path which led to the water's edge. The officer of this post received several wounds, but he was taken prisoner with his detachment.'

87 The family name Le Borgne is perhaps linked to the seventeenth century fur-trader, Emmanuel Le Borgne. If so, it would be likely that Le Borgne was a prominent member of society and thus a likely candidate for a militia commander.

and that they should follow the route of the other regiments to take the heights close to the town.

The regiment arrived at 9 o'clock, and took its place between Languedoc and Guyenne. Royal Roussillon joined the line a half-hour later and took the left. Some platoons of colony soldiers and Canadians fired on the English from behind bushes and rocks, ahead of the two armies. The English, who had field guns, discomforted us greatly with their grapeshot. At 9 o'clock we sent for two 12-pounders from the town which were placed on the right. They made several discharges. The rest of the militia of the government of Québec arrived at the same time. M. de Montcalm travelled to the front of the army which consisted of 2,500 men, asked the soldiers if they were tired, and observed the movements of the enemy. Having seen them reinforcing their position and fearing they would turn our right flank, he ordered them to march.

The regiments were brought forward eagerly. They had not gone one hundred paces when the Canadians who formed the second rank and the soldiers of the third [rank] gave fire without any order, and, following their custom, lay down to reload. This false move severed all the battalions. The greater part of the soldiers of the first rank were killed or wounded by the volleys they received from the English who were posted on an elevation. Those who had gone to ground stood up, made an about face and took the road to the town, and entered into the suburbs without any possibility of rallying. M. de Montcalm was wounded in the lower stomach and thigh and was carried into the town.

The *major-général* ordered that the troops line the walls of the suburb; a quarter of an hour later each battalion sent a piquet into the town and the rest of the army held the bridges.

M. le marquis de Vaudreil, before the rout, had come up onto the heights and rallied the Canadians who, after being fired on a few times by the English, withdrew. The Guyenne, Languedoc and Béarn Regiments were formed before the mill to allow the militia of the governments of Québec, Montréal and Trois-Rivières to pass over the bridge. They themselves crossed the bridge together and were replaced by La Sarre and Royal Roussillon. They went into the redoubt, lined the walls, and provided workers to demolish the second bridge and mix the gunpowder which was in the barn of the mill. At midday, La Sarre and Royal Roussillon crossed the bridge and formed on the main road. The battalion commanders and the first captains were ordered to meet with M. de Vaudreuil who wished to assemble a council of war to decide the course to take.

The five battalions, especially La Sarre and Guyenne, were sorely punished. From Béarn, MM. de Tignes and Maubeuge, captains, were both killed, Figuiery and Tourville, captains wounded, Malartic had a horse killed under him and several musket balls through his coat.[88] The council of war decided that the army should

88 Pierre Maubeuge d'Herbigny was born in Ardennes in 1728. He would die of his wounds on 12 October 1759. Étienne-Guillaume Figuery was born at Castelsarrasin (St-Sauver), Tarn-et-Garonne. He started his career in the cavalry as a cornet in the Beaucaire Regiment in 1744 but transferred into the Béarn Regiment in 1746. He survived his injuries and returned to France with his wife in October 1760. I have found no record extant of de Tignes or Tourville.

retire behind the Jacquartier River.[89] The regiments returned to camp after an hour, leaving a 60-man guard on the bridge; an exact roll-call found that many officers, soldiers, and Canadians had been killed or captured. At 5 o'clock the troops took supplies, flour and meat. An order was read to leave the camp standing and to take only those tents which were absolutely necessary.[90]

The army was put to march at 9 o'clock in a single column in the following order: the government of Québec, 600 men of those of Montréal, the government of Trois-Rivières, the brigade of La Sarre formed of the five battalions,[91] the artillery and the equipment escorted by the bridge guard. It took the road to Charlesbourg, which they passed at 3 o'clock in the morning on the 14th of September. It continued this route, making a stop at 6 o'clock at Lorette. Many people were missing here as the march through the night had been too fast. At midday it made another halt at la Cense de Pauvres,[92] and arrived at Pointe aux Trembles at 5 o'clock where they lodged in the barns. We learned that M. de Montcalm had died at 4 o'clock in the morning, and that the English were not yet at Beauport.[93]

15th September

The army left at daybreak. It stopped for a long time on the left bank of the Jacquartier River, because the bridge, which had been broken for some days, had not been repaired. It crossed at midday and lodged in the barns which border the right bank.

---

89 Note by Gaffarel – Vaudreuil, Bigot and Bougainville wished to try for a second time on the fortunes of battle: the officers were of the contrary opinion. Montcalm, who still lived, merely outlined the options, fight, surrender or retreat, and did not give an official opinion. See the letter of Bigot to the Minister of War: 'He thought that there should be another attack at daybreak the next day, having assembled all of our forces, including those of M. Bougainville, whose majority had not yet been added to those in the city or camp. I was also of this opinion; but all the officers in council insisted on making a retreat to Jacques Cartier.'

90 Note by Gaffarel – The retreat was made with such haste that not only the tents, but the ammunition and ten days' worth of food were given up. See the letter from Bigot to the Minister of War (15 October 1759): 'we abandoned most of the tents, army equipment and ten days of food as I had had great difficulty in bringing up carts, because they could not reach us by water as it was too dangerous.'

91 These were the regular battalions La Sarre, Languedoc, Béarn, Guyenne and Royal-Roussillon that had fought on the Plains of Abraham.

92 Unknown location.

93 Note by Gaffarel – This dry hint is the limited expression of grief from Malartic. It seems that he felt little sympathy for Montcalm. He much preferred Lévis. His companions did not feel the same as him. 'I will never forgive myself for losing my general,' wrote a French officer. 'How great a loss for us, for this country and for the State! He was a good general, a zealous citizen, a solid friend and father to all of us. He was taken at the very moment he could enjoy the fruits of a campaign that M. de Turenne would not have disavowed himself of. Every day I seek him and every day my pain grows deeper.' – See letter of Bernier, *commissaire de guerres*, to the minister of war: 'Would you pardon me to finish by throwing yet more tears on the tomb of the Marquis de Montcalm? The colony weeps and will for a long time feel the loss. The military has lost a zealous protector who could find charm in the greatest fatigues with the desire to earn his praise.' From the Memoirs of Captain Pouchot: 'The purity of his intentions and selflessness of Montcalm always equalled his valour.'

16th September

The army rested. Many stragglers caught up. M. de Vaudreuil had had news from M. de Bougainville who was at Saint-Augustin. He also received word from Québec. He has sent a convoy of food by land and water for that town.

17th September

More men who had stayed behind re-joined. M. le chevalier de Lévis arrived at 10 o'clock. His return has spread joy.[94] He announced that we would move forward tomorrow, saying that, although having lost a battle, he must not abandon 10 leagues of country. M. de Bougainville has fallen back from Pointe aux Trembles and M. Repentigny on Ancienne Lorette. Many of the Canadians deserted, and almost all the savages have taken the roads back to their villages. M. de Lévis has sent out a guard for Sainte-Anne who are ordered not to let anyone past without permission.

18th September[95]

The army took food for two days, the ration composing of five *quaterons* of bread made without having the bran extracted, and a half-*livre* of meat. It crossed the Jacquartier River and camped at Pointe aux Trembles. M. de la Rochebeaucourt [commander of the *Corps de Cavalerie*] said that he would head towards Québec with the cavalry, who carried 60 *quintaux* of biscuit.[96] M. de Bougainville went to Saint-Augustin, and M. de Repentigny to the bridge of Lorette.

94 Note by Gaffarel – Lévis was held in high esteem by the soldiers as well as the officers. See the end of this present volume given by Malartic of this campaign. Here is the letter in which he announced to the minister of war his taking of command: 'From the camp of Saint-Augustin, the 21st September 1759. It is with the deepest sorrow that I have the honour to give you the account of the loss of M. le marquis de Montcalm who died of his wounds on the 14th of this month. This carries all the regrets of the army as well as my own. When the sad news reached me, I was on the frontier of the upper country whose defence was entrusted to me. I left immediately to come as replacement. You know, Monseigneur, of his zeal and talents. I will make my best effort to follow in his footsteps, and merit the thanks of the King, your kindness and protection.'

95 Note by Gaffarel – Lévis had resolved to go to the aid of the garrison of Québec and take the offensive. This was indeed the manoeuvre suited to the circumstances (see the account of Joannès), but the garrison of Québec was ill-prepared. According to Joannès, ' most militia and sailors harboured ill will. The worst of this was that the officers of these troops were held and beaten, two with their swords. They threatened nothing less than to abandon their posts and leave their troops. Many of them had already escaped and deserted.' See the letter from Lévis to Marshal de Belle-Isle (1 November 1759): I took to repair the fault that had been made and engaged the M. de Vaudreuil to return with the army to rescue the place. I represented to him that it was the only way to prevent the escape of the Canadians and Indians who were returning home, and at the same time reviving everyone's courage; by marching forward, we repatriated many stragglers, and the habitants of Québec re-joined the army etc.'

96 Note by Gaffarel – The garrison of Québec did not have any food; it was for them that M. La Roche-Beaucourt carried the biscuit, riding ahead with the cavalry.

19th September

Rumour that the town had surrendered.[97] The army resumed its march at 6 o'clock. M. Daubrespy, captain of Béarn,[98] who came from Québec told us that the place had capitulated yesterday with the following conditions; that the garrison come out with the honours of war with two cannons and a mortar, to be embarked together and returned to France, that no harm will come to the habitants for having taken up arms for the defence of their country, having been compelled, and the subjects of the two kings being militia will ensure the conservation of the goods of those absent, the main houses will be safeguarded on the delivery of the gates of the town, Catholics will be free to publicly follow their religion, that if the Bishop wishes to return to the city he will be his own master.[99] MM. de Vaudreuil and Lévis disapproved of this capitulation, as the city did not lack food, as the cavalry had delivered it before the surrender,[100] and the general had given word to the commander that he would come to their aid, and that the enemy had not yet established their batteries.[101] The army

97 Note by Gaffarel – On 15 September de Ramezay, governor of Québec, had held a council of war attended by a *lieutenant-colonel* and 13 captains. Apart from M. Jacau de Fiedmont, they unanimously agreed to surrender. The habitants of Québec, having at their head Jean Panet, notary and public prosecutor, and Jean Taché, trusted merchant, had prevailed on Ramezay to insist on surrender.

98 Daubrespy had taken part in the council of war on the 15th.

99 Note by Gaffarel – See the principal articles of the capitulation signed on 18 September by Ramezay and Brigadier Townshend.
I. The garrison of the town composed of the regular troops, the marines and sailors, leave the town with arms and baggage, drums beating, matches lit and two cannon and twelve rounds for each piece, and they will be shipped as conveniently as possible to the first port they arrive at in France.
II. The habitants will be protected in the possession of their homes, goods, effects and privileges.
III. The said habitants will not be called out for bearing arms in the defence of the town, since they were compelled, and that the habitants will receive two crowns for serving in the militia.
V. The said habitants will not be transferred or required to leave their homes, until a definitive treaty between His Most Christian Majesty and His Majesty of Britain has regulated the situation.
VI. Free exercise of the Roman religion, safeguarded granted to all religious people including the Bishop, who can come and freely exercise the functions of his state, when it is deemed appropriate, until the possession of Canada has been decided between His Most Christian Majesty and His Majesty of Britain.

100 Note by Gaffarel – According to the minutes of the Council of war on 15 September there remained food of all kinds, from 15,000 to 16,000 rations to feed 2,200 combatants, 2,600 women and children, and from 1,000 to 1,200 non-combatants.

101 Note by Gaffarel – Yet Vaudreuil, before leaving the Beauport camp, sent this note to Ramezay. 'We notified Mr. Ramezay he should not wait until the enemy prevails in assault. As soon as he lacks food he will hoist the white flag and send the most capable and most intelligent garrison officer to propose capitulation.' Ramezay nevertheless weakly abused the permission to surrender. He had notice of the arrival of Lévis. He had already received some of his riders. He should have, as advised by Joannès and Fiedmont, shut himself up in the upper town and resist fiercely, but, as written by Joannès, 'the officer, who has never seen war in the woods, was unaware of the how to defend a position; it is assumed, because he did not acquiesce to this opinion, he fell back to the orders he had from the Marquis de Vaudreuil not to risk to getting carried away with sword in hand.'

camped before the Calvary of Saint-Augustin, and M. de Bougainville occupied the bridge and environs of Lorette.

20th September

The army stopped to wait for food which could not get here because of the bad weather and bad roads. Part of the army was forced to fetch it from more than three leagues away by the less practicable roads, and the others received flour. Several individuals arrived from Québec, praising the good treatment of the English. The courier from Montréal told us that all was calm in the *pays d'en haut*, that the English have demanded one of our officers who went to Fort St-Frédéric carrying news of the peace, where they attempted to unsuccessfully burn one of our barques.[102]

21st September

The army retired to Pointe aux Trembles and M. de Bougainville to Saint-Augustin. Food was given out for 2 days.

22nd September

The army stayed and provided workers to the habitants to help cut the harvest. Several officers and merchants came from Québec saying that the English have put a lot of artillery into the city, are putting up the walls and repairing the largest houses, that they expect to leave a garrison of 4,000 men, and to leave 3 frigates in winter harbour.[103] We removed the ammunition we had left at Saint-Augustin. The army was given meat for one day.

23rd September

The army stopped and provided workers for the harvest.

24th September

The army returned to Jacquartier. The Royal Roussillon and Guyenne Regiments camped on the right bank of the river Portneuf, those of La Sarre, Languedoc and Béarn with the people of Québec and Trois-Rivières on the left river bank, the government and town of Montréal militia on the right bank of Jacquartier.[104]

---

102 The 'peace' would seem to refer to the settlement that had been made with respect to Quebec.

103 General Murray took command of the remaining army and the town of Québec. Most of the army stayed apart from the grenadiers and the siege artillery, although only one hundred rangers were retained. Admiral Saunders feared leaving ships in the St. Lawrence over winter and only a couple of sloops remained. Stacey, Quebec, p. 183.

104 Note by Gaffarel – Lévis, with the remnants of his regiments, took on a great responsibility and established his winter quarters facing the English. It was not possible to imagine resistance. Lévis himself was very discouraged. Here is his letter of 1 November to Marshal

25th September

The army has been occupied establishing barracks. Several tents and marmites were given out.

26th September

The engineers have traced out the works that M. de Lévis wishes to make on the bridge of Jacquartier. The sick have been sent off in bateaux which will fetch munitions and food. Several merchants coming from Montréal passed to go to Québec.

27th September

The works were started. The regiments made fascines and oars. One of our surgeons came from Québec saying that the English had made it difficult for our soldiers and officers to leave the hospital, wishing to keep them as prisoners despite the agreement.[105]

28th September

Fascines continued to be made and two hundred workers were supplied to begin a hornwork, which would cut across Pointe Jacquartier. M. de Vaudreuil received passports to be able to send officers to Québec to treat in the exchange of prisoners, and sent two *goelettes* to load the equipment of the officers. A courier from Montréal told us that an English officer and eight soldiers had been captured. He had recently set out from Fort St-Frédéric with orders to follow the River au Sable to the area around Présentation and, after a successful reconnaissance, sent half of his detachment to Chouaguen with an account to General Gage and the rest to Fort St-Frédéric to inform General Amherst, who proposed to come and attack the Isle aux Noix.[106] A second courier from Montréal told us that a party of English had disembarked at Bay of Missisconi [Michiscouy].

29th September

M. de Vaudreuil and the Intendant left for Montréal. Three officers and thirty wounded soldiers arrived from the hospital of Québec. M. de Bougainville who will go to discuss the exchange of prisoners, came to take the orders from M. de

---

de Belle-Isle; 'We must admit that we are very unhappy. When we had hoped to see the campaign end with glory, everything turned against us... I will do my utmost to preserve the rest of this unfortunate colony for the winter, and wait for aid that I appeal to his Majesty to send us in the first days of May. If the King judges not to give us aid, I must warn that he cannot count on us to last until the end of May. We are obliged, despite poverty and destitution, to keep our courage, having no other resource to put to use.'

105 Note by Gaffarel – The general hospital, on the bank of the Saint-Charles River, was filled with around 1,200 wounded and sick of both nations.

106 The River au Sable is now called Ausable River, New York.

Lévis. The number of workers was increased. The regiments provided many fascines and piquets. The bateaux sent to the fleet to fetch ammunition have returned with nothing.

30th September

M. le chevalier de Montreuil has taken command of the troops of M. Bougainville. The number of workers was increased. The treasurer left for Montréal. The Intendant said to give bills of exchange for the troops and the *munitionnaire*. The guard who left the hospital of Québec returned.

1st October

The number of workers was increased.

3rd October

All the battalion commanders assembled with M. de Lévis to arrange the finances. M. Bougainville returned saying that the English were surprised to see him and that they were tempted to make him a prisoner. They do not wish to honour the agreement and regard all the sick and injured who remain in the hospital as prisoners.

4th October

Work as normal. Our Canadians brought in twenty cattle taken from the suburbs of Québec.

7th October

Malartic left with orders of the general, according to the request of the five battalions, to go to Montréal to ask for bills of exchange for the regular troop's subsistence from the 1st of May until the 1st of November and work on the establishment of quarters of the seven battalions, who will winter in the government of Montréal. He arrived at 9 o'clock, finding the roads very bad and learned that the Intendant had been forced to give bills of exchange to the merchants, according to the just representations they had made. An announcement was made to prevent the drawing of bills of exchange until tomorrow up to the 15th inclusive.[107]

107 Note by Malartic – The assembled orders for the bills of money were for the sums of 20 *sol*, 3, 6, 12, 24, 48 and 96 *livres* which were reported in the month of October to the treasurer, who gave receipts which could then be converted to bills of exchange against the treasurer of the colonies, payable in three years. There were also printed cards with the arms of the king of 5, 10 and 20 sol. 3, 6, 12 and 24 *livres*.

11th October

Another proclamation was made to announce that the withdrawal of bills will finish on the evening of the 13th, which raised many cries. It was learned that a party of one hundred and fifty English came to the village of Saint-François on the 6th, where they surprised the Abenakis, killing and capturing a few, including women and children, setting fire to the village and retiring quietly. The Abenaki recovered from their surprise but did not wish to pursue, although it would have been easy to reach and harass the enemy party.[108]

12th October

Two officers of those who remained at Québec arrived with permission from the English general.

13th October

The withdrawal of bills ceased. Several individuals did not have time to receive theirs.

15th October

News from Isle aux Noix informed us that one of our barques has been chased fiercely by an English brigantine of twenty-eight cannon and was forced into the Bay of Missisconi [Michiscouy]. It is believed that the English army are marching toward the said island.

16th October

Malartic went to work in assisting lodging the troops in the parishes of Longue Pointe, Pointe aux Trembles, Riviere des Prairies, le Sault des Recollets and l'Isle Jésus. The habitants told him that they had heard cannon shots and that they had received orders to be ready to move.

17th October

He [Malartic] continued to establish lodgings in the parishes of Terre-Bonne, la Massecouche [Mascouche], la Chenaie and l'Assomption. He met two officers who were assembling the Canadians, who communicated to him the orders of M. de Vaudreuil, which required him to lead them to Saint-Jean with the utmost haste, as the enemy was marching to attack the Ile aux Noix.

---

108 This was the infamous St. Francis Raid, launched by Robert Rogers and a band of volunteers hoping to find loot. They ambushed a village half empty, killing women and children. Roger's party was pursued by vengeful Abenaki and had a make a gruelling return through the woods facing starvation. For a detailed work on this action see Stephen Brumwell, *White Devil, passim.*

18th October

He [Malartic] returned to Montréal to take orders from M. de Vaudreuil. He learned that M. de Rigaud has gone to La Prairie to take command of all the assembled Canadians; that an English officer with seven soldiers surrendered to our barque, having taken refuge in the Missisconi Bay; we learned he had departed Fort St-Frédéric twenty days ago under the order of General Amherst entering the Chazé River, and back through the strip of land towards Saint François to see if General Gage had arrived there; that on not finding him there, he returned to Lake Champlain, and that following his orders he presented himself to the first barque with two masts that he met which he was astonished to find was French.[109]

19th October

A courier from the Isle aux Noix told us that they awaited the enemy, that the commander of the schebeks had spotted the English fleet which had run aground; they set them on fire and came by land with their equipment. M. de Vaudreuil sent a courier to share the news with M. de Lévis and ask for troops. Malartic left at noon to determine the lodgings in the parishes of Repentigny and Saint-Sulpice.

20th October

He [Malartic] continued to work in the parishes of la Vallée au Tray [Lavalterie], Lanoraye, Berthier, the islands of Pas and Saint-Ignace, and went to sleep at Sorel.

21st October

He went up the Chambly River to go to Saint-Ours, Saint-Antoine and Saint-Denis.

22nd October

He went to Saint-Charles and returned to Saint-Denis and Saint-Ours where he made a small portage to cross to the right bank of the river.

23rd October

He established lodgings in the parishes of Vercher, Varennes, Boucherville and Longueuil.

24th October

He was at La Prairie. M. de Contrecoeur, who commanded there, told him that M. Rigaud is camped at la Tortue to stop any party that wished to invade by the

109 The Chazé river leads towards Montréal from Lake Champlain, near Point aux Fers. Today known as the Chazy River, New York.

Chazé River; that M. de Bourlamaque had said in his last letter that cannon were heard around the area of Faucault Mill, where he believes the English army to be encamped. He embarked for Montréal. The contrary wind forced us to halt above La Prairie. He went to Longueuil and entered the town. M. de Bastard who commanded the troops who were aboard the schebeks and who arrived at the same time, said that they almost died of hunger and misery in the woods and that he would have had trouble finding a way out if it was not for finding an officer and twenty Scots who met him and took him across all the rivers which they found on their way. The officer said he had left Fort St-Frédéric with all the army, and that the Scots were responsible for making paths for portages.

25th October

M. de Vaudreuil ordered that M. de Rigaud to come to camp at La Prairie. M. de Bourlamaque informed that he expected to be attacked. A courier from the Isle au Galop told us that the army which had been at Chouaguen had retired, that four hundred men remained and a corvette of twenty-two guns was being constructed. News from Michillimakinak coming via Détroit, where M. de Rocheblave retired in good order after the defeat of the detachment from the Belle Riviére.[110] The savages of these two parishes still appear attached to us.

26th October

Nothing of interest.

27th October

It appears that if the enemy has moved forward then they have already retraced their steps. A courier from Jacquartier announced to us the departure of the Canadians of

110 Philippe-François de Rastel de Rocheblave, sometimes called the Chevalier de Rocheblave, came to New France during the Seven Years War and seems to have fought in the Ohio region. He was at Fort Chartres in 1760, and in the following years he established himself at Kaskaskia as an officer in the colonial regular troops. Around 1765 he moved from Kaskaskia, which had passed into British hands, to Sainte Genevieve (Missouri) on the west bank of the Mississippi in territory that France had ceded to Spain. There he took command of the Illinois country for the Spaniards. After quarrelling with the Spanish governor in New Orleans, he re-crossed the Mississippi around 1773 or 1774 and settled once more at Kaskaskia, where he soon became the commandant, this time in the service of the British. In July 1778 he was taken prisoner by American troops under George Rogers Clark and sent to Virginia. Evidently having escaped, in the spring of 1780 he reached New York which was still in British hands. Shortly after the Revolutionary war ended, he settled with his family in Montréal, and from 1789 they lived at Varennes. Rocheblave took an interest for a time in the fur business, and from 1792 until his death on 22 April 1802 he served as member for Surrey in the Lower Canadian House of Assembly. In May 1801 he was appointed clerk of the land roll. Malartic here noted, 'It was unfortunate that this officer who had made better arrangements was not old enough to be the commander in chief of this detachment as he could have saved Niagara'.

the government of Montréal, who went down the River Chambly and were followed by Royal Roussillon, Guyenne, and a detachment of colony troops. M. de Vaudreuil sent orders to two regiments to occupy the parishes from Sorel up to La Prairie.

28th October

M. de Vaudreuil sent orders to M. de Rigaud to remove his camp, return with the troops and to send the habitants to their homes. A courier from Jacquartier who left before the one which arrived yesterday, told us of the death of several wounded officers; and that M. de Lévis had removed grain and cattle on which the English had designs.

29th October

M. de Rigaud arrived. The news from Isle aux Noix was that the English were not approaching. M. de Vaudreuil dispatched a courier to propose a prisoner exchange to General Amherst.

31st October

Malartic finished the work on the bills of exchange with difficulty, and he heard said that, despite the short time allowed for withdrawal, the receipt was for thirty-six millions.

1st November

We learned that Béarn left Jacquartier on the 29th.

3rd November

Very bad weather. I have been at Repentigny to wait for the regiment. I went back on the 4th to bring the shoes which were embarked in my bateau and I arrived on the 5th, an hour before the regiment.

6th November

Béarn crossed the Assomption River to get to their quarters.

7th November

I have been to Montréal. I dined at M. de Vaudreuil's with all the English officers, who will be released shortly. General Amherst has responded to M. de Vaudreuil with an acceptable agreement, that he will return all the officers and soldiers he has received and send the rest back to France.

10th November

The English prisoners have left. We learned that the Acadiens captured eight small vessels and asked permission to race them.

12th November

M. de Vaudreuil held several councils with the Abenaki, who ask to spend the winter at the top of the Assomption River, to be able to return often to Montréal to consume food supplies and ruin the habitations through which they pass.

13th November

M. Lévis arrived from Jacquartier. The Abenaki have changed their advice, after an offer from the Iroquois, to spend the winter six leagues from Sault. A courier from Jacquartier told us that the English have sent two thousand men and eight cannon to Lorette, to pursue the French in those parts and administer the oath of allegiance to the habitants. They have made entrenchments from the bridge. M. de Bougainville, who was on the march to return, stopped at Maxkinongé, where he waited for orders from the generals.

I made visits to the quarters occupied by the regiments, which were at Longue Point, Pointe aux Trembles, Riviere des Prairies, le Sault des Recollets and Sainte-Geneviève. The regiment of La Reine occupied the parishes of Chambly, Saint-Charles, Saint-Denis and Saint-Antoine with Saint-Ours; Guyenne the parishes of Sorel, Contrecoeur, Vercher and Varennes; Royal Roussillon, Boucherville, Longueuil and La Prairie; La Sarre, Isle Jésus, Terrebonne and la Massecouché [Mascouche]; Berry, la Chenaie, l'Assomption, Repentigny, Saint-Sulpice, La Valtrei [Lavalterie], Aultray [Autray], La Nokaie [Lanoraye], Berthier, les Isles des Pas and Saint-Ignace; Languedoc, in the government of Trois-Rivières. The regiments of La Sarre, Languedoc and Béarn each left a piquet at Jacquartier; M. Dumas commanded on this frontier, there were five hundred men in the fort and three hundred at Pointe aux Trembles which was commanded by M. de Repentigny. The regiments of La Reine and Berry left three piquets at Isle aux Noix, where M. de Lusignan commanded with many of the colony troops. Royal Roussillon and Guyenne sent two piquets to Saint-Jean, where M. Valette, captain of Royal Roussillon, commanded. M. Desandrouins, engineer, commanded at Fort Lévis which was garrisoned by colony soldiers and Canadians. M. le chevalier de Lacorne, who has arrived, has left this frontier tranquil.[111]

111 Fort Lévis was hastily constructed on an island in the middle of the Saint Lawrence, near its confluence with the Oswegatchie River in 1759 after it was decided that the fort at Présentation was untenable. On Map 2 the island would have been between 'The Gallops' and Fort Présentation. It is now called Chimney Island and any remains of the Fort were lost in the dredging of the St. Lawrence Seaway construction.

21st November

I have been at Montréal. I heard that the officers who conducted the English have returned. They said that General Amherst is still with his army at Fort St-Frédéric, they were showered with civilities there and kept some of our bateaux to return our prisoners. Consequently, the troops who occupy the south were ordered that the habitants should hold ready to march with food for six days.

24th November

Deserters from Québec reported that the detachment which had gone to Lorette had returned to the town and that there no more ships on the river.

28th November

A courier from Jacquartier told us that our vessels passed happily past Québec.[112]

29th November

A man concerned with the arming of our vessels arrived from Jacquartier and told us that five ships have fortunately passed by there but that five were lost opposite the Chaudière Falls, where they were submerged; the English sent a well-armed *goelette* to burn them; that forty-five men of the said *goelette* collided with the *Elisabeth*, which it set ablaze; Captain Canon seeing this gave a well-armed chalouppe to M. de la Giraudais, his second, and charged him with seizing the *goelette* which was taken and boarded, and who killed eight men and made eleven prisoners.

At the beginning of December there was nothing of note. M. Dumas wrote that the English had twelve hundred men on guard daily at Sainte-Foi, Charlesbourg, Lorette and Saint-Augustin, the Isle d'Orleans and Pointe Lévis to cover the woodcutters, who have difficulty providing the required amount.[113] Two sentinels froze at Québec; our parties sometimes captured men from the advance posts.

20th December

M. Pouchot arrived from Saint-Jean with all the officers and regular troops captured by the English, two from the Colony, and one hundred and sixty-eight soldiers or

112 Note by Gaffarel – These vessels carried Mercier [the artillery commander] back to France. After establishing his winter quarters, Lévis sent Mercier to Paris to inform the King of the situation in Canada and ask for aid. See his letter of 1 November to Marshal de Belle-Isle: 'Without supplies of war or food, it will be impossible for us to make any expedition or enterprise this winter; we will be blessed if we can support ourselves. We have finished eating most of the remaining oxen and horses. We have to feed in the region of three to four thousand people, including savages, which will completely consume the few resources that remain in the colony.'

113 Note by Gaffarel – Garneau (Canada, II, 333) found the register of orders of payment of Murray's troops in the archives of the provincial secretariat at Québec. On 24 December 1759, there were 8, 204 men present not including officers.

Canadians who were ordered to go to their quarters, and he was to go to his company. At La Prairie they received contrary orders to come to Montréal where they arrived on the 24th; they praised their good treatment and honesty of the English, saying they had suffered much poor weather and setbacks caused by the bad roads and the cold.[114]

114 Note by Gaffarel – Pouchot could have added famine to these setbacks. On 1 November 1759, a barrel of wine cost 700 *livres* in Canada, bread 8 sous per *livre*, 40 *sous* for bacon, 20 *sous* for beef, a cabbage 20 *sous*, a dozen eggs 50 *sous*, a pair of shoes 20 *livres* etc. See Dussieux, op. cit.

6

The Year 1760

This year witnessed the end of French rule in Canada. General Lévis made a desperate strike to recover Québec. At the Battle of Sainte-Foy he forced the British army to retire inside the walls of Québec but was at the mercy of the international supply situation. The first ships to enter the Saint-Lawrence that year were British. Withdrawing to Montréal, Lévis' army was determined to fight to the last in a bid to recover some of the honour which the army felt had been lost by the submission of Louisbourg: In the end, though, it would come to naught. British armies approached from Lake Ontario, Lake Champlain, and Québec. Vaudreuil ordered the army to surrender. General Amherst churlishly refused the honours of war and so Lévis had his regiments' flags burnt and left New France without meeting Amherst. Malartic's sense of relief at the end of the war is palpable in his journal entries. The tension which had been building over the last two years is suddenly gone as he lets his observations wander to more mundane matters.

1st January – 14th February

Several of the officers, held by the English as prisoners, arrived at Montréal; the generals wished them to return back to Québec as they had come back on parole as avowed prisoners; M. de Bellecombe returned at the beginning of January 1760, to give a proposition to General Murray, commander of Québec, which it was hoped would be agreeable to him on the subject of these prisoners.[1] There were preparations for an expedition which would appear to menace Québec including refitting the artillery to enable it to travel on the ice, and making ladders of different heights and other seasonal equipment. Nothing was neglected in picking up supplies. Several of the outposts were lacking.

The habitants were ordered to make ready to leave at the first notice with food for six days for themselves as well as the soldiers who are lodged with them.[2] Almost all the mills are idle, the water being too high. The inhabitants have difficulty in getting

1 Guillaume Léonard de Bellecombe was *aide-major* of Royal Roussillon. He was captured at the Battle of the Plains of Abraham after being wounded. He later went on to be governor of Pondicherry.

2 Note by Gaffarel – 'It was not without incredible difficulties that the troops could be put into a fit state to make this campaign. The fully exhausted colony not only lacked food, but also all that was necessary to equip and encamp the troops.' *Relation de la second bataille de Québec et du siege de cette ville.* (Depot de la guerre, vol. 3574, p. 32)

flour. Daily trains loaded with provisions and equipment for Jacquartier and return with wine and eau-de-vie. These liquors are down a quarter on the price they were sold previously. M. de Boishébert left on the 15th of January to go the banks of the Riviere du Sud to keep up the good dispositions of the inhabitants, and try and take food from these parts which it has in abundance. M. de Bellecombe returned on the 20th with an English officer that M. de Murray sent because he is prisoner. The general would not accept our proposals and responded saying that he would follow the rule established by M. Amherst, his general. M. de Lévis ordered all the officers of the regulars who were regarded by the English as prisoners should leave immediately for Québec.

The commandant of Fort Lévis sent one hundred men from his garrison, not having the necessary supplies for them. Some were frozen on the road; the cold being very severe this month. A courier from Jacquartier told us that the English have a detachment in the south;[3] that M. de Saint-Martin has been sent into the same parts to scout their movements. Four Acadians arrived who have, with the help of the savages, stolen the boats of the English.

We learned from Jacquartier that they have found a way to take many things from Québec; that the tracks of a lost courier were found under the Falls at la Chaudière, that in this spot he reprised his correct route; there was picked up a letter from a merchant who asks his correspondent in Boston for some good shoes for the Spring; he complains that they are lacking in many things. The English have deliberated on burning down the neighbouring parishes of Québec, and the general hospital, because that is where the French can approach from. Several of the officers favoured this but General Murray rejected it, as it would expose them to breaking their word to the Canadians when they made their oaths of allegiance, and that by doing this they would increase our forces in sending us more than twelve hundred men who would not only fight as enemies, but with personal enmity to all those in Québec. His advice prevailed.

Scaling ladders were being made in the all neighbouring parishes of Jacquartier. A sergeant and six French soldiers in the service of the English received orders to go to Lorette to stop an Acadian suspected of corresponding with our outposts, he returned to Pointe aux Trembles with his detachment. M. de Repentigny sent him to M. Dumas.

M. de Saint-Martin spent several days at Pointe Lévis. The river is solid before Québec; the ice is so strong that the English often skate, giving great pleasure to the savages who have already captured six. A secretary of M. de Vaudreuil was charged with beginning to make a tour of the parishes of the government to record the state of the boys and ability to march, prevailing on all the inhabitants to be ready and prepare food for six weeks for themselves and the soldiers who lodge with them. He

3 Lt. Col. William Haviland was now installed as commander of Fort Crown Point and Ticonderoga, as Fort St-Frédéric and Carillon had been renamed, and had as a garrison the 27th Foot, two companies of rangers, and half of the late General Forbes' 17th Foot. Douglas R. Cubbison, *All Canada in the Hands of the British: General Jeffrey Amherst and the 1760 Campaign to Conquer New France,* (Norman: University of Oklahoma Press, 2014), p. 93.

found the inhabitants making their best efforts.[4] M. Bougainville has left for Sainte-Anne to go on to Jacquartier and Pointe aux Trembles.

15th February

A courier from Jacquartier told us that the English have attacked M. de Saint-Martin at Pointe de Lévis. Abbé Piquet arrived from Présentation with two officers and twenty-five savages, who came to ask Ononthio if they could accompany the expedition to Québec.

16th February

Letters from M. Dumas and Saint-Martin were received from two couriers from Jacquartier. The latter gave an account to M. de Vaudreuil saying that a detachment of six hundred men had made a sortie from Québec and gone to Pointe de Lévis. He was arrayed advantageously for combat and held up the first attack without losing an inch of ground, but that in the heat of battle he was informed of another detachment of six hundred which sought to flank him so he thought best to retire; he made it in good order by the Etchemin road where he crossed the river of that name, and positioned himself on the left bank to await the aid and reinforcements he had asked from M. Dumas. He lost only five men. He asked M. le general for permission to go and take his revenge.

We learned from the Isle aux Noix that a party of eighty savages attacked a convoy between Fort St-Frédéric and Carillon, and made some prisoners, that they took a train loaded with snowshoes, shoes, deer and crates of muskets, and that they lost five others. The prisoners say that Colonel Johnson is at Carillon with many savages, that Captain Rogers is also there and that soon they will send a considerable party against our frontier. Someone coming in from Pointe aux Trembles, assured us that he was an inhabitant of Lorette and that on the day of the combat of M. de Saint-Marin, he had seen fifteen trains of wounded return to Québec.

18th February

A courier from Jacquartier reported to have seen M. de Bougainville on the alert at Pointe aux Trembles as the English have reinforced their posts and moved ahead of Saint-Augustin, where they have captured one of our soldiers, and that M. Dumas has recalled M. de Saint-Martin.

4 Note by Gaffarel – The Bishop, Dubreuil de Ponbriand [sic], a refugee in Montreal, had, in a pastoral letter, recommended the faithful to pray for, 'those who have sacrificed for their country. The name of the illustrious Montcalm, those of the many respectable officers, those of the soldiers and militia who will not leave your memory.' This call, when it spoke of taking up arms, made a great impression.

20th February

The savages have arrived from Isle aux Noix with their prisoner who rubbished the last news. They assure that Colonel Johnson is not at Carillon, that there are few savages; that the trains were loaded with clothing and equipment for the garrison of Fort St-Frédéric, and that there will be a detachment coming out from the two forts in the next few days.

23rd February

A courier from Jacquartier told us that the English are approaching Pointe aux Trembles, that they have captured a soldier, that M. Dumas prevented their plan by withdrawing the troops under M. de Saint-Martin, whom he has brought back to Saint-Antoine, M. Bougainville has returned from visiting all the posts along the frontier of Jacquartier. There is an increase in the number of transports which depart everyday loaded with different munitions.[5]

24th February

M. de Bourlamaque left for Jacquartier. All the priests have received a letter circulated from M. le general and the Intendant which prescribe them to supply all the corn they have, and that if they make any difficulties they will have their authority removed. It is learned that M. de Saint-Martin sent news from the Etchemin River that he had killed some men and captured 6 from a detachment which had been scouting around these parts. A great thaw is raising fears that the ice will recede. An order was sent to the inhabitants to have the biscuit they have prepared put into barrels for storage. The commanders of the regiments were warned to make ready to leave at the first order.

Several couriers from Jacquartier told us that M. de Saint-Martin has approached Pointe de Lévis to engage the English who made a sortie; that three thousand men marched against him; that he retired at their approach keeping up a constant fusillade; that he was pursued up to the Chaudière Falls, and that he lost four men.

3rd March

M. de Bourlamaque arrived from Jacquartier, where he had prepared the dispositions for the projected expedition; he sent back all the detachments which were near Québec, which were not of great use, and because General Murray had burned eighty houses on Pointe de Lévis. An order was issued to all merchants to send all their merchandise they have remaining to the King's magazine. Daily auctions are held which show that many people fear for the colony.

5 Note by Gaffarel – The biggest problem was procuring food. See the Letter from Vaudreuil to Lévis cited in Garneau (Canada, II, p. 342): 'we have, after much care, gathered all the resources of the colony, both comestibles and munitions of war; both are very mediocre, and if not sufficient let us also use all expedients that our zeal suggests to supplement them.'

6th March

News from the Isle aux Noix which tells us that the savages who were scouting gave notice that they found tracks in the woods of a detachment of five hundred men. An officer who arrived from Saint-Jean the day before yesterday said that while scouting, he saw five men near the Sable River and then nearly thirty. He believed the purpose of this detachment was to come and burn Sault Saint-Louis, to ravage these parts, or to burn the two frigates which are at Sorel. M. de Vaudreuil engaged the savages to go and investigate these parts. All the officers of the troops who are in the south have received orders to return to their quarters, and the crews of the frigates to return on board ship.

7th March

The savages departed.

8th March

We learned from three couriers from Acadia that the savages often go to the English forts to fetch the things they need in return for beaver pelts; that the parishes and their missionaries are disposed to make peace, fearing that if they do not accept it, they will be driven to the wilderness. A public order was proclaimed that requests all individuals to bring all the gunpowder they have to the King's magazine. They will be payed 3 francs per livre. Work continues with the greatest spirit in preparation for the expedition to Québec.[6] The troops have begun to be equipped. The artillery has been sent down the River Chambly which will then be shipped on the vessels at Sorel.

We learned from Isle aux Noix that the French and savages who returned from the scout agreed that they had found tracks and marks at Pointe aux Pins from the camp of M. Pouchot from the beginning of winter, and that on their return from Fort St-Frédéric in Missisconi [Michicouy] Bay they saw the old tracks. People who come from Québec say that the English have great quantities of flour, and that they are constructing redoubts at Pointe de Lévis.

13th March

M. de Repentigny wrote that the river is flowing before Québec; that the ice has moved up much further because the English have cut down much of the wood.

6 Note by Gaffarel – See the beautiful letter circulated from Lévis to battalion commanders (29 November 1760) announcing the projected expedition: 'In carrying out this expedition we must mark the debt of gratitude we owe to the colony which has fed us all the time we have been here. The inhabitants have received the soldiers as if they were their children... All these reasons are quite pressing to a nation who has honour at its principle and is prepared to sacrifice all, if necessary, to save against loss of religion in the colony and the cruel slavery that the English will not fail to subject on the Canadians.'

15th March

M. Rigaud said that the inhabitants and savages of Trois-Rivières have assure that they have seen a body of seven to eight hundred men around Nicolet which spread alarm in these parts, *la générale* was beaten in the town. M. de Longueuil has gone to raise everyone to prepare for campaign, and sent an envoy to the Regiment of Languedoc with orders to assemble and wait ready for decisive news.

16th March

M. Longueuil said to the general that a Jesuit had written to him of a savage who had been hunting before Nicolet who saw two men, then eight dressed in red, he immediately killed his dogs so as not to be discovered, and came as fast as his legs would carry him, he [Longueuil] sent a detachment of two hundred men under orders of his son with three other officers to go and seek the enemy in those parts, which have been spoken about for several days. The bakery at Jacquartier has burnt down with a portion of the magazine. If the wind had not changed the powder magazine could have been at serious risk.

17th March

M. Pouchot went to go and take command on the frontier of Fort Lévis and relieve M. Desandrouins leaving him free for the siege of Québec. M. Bougainville arrived from Isle aux Noix. One hundred and fifty savages were equipped and left immediately tasked with taking prisoners from around Fort St-Frédéric. M. Diverny, an artillery officer, came to return an account of the artillery that has been delivered to Sorel. We learned that a detachment of five hundred English had surprised the patrol of cavalry who were coming up to this post, repelled the guard and burnt the mill at Saint-Augustin with a few houses. M. de Repentigny said that if it were him he would have given the signal to oppose the retreat of this detachment. The engineers MM. Desandrouins and Fournier have arrived. M. Bougainville left to take command on the frontier of Isle aux Noix. M. de Lotbiniére, engineer, went with him.

4th April

The rivers have begun to flow. The regiments received the details of the Canadians who will campaign with them.

5th April

M. de Montegron said that the party of savages has returned and that they took 9 prisoners, comprising 3 officers that were taken under Fort St-Frédéric; that despite everything he said to the savages to persuade them to stay there, they wished to return. The regiments received orders to send men to fetch the bateaux allocated to them. The melting of the ice is not responding to the troops' eagerness to leave.

13th April

Men and horses designated to form a troop of cavalry were assembled; all the horses from the town in a fit state were pressed into service. The first division left on the 14th and the second on the 15th.

17th April

M. de Lapause, *aide maréchal général des logis de l'armée*, and M. Desandrouins, engineer, left for Pointe aux Trembles. All the regiments fetched their bateaux from Montréal; those of La Sarre and Béarn could not enter onto the river which is still frozen, and remained at the end of the island. Many colony soldiers arrived, who will compose two battalions which will be formed.

18th April

M. de Montegron, famous partisan held in high esteem, drowned while hunting; an ice bank capsized the boat which bore him. Munitions, artillery and its equipment were embarked onto a *flûte* [transport] and a *goelette*. M. de Bourlamaque and the *major-général* have left for Jacquartier.

20th April

The regiments of Royal Roussillon, Guyenne and Béarn have left their quarters with the Canadians who will serve with them. A party of the Battalion of Montréal has also embarked. Béarn has been lodged in the parish of Repentigny. They have had difficulties in boarding because of the ice.[7]

21st April

Béarn left early but were forced to stop at Autray, so as not to block up the entrance to Lake Saint-Pierre, where the other regiments are held up by a violent north-east wind. M. le chevalier de Lévis passed at 3 o'clock in the afternoon.

22nd April

Good weather. The regiments of Royal Roussillon, Guyenne, Berry and Béarn, and a portion of the two battalions of the marine have crossed the lake and camped before Trois-Rivières.

7 Note by Gaffarel – The English, despite precautions taken, were on their guard. On the 21st Murray informed the population of Québec that they should be ready to evacuate within three days. This order was executed on 24 April.

23rd April

Wind from the north-east and rain. The regiments are lodged in the parishes of Sainte-Anne, Grandines and Deschambault. M. le chevalier de Lévis said tomorrow we would arrive at Pointe aux Trembles.

24th April

The regiments of la Reine, part of La Sarre, Royal Roussillon, Guyenne, Berry, and Béarn, with several companies of Languedoc have arrived at Pointe aux Trembles and are camped before the church, having had much trouble pulling their bateaux overland because of the ice. The frigates and *goelette* moored at midday and M. de Lévis arrived at the same hour.

25th April

All the army has reunited at Pointe aux Trembles and have been ordered to hold ready to march. Ammunition has been distributed. Three cannons were landed which would follow the army. We sent out a party ahead to gather news of the enemy who are believed to be at Cap Rouge. They threatened the inhabitants of Saint-Augustin that they would come to burn down the village. The army took bread for one day.

26th April

The army embarked at 8 o'clock, and arrive at 10 o'clock despite the north-east wind from Saint-Augustin. They have dragged the bateaux far enough so that the *bordages* [keels] will not leave a trail leading to their hiding place. They have been ordered to make supper and be prepared to march at 3 o'clock with food for three days and provisions of cartridges: they began to march at the prescribed hour, leaving two men to guard each bateau, climbing the slope of Saint-Augustin and taking the road to Lorette. Around 5 o'clock a violent storm arose followed by strong rain. By 10 o'clock the army was lodged in the houses of Lorette.

27th April

The rain continued. At 6 o'clock the *major-général* carried orders to the La Sarre Brigade, composed of that regiment and Béarn, to put them into motion. The general had stopped half a league from the lodgings which required him to wait for the weather to clear. At 10 o'clock the army began to march in a single column, the grenadiers forming the advance guard. At midday it arrived at Sainte-Foi; the advance guard commanded by M. de Bourlamaque has been posted at the end of this parish, opposite a body of fifteen hundred Englishmen who blocked them. They repelled a detachment of Scots who wished to fall upon our savages.

At 2 o'clock we saw the church of Sainte-Foi on fire and the roof blown off. M. de Bourlamaque informed M. de Lévis that the English had retired. The general ordered him to pursue them with the grenadiers and cavalry, who would be followed by the whole army who would go to lodge in the houses of Sainte-Foi at 6 o'clock. The grenadiers closed near to the English rear guard and forced them to return to the town. This march was hard as it was painful. All the officers had walked on foot and had to suffer as their soldiers did from rain, snow and the inconvenience of marching through knee deep water.

28th April

The English fired several cannon shots on the grenadiers and Canadians that the general had posted close to the town. At 7 o'clock all the army moved forward to take some more houses. The commander of the grenadiers informed that the entire garrison had come out, the general ordered *la générale* beaten and to join together [the Canadians and grenadiers]. They met and formed at the head of the army, which was put into motion to go and attack the English posts on the heights with considerable artillery; our brigades formed under fire from the said artillery, but did not prevent one from forming line and the other staying in column, waiting for the ground to permit them to deploy: the English posted the larger part of their forces and made the strongest efforts on the mill and two hills occupied by the grenadiers.[8] M. de Bourlamaque, who was posted there, seeing that all the enemy forces were encircling him, was forced to retire with the grenadiers. He was wounded while ordering this movement and had his horse killed under him. He had to be taken to the field hospital.

However, our army still continued to advance, the left formed by the Brigade of La Sarre marching forward without firing, although punished by the grapeshot of the English. The general sent two officers with orders for them to make an about-face and take post between some houses behind them. Malartic, major of said brigade, was very distressed on receiving this order and brought it to the piquet of Béarn, who had the right of the brigade, to command the about face. M. de Barraute, captain of distinction of the said piquet, told him and all the soldiers; "Our major, if we make an about face, the enemy will follow and defeat us. March on them without firing and we will beat them." The major could not execute the order and moved forward fifteen paces so that the brigade saw that it was necessary to move forward. A minute later, M. Dalquier, *lieutenant-colonel* commanding the said brigade, came to him and said, "Major, I take it upon myself to violate the order of the general. Let us use the ardour of our soldiers. We will not fire but rush the enemy with the bayonet and will vanquish them."

The brigades of the Marine, Berry, and Royal Roussillon made the same manoeuvre. At the same time the grenadiers retook the mill and the hills which had been abandoned. A few minutes later M. de Lévis came to the brigade of La Sarre and said to M. Dalquier. "You have rendered the greatest possible service to your King by not turning about. Hold five minutes: I promise you victory." The general, who

8 Murray had 3,866 men on the field and had twenty cannon and two howitzers deployed. In contrast Lévis only had three cannon and around 5,000 men on the field. Stephen Brumwell, *Redcoats: The British Solder and War in the Americas, 1755-1763* (Cambridge: Cambridge University Press, 2002), p. 257.

was posted on the right, saw M. de Poularies, *lieutenant-colonel* and commander of the Royal Roussillon Brigade, arrive. He made part of his brigade quarter wheel to the left to hold the flank of the English, which was at this moment beginning to retreat and taking the road to the town. They had abandoned their artillery, which consisted of twenty-two cannons and a howitzer, all cast, lots of ammunition and a large amount of tools. We captured eighteen officers including a colonel and sixty soldiers. Their losses must be considerable because from the beginning of the battle, which lasted over five hours, several carts removed their dead and wounded. Our losses were seven or eight hundred killed or wounded, including sixty officers.[9]

I was wounded by a piece of grapeshot that struck my chest as I was marching forward. The blow knocked me over and caused a great commotion. Returning to my senses I found myself between the hands of a sergeant and a soldier, who wished me to get up. I begged them to let me die on the spot. They raised me up despite my protestation and I felt something cold slide down my stomach. I opened my vest and found the lower part of my left breast pierced as big as a fist and very dark. I found below this the bloody piece of grape. I was put into the hands of a surgeon who opened this contusion with twelve strokes of the scalpel.

The battalions were reduced to a few people by the end of the battle: it was this which prevented the general following the enemy as quickly as he wished and possibly entering the city.

To show how difficult it is in a lively action for all the officers to see their commander, I can relate that a moment before M. Dalquier came to see me, a captain, who did not like this commander [Dalquier], came to tell me that he was not at his post and that as such he commanded the brigade. I proved to one and the other my discretion, believing it to be prudent here. The savages, who had not been of any use during the action, plundered the equipment and haversacks they brought back, and as soon as they saw us masters of the field of battle, went to lift scalps. They took several from the French. We had suffered much from the enemy cannon loaded with grapeshot. The discharges which swept through us at close range caused our greatest loss. The Canadians of the four brigades of the right, those who had been in the intervals or in front of the brigades, fired at length and very timely. They did much harm to the English. As soon as the general gave the orders to press them, he sent a guard to take the general hospital, where he transported the wounded and those of the English who remained on the field of battle. I arrived there at 6 o'clock. We were very well received by the *hospitaliers*, and we found there close to six hundred, including French and English.[10]

9 Murray had to spike all but two of his guns and recorded 292 killed, 853 wounded and 53 prisoners. Stuart Reid, *Québec 1759: The Battle That Won Canada* (Oxford: Osprey, 2003), p. 91.

10 Note by Gaffarel – The spectacle was heartbreaking. See the letter cited by Garneau (Canada II, 350), written by a Sister of the general hospital. 'If only there were a pen other than mine to paint the horrors that we had to see and hear during the twenty four hours while the wounded were transported, the cries of the dying and the suffering of all concerned. In these moments there must have been a supernatural force which kept them enduring without dying. After having taken more than five hundred beds that we had in the King's magazine, there were still many more of these poor souls in this unhappy place. Our barns and our stables are full. We

Our brigades began to entrench near to the town whose artillery killed some of our men. Our fleet moored at noon near Samos.

On the 22nd the English had sent out all the French from the town. On the 26th they pulled back all the troops and artillery that had been at Lorette, and on the 27th those of Cap Rouge where they had left some cannon. They had burnt many muskets and ammunition in the church of Sainte-Foi and abandoned a few guns; they heard about the march of our army from a gunner who fell into the water at Saint-Augustin. He drifted on a piece of ice to the Isle d'Orleans, where the tide pushed him into the cul-de-sac of Québec. Sailors, having heard the man's cries, rushed to him, picked him up and carried him to General Murray who cared for him. As soon as the man had recovered his senses, he was very surprised to be in the middle of the English and was forced to admit that we were coming.

29th April

The enemy fired greatly on our workers.[11] Some of them were killed and wounded. Several of the officers and soldiers wounded yesterday have died. All our bateaux have arrived and been unloaded. The artillery was mounted and the munitions at the camp. A trench was opened at night fall, starting from Buttes-à-Neveu, circling all the ground from the said heights to Porte Saint-Louis.[12] The English have troubled our workers who have difficulties removing the earth which is still frozen.

30th April

The English made a sortie at daybreak. The officer commanding took all the men with him into the trench. There were 10 of them killed and 4 of our men. At midday a frigate was seen going down river. It is believed it carried our deserters. Five

had in our infirmaries seventy two officers of whom thirty three died. We saw arms and legs amputated. Clothes were lacking which caused additional distress. We were forced to give our sheets and shirts... This battle was not like the first one. We could not rely on the support of the hospitals of Québec, the English had taken possession of those houses and those of the Ursulines and their individuals to lodge their own wounded who were in greater numbers than ours.'

11 Note of Gaffarel – Murray had decided to prolong the resistance until the arrival of the supply fleet. On 29 April Murray addressed this beautiful order of the day to his army. 'If the day of the 28th of April was unlucky for the British army, the affair was not desperate enough to lose all hope. I know from experience the bravery of the soldiers that I command, and I am confident that they will make their best efforts to recover that which is lost. A fleet is expected with reinforcements for us. I invite the officers and soldiers to bear their hardships with patience, and beg them to exhibit good heart at every peril; it is a duty they owe to their King, their country and also to themselves.'

12 The Buttes-à-Neveu were rocky heights on the Plains of Abraham. Montcalm had assembled his army there at the Battle of the Plains. They overlooked the city and were a good site for artillery to fire on the city. Today they have been partially built on and partly landscaped as part of the Plains of Abraham National Park. The Porte Saint-Louis was one of Québec's bastioned gates, to the right of the besieging army.

battalions relieved the five who had manned the trenches. The besieged have troubled them. We began to construct three batteries.

1st May

The same number of troops and of workers in the trenches as yesterday. The fire from the besieged was very lively. Our fleet disembarked artillery, munitions, forage and equipment for the hospital. The roads are very bad which causes great difficulties in getting the items to their destination. The defenders opened up their embrasures and attacked on all fronts. General Murray sent food for his sick in the hospital and asked for *pruche*, which is excellent at protecting against scurvy.[13]

2nd May

Guards and workers for the trench as normal: the same care was taken by the enemy to harass them. General Murray made a sortie out of Québec against some of the few Frenchmen on guard. Many Canadians from the surrounding parishes arrived.

3rd May

Guards, work on the trench and bombardment from the defenders as normal. They set fire to all the houses they hold from the palace to the Canoterie.[14] A few of their men deserted. After sunset they redoubled their fire which killed several men.

4th May

Guards, trenches and fire of the enemy as normal. During the night we received much fire from the tip of the Isle d'Orleans. We found some cannon at Samos, and a mortar and 50 shells at Beauport. One of our pilots captured by the English escaped them at Kamouraska, where he arrived. He reported that the frigate [that he was piloting] was hit twice, which caused a leak but continued on its way. M. Lévis has sent a drummer carrying spruce to General Murray, who sent him some cheese from *Exther.*[15]

13 Pruche is spruce. Spruce beer was brewed in Canada to ward off scurvy. Gaffarel's edition contains the bizarre error of transcribing the word as Perruche which means parakeet. See the letter from Lévis to Bellecombe, 4 May 1760. H.R. Casgrain (ed.) *Lettres du chevalier de Lévis Concernant la Guerre du Canada (1756-1760)*, (12 vols. Quebec: Demers & Frère, 1889-95), Vol.2, pp. 300-1.

14 The Canoterie was a hanger, built at the end of the seventeenth century, which was used to store canoes and was located around the present-day street, Côte de la Canoterie. The waters of the St. Charles River used to come up to present day Rue St.-Paul.

15 It was Cheshire Cheese; see Casgrain (ed.) *Lettres du chevalier de Lévis*, Vol. 2, p. 300.

5th May

Work and guards as normal. With much difficulty, a battery of cannons and mortars has been completed. The fire of the besieged was not as lively as the preceding days. M. Lévis has sent for the English officers who are in the general hospital to be sent to Québec. The general sent some pieces of game to M. de Murray who delivered three barrels of wine to the hospital for his wounded.

6th and 7th May

Work, guards and the trench as normal, as was the fire of the besieged. General Murray sent a bateau to the hospital loaded with food. Great wind from the north-east.

9th May

Continuation of the north-east wind. Work, guard, trenches and fire of the besieged as normal. At 11 o'clock a vessel was spotted rounding Pointe de Lévis. It anchored in front of it. We hoped for a moment that it was French. It proved to be English and responded to the signals from the town. It sailed at 3 o'clock and moored very close to the lower town.[16]

10th May

Continuation of the north-east wind and bad weather. At daybreak we saw a *goelette* tack around the tip of the Isle d'Orleans to Pointe de Lévis, where she came across to the town. Guards, work and the fire of the besieged which lasted until 5 o'clock when it stopped amid cries of joy and to which the guards of the trenches responded with 'Vive le Roi!'[17] General Murray sent an officer to the hospital charged with a

16 Note by Gaffarel – From Knox (Garneau, Canada, II, 353): 'The circumstances were such that if the first fleet to enter the river were the French, the place would fall into the hands of its former masters. So everyone, besieged and besiegers, turned an anxious eye down river, from which they hoped salvation would arrive.' See a letter from Vaudreuil to the minister of war (22 June 1760): 'It is unfortunate that the just actions of M. Berryer were susceptible to delay; the relief which was intended, however modest, joined with the measures we had taken would have put the colony out of danger and one French would effectively have brought about the surrender of the town of Québec.' – Department of war, vol. 3, 574. p. 67. Letter from Bourlamaque to Crèmille, deputy minister of war: 'We have had the pain of seeing the English squadron arrive instead of the vessels we expected and were forced to withdraw with great success. Now, without hope of receiving any help, we remain with patience and courage. M. le chevalier de Lévis, worthy of a happier success, neglects nothing to maintain the one and the other.'

17 Note by Gaffarel – From Knox [a British Captain of the 43rd Regiment] cited by Garneau (Canada, II, 353): 'We remained in suspense for some time, not having enough eyes to keep watch; but we were soon convinced [the ship] was English. One cannot express the joy which then carried the garrison. Officers and soldiers went up on the walls facing the French and raised hurrahs continually for more than an hour, raising their hats in the air. The city, the enemy camp, the port and neighbouring country rang with our cries and the rolling fire of our guns because the soldiers, in their delirious joy, did not tire of shooting for a considerable time.'

letter and gazettes, who wished to present himself to M. de Lévis. I did not wish to allow this and I promised him I would pass on the details to our general and send him his response soon. A courier from Montréal told us that there is no news from the *pays d'en haut*.

11th May

Good weather, services and trials of the siege as normal. The fire of the besieged was very lively which killed and wounded some of our soldiers. At 8 o'clock our general went to unveil our batteries which fired fiercely all day even more so than the enemy's. M. Barraute was wounded in the head by shrapnel from a shell. We suffered the misfortune of his loss a few days later. One of the *goelettes* passed below the town on the evening tide. The fire of the besiegers did not stop it.

12th May

Our cannon balls have knocked down many of the *saucissons* and destroyed some barricades. Our fire was greater than the enemy's.

13th and 14th May

Service as normal. The fire of the besieged has been greater than ours; this is because four of our cannon have burst and our powder was wet.[18] Several wounded and sick have left for Trois-Rivières and Montréal.

15th May

Service as normal.[19] The fire of the besieged was greater than our own. A violent north-east wind made us believe that the English fleet must be approaching.[20] At 7 o'clock in the evening two vessels were seen rounding Pointe de Lévis. We first considered them French and then English, seeing them respond to signals from the town. They anchored near the walls of the lower town. At 11 o'clock the savages

18 Note by Gaffarel – See the letter from Lévis to Vaudreuil, 13 May 1760: ' Our batteries are in a bad state ... with few large pieces and not of good quality we are unable to make a breach... In these unfortunate circumstances, I am obliged to delay and seek to gain time, in my taking the position to receive the help we can get from France.'

19 Note by Gaffarel – Letter from Lévis to Vaudreuil, 15 May 1760: 'Morally we are doing everything we can do, but we are not fortunate. It is time for this to end one way or the other, I think it will not be long, as we wait for the great north-east wind we are on the great sea.'

20 Note by Gaffarel – The English admitted that if they saw even one French ship of the line, they would have capitulated. See Desandrouins: *Conversation I had with Sir Holland, acting chief engineer during the siege of the Québec, 13th September 1760*: "We admired your work... You were no doubt waiting for help from France? But in the meantime I took my precautions..." – "Ah! A single ship of the line and the place would be ours!" – "You are correct!" – See a letter from Lévis to Berryer (28 June 1760): 'A single frigate arriving before the English fleet would have decided the surrender of Québec and provided for Canada for this year.'

led two prisoners to our general who assured that they were ships of war. M. Lévis commenced his dispositions for lifting the siege and the retreat.

16th May

A vessel of 74 cannons has sailed above the town with two frigates to give chase to our own, including one which failed to sail.[21] They fired several broadsides at the English, who pursued the *Atalante* and two *flûtes* who tried to escape into the Cap Rouge River.[22] The ship moored at Sillery, where it shelled our bateaux. The ten battalions were brought up to the trenches, on which the English gave the most tremendous fire. Several Canadians began their retreat, some back to their homes; the others took the route to Cap Rouge, where we hope they will wait for the army. All the wounded in a fit state to march left for Cap Rouge, the others stayed at the general hospital and the field hospital. The savages got drunk, raided the camp and made a lot of mess. They killed a grenadier and wounded another. To stay their fury, a grenadier was forced to kill one in self-defence as he wanted to cut his throat.

M. le chevalier de Lévis said to me that I should go to his house, and was ordered to remain at the general hospital in command and make the arrangements with the English general to re-establish our sick. The general put the army into motion at 9 o'clock in the evening and gave the rear guard to M. Poularies, which he did with the ten companies of grenadiers in the best possible order.

17th May

I sent a drummer with a letter to General Murray from M. de Lévis. At 10 o'clock Colonel Burton came to visit our sick on behalf of the general. A body of one thousand five hundred men came out of the town to take the road to Sainte-Foi, where I sent several sick who had remained. The English officers came to see the ladies of the hospital; we were overwhelmed with honesties, told about the battle, praising the

21 The larger ship here was the *Vanguard*, a 70-gun ship commanded by Commodore Robert Swanton. The two frigates were the *Diana*, 36 guns, commanded by Captain Alexander Schomberg and the *Lowestoft*, 28 guns, commanded by Captain Joseph Dean. It was the *Lowestoft* and the *Diana*, which most of the work pursuing the French vessels. The *Vanguard* was used to fire on the French army as described by Malartic in this entry. Laird Wm. Clowes, *The Royal Navy – A History from the Earliest Time to the Present* (Sampson Low, Marston and Company: London, 1898),Vol. III, p. 227.

22 *L'Atalante*, launched from Toulon in 1741 was a fifth rate, 32-gun ship. It was sunk in July of this year. Note by Gaffarel – The commander of this frigate, *l'Atalante*, was called Vauquelin. After exhausting his ammunition, he landed all men capable of service and shut himself on board with his injured. The English called on him to raise his flag. Vauquelin responded proudly that he would not surrender his men or his flag. The English responded to his courage and treated him with respect. On this interesting story see M. Gabriel Gravier, *Notice sur Jean Vauquelin de Dieppe, le heros de Louisbourg et de la Pointe aux Trembles* (Rouen: Espérance Cagniard, 1885).

provision of our general and assured that we had taken our revenge from the 13th of September.[23]

18th May

General Murray sent a major to fetch me, and I was accompanied by the *chirurgien-major* [surgeon-major]. This general, who is a man of spirit, received me very graciously as did all the officers who were with him. He showed great surprise when I asked him for food, many prayers being afforded to me and it was agreed on the condition that I would return food in kind. I could neither promise nor refuse. I was permitted to inform M. de Lévis, and I returned an account to him as soon as I had returned to the hospital. M. de Murray had initially authorised me to send my letter with a soldier of my guard. He since said to me that he would take on responsibility of delivering it.

19th May

Admiral Colvill has arrived with the ships which were wintering in Halifax.[24] I dined with M. de Murray. He had a great many questions on the battle of the 28th. The general extolled greatly M. de Lévis' dispositions, speaking with me of his great respect and honour of the troops; after dining, he did me the honour of asking my opinion on the motives for coming out with his garrison on the 28th. I replied that, presumably, he had hoped to be as happy as on the 13th of September as he would have the glory of taking Canada without the aid of the other English generals. He thanked me and started to laugh. I received the response of M. de Lévis which told me that he could not send food; that, according to the agreement, the English must provide for us and that he would send down bateaux to take the wounded in a fit state from the hospital. I sent this response to General Murray who asked I go and see him tomorrow morning.

23 Note by Gaffarel – On this same day Malartic addressed the following letter to General Lévis. 'I sent a drummer this morning with your letter to General Murray, and I asked for his permission to speak to him conforming to your instructions. I have the honour to report what he has told me. All the English agree that on the 28th, we had taken revenge for the 13th of September. They pay tribute to the valour of the troops and the skill of your arrangements and your withdrawal, forced upon you by the arrival of the fleet. As such you must be very quiet on the relations which will arrive from Europe; the English say that there is no grace of favour in France to which you cannot claim.'

24 Alexander Colvill, 7th Baron Colvill, had joined the Royal Navy at 15 in 1733 as a volunteer, his family having little wealth or connections. He had commanded several vessels by the time he was appointed a commodore and commander in chief of the vessels in North America for a brief period over the winter of 1757/8. Although Captains more senior to Colvill arrived in North America later in the war he was permitted to remain as commodore. It has been considered that Colvill's decision to put Swanton and his ships into the St. Lawrence on 16 May was a decisive factor in preserving Murray at Quebec as it denied the Saint Lawrence to the French ships. Colvill remained in command in North America until 1766 and died four years later in England.

20th May

At 7 o'clock I returned to the house of the general who, after the ordinary niceties, told me of his great astonishment that M. de Lévis would not send food. He said to me that if we did not return that which had been supplied, he would hold all those in the hospital as prisoners, before accounting for his conduct to his nation and being forced to feed men who, in ten days, would be fighting against him. I gave him the representation of the instructions of my general and the agreement allowed to me. He replied that he knew nothing more useless than an agreement in America, that we observe them when it is convenient and infringe them when they are not, and they do the same.

20th-25th May

Several merchant vessels arrived.

26th May

M. de Senneville, lieutenant of cavalry, came carrying letters of M. de Lévis to me, which told me that it was impossible for him to deliver provisions of food for our sick;[25] that he was sending a *goelette* to fetch those who were in a state to travel, and that if M. Murray kept them, he would report of his honesty and be assured that they would be well treated. The general wrote to M. de Lévis, and I said I would deliver it to him.[26] I then charged it with the lieutenant of cavalry who left at 6 in the evening.

29th May

The *goelette* arrived. M. Murray refused to let any officer or soldier embark, regarding all as prisoners as he had fed them. I represented to this general that it would do great harm to many of my friends, who were to be appointed battalion commanders, captains of grenadiers and captains. He took me by the arm and said to me, "Your comrades are my own, the enmities of our kings are not ours personally, I regard you as my brother, I would despair at undermining their progress and I will give passports for those that you ask." Immediately he sent for eight of the officers who would not have been appointed to vacancies had they remained in the hospital;[27] he

25 Note by Gaffarel – Three letters are preserved from Malartic to Lévis and the responses of the latter, relating to the treatment of prisoners (23, 25, and 26 May.) See *Casgrain, Lettres de divers particuliers au chevalier de Lévis*, Vol.10, pp. 214-231.

26 Note by Gaffarel – See the letter from Murray, 26 May: 'I am mortified that the circumstances do not allow me to do all that you desire of me. It is impossible for me to return your sick if I have to provide their food. I cannot ignore the fact that you do not have all the facilities to provide subsistence for your troops without removing the provisions of the habitants, and that would make it essential for you to nourish those left at the general hospital until they were well enough to do us harm. My duty, I believe, obliges me to follow my current action. In all that is not incompatible with this duty, I shall be glad to give you evidence of the perfect esteem, etc.'

27 According to a letter from Malartic to Lévis, these officers were MM. Dalquier, Duparc, Pinsure, Savournin, de Fontenay and Lenoir. See *Casgrain, Lettres de divers particuliers au chevalier de Lévis*, Vol.10, pp. 214-231.

promised to let the *goelette* take on some refreshments that I had been allowed to buy for M. Lévis and our officers. At 6 o'clock, he stopped the guard, who had been left to me at the hospital, and conducted them to the prisons of the town, as well as the eight wounded soldiers, who began to march. I accompanied them and told the general that I wanted to follow the fate of the guard entrusted to me. He responded, "It is useless that we enter into a dispute on this regard, I have given an account to the King of England of my conduct, I have written to M. de Lévis. From the letters of this general, you have not been left at the hospital as an officer of the guard, but as a commander to meet the needs of the patients and inspect all those who were there."[28]

30th May

M. Murray prevented the departure of a frigate for Europe and charged it with delivering all the letters that we wished to write. A corvette arrived from Boston which reported that an officer had left from Québec during the winter to carry news to General Amherst.

1st June

At 11 o'clock in the evening, I received, via M. de Senneville, the letter from M. de Lévis, which ordered me to remain at the hospital for several days more.

2nd June

On my way to disclose M. de Lévis' letters to M. de Murray I met him. I found him on the road going towards the Falls. He proposed that I accompany him. I could not accept. He assured me that he persists in the resolution to hold our sick and wounded. Twenty-one of our soldiers have escaped the prisons of the town, fooling the guards, dressing and acting like the English. A detachment was sent in pursuit who brought back three; the general seemed very angry on his return and said that he will break the duty officer and hang the sentries. According to spreading news, General Lévis is preparing to come and fetch his sick, as such the general traced a redoubt that surrounds the mill of the hospital and increased the hospital guard to two officers and sixty soldiers.

---

28 Note by Gaffarel – Letter from Malartic to Lévis, 30 May 1760: 'I have the honour to give you the account that I have been the most unfortunate ambassador in the world. I did what I could and knew, and was successful in this regard. M. Murray sent for my guard yesterday, regarding them as prisoners. I went to him and demanded the reason, and to tell him I would follow their fate; he responded that he would have no more of the agreement, that it was unnecessary for us to continue with protests, that you would demand, and that he has given an account to the King of his actions.' See the letter of protestation from Lévis to Murray (4 June 1760), and the response of Murray (7 June). Complaints of Lévis to Amherst, commander in chief (14 June).

3rd June

The commander of the guard of the hospital received orders to visit and pack up the boxes and effects of the French officers that the general has permitted to embark on the *goelette*. This visit was made with the greatest openness and honesty. At 9 o'clock in the evening, a large chaloupe came to take these effects. An officer and nine surgeons, for whom I had gotten passports, also embarked on it. The general drew me into a window recess and asked: "Do you think that we will give back Canada? I am not sufficiently versed in politics to see far ahead. If we are wise we will not retain it. It is necessary for New England to have a barrier to gnaw at and we will give it one to keep it occupied by not retaining this country."[29]

4th June

Seeing my presence at the hospital as useless, I went to ask M. de Murray permission to go and see M. de Lévis. The general agreed with all possible grace, assuring me that he did not regard me as a prisoner, that I would be master of the decision of staying with M. de Lévis or returning, and filled me with politeness and offers of service. I had the sorrow of seeing several of my comrades die in this hospital: from La Sarre, Palmarolles,[30] battalion commander, and some others; from Berry, M. de Trecesson, commander,[31] Derlein, de Preissac,[32] captains and some others; from Béarn, Monderon, Barraute and Vassal, captains;[33] Salvignac and Tautabel,

29 Note by Gaffarel – This was however not the opinion of the ministers and the English nation, however they had not made their final resolutions, as such on 12 September 1760, after the capitulation of Montreal, the *commissaire de guerre*, Bernier, wrote again to Lieutenant Général de Crèmille: 'If this country is no longer to fall under the dominion of France, it will be an infinite loss; if it is returned it can only be good, if you look on it as a building returned to its foundations, and that will destroy the shadowy interest, which is the unique and ancient cause of its loss; everything must be renewed, or fear that leavening corruption will remain.'

30 Captain François-Charles Bertran de Palmarole (Palmarolle), joined the army in 1734 as a second-lieutenant and was born in 1714. He rose to the rank of captain in July 1740 and then rose to command the company of grenadiers in 1756. He became battalion commander in October 1759.

31 Marie-Joseph-Toussaint Carné de Trécesson was the *lieutenant-colonel* of the 3rd battalion of the Berry Regiment. He was born in January, 1715 in Finistère and began his military career in 1729 as a cadet, remaining with the regiment for the duration of his service. He died on 17 May in Québec's general hospital.

32 Derlein is Jean-Gérard Preissac d'Arlens, a captain from the 2nd Battalion of Berry. He was born in 1727 and became a captain in 1747. He was made a chevalier of Saint-Louis on 13 February 1760 but died of his wounds in the Hospital on 9 May. There is some confusion over the second man here. It could simply be a transcription error in that the transcribers indicated two people whereas Malartic meant one (Preissac also being a part of d'Arleins name). There were two more Preissacs in the Berry Regiment and a further two in the Guyenne Regiment. One of Berry's other Preissacs was hospitalised in Louisbourg, the other, Henri Preissac d'Esclignac de Cadillac, was present at the Battle of Sainte-Foy but survived and took over command of the company of grenadiers from Captain Villemontel who was killed.

33 Jacques Bargeton de Montredon was an old soldier, having been born in February 1696. He was senior captain of the regiment and became captain of grenadiers in 1757. He was hospitalised on 23 April but did not die of his wounds until 23 July. Germain Vassal de

lieutenants;[34] from the Marine, Saint-Martin, Laronde, Meloise and others whose names I cannot remember.[35]

5th June

A warship and five merchant vessels arrived from Ireland. I was at the house of General Murray to visit and thank him when an interpreter who read my passport assured me that I carried one for a prisoner. The general showed great surprise and assured me that it was the fault of the secretary, and immediately made up one which I desired. I thanked him and left as good friends. At 11 o'clock I returned to the hospital to take leave of my comrades and our soldiers. I left at 1 o'clock. By 6 o'clock I reached Pointe aux Trembles, where I stayed a half-hour with the commander of the cavalry, and then arrived at the fort at Jacquartier at 8 o'clock. This place was commanded by M. de Repentigny, at whose house I slept.

6th June

I left at a good hour. At Cap Santé I encountered a courier from Montréal charged with news for General Murray. At 7 o'clock I arrived at Deschambault where I spent an hour with M. Dumas, commander of that frontier. At Batiscan, I found M. de Montbeillard, commander of the artillery, who was constructing bridges on this river as well as those of Sainte-Anne, Champlain and the Chenaux. I was forced to stop at Cap Madelaine at 4 o'clock by a strong north-easterly wind and the unwillingness of other passengers and spent the night there.

7th June

Very bad weather. I arrived at Trois-Rivières at 6 o'clock, and spent two hours going to visit and talking with M. de Longueuil, governor. I embarked at 8 o'clock to go to l'Abbadie. The canoe was full of water and I abandoned it and set to on foot, despite the bad weather and villainous path. I slept at Maxkinongé.

Monviel was born in 1723 at Lot-et-Garonne. He married Charlotte Boucher de La Perrière at Boucherville in 1758. He died of his wounds in the hospital on 14 May. Barraute is listed as a captain of Bearn although no other information is extant.

34 Henri de Salvignac became a lieutenant in 1746 and died in Quebec on 17 August 1760. Pierre Tautabel de Fréjarise was born in 1729 and joined the Bearn Regiment after various service on 1 April 1755. He died during the battle of Sainte-Foy.

35 St-Martin (see Malartic's entry of 8 September 1756, p. 90) was recorded as wounded at Sainte-Foy, although information is scant so is quite possible that he perished there. Laronde could be one of the sons of Louis Denys de la Ronde (1675-1741), a senior marine officer, either Phillipe or Pierre-François-Paul. Meloise was Louis-François Renaud d'Avène des Méloizes, part of a Canadian military dynasty. Louis died in the battle and his brother Nicolas was also wounded.

8th June

The bad weather continued. I left at daybreak by canoe. I changed it after a league. I landed at the Chennail du Nord [North Channel] to reach Berthier by foot, which [the North Channel] is missed out by canoes and canoeists for fear of capsizing. At Mauvrey I met a courier who had come from Deschambault. I arrived at Montréal at 11 o'clock at night. M. Vaudreuil and M. de Lévis showed great pleasure to see me, assuring that they would keep me and asked many questions about the general hospital, the events at Québec and what I believe the enemy to be doing. These generals told me that M. de Langis, who went to scout with a party of savages, was fired on at Pointe aux Fers by a large party of English and retired with some wounded and without having taken a prisoner.

10th to 15th June

News from Fort Lévis, from Isle aux Noix and Deschambault. All very quiet on these frontiers.[36]

16th June

We learned that M. de Murray has delivered the refreshments that he permitted to be shipped. Two officers arriving from Québec said that when they left there were thirty merchant ships anchored. M. de Vaudreuil made a general order to the Canadians, who were ordered to march in two divisions: one following the battalions and the other to go to a specified destination. M. de Lévis wrote to the commanders of the regiments for the information of items which need to be provided to put them in a state to camp and to prevent holding up a march at the first notice. He urged them to make a review of the Canadians who will be under their orders.

21st June

We learned that M. de Murray had sent a French officer to Louisbourg, and that he was sending all those who could travel from the hospital back to France.

22nd June

My servant, whom I had sent to Québec to fetch my equipment, came back and gave me a very honest letter from the major-general [Murray].

36 Note by Gaffarel – Bougainville was charged with the defence of the Ile aux Noix, but he thought the situation was desperate. On 16 June 1760 he wrote to the minister of war, 'The enemy now threatens us from all sides, and although reduced by our victory to a handful of people, we will defend this colony to the last extremity. The sense of such a critical position, the miseries of all kinds which envelop us, the lack of almost all meat, the evils of the past, present and future do nothing to diminish the courage, ardour and zeal of these troops in the service of his Majesty.'

23rd June to 1st July

Frequent couriers which tell us nothing of interest.[37] M. de Bonnot, captain of Guyenne, left with all the English prisoners and was stopped at Pointe aux Fers by the commander of the barques, which have been held up for some days waiting for the orders of his general, and were then conducted to Fort St-Frédéric, where they will be sent on to New York to be traded in a prisoner exchange. A party of English have burnt some houses at Sainte-Thérèse over the last two days and taken twenty men prisoner. A grenadier of the La Reine Regiment who was in the woods put the English party to flight by shouting, "Advance comrades!"

1st July

M. Pouchot wrote from Fort Lévis that one of his parties had captured two prisoners who assured that the English were assembling an army at Chouaguen and were waiting on General Amherst.[38] M. de Saint-Simon, arriving a little later from Acadia, came with packets from the Court carried by three vessels which left Bordeaux in the month of April, whereon they approached the coast of Acadia, he [Saint-Simon] left on the 9th to carry dispatches and the orders of these three vessels. M. de Lévis went to visit the Isle aux Noix and its surroundings.

13th July

Two officers of the Marine arrived from Acadia carrying packets of letters from the Court. They said that the three vessels were in Chaleurs Bay and that they had not seen any of the other vessels that had left with them.[39] If they had sent these vessels out in February, we would have retaken Québec and preserved Canada.

14th July

Two sailors arrived who had come from the bay of Acadia, where their vessel had wintered leaving for France in the month of August. MM. Langlade and Outelas, who left here some days ago with the savages to take prisoners from under Fort St-Frédéric, returned reporting that they had been up to the house of Hoquart; here

37 Note by Gaffarel – The situation was already desperate and the French were fighting more for the honour of the flag. They did not have much powder and ball for combat; a total of 312 cannonballs from an official report. They were lacking food and even bread: As Lévis wrote to the minister of war on 30 June, 'We will attempt to gather our forces; if the enemy do not measure their movements we will attempt to take the opportunity to fight the first advancing bodies of their troops. It is the only option which remains. We are not in a fit state to hold a campaign: food, munitions, all are lacking. It is surprising that we still exist.'

38 Pouchot, taken prisoner at Niagara, had been exchanged. He was sent to Fort Lévis, an important position, just below Présentation, at the head of the Saint Lawrence rapids; he had a garrison of only 200 men.

39 Note by Gaffarel – Chaleurs Bay is around 140-150 km long, 32km wide and an excellent port. The inhabitants, mostly former Acadians, engage in fishing. The Indians named it Ecketma Nemanchi or Lake of the Fishes. It was re-named by Jacques Cartier.

they found an outpost but were discovered; they exchanged fire for a long time but were forced to retire without taking a prisoner. They said they had made a good reconnaissance of the fort and had seen six hundred tents around it. A savage who came from Chouaguen said they had seen troops embark destined for Détroit. The news from Fort Lévis told us that there were five thousand men at Chouaguen, that more arrived each day and they were waiting for General Amherst. M. Desandrouins went to scout the islands and entrance to Lake Saint-Pierre and trace out a small fort on the island of Sainte-Thérèse.[40]

18th July

M. Dumas reported from Deschambault that he had been informed that M. de Murray had embarked on the 14th with two thousand five hundred men.[41]

19th July

The courier from Deschambault told us that the English fleet had been opposite point aux Trembles on the 15th.

20th July

The news from Deschambault said that thirty-nine frigates or small boats had gone up the Richelieu on the 16th, and that fifty others were disposed to head up river.

24th July

We learned that the English disembarked at Platon; that M. Hertel, who commanded a small detachment, was wounded and captured; that he died of his injuries and that M. de Murray had sent his body and remains to Jacquartier. M. de Lapause went to reconnoitre the River de Maxa [Yamaska] and the country it crosses.

M. de Bourlamaque went to make defensive dispositions at the entrance to the lake and opening of the River Chambly.

25th July

The courier from below says that the English fleet is at the same anchorage; that a body of six hundred men have disarmed the Canadians in the south and made them swear allegiance and treated them kindly. The news from the Isle aux Noix is

40 Lake Saint-Pierre is formed by the Saint Lawrence and is two leagues above Trois-Rivières, and an equal distance from the confluence of the Richelieu River.

41 Murray left Québec on 14 July. He had received reinforcements of Royal Navy vessels which gave him total superiority on the river but with almost 2,500 of his men sick and wounded from the arduous winter, the Battle of Sainte-Foy, and resulting siege of Québec he could only spare around 2,000 men for the offensive, cobbled together from various battalions. Cubbison, *All Canada in the Hands of the British*, pp. 68-72.

that we have two parties on campaign, one against Fort St-Frédéric and the other in Michiscouy Bay, where they have found the tracks of a party of thirty men. The news from Fort Lévis is that the English are in force at Chouaguen.

25th and 26th July

Couriers arrived from all fronts. The fleet is opposite the Grandines and at the base of the Richelieu.

27th July

M. de Bourlamaque returned but could not find any countryside that he thought suitable to defend.

28th July

A courier from Deschambault told us that the whole fleet except a frigate of forty cannon, went up the Richelieu and reunited at the Grandines. M. de Lévis has requested all the regimental commanders to order their officers to levy grain in the areas they occupy, which will be paid by appointment with the generals and the Intendant.[42] I left on the 28th with this objective and I found four hundred and seventy-two *minots* of grain. I learned from the Sault des Recollets that the La Sarre Regiment will leave on the 31st to go and entrench the islands at the entrance of the lake.

30th July

I returned to Montréal. I learned that the ships were at Batiscan and Champlain; that some cavalrymen were wounded passing the river by fire from the vessels.

31st July

The courier from Trois-Rivières announced that the fleet had set sail; that the wind was not strong enough to push away; that M. Dumas has sent his equipment into the town and reckoned he would return in the night.

1st August

The courier told us that the fleet was moored opposite Cap Madeleine. The letters from Jacquartier announced that another fleet of twenty boats had left Québec to come up river. M. de Bourlamaque went to see the work which is being done on the lake and returned on the 5th. A courier from Trois-Rivières told us that the fleet had

42 Note by Gaffarel – Letter from Lévis to the minister of war, 'We will try every means to rescue the colony; but our situation is so unfortunate that we need miracles; our armies will have only bread to survive, and poor bread at that.'

quickly passed the town without firing a single shot and moored a league and a half above the town.

6th August

M. de Lévis left to go and see the works at the entrance of the lake and returned on the 7th. The Béarn Regiment sent one hundred men to the island of Sainte-Hélène to construct batteries. The Guyenne Regiment left for the Isle aux Noix. M. de Bougainville said that the schebeks are approaching his position and have the appearance of making an advance guard. The Regiment of Royal Roussillon was ordered to go to Saint-Jean and the inhabitants of the South to hold ready to march. The courier from Trois-Rivières informed us that the fleet has entered the lake; that the English detachments in the south have come up as far as Bettancourt [Bécancourt].

9th August

M. de Bourlamaque left for Sorel.

10th August

News from Fort Lévis. M. Pouchot said that the savages have brought him a prisoner who said that General Amherst is at Chouaguen with ten thousand men. The courier from Trois-Rivières told us that all the vessels have entered the lake; that the second fleet has put six hundred men ashore at Batiscan who are ready to take the oath of allegiance from the inhabitants and force them to lay down their arms with their captains.

11th August

The news announced that the ships are coming. Orders were sent to M. Dumas to abandon Trois-Rivières and let the regular garrison track the vessels up to Berthier, where they would receive new orders. The Béarn Regiment sent their grenadiers and forty soldiers who knew Sainte-Marie to begin making batteries. The first battalion of the Marine received orders to go and camp at l'Isle Saint-Hélène.

12th August

We learned that the ships have penetrated the islands; that M. de Bourlamaque has retired to Sorel with the La Sarre Regiment and the third battalion of Berry following the movement of the fleet to the south, which was also observed by the barque *la Marie*, which retired as they advanced.[43] Twelve soldiers of different regiments arrived who had deserted from the hospital of Québec to re-join their companies.

43 Note by Gaffarel – The situation was desperate. As Lévis wrote to the minister of war on 7 August, 'It seems that their project is to come to Montréal or Sorel to facilitate their meeting

13th August

Different advice tells us that the ships are lined up before Sorel; that a few have passed before Berthier. At midday, a courier from M. de Bourlamaque told us that the vessels were at Valtrie [Lavalterie] and that he was following them. The same courier was sent with orders. Béarn received one to assemble tomorrow at Pointe aux Trembles, where they will find others.

14th August

We learned that M. Dumas, yesterday from the evening until 7 o'clock, was at Lanoraye; that the English barges have taken the route from Sorel; that the ships are left drifting to follow them; that once M. Bourlamaque was informed, he countermarched to follow the barges. M. de Lévis left for Berthier. A portion of Béarn arrived at 4 o'clock at Pointe aux Trembles; the companies which are at Sainte-Geneviève were not able to attend.

15th August

Very bad weather. We learned that the vessels are in the islands [at the head of Lake St.-Pierre]; that a detachment was sent to Saint-Ignace and captured all the livestock; that M. de Lévis is at Berthier with the troops of M. Dumas and that M. de Bourlamaque has returned to Sorel.

16th August

The companies from Sainte-Geneviève have reached us. The Canadians were sent back home, the south-west wind is holding the ships in place. The couriers passing during the day said that our troops and vessels are in the same places as yesterday.

17th August

Wind from the north-east. A courier passing at midday said that the fleet set sail at 6 o'clock. The Béarn Regiment received orders to march to protect the entrance of M. Dumas into the islands. Ordnances were sent to all the parishes to recall the Canadians, put a strong guard on the end of the island, and for all to hold ready to march. The wind calmed at 3 o'clock, we judged that the fleet would be obliged to anchor. We learned that the enemy had arrived at the Isle aux Noix and that General Amherst embarked at Chouaguen to come and besiege Fort Lévis. M. de Montreuil

with M. Amherst. We have naught to stop them as there are several possible routes, we lack artillery and powder; it is only by demonstrating a defence that we delay their march.' See a letter of the same to Berryer (28 June 1760). 'We are not in a state to take to the field lacking food ammunition and everything in general; it is surprising that we still exist. All that remains is the good will and courage of our troops, though the battalions have exhausted officers and old soldiers and are extremely weakened.'

passed at 10 o'clock at night, telling us that he left M. de Lévis at Berthier and that the fleet was anchored.

18th August

M. de Lévis returned the guard that Béarn had sent to the coast of the island, and said they were not needed there as the wind was from the north-east. We learned that General Amherst has marched on Fort Lévis, that the army of Lake Champlain has made its descent from north and south on Isle aux Noix and that they are entrenching. M. de Vaudreuil sent orders to all the parishes for all the Canadians who make up the second division to take to the field with arms, baggage and food for eight days, some to Saint-Jean and the others to Montréal, where they will learn their destinations.

19th August

I was at Montréal. I learned that the army on Lake Champlain has made batteries to pound Isle aux Noix. It is believed that Fort Lévis is besieged. M. le chevalier de Lacorne must leave with a considerable detachment to make or occupy an outpost, where he will scout, once he has learned if it is possible to approach Fort Lévis. M. Bourlamaque broke the head of a Canadian who was charged with a letter from M. de Murray for the commander of the army on Lake Champlain. This general said that his army was in a good state, that the two regiments arriving from Europe were complete and carried themselves well, though piled into transports, that when Lord Raulo joins them with troops coming from Louisbourg, he will take the route to Montréal, whether he has news of M. Amherst or not, his army is sufficient to cope with M. de Lévis.[44]

20th August

I was at Montréal making the arrangements for the pay of the regiment which must, by order of the minister, be given in letters of exchange for the first term and the balance settled by appointment. M. le chevalier de Lacorne left at midday. No news from Fort Lévis; that from l'Isle aux Noix tells that the English continue their batteries and make a portage to capture the river to the south; from Berthier that our armies of the north and south are in the same position.

---

44 Andrew Rollo, 5th Baron Rollo, started his military career late in life, joining the army at the age of forty, distinguishing himself at the Battle of Dettingen in 1743. He rose through the ranks to receive the lieutenant-colonelcy of the 22nd Regiment of Foot in 1756. He and his regiment were present on the New York frontier in 1757, and were veterans of the siege of Louisbourg. He remained there until setting sail with the 22nd and 40th regiments to join Murray and his army on 18 August. On 22 August he led his regiment on a raid against Sorel, privately expressing his distaste at waging war against civilians. In 1761 and 1762 he went on to be involved with the successful British captures of Dominica and Martinique. He died in Leicester, England, 1765.

21st August

Nothing of interest.

22nd August

I have been in Montréal. I learned that the English hold ready to demolish the bridge of the Isle aux Noix, that they have been swept with fire but this has not forced them to surrender, that M. de Saint-Luc returned to Saint-Jean and that he sent four savages to attempt to take a prisoner.

23rd August

Wind from the north-east. We held ready to march. We summoned up our Canadians. We had sent a guard to the end of the island [of Montréal], a detachment of thirty-six men in a bateau to go La Valtrie [Lavalterie] and the same to Berthier and, if finding no opposition, to collect and return the bateaux which are scattered along the shores. An officer sent by M. Dumas told us that the fleet sailed this morning and were progressing. At 7 o'clock some soldiers of the detachment that had left in the morning brought in a canoe saying it was taken from a Canadian of Berthier, that the fleet could not make more than a league, the wind having dropped. M. de Lévis went to Pointe Claire to order M. de Lacorne to leave. We brought up 12 bateaux to the town.

24th August

No news from Fort Lévis. It is said from Saint-Jean that the Isle aux Noix is being heavily bombarded.

25th August

Our detachment brought in three bateaux. The English fired on a soldier who was returning by land.

26th August

I reconnoitred the island of Sainte-Thérèse and its surrounding channels, which are between this island and that of Montréal. I found that this was deep enough to support a ship of three hundred tonnes. On my return I found an engineer tasked with arranging everything for the passage of M. Dumas. At 6 o'clock the *major-général* ordered us to approach Longue Pointe to find houses necessary to lodge Dumas's troops. We have learned that the English have taken a *Diable* and one barque which was behind Isle aux Noix after it had been struck by a battery they had established opposite.

27th August

At day break we learned that M. Dumas had begun to march yesterday evening at 7 o'clock, as it had to be early to cross the river which he proposed to do at the Assomption River, where we had sent him six bateaux and two more at the end of the island. A courier from Trois-Rivières announced that eight large vessels were coming up river. The cavalry arrived at 9 o'clock on the shore of the island, followed by the artillery, the piquets, and after midday M. Dumas, who occupied the parts from the said tip to Pointe aux Trembles. At 11 o'clock we had discovered the fleet opposite Repantinie [Repentigny]. They continued on their route and appeared at 2 o'clock at the end of the island of Sainte-Thérèse, and moored between this island and the Isle aux Foins and 5 o'clock. At 7 o'clock some ships sailed around for half an hour to find a better mooring.

28th August

The fleet sailed at 7 o'clock. The wind calmed at 8 o'clock and they anchored. The Béarn Regiment which marched to follow them stopped opposite the boats of the advance guard. No news from Fort Lévis. The gossip is that the English had finished their portage of barges to invest the Isle aux Noix, M. de Bougainville is considering evacuating.

29th August

Wind from the south-west. I was at Montréal. I learned that the Isle aux Noix was evacuated on the 27th in the evening and that M. de Bougainville has left a lieutenant and thirty men to capitulate.

30th August

The fleet is resting on their anchors. The barges and canoes have been coming and going to sound the depth of the river. The savages say that M. Amherst has besieged Fort Lévis and that M. Pouchot defends with vigour.

31st August

The wind is tranquil. The English have disembarked at Varennes in the number of five hundred. They took position at the church, where they then split into small detachments who burned and pillaged some houses. M. de Bourlamaque, who was at Longueuil, made observations with detachments that took a prisoner who said that there were three thousand men in the fleet, including those from Louisbourg; that the detachment disembarked at Varennes was six hundred men and three cannon. The troops from the Isle aux Noix have retired with those troops who were at Saint-Jean in line of battle [i.e. in good order]. M. de Lévis went to camp with the troops of M. de Bourlamaque.

1st September

A courier from chevalier de Lacorne told us that this officer had made his approach to Fort Lévis to see that the English were now its masters and that they were preparing to descend the rapids.[45] News from Chambly where the English have not yet attempted a move. A canoe passed by but did not wish to come near the fort.

2nd September

I was in town for the enquiry into the state of all the corps of troops and their distributions which have scattered to the winds [i.e. rations were missing]. I left at 5 o'clock. On arriving at Longue Pointe I saw several ships under sail and they lay opposite the first houses of Pointe aux Trembles. I arrived at the fort at 7 o'clock. I found the assembled regiment which was ready to march at 9 o'clock to follow the advance guard of the fleet. It halted at 11 o'clock at the house of Preville. Two ships of three masts and three *goelettes* were moored opposite. M. Dumas posted several piquets on our left.

3rd September

The fleet was still. I was ordered to the town. I was told that M. de Lévis is to the south, presumably to withdraw the troops under MM. Bourlamaque and Roquemaure. M. de Lacorne said that General Amherst is above Long Sault. Several soldiers of our battalions that are in the south have deserted to stay with the habitants. Water bearers of the regiment, composed of four trusted soldiers, were captured whilst engaged around the fleet.

4th September

The vessels of the advance guard set sail and came up to the Migeon Stream.[46] Two piquets of Béarn followed with orders to stay between them and the town: the company of grenadiers was placed near the church at Longue Pointe. I was ordered to the town. I found MM. Lévis, Bourlamaque, Bougainville and Roquemaure had returned. The regiments of La Reine, R. Roussillon and Guyenne occupied the suburb of the Recollets, those of La Sarre and Berry the ground from Porte de Québec up to the Migeon Stream, Béarn has been charged with guarding from the Migeon Stream

45 Note by Gaffarel – Fort Lévis had effectively capitulated on 26 August but after this the ramparts were destroyed, the cannon put out of service, the officers and a third of the garrison killed or wounded. From the memoirs of Captain Pouchot, 'On the morning of the 26th the enemy came and were extremely surprised to see only a few soldiers and sixty militia in scattered positions which were surrendered. They asked M. Pouchot where the rest of the garrison was; he responded that they could see them all.' Pouchot had held back 11,000 soldiers over 12 days with 200 men.

46 A small water course on the island of Montreal, north of the city and marked on Map 4.

up to Pointe aux Trembles and M. Dumas, who controls the Languedoc Regiment, from Pointe au Tremble up to the end of the island.[47]

5th September

M. de Lévis visited his outposts from the town to the end of the island. I was ordered to the town. I saw the Royal Roussillon Regiment file down to go and guard the ground between the Sœurs and Migeon Streams.

6th September

We learned that the army of M. Amherst, who was at Cèdres yesterday, arrived at Pointe Claire this morning; that the detachment of cavalry which was observing [him] has withdrawn. At midday we saw a column of twelve hundred men file from Boucherville to Longueuil, where they halted and Canadians arrived from all over to swear the oath of allegiance.

7th September

The fleet has not made any movement. An order expedited to La Chine, told us that the enemy had arrived. M. de Lévis went out with two companies of grenadiers to make a reconnaissance. This general ordered the regiments to hold ready to march, and sent the *major-général* to recall the corps of M. Dumas. The Regiment of Béarn received orders to retire behind the Sœurs Stream. At 6 o'clock, another order to send the grenadiers to the house of Montigny, and to march behind the Migeon Stream; at 7 o'clock the march was hastened to occupy the first houses of the suburbs, where they arrived at 10 o'clock. They found M. de Bourlamaque who stopped it and ordered that, once M. Dumas had reached the house of Montigny, the grenadier company of La Sarre will occupy the redoubt guarded by the one of Berry; that those of Languedoc and Béarn and of the Marine will be in the three houses nearest the redoubt; that Béarn will occupy all the gardens and palisade fences from these three houses up to the town, where the regiments of Royal Roussillon and Berry have just returned.[48] M. Dumas and the companies of grenadiers executed these orders at midnight. Béarn began to form line along the main street of the suburb, forced to wait until day to reconnoitre all that they must guard. The cavalry remained between the house of Montigny and the Migeon Stream. The regiments of La Reine, La Sarre and Guyenne retired into the town at 6 o'clock.

47 The Porte de Québec was the town gate which faced north with the road leading to Québec.

48 Although Montreal had stone walls and a ditch, its long shape did not lend itself to Vauban-style Pointed bastions. Its outlying smaller forts were constructed to protect civilians against raiding Iroquois earlier in the century and none of their defences were of any use against a European style artillery siege. Chartrand, *French Fortresses in North* America, pp. 32-44.

8th September

Languedoc, Béarn and the troops under the orders of M. Dumas sent their piquets into all the gardens, from the redoubt up to the town. M. de Bougainville left at 6 o'clock to go and propose a capitulation to the English general, and was well received.[49] M. Bougainville left M. de Las, captain of La Reine, as a hostage and took a Scot in exchange.[50] He gave an account to our generals of all that had been agreed with General Amherst, who agreed to a ceasefire until noon.

MM. de Lévis and Bourlamaque made a visit to the posts of the suburbs. M. de Bougainville returned to the English camp at midday and returned at 3 o'clock with M. Abercrombie, aide-de-camp to M. Amherst, and M. de Las.[51] The fleet made no movement. At 4 o'clock we had notice that M. de Murray had disembarked at Pointe aux Trembles and that he was near to Longue Pointe. The *généralle* was beat in the suburbs and the town. All the troops ran to their arms. M. de Lévis went to reconnoitre the enemy. This general said to us on his return to rest; that there is only a small detachment between Pointe aux Trembles and Longue Pointe.

At 8 o'clock, we heard that M. de Murray was at the Sœurs Stream and was preparing to cross it. M. de Bourlamaque informed him that they were in talks and that there is a truce. It allowed soldiers to aid the people of the *munitionnaire* to empty the magazines which were outside the town. At 10 o'clock M. de Murray sent an officer to ask permission to cross the town to go and talk to General Amherst. He was stopped at the first guard post and was guarded up to daybreak so as not to expose him to the insults of the savages. M. de Bourlamaque has been holding back on M. de Murray's request.

9th September

M. de Murray wrote to M. de Bourlamaque to express his surprise that he had received no response and believes he is being played. M. de Bourlamaque went to see him. At 6 o'clock the *major-général* ordered the regiments of Languedoc and Béarn to enter the town and camp on the Champ de Mars. All the commanders of the

49 Note by Gaffarel – Letter of Bernier, *commissaire de guerre*, to Crèmille, *lieutenant-général* (12 September 1760): 'Montréal is without defence apart from the debris our battalions and those of the colony, exhausted for several days by the desertion of soldiers and without the help of the inhabitants, who have long shown this example due to the fear of having their homes burnt. It was feared that Montréal would be reduced to ashes from the first moment the enemy should use artillery, or that, if allowed to give the appearance of a siege, they could be obstinate and take it at will and with it the entire colony.' See an anonymous report addressed to Marshal de Belle-Isle (Department of War, vol.3,574, piece 112): 'Montréal is a town surrounded by a single wall, to protect against savages rather than against troops. It is full of an infinite number of people who have taken refuge there after the destruction of Québec and the various razing campaigns. These people streamed in crowds to implore Vaudreuil to save their lives and property at the hands of the savages who had gathered from all quarters to the English.'

50 Probably Joseph-Alexandre Lassée de Maron (1727-1793), captain of La Reine. He was made a chevalier of Saint-Louis in 1771.

51 Captain James Abercrombie of the 42nd Regiment and aide to Amherst was probably not related to the erstwhile commander Major General James Abercromby.

regiments, captains of grenadiers and majors were ordered to go to see M. de Lévis at 7 o'clock. This general communicated to them the representations that he had made verbally and written to M. de Vaudreuil, not to capitulate under the harsh terms of laying down their arms and not serving again for the rest of the war.[52] He outlined that he [Vaudreuil] could agree to this capitulation for the Colony if he wished, and requested that he be allowed to pass with his regular troops onto the Island of Sainte-Hélène, where he would force the English to accord an honourable capitulation. He also communicated the order Vaudreuil gave to him in writing to confirm this capitulation, he responded that his troops were sent to defend this Colony, that they had preserved it much longer than it had been hoped, and that they had no other use than to procure an advantageous capitulation to the Canadians by sacrificing those troops, who were very sensitive to this.[53] At midday M. Dumas entered the town leaving the cavalry outside. Coats, waistcoats, pants, hats and cloth were

52 Note by Gaffarel – Amherst, the general who surrendered at Kloster Zevern, wished to take his revenge on Canada. He was merciless and refused military honours to soldiers who well deserved them. Vaudreuil, on his side, did not show enough energy for an honourable capitulation. This can be understood through the complaints of Lévis in his official report: 'I have no other part in the capitulation other than to protest against the treatment done to the regular troops, which should be given more attention on the part of M. de Vaudreuil and more respect from General Amherst. My efforts on this occasion have not allowed me to receive General Amherst, or make to him personally, the niceties used in similar circumstances between generals. I felt to mark my resentment and at no point stomached the reasons that the English general gave for his conduct, namely that it was in recompense for the cruelties committed by the savages, which whom our troops were associated.'

53 Note by Gaffarel – Lévis protested in writing along with the senior officers against the treatment made to the army and wished to remain outside the capitulation. The officers followed his example and several regiments burnt their colours. See the *archives de la guerre*, vol. 3,574 no 129.

The principal articles of the capitulation of Montreal were; I. The entire garrison of Montreal must lay down their arms and serve no longer for the whole of the current war, effective imminently after the signing. – III. The troops and militia *of Jacque Cartier, Sainte-Hélène and* other forts should serve no longer in this war and lay down their arms. – V. The troops who are in the field must like the others lay down their arms. – IV. The militia will return home without any interference under any pretext whatsoever, for having borne arms. – XVII. The officers and soldiers will be embarked to France in vessels that will be sufficient for their number and as convenient as possible. The officers of troops and marines who are married can take their families with them, and all will be free to embark their servants and baggage. – XXVII. The free exercise of the catholic, apostolic and roman religion remains in its entirety, so that all states of people of the town and country, remote locations, can continue to assemble in their churches and frequent the sacraments as before, without being disturbed in any way, either directly or indirectly. – XXXVI. If, by peace treaty, Canada remains part of His Majesties Britain, all the French, Canadians, Acadians and others who wish to retire to France will be allowed by the English general, who will procure their passage; and yet, if by this decision there are French of Canadian traders or others who wish to go to France, the English general will also give permission. XXXVII. The Canadians will retain full ownership and possession of their property, manorial and commoners, movable and immovable goods, furs and other effects, even their street buildings will not be touched under any circumstances whatsoever. – XL. The savages or Indian allies of His Most Christian Majesty; will be maintained in the lands they inhabit, if they want to stay there; it shall not be questioned under any pretext whatsoever for taking up arms and serving His Most Christian Majesty.

distributed to the soldiers in exchange for what is due to them for the equipment of the campaign. At 6 o'clock M. Abercrombie carried the signed capitulation to M. de Vaudreuil. Colonel Haldimand came to take possession of the town and the commander.

10th September

The troops received orders to assemble for review by M. de Lévis; this was then countermanded. They laid down their arms at 7 o'clock, after which they passed in review by M. de Lévis and the *commissaire*. They were told that some officers and soldiers would be sent to fetch equipment that had been left in the parishes where they spent the winter.

11th September

Colonel Haldimand announced yesterday that permission was given to supply the necessary bateaux. General Amherst came to dine with M. de Vaudreuil, who was not able to invite a single regular officer to dine with him.

12th September

M. de Vaudreuil went to dine with General Amherst. I went, with the permission of my superiors, to dine with M. de Murray, who greeted me openly, seating me at his side and giving me the honour of saying, "You must all be well contented. You have covered yourselves in glory to defend, for six campaigns, this colony which we should have taken in one, if we had done all that was in our power."[54] I was honoured to respond that we would be content if not for the hard capitulation which was imposed. The general seized me by the arm and assured me that I did not understand that I was my own master; that after the passport he had given me on my departure from Québec, I was supposed to be still at the hospital and therefore, free. I thanked him and told him that I could not accept this kind offer without the permission of my superiors, who counselled me to profit from it. The next day I reported to the general, who gave me a certificate from General Amherst which stated that I could continue to serve.

---

54 Note by Gaffarel – Lévis, despite his modesty, had made the same testimony of his soldiers. He wrote to the minister, 'They were prodigious in valour, they gave, as did the inhabitants themselves, repeated evidence, especially on the 28th of April, that the conservation of Canada would not depend on their zeal, nor courage, and that is was a suite of misfortune and fate that for some time this country was exposed by the relief from France not arriving at the critical moment. So poor as they were, united in their last success, they were determined to retake Québec.'

13th and 14th September

Several canoes loaded with furs arrived from Michilimackinac and other posts. The English sent out detachments for all the outposts and for Détroit.[55] They contained many savages; they hung one that fled into a house, and have sent detachments into the different parishes of the island to stop the domiciled savages from ravaging. All the troops received orders to hold ready to leave. The La Sarre Regiment embarked in two large ships; Languedoc in a *goelette* and several bateaux. They received food comprising of one and a half *livres* of flour and half a *livre* of bacon per day for each officer, soldier and passenger.

15th September

The regiments of La Reine, Royal Roussillon, Guyenne and Berry have embarked in the large boats and *goelettes*. That of Béarn and the two battalions of the Marine were ordered to embark at 2 o'clock in the small bateaux. One hour later this was countermanded due to lack of bateaux. They were given a supplement of food for two days. MM. de Vaudreuil, de Lévis with the staff and the Intendant made dispositions to leave. A proclamation was made to warn everyone who wishes to see the Intendant to present themselves within three days. M. de Vaudreuil and the Intendant made a manifesto to engage M. Amherst to give ongoing orders and trusts and he promised to make payments and carry out all that he could.[56]

16th September

The Béarn Regiment embarked in a *goelette* and five bateaux, which were very crowded. The two battalions of the Marine were also embarked in these ships. They were ordered to follow the 48th Regiment who, going to garrison Trois-Rivières, would serve as their escort. Our *goelette* reached the wide river at 1 o'clock and was allowed to drift with the current. The wind passed from the north to the west, we set sail and left the ships which carried the troops and all the others between l'Isle Sainte-Thérèse and Varennes in front of Longue Pointe. It [the *goelette*] moored at 8 o'clock before Saint-Sulpice.

55 Note by Gaffarel – By the capitulation of Montreal, de Belestre, commander of Détroit, and all the other outpost commanders, as well as three to four hundred Canadian families, left to themselves, had to bow before this *fait accompli*. Major Rogers received their submission.

56 Note by Gaffarel – Vaudreuil, Lévis and Bigot had no illusions as to the value of the Canadian bills of exchange. Lévis wrote to the minister, 'The paper which remains is completely discredited, and all the inhabitants are in despair. They sacrificed everything for the conservation of Canada. They are now ruined, destitute; we must neglect nothing to re-establish their confidence.' The outrageous speculations increasingly discredited this paper. In 1765 Canadians were invited to draw on their paper money which they still held, 1639 deposit slips were prepared but, left to stock trading, their value had been absorbed by this speculation. It was only in March 1766 that a new agreement liquidated what remained of the Canadian paper. (Garneau, *Canada,* II, p. 365)

17th September

Wind from the south-west. We set sail at 6 o'clock, and were grounded at 7 on the shores of the flat islands. We were released at 10 o'clock, and passed Sorel by midday where we found several vessels destined for Montréal. We entered the lake [St.-Pierre] at 3 o'clock, and beached at 4 o'clock and were unable to get back afloat.

18th September

We discovered several bateaux, which we signalled to dock with us. They did not see us and continued their journey. We sent to ask for help from Trois-Rivières. At 8 o'clock we began to remove our ballast. We were freed at 9 o'clock, having sailed away with a good south-west wind, leaving the lake at 4 o'clock, having been stopped by a bateau bringing a port officer and several English sailors who moored us at Trois-Rivières and were presented with a barrel of flour. The officer sent to Trois-Rivières to ask for help came back to tell us the M. Burton, governor of the said town, cannot spare us a pilot.

19th September

Wind from the north-east. We had received bread that was sent to be baked at the town. At 10 o'clock, we were ordered to go back to open water. We had taken twelve French sailors to augment our crew. We traversed the channels, rounded Cap de la Madeleine, having to tack around the Pointe Saint-Ignace, and were obliged to moor at midday opposite the church at Madeleine. The wind was contrary; we landed twelve men ashore to cook bread. At 4 o'clock, the wind having calmed, we set sail having left the chaloupe ashore to bring us the bread, having rounded several shores; we let ourselves go with the current and moored within a league of the Cap.

20th September

Wind from the north-west. We began on our journey at 7 o'clock, having to do much tacking without advancement and moored before Champlain at 9 o'clock. At 4 o'clock, the wind fixed to the north-east and tormented us all night.

21st September

Continuation of the north-east wind.

22nd September

The wind dropped in the night and rose from the south-west at daybreak. We sailed at 6 o'clock, rounding Pointe de Batiscan and then beaching at 9 o'clock opposite the mill at Sainte-Anne, on a great sandbar, such that those from above could not help us. We sent a canoe to land to find a pilot who could help us. We worked to repair our chaloupe which was damaged. We had a great deal of trouble, having no hammer or nails. We sent the chaloupe to land at 3 o'clock to go and meet the canoe which could not reach us, the wind and current being too strong.

23rd September

Two English bateaux wished to come aboard but the wind stopped them. The chaloupe and canoe joined us with a good pilot who immediately cast a second anchor to try and pull us out. We turned a great deal but without success. We had sent an officer to Sainte-Anne to see if they have bateaux so that we could unload the *goelette*. A sergeant was charged with a letter for our commander and sent to Trois-Rivières, which asked for aid and food as we were beginning to run low. We sent many of the soldiers ashore. A large English chaloupe stopped by us; the commanding officer made many soundings around the *goelette*, casting another anchor which turned us but without being able to free us. He left us at 11 o'clock recommending that we unload the *goelette* as soon as we could. Two bateaux then arrived on which we embarked several soldiers who went to Saint-Pierre. We kept the sailors on board and a few soldiers to help with manoeuvring. A *goelette*, commissioned by the owner of our own, came to anchor beside us. The captain came aboard with his pilot to see how it could be freed. He then returned to his boat, promising to return on the evening tide. The captain who commanded our ship ordinarily, and now appointed pilot to the English commander, came aboard to prove his second's ignorance. Several English bateaux passed which were giving a regimental officer passage to Québec. At 4 o'clock the wind was thrown to the north-east and freshened. At 8 o'clock, the owner of the *goelette* returned, made soundings all around, much turning of the capstan, and not succeeding said he would return on tomorrow's tide.

24th September

Continuation of the north-east wind which was fresher than yesterday. At 8 o'clock our pilot began to work, and sent an anchor out much further than the previous one and took it to where the tide plucked us from our sandbar and we moored at 11 o'clock in the main channel. At 11 o'clock the owner came up in a large English chaloupe and was glad to find the task completed. At 1 o'clock we landed, having rounded Saint-Pierre which is a pretty coast and very steep; we returned aboard at 5 o'clock.

25th September

Very strong wind from the north-east. The sergeant who left for Trois-Rivières arrived at 10 o'clock in a bateau loaded with two barrels of flour, one of bacon, one of oatmeal and peas, and fifty livres of butter that was sent to me by Colonel Burton with a very honest letter. I distributed part of these supplies to the soldiers and sailors who waited impatiently, as yesterday we had to make bread on land.

26th September

Continuation of bad weather. Several officers have been on land to buy bread and vegetables.

27th September

The wind and weather are as bad as the other. Two *goelettes* passed to go to Trois-Rivières. The commander of the fleet moored at Batiscan said to us to come and fetch food and asked for the nominal roll of all those on board our *goelette*. I presented this to M. Dalquier who ordered a field officer to take it to the commander. The officer returned at 3 o'clock in his bateau loaded with butter, flour and tallow. At 4 o'clock a bateau from Québec arrived to take the effects of the people from the *commissaire de guerre*, who had arrived at Trois-Rivières. The wind eased in the evening.

28th September

The wind returned from the north and calmed around 10 o'clock. A *goelette* moored in front of ours set sail. We worked to follow it. We had great difficulties in freeing our cables which were trapped under stones. We called the men who were on land to fetch wood, and were able to set sail after midday. We tacked around several shores to round two or three capes. We then had the wind behind us to reach the Grandines where we moored at 6 o'clock.

29th September

The wind was fixed to the north east and gave us a great shower of rain. At 8 o'clock we passed two English *goelettes* going up river. One beached a quarter league from ours. We sent our *chaloupe* with our best sailors who re-floated it.[57] The captain came back with them to thank our commander, who offered him a few bottles of Spanish wine, and asked for a clever *maître* [naval petty officer] which we lent him. At midday the wind freshened and tormented our *goelette*. The pilot wanted to be relieved. He worked to find a sheltered anchorage to resist the wind and cast an extra anchor to be safe. The river was very restless all night which harassed us.

30th September

The same wind and rain. Several bateaux and *goelettes* passed going upriver to Trois-Rivières. At 4 o'clock the pilot found the river and the wind reluctant to appease and made hard work to bring up the anchors, the cables being very twisted. He made sail and anchored at the end of the day opposite Saint-Jean where we were more sheltered from the wind, which calmed at night.

57 Larger vessels like the *goelette* Malartic was travelling in would carry their own smaller vessels such as this *chaloupe* to reach the shore.

1st October

We set sail at high tide, having moored opposite Saint-Pierre, where we put ashore to go and buy food. I wrote, by order of M. Dalquier, to the commander of the fleet to ask him for food. He responded that he would supply us, if we came to meet him.

2nd October

Four soldiers escaped during the night and deserted to return to Montréal. We raised anchor at sunrise, sailed, ran a line to go around several capes, and drifted to below Cap Santé where we set anchor. I sent a request for food to the commander of a frigate moored below the Richelieu. He kindly acquiesced.

3rd October

We sailed at daybreak and moored at midday before Pointe aux Trembles. We had sent the chaloupe to Sainte-Antoine to fetch wood. The wind was fresh from the north-east which impaired the help of the evening tide.

4th October

We set sail at daybreak and moored after an hour before Saint-Augustin and profited from the high tide of the evening to get up to Cap Rouge.

5th October

We sailed at daybreak. We found ourselves before Québec a little before 8 o'clock. The Captain of the port, who came aboard, moored us between the first vessels. The captain of the *goelette* went aboard the commander of the fleet's ship, who sent with him Commodore Shuenton [Swanton], charged with the details of embarkation. Several officers went into town to see M. de Lévis, who testified their regret that we did not arrive earlier, as we would already have left and been shipped home.[58] At midday I went down to the town to request food and returned aboard to have it fetched. I found an officer who told me to go aboard the flagship in an hour. As I prepared to descend in the canoe, an English officer came to order me to prepare ten officers and one hundred and seventy soldiers that the chaloupe would come to

58 Note by Gaffarel – In his report to the minister of war (27 November 1760) Lévis told of the extreme difficulties in descending the Saint Lawrence. 'After the battalion had left Montréal, I followed with M. de Bourlamaque resolving to be the last to leave Québec, so by my presence to obtain from the English commander all possible commodities for their transport. Despite my sorrows and my care they suffered extraordinarily: 1st Because of the few vessels supplied by the English; 2nd by a terrible north-east wind which kept the river endangered for 22 days, and put several vessels out of service, which forced the English to cram them in to their remaining vessels, though they had exceeded their ordinary rule of men per tonne; 3rd finally, as everyone lacked their own things; it was necessary to buy comforts for the crossing from the English merchants, and the hard situation for the majority of having nothing to eat other than the rations of a common sailor.'

take to embark on a brigantine in an hour. I had great difficulties as the officers and many of the soldiers were in the town. At 4 o'clock I had embarked all that I could and left on the first chaloupe to look over the brigantine, that I found very small to carry all the men. I returned aboard our *goelette* to embark the remaining men, who I followed. The officer charged with embarkation prescribed we should stay aboard, assuring us that the captain would order us to leave on the low tide. He went to give an account to the Commodore, and returned a quarter hour later saying that our commander had arrived at the same time as he was going to town. Our commander embarked immediately to go and make representations to M. de Lévis on how we have been embarked and the little time we have had to get provisions. At 8 o'clock I received orders to go to our general, who having asked me some questions gave our commander the option of leaving in the brigantine or staying in the town and waiting for a more convenient vessel. He decided to leave in the brigantine.

6th and 7th October

The soldiers and officers who we were awaiting re-joined us. We were given some passengers which brought the number to one hundred and seventy. We were given the following supplies: for Wednesday, two pounds of biscuit, half a pint of oil, a pint of peas and two pints of oats for three men; for Thursday two pounds of biscuit, four pounds of bacon and a pint of peas; for Friday the same as Wednesday; for Saturday two pounds of biscuit and four pounds of salt beef; for Sunday the same as Thursday; for Monday two pounds of biscuit, half a pint of oil and two pints of oats; for Tuesday the same as Saturday. It took much effort to raise the anchor without success. Several vessels were sent, which detached and finally lifted our anchor with that of a frigate which had become tangled in our cables.

8th October

We had barely set sail when we had to weigh anchor again last night. The wind calmed. At 10 o'clock we drifted and moored at high tide opposite Saint-Jean.

9th October

We followed the tide and moored at the end of the traverse. We lifted anchor at 6 o'clock and by eight were up to Cap Tourmente.

10th October

Having left with the tide, we rounded Cap Tourmente, ran a line passing le Gouffre, above which we were forced to anchor so the current would not drag us into it. Our captain gave the signal that we were in difficulties to the chaloupes and vessels moored along the Isle aux Coudres. They came in an hour, pulling us out of the current and moored in a channel. We lifted anchor at low tide to approach close to the Isle aux Coudres.

11th October

A great calm, the tide carried us near to the vessels. At 11 o'clock a wind rose up from the south-west, the commanding vessel gave two cannon shots to signal to set sail. We hoisted sails and had to wait half an hour for our bateau that went down river to fetch our pilot, water and wood. We re-joined them at 2 o'clock, having made good progress and sailing past two ships which had set off much earlier. At sunset the commander fired two cannon shots to signal mooring. He cast the anchor having made eight leagues. At 8 o'clock a large vessel moored too close to ours and caught us on their anchor, we approached and broke the tip of our bowsprit. We ran in great danger and would have been difficult to disengage had it not been for a soldier of the marine on the other vessel who cut the cable despite the opposition of the captain. We worked on repairing the damage.

12th October

We fixed our bowsprit and set sail at 8 o'clock, the wind set from the north-west and we carried on our route. We passed several vessels which were ahead of us. We came across the Isles Blanches, Pont à l'Eau-de-vie and l'Isle Verte, and at the end of the day we could make out the island of Bic. We ran a line during the night.

13th October

Wind from the north-east; Today we found ourselves by the Bic traverse, thirty-two leagues from l'Isle aux Coudres. We ran along the coast all day and reached St-Barnabé by evening. At 8 o'clock the wind swung from the south and we carried on our route during the night.[59]

14th October

The wind returned to a north-easterly and we were given much rain. We had tacked all day without making much progress. After sunset the wind changed to north-west and we made up for this during the night.

15th October

The north-west wind continued which after sunrise blew from the west. We had ranged to the south, having sighted Cap des Rosiers at 9 o'clock we passed Mont Notre-Dame and Gaspé. The fog prevented us from seeing Anticosti that we passed by to the north. We made a good route all day, having the wind behind us, which greatly tormented us by rolling continually.

59 This illustrates the difficulties of travelling the St. Lawrence against the wind. Isle de St-Barnabé is too small a scale to be seen on Map 9, however it is just a little way out from the coast of Rimouski.

16th October

The wind came continually from the west. We sighted the islands of Madeleine, up to Oiseaux. We made good progress all day travelling 8 or 9 *nœuds* [knots].[60] At sunset the wind moved to a south-westerly, which gave us great pleasure.

17th October

At daybreak, we saw the islands of Saint-Paul, Île Royale and Newfoundland. From 8 o'clock we went full sail, ahead of the other ships. At 9 o'clock we discovered a warship which haunted the coast of Newfoundland.

18th October

Wind from the north-west. We saw the islands of Saint-Pierre. We went at midday to Banc Vert, where we caught thirty cod. The winds passed south south-west and we had calm in the evening.

19th and 20th October

Mist and wind from the south south-east which forced us to tack and go to the north to avoid land.

21st October

Very strong wind which greatly bothered us. The crew has been constantly on deck or in the rigging to avoid damage. From 4 o'clock until evening, the wind blew from the north-west and we made progress. At 6 o'clock there was a great fog which calmed the wind.

22nd October

The fog continued. The wind lifted from the south south-east, and though somewhat close [to the wind], we carried on route. It dropped during the day.

23rd October

The wind returned at 1 o'clock in the morning from the south south-east, and we started on route until 7 o'clock; a heavy rain and then calm, we made good progress until the end of the day; then it blew from the east. It was furious all night and we were greatly inconvenienced.

---

60 According to Diderot's Encyclopédie, the French knot is not particularly specific, being spaced at 42 to 50 *pied*. "Noueds (Marine)" in *Encyclopédie, ou dictionnaire raisonné des sciences, des arts et des métiers, etc.*, eds. Denis Diderot and Jean le Rond d'Alembert. University of Chicago: ARTFL Encyclopédie Project (Spring 2016 Edition), Robert Morrissey and Glenn Roe (eds), http://encyclopedie.uchicago.edu/. Vol 11. p. 185.

42th October

Strong thick fog. The east wind continued which greatly agitated the sea and bothered us greatly.

25th and 26th October

The wind is constantly held in the east. The crew can do little more than avoid bird droppings.

27th October

A little calmer but the fog continues. We learned of a ship which had the wind on us. We stopped it at 4 o'clock in the afternoon. It had come from Neufcastle [Newcastle, northeast England], which it had left forty-two days ago.

28th October

The wind lifted from the north-west, being weak and bringing lots of fog. It passed to the south at 8 in the evening, and much fresher, to our great displeasure.

29th, 30th and 31st October

Wind from the south-west which was so good that we made nearly two leagues per hour.

1st November

Continuation of the south-west wind. At 6 o'clock in the evening, the wind changed and dropped during the night.

2nd November

Light wind from the north-west and fog. At midday it blew from the north-east and greatly agitated the sea.

3rd November

Continuation of the northeaster. We sighted a vessel at midday which was down wind and seemed to hold our route.

4th November

South-easterly wind. We gave chase to the ship we saw yesterday and caught up with it at noon. It was English, coming from Carolina, which it left thirty-one days ago. At 9 o'clock the wind picked up from the south-east and continued us on our route during the night.

5th November

Wind from the south. We sighted a vessel which had the appearance of a privateer. It gave chase for two hours then changed course, not being able to catch up with us. At the end of the day, the wind freshened much which agitated the sea and we were greatly distressed. The waves flooded our deck.

6th, 7th, and 8th November

Wind from the south-west which has greatly eased our path. On the 8th and the end of the day, it changed to the north and held the sea in agitation so much that we were forced to heave-to. The brigantine took on water in all parts, a great deal coming into our cabin.

9th November

A tempest. From 6 o'clock in the evening it calmed a little. We set sail but did not progress far due to the height of the waves.

10th November

The wind returned from north north-east and we were greatly tormented. By the end of the day, we were obliged to heave-to.

11th and 12th November

Wind from the north-east. We ran the line. Two ships were sighted which seemed very large. We stopped by them at 3 o'clock in the afternoon to ask for refreshments and liquor but they did not want to sell us any, though one, Dutch, came from Malagua [sic. Malaga] and the other Danish, the Canary Islands. We immediately worked to continue our line.

13th, 14th and 15th November

Continuation of the north-east wind which greatly bothered us.

16th November

Good weather and a light north-easterly. We discovered a vessel which we steered for. We approached it at 9 o'clock and recognised it as Dutch and hailed her. They responded that they had come from Surinam. We asked them if they wanted to sell any sugar or liquors. The captain said that he had none, that he was lacking in everything, the gale of the 10th having already taken his launch, his jolly-boat and a man who had been on deck. I had gained the trust of our captain who told me that he would put his jolly-boat in the water so that we could go aboard the Dutch ship. At midday one of my comrades, the captain, my servant and I, embarked with difficulty in the rowboat, we came up to the Dutchman and boarded her. We found a captain who inspired us with reverence, this being his sixty-sixth campaign. After having sung misery, he made us take spiced bread and rum which we found good. He gave us four bottles [presumably rum], two of vinegar and a cheese. His crew sold us four barrels of raw sugar, some bags of coffee and two bottles of lemon juice. For all of these stimulants we paid dearly, which gave them great pleasure. We visited all the cabins of this vessel, which was a great merchantman, and found them very clean. We thanked the captain and separated from him very happy with our refreshments and he with our money. We easily got aboard our ship. The sea was calmer and we sent a barrel of beef and bacon to the Dutch.

17th and 18th November

Good weather and calm. Several of the French sailors judge that we are near the coast of France by the colour of the water. Some birds confirmed this opinion.

19th November

Wind from the north-west which blew from the north at 8 o'clock to keep us on route. At 10 o'clock in the evening we saw a vessel by the light of the moon which passed down wind.

20th November

Our captain made a sounding and found the bottom was a hundred fathoms. He judged from the colour of the earth brought up on the probe that we are one hundred leagues from Belle-Isle.[61]

21st and 22nd of November

Wind from the north threw us so far to the south that the captain feared that we would not reach a French port but have to enter one in Spain. He made soundings often and always with success.

23rd November

Light wind from the north. We made small progress. At 8 in the morning it was announced, to our great satisfaction, that land was sighted. Our captain believes it to be the islands of Ré and d'Oléron.[62] One of the sailors from the Isle d'Oléron was in the tops assured that he recognised his homeland. We steered to run several lines to reach the entrance between two of the island without success. We saw several fishing boats.

61 Island just off Quiberon, South Brittany, France.

62 These two islands marked the north and south of the bay which leads into the French harbour of La Rochelle.

24th November

We passed between the islands having moored near that of Ré. We profited from the tides to reach the harbour of La Rochelle. We saw several English vessels opposite the Isle d'Aix.[63]

25th November

We moored in the harbour of La Rochelle at 4 in the morning. What joy! I embarked immediately in the jolly-boat to go and inform the commandant of this place of our arrival. I was pleasantly surprised on disembarking to learn that MM. de Borée and d'Avisard, my old comrades, are now lieutenant of the king and the other major; I was awakened by the lieutenant of the king, who, after having said to me that ours was the first vessel to arrive from Canada for a long time, engaged me for lunch and to rest. At 7 o'clock I spoke with the *commissaire de la marine* who commanded that the chaloupes of the port would fetch our battalion. He conducted me at 11 o'clock to M. le comte de Narbonne, *maréchal de camp*,[64] employed in the province, who gave orders that we would be lodged in the town. The battalion entered the town at 5 o'clock.

M. le maréchal de Senecterre, commander of the province,[65] arrived on the 26th and decided that our battalions would rest for eight days at la Rochelle, whence they will go to Niort, where they will stay until they receive new orders.

63 A tiny island in the middle of the bay.

64 Jean-François, comte de Narbonne Lara, (1718-1806), was a nobleman who was commander of the upper Languedoc region. He was father to Louis-Marie-Jacques Amalric, born in 1755 who followed his father into the military and later became a diplomat serving Napoleon during the later years of the First Empire.

65 Jean-Charles de Saint-Nectaire (vulg. Sennecterre), marquis de Brinon-sur-Sandres and Pisani, baron de Didonne & Saint Germain-sur-Vienne, came from an ancient noble family from the Auvergne. *Dictionnaire généalogique, héraldique, chronologique et historique : contenant l'origine & l'état actuel des premieres maisons de France, des maisons souveraines & principales de l'Europe* ... (Paris: Duchesne, 1757), Vol, 3, p. 241.

Afterword

Written After the Events

I add to this that I have written on Canada that, if M. le marquis de Lévis had been commander-in-chief, the English would not have taken it.[1] After the English abandoned the camp at the Falls, this general would have carried the largest part of his forces on to the heights of Québec and would have watched very closely the movements in these parts; if he had been with the army on the 13th of September 1759, he would have been opposed to our attack; he would have wagered ten to one that the army's attack would be beaten, being obliged to descend from the heights that they occupied, following a sunken path that separated the two armies: and, supposing that even if it was necessary to attack, he would have formed three columns with the five battalions, placing the Canadians in the gaps allowing them to fire and march following their style; I am persuaded that we would have been the victors. The battle of the following 28th of April proves this. We then would have been able to attack the English on the 14th of September who, having lost their general, would have been at least as disadvantaged as ourselves.

If M. Berryer, minister of the marine, had wished to risk, at the end of January or the beginning of February 1760, several merchant vessels loaded with canon and munitions, then we would have managed and taken Québec. M. le marquis de Lévis had written to the minister who responded that he should hold Canada until the end of June: he replied that he could last the whole campaign if he received these vessels loaded with cannons and munitions, and in consequence descended with

1 Gaffarel – If Malartic had a good opinion of his general, Lévis also made much of him. Here, noted in his correspondence, notes which he gave on him:
Campaign of 1759. Asked for a gratuity. 'An Officer whose zeal, talent and intelligence merits distinguished awards.
Campaign of 1760, for the Battle of Sainte-Foy, 28 April, requested for him the rank of *aide-major général* and a pension. 'He is a distinguished officer whose birth, talent and propriety are all that you can wish of him, he was wounded at Carillon and recently on the 28th.'
In December 1760 he asked for the rank of *lieutenant-colonel* or a pension. 'This is an officer of distinction of long service, and merits the most grand praise, with talent, birth and propriety and all that you can do for him.'
Memoir of graces asked for after the war. Asked for M. de Malartic a pension according to M. de Mazerac: 'He is the first of the *aide-major* who served in Canada. He continued acting in the function as a *major-général*. Seriously wounded in two separate affairs; this is an officer of great merit, and this grace can only have universal approval.'
[It is worth noting that, while Montcalm was long dead, by the time of writing in the 1780s, Lévis had enjoyed a long and successful military career and was promoted to Marshal of France in 1783.]

the army onto the ice, to go and receive them. M. Murray has said that, if he had seen the arrival of the white [Bourbon] flags, he would have been forced to capitulate: he sent for the first of our cannonballs which fell into Québec, which gave him great pleasure because it showed him that our powder was damp. This general said some very honest things to us and wished us a good crossing. He assured us that the English would return Canada to France on the condition that general M. de Lévis did not return as governor general as they would not be able to take it back.

I was surprised to learn that one battalion that had shown good service was to be broken up;[2] I cannot and do not wish to ignore the fact that a senior officer, under whose orders I had been during several campaigns, testified the utmost surprise at this to M. le duc de Choiseul. The minister responded that the officers would not be forgotten and that he was charged to find places for those who merited it. In my particular case, I was greatly praised. He gave me the majority of the Royal-Comtois Regiment at the end of April. I was not informed until the first days of June. I was very eager to go and thank M. le duc de Choiseul, but could not find him at home; I carried the news to M. Dubois who told me that the Royal-Comtois Regiment was embarking shortly and to join it as soon as possible.[3] I assured him that I was ready to leave. He made several jokes that he didn't think that I was, and finally finished by telling me that I had been named Colonel of the Vermandois Regiment and had been since the 5th of June.

2 In the reorganisations of 10 December 1762, Malartic's 2nd battalion of Béarn was broken up. This also happened to the regiments of Guyenne, Berry and Cambis which had also served in North America. Pajol, *Guerres*, vol. 7, pp. 94-5.

3 The Royal-Comtois Regiment was posted to the Ile d'Oléron, an island just of the west coast of France. Pajol, *Guerres*, vol. 7, p. 171.

Appendix I

Native American Tribal Names in French and English

It is not the intention here to give a potted history of Indian tribes as this is outside the scope of this book, but these translated names should assist further study.

Abenaki – Abenaki
Aouias – see Ouias
Christinaux – Another name given to the Crys or Cris in the 17th and 18th Centuries.
Chaouanons – Shawnee
Cicachas – Identified as a Louisiana tribe who originally fought with the French but then reached agreement with them.[1]
Crys/Cris – Cree
Folle Avoines – Menominee (French name is literally Wild Rice people)
Hurons – Hurons (now more commonly referred to as the Wyandot or Wendat)
Iroquois (cinque nations) – Iroquois (Five Nations)
    Onontaguès – Onondagas 300 warriors
    Sonnontoins – Senecas 700 warriors
    Goyogoins/Goyoguans – Cayugas 350 warriors
    Onoyotes/Onazote – Oneidas 250 warriors
    Agnis, Agnés, Agniers or Mohacks – Mohawks 150 warriors
    Tascarorins – Tuscaroras 100 warriors[2]
Katibas/Kaṭawbas – Catawba
Loup – Delaware, mostly those living over the Appalachians in the Ohio valley
Miamis – Miamis
Mississaguès – Mississauga
Moraygnans/Moraignans[3]

1 See *Histoire Philosophique et Politique: Des Établissemens & du Commerce des Europeans dans les deux Indies, Tome Dix-septieme,* (La Haye: Gosse Fils, 1774) p. 381 James F. Brooks has tentatively suggested the name could be used for the Comanches, see James F. Brooks, *Captives and Cousins: Slavery, Kinship, and Community in the Southwest Borderland,* (Chapel Hill: University of North Carolina Press, 2002), p. 15.
2 These figures come from a table in the English translation of Pouchot, *Memoir*, vol. II, p. 260. It shows the rough number of able-bodied warriors and is based upon figures drawn up by William Johnson in the autumn of 1763.
3 Moraignans are mentioned in terms of capitulation made between Amherst and Vaudreuil

Nippisingués – Nepissings
Outaouas – Ottawas
Ouias/Aouias – Weas
Pouteoutamis – Potawatomis
Pous – Unknown
Sauteurs – Ojibwe/Chippewas, (French name means 'people of the falls')
Sault – Indians of the Sault[4]
Serokis – Cherokee
Tetes-Plattes – Flathead
Scious – Sioux

in 1760 in Article 9. 'The British General shall engage to send back, to their own homes, the Indians and Moraignans, who make part of his armies, immediately after the signing of this present capitulation.' *A Collection of the Acts Passed in the Parliament of Great Britain and of Other Public Acts Relative to Canda,* (Quebec: Desbarats, 1800) p. 8. They appear to have been a tribe or group who lived in the Ohio valley although Bougainville seems to be the only other source where they are named specifically. R. Douglas Hurt, *The Ohio Frontier: Crucible of the Old Northwest, 1720-1830* (Bloomington: Indiana University Press, 1996), p. 20.

4 Sault St Louis, sometimes simply shortened to the Sault was called Caughnawaga by its people (Kahnawke today) and was a village of Christian Mohawks who had moved away from their traditional lands. The towns of New France had several of these mission villages which had come about in the seventeenth century. Jesuits had sought to convert various tribes of Native people and had been particularly successful at the time when the Iroquois were waging a fierce war against the Hurons and other Algonquin people around the great lakes, epidemics and disease were rife. Those that sought salvation converted to Catholicism and settled in villages around Montreal, some with their own missionary living with them. This caused upset when Catholic Iroquois and their southern tribes people were called upon by European powers to fight each other. See MacLeod, *The Canadian Iroquois and the Seven Years War, passim*; Moogk, *La Nouvelle France,* pp. 40-50; Richter, *Ordeal of the Longhouse,* pp. 105-132.

Appendix II

Historical French weights and measures

There was still a great deal of variation from place to place in weights and measures in different parts of France. The government controlled weights and measures in Canada and so presumably they used the Parisian standard which is quoted below, rather than regional variations.[1] The numbers below come from: A British Merchant, *Commercial tables. Exhibiting a View of the Weights, Measures, Coins, and Monies of France, compared and equalized with those of Great Britain,* (Salisbury: E. Easton, 1790).

Weights

Once – ounce.
Livre – pound. The French *livre* was just over 1lb 1oz in English weight.
Quarteron –a quarter Quintal or 25 *livres.*
Quintal, (pl. *Quintaux*) – 100 *livres.*

Measures

Pouce – Inch
Pied – Foot. This is equivalent to 1.066 of an English foot.
Aulne/Aune – Yard. This was the measure for cloth and was 44 *pouce* or 47 English inches
Toise – 6 *pied.* Used both on land and sea unlike the English Fathom.
Arpents – 180 *pieds.*
Lieue – 2,000 *toise.* Translates as a league. Around 2.4 miles.

Liquid Measures

Chopine –Half a Parisian pint, which was much larger than the English equivalent at about 1 quart. A *Chopine* was about the same as an English Pint.
Pot – Two Parisian pints or 2 English quarts.

1 Allan Greer, *The People of New France,* (Toronto: University of Toronto Press, 1999), p. 53.

Dry Measures

Boisseau – the standard measure and the equivalent to around 2.8 gallons.
Minot – 3 *Boisseau* and the equivalent to an English bushel (8 gallons).

Currency

Like the old British system, France worked in *Livres*, *Sols*, and *Derniers* – as pounds, shillings and pence. *Livre*, like the weight, translates as a 'pound'. There were two types of *Livre*, the '*Livre Parisis* and the *Livre Tournois*, deriving their names from the Cities of Paris and Tours: the *Livre Parisis* was more valuable by one fourth part, than the *Livre Tournois*, but the former had not been in use since the time of Louis XIV.'[2] Sometimes the name *franc* is given instead of *livre* but they are the same. It was recorded that the coins in circulation were mostly *sols*, of which there were twenty *sols* in the *livre*. Three *livres* made an *ecu* or half a crown. As seen in Malartic's journal, coin was scarce as the war dragged on and the Canadian government was reduced to writing out bills of exchange on the backs of playing cards. Every October these bills could be brought to Quebec or Montreal to be changed to bills of exchange which could be drawn on the Treasury of France. Losses were incurred in all of these transactions as each financier took their cut.[3]

2 British Merchant, *Commercial Tables*. p. v.
3 Kalm, *Travels into North America*, vol. II, p. 234-6.

Bibliography

Note that this does not include the works cited or quoted by Gaffarel in such of the original footnotes as have been retained in the translation. Gaffarel was not consistent in his citations and the translator has sought to find his sources wherever possible.

Primary Documentary Archive Collections

When Gaffarel refers to documents in the army archive, these are now under the purview of the Service Historique de la Défense, located in Vicennes, France. http://www.servicehistorique.sga.defense.gouv.fr/.

CO5 (Colonial Office Records). National Archives, United Kingdom.

Printed Primary Sources

Anon. *A Collection of the Acts Passed in the Parliament of Great Britain and of Other Public Acts Relative to Canada* (Quebec: Desbarats, 1800).

Anon. *Instruction sur l'exercice de l'Infanterie,* (Paris: L'Imprimerie Royale, 1754),

Allingham, William, *The New Method of Fortification, As Practised by Monsieur de Vauban, Engineer-General of France. Together with a new Treatise of Geometry* (London: A. Bettesworth, 1722).

Bougainville, Louis Antoine de (trans. Edward P. Hamilton), *Adventure in the Wilderness: The American Journals of Louis Antoine de Bougainville, 1756-1760* (Norman: University of Oklahoma Press, 1964).

Casgrain, H.-R. (ed.), *Collection des manuscrits du maréchal de Lévis* (12 vols. Quebec: Demers & Frère, 1889-95).

de Joannés, Major de Quebec, 'Memoire sur le campagne de 1759' in A.G. Doughty and G. W. Parmelee, *The Siege of Quebec and The Battle of the Plains of Abraham* (Quebec: Dussault & Proulx, 1901) Vol. 4. Appendix Part I pp. 219-230.

de Léry, Gaspard-Joseph Chaussegros, "Journal de la Campagne d'Hiver, du 13 Février au Neuf Avril 1756." *Rapport de l'Archiviste de la province de Québec,* 1926-7, pp. 372-405.

Johnson, William, *The Papers of Sir William Johnson* (Albany: University of the State of New York, 1921).

Kalm, Peter, (trans. John Reinhold Forster), *Travels into North America,* (London: T. Lowndes, 1771).

O'Callaghan, E. B., John Romeyn Brodhead, and Berthold Fernow (eds.), *Documents Relative to the Colonial History of the State of New York* (Albany: Weed, Parsons and Company, 1853).

Montcalm, Louis-Joseph de, *Journal du marquis de Montcalm durant ses campagnes en Canada de 1756 à 1759* (Québec: Demers & Frère, 1895).
Pouchot, Pierre (trans. Franklin Benjamin Hough), *Memoir upon the late war in North America,* (Roxbury: W. Elliot Woodward, 1866).

Secondary Sources

Anon. *Dictionnaire généalogique, héraldique, chronologique et historique : contenant l'origine & l'état actuel des premieres maisons de France, des maisons souveraines & principales de l'Europe ...* (Duchesne: Paris, 1757).
Alberts, Robert C., *The Most Extraordinary Adventures of Major Robert Stobo* (Boston: Houghton Mifflin, 1965).
Bearor, Bob, *The Battle on Snowshoes* (Bowie: Heritage Books, 2005).
Bearor, Bob, *Leading by Example* (Bowie: Heritage Books, 2007), Vol. 3.
Bonaparte, Darren, *The History of Akwesasne from Pre-Contact to Modern Times.* http://www.wampumchronicles.com/history.html [accessed 16/7/2016].
Brasseur de Bourbourg, Abbé, *Histoire du Canada: de son Église de Ses Mission,* (Paris: Société de Saint Victor pour les Propagation des Bon Livres, 1852).
British Merchant, A, *Commercial tables. Exhibiting a View of the Weights, Measures, Coins, and Monies of France, compared and equalized with those of Great Britain* (Salisbury: E. Easton, 1790).
Brooks, James F., *Captives and Cousins: Slavery, Kinship, and Community in the Southwest Borderlands* (Chapel Hill: University of North Carolina Press, 2002).
Brumwell, Stephen, *Redcoats: The British Solder and War in the Americas, 1755-1763,* (Cambridge: Cambridge University Press, 2002).
Brumwell, Stephen, *White Devil* (London: Orion, 2004).
Castle, Ian, Fort *William Henry 1755-57* (Oxford: Osprey, 2013).
Chartrand, René, *Canadian Military Heritage Vol. 1 1000-1754* (Montreal: Art Global 1993).
Chartrand, René, *The Forts of New France in Northeast America* (Oxford: Osprey, 2008).
Chartrand, René, *French Fortresses in North America 1535-1763* (Oxford: Osprey, 2005).
Chartrand, René, *The French Soldier in Colonial America* (Ontario: Museum Restoration Service, 1984).
Chartrand, René, *Louisbourg 1758: Wolfe's First Siege* (Oxford: Osprey, 2000).
Chartrand, René, *Montcalm's Crushing Blow: Oswego 1756* (Oxford: Osprey, 2014).
Chartrand, René, *Ticonderoga 1758: Montcalm's Victory Against all Odds* (Oxford: Osprey, 2000).
Chartrand, René, *Tomahawk and Musket: French and Indian Raids in the Ohio Valley 1758* (Oxford: Osprey, 2012).
Child, Hamilton, 'History of German Flats, NY' in *Gazeteer and Business Directory of Herkimer County, NY* (Syracuse, New York: H. Child, 1869).
Crouch, Christian Ayne, *Nobility Lost: French and Canadian Martial Cultures, Indians, and the End of New France* (New York: Cornell University Press, 2014).

Cubbison, Douglas R., *All Canada in the Hands of the British: General Jeffrey Amherst and the 1760 Campaign to Conquer New France* (Norman: University of Oklahoma Press, 2014).

Demos, John, *The Unredeemed Captive: A Family Story from Early America* (New York: Vintage Books, 1995).

Dull, Johnathan R., *The French Navy and the Seven Years War* (Lincoln and London: University of Nebraska Press, 2005).

Dunnigan, Brian Leigh, *Siege 1759: The Campaign Against Niagara* (Niagara Falls: Old Fort Niagara Association, 1996).

Dussieux, L., *Le Canada sous la Domination Française d'apres les Archives de la Marine et de la Guerre* (Paris: Jacque Lecoffre, 1862).

Ekberg, Carl, *French Roots in the Illinois Country: The Mississippi Frontier in Colonial Times* (Champaign: University of Illinois Press, 2000).

Falconer, William, *An Universal Dictionary of the Marine* (London: T. Cadell, 1769).

Fournier, Marcel (ed.), *Combattre pour la France en Amérique: Les soldats de la Guerre de Sept Ans en Nouvelle-France* (Montreal: Société Généalogique Canadienne-Française, 2009).

Gabriel, Charles Nicolas, *Le maréchal de camp Desandrouins, 1729-1792* (Verdun: Renvé-Lallemant, 1887).

Garneau, François-Xavier, *Histoire du Canada Depuis sa Découverte Jusqu'à Nos Jours* (Quebec: John Lovell, 1852).

Grandtner, Miroslav M., *Elseviers Dictionary of Trees: Vol. 1: North America* (Amsterdam: Elsevier, 2005).

Gravier, Gabriel, *Notice sur Jean Vauquelin de Dieppe, le heros de Louisbourg et de la Pointe aux Trembles* (Rouen: Espérance Cagniard, 1885).

Greer, Allan, *The People of New France* (Toronto: University of Toronto Press, 1999).

Humbert, Greg J., *A Compendium of the Catholic Health Association of Canada* (Ottawa: CHAC, 2004).

Hurt, R. Douglas, *The Ohio Frontier: Crucible of the Old Northwest, 1720-1830* (Bloomington: Indiana University Press, 1996).

Jennings, Francis, *Empire Of Fortune: Crowns, Colonies and Tribes in the Seven Years War in America* (New York: W. W. Norton, 1990).

Jennings, Francis, *The History and Culture of Iroquois Diplomacy: An Interdisciplinary Guide to the Treaties of the Six Nations and Their League*, (New York: Syracuse University Press, 1985).

Kennett, Lee, *The French Armies in the Seven Years War* (Durham, North Carolina: Duke University Press, 1967).

Kemmer, Brenton C., *Redcoats, Yankees and Allies: A History of the Uniforms, Clothing and Gear of the British Army in the Lake George-Lake Champlain Corridor 1755-1760* (Bowie: Heritage Books, 1998).

Kent, Timothy J., *Birchbark Canoes of the Fur Trade* (Detroit: Silver Fox Enterprises, 1997).

MacLeod, D. Peter, 'The French Siege of Oswego in 1756: Inland Naval Warfare in North America' in *The American Neptune* 49 (1989), pp. 262-71.

MacLeod, D. Peter, *The Canadian Iroquois and the Seven Years War* (Toronto: Dundern, 2012).

McDermott, John Francis, A *Glossary of Mississippi Valley French, 1673-1850* (St. Louis: Washington University Press, 1941).
Moogk, Peter N., *La Nouvelle France: The Making of French Canada – A Cultural History* (Lansing: Michigan State University Press, 2000).
Nester, William R., *The French and Indian War and the Conquest of New France* (Norman: Oklahoma University Press, 2014).
Pajol, Charles-Pierre-Victor, *Les guerres sous Louis XV* (Paris: Firmin-Didot: 1881).
Pengel, R.D., *French Infantry Regiments 1740-1762* (Doncaster: Imperial Press, 1982).
Podruchny, Carolyn, *Making the Voyageur World: Travellers and Traders in the North American Fur Trade* (Lincoln: University of Nebraska, 2006).
Preston, David, *Braddock's Defeat: The Battle of Monongahela and the Road to Revolution* (New York: Oxford University Press, 2015).
Raynal, Guillame-Thomas, *Histoire Philosophique et Politique: Des Établissemens & du Commerce des Europeans dans les deux Indies* (La Haye: Gosse Fils, 1774).
Reid, Stuart, *Quebec 1759: The battle that won Canada* (Oxford: Osprey, 2003).
Richter, Daniel K., *Ordeal of the Longhouse: The Peoples of the Iroquois League in the Era of European Colonization* (Chapel Hill: University of North Carolina Press, 1992).
Scadding, Henry, *Toronto of Old: Collections and Recollections Illustrative of the Early Settlement and Social Life of the Capital of Ontario* (Toronto: Adam Stevenson & Co., 1873).
Stacey, C. P., *Quebec, 1759: The Siege and the Battle* (Montreal: Robin Brass Studio, 2002).
Steele, Ian K., *Betrayals: Fort William Henry & the "Massacre"* (Oxford: Oxford University Press, 1990).
Steele, Ian K., *Setting All the Captives Free: Capture, Adjustment and Recollection in Allegheny Country* (Quebec: McGill-Queens University Press, 2013).
White, Richard, *The Middle Ground: Indians, Empires, and Republics in the Great Lakes Region, 1650-1815* (Cambridge: Cambridge University Press, 2011).

Maps

For the maps in this book I consulted period maps which are freely available and well worth investigating. Both of these French services are leading the way in public access and other institutions could learn much from them. Gallica (http://gallica.bnf.fr/.) is the online search catalogue of the Bibliotheque Nationale de France. Its images are high resolution and the catalogue is huge. The Archives Nationales d'Outre-Mer (ANOM) have a fantastic online database full of high resolution images called Base Ulysse (http://anom.archivesnationales.culture.gouv.fr/ulysse/). Specific maps that were consulted for this volume are as follows:

Carte du fleuve Saint – Laurent depuis Montréal jusqu' au Fort Frontenac, 1740. Available at *http://gallica.bnf.fr/ark:/12148/btv1b5968885n*
Carte générale des paroisses et missions établies des deux côtés du fleuve St Laurent depuis Rimousky en montant jusqu'au Côteau des Cèdres, 174? Available at *http://gallica.bnf.fr/ark:/12148/btv1b530529320*

Carte du Lac Champlain depuis le Fort de Chambly Jusques au desus du Fort St Frederic dans la Nouvelle France, 1739. Available online at ANOM.

Carte du Lac Ontario 1757, Copy of 1890. Held in Toronto Reference Library, Baldwin Collection, B2-42a CabII. Available online http://www.torontopubliclibrary.ca/detail.jsp?Entt=RDMDC-B2-42A&R=DC-B2-42A

Carte du Lac Ontario et de la Rivière jusques au dela de L'Isle de Montreal celle de Niagara et partie du Lac Erie, 1726. Available at http://gallica.bnf.fr/ark:/12148/btv1b5968948q

Carte de l'isle d'Orléans et du passage de la Traverse dans le fleuve St Laurent, 1744. Available at http://gallica.bnf.fr/ark:/12148/btv1b8490648f

Carte de la région comprise entre le lac Champlain et la rivière d'Hudson, avec les forts Saint-Frédéric, Vaudreuil, Georges et Lidius, 27 October 1756. Available online at ANOM.

Le fleuve Saint-Laurent représenté plus en détail que dans l'étendue de la carte, 17??. Available at http://gallica.bnf.fr/ark:/12148/btv1b530090651

New Map of the province of Quebec according to the royal proclamation of the 7th of October 1763 from the French surveys connected with those made after the war / by Captain Carver, and other officers in his Majesty's service, 1775. Available at http://gallica.bnf.fr/ark:/12148/btv1b53029844d

Partie du fleuve St Laurent depuis Québec jusqu'au lac St François, 1764. Available at http://gallica.bnf.fr/ark:/12148/btv1b8595964c

Plan des Terres des Environs du fort St Frederic, marquées par le Sr Boiscler en 1739, sur laquelle carte sont aussi raportées les sondes qu'il a observées, 1739. Available online at ANOM.

Online Databases

Three Decks. www.threedecks.org. A catalogue of ships from the age of sail.

Dictionary of Canadian Biography online. http://www.biographi.ca/en/ A very useful resource covering all major figures in Canadian history.

The Virtual Museum of New France. http://www.historymuseum.ca/virtual-museum-of-new-france/population/pays-den-haut-and-louisiana/.

Commission de Toponymie de Québec. http://www.toponymie.gouv.qc.ca/ct/english.aspx. Excellent for finding obscure villages or landmarks in Québec province.

La Base de données lexicographiques panfrancophone (BDLP) http://www.bdlp.org/. An online database of various Francophone colonial dialect words, organised geographically.

Index

From Reason to Revolution series – Warfare c 1721-1815

http://www.helion.co.uk/published-by-helion/reason-to-revolution-1721-1815.html

The 'From Reason to Revolution' series covers the period of military history c. 1721–1815, an era in which fortress-based strategy and linear battles gave way to the nation-in-arms and the beginnings of total war.

This era saw the evolution and growth of light troops of all arms, and of increasingly flexible command systems to cope with the growing armies fielded by nations able to mobilise far greater proportions of their manpower than ever before. Many of these developments were fired by the great political upheavals of the era, with revolutions in America and France bringing about social change which in turn fed back into the military sphere as whole nations readied themselves for war. Only in the closing years of the period, as the reactionary powers began to regain the upper hand, did a military synthesis of the best of the old and the new become possible.

The series will examine the military and naval history of the period in a greater degree of detail than has hitherto been attempted, and has a very wide brief, with the intention of covering all aspects from the battles, campaigns, logistics, and tactics, to the personalities, armies, uniforms, and equipment.

Submissions

The publishers would be pleased to receive submissions for this series. Please contact us via email (andrewbamford18@gmail.com), or in writing to Helion & Company Limited, 26 Willow Road, Solihull, West Midlands, B91 1UE.

Titles

No 1 *Lobositz to Leuthen. Horace St Paul and the Campaigns of the Austrian Army in the Seven Years War 1756-57* Translated with additional materials by Neil Cogswell (ISBN 978-1-911096-67-2)

No 2 *Glories to Useless Heroism. The Seven Years War in North America from the French Journals of Comte Maurès de Malartic, 1755-1760* William Raffle (ISBN 978-1-911512-19-6) (paperback)

No 3 *Reminiscences 1808-1815 under Wellington. The Peninsular and Waterloo Memoirs of William Hay* William Hay, with notes and commentary by Andrew Bamford (ISBN 978-1-911512-32-5)

No 4 *Far Distant Ships. The Blockade of Brest 1793-1815* Quintin Barry (ISBN 978-1-911512-14-1)

Books within the series are published in two formats: 'Falconets' are paperbacks, page size 248mm × 180mm, with high visual content including colour plates; 'Culverins' are hardback monographs, page size 234mm × 156mm. Books marked with * in the list above are Falconets, all others are Culverins unless otherwise noted.